Blueprints for Thinking in the Cooperative Classroom

Second Edition

James Bellanca

Robin Fogarty

With Foreword By

Arthur L. Costa

IRI/Skylight Publishing, Inc.

Palatine, Illinois

Teaching Aids for *Blueprints* Lessons

Videos
- Blueprints for Thinking in the Cooperative Classroom Video Package (the eight videos in this package are also available separately)
  (IRI/Skylight Publishing, Inc.)
- How the Elephant Got His Trunk (EBEC)
- The Lion and the Mouse (EBEC)

  ENCYCLOPAEDIA BRITANNICA EDUCATIONAL CORPORATION
  Attn: Customer Service
  Britannica Centre
  310 S. Michigan Avenue
  Chicago, IL 60604
  1-800-554-9862
  1-312-347-7900 ext. 6566

Posters
- How's Your Team Building? (IRI/Skylight Publishing, Inc.)
- Have You Asked a Fat Question? (IRI/Skylight Publishing, Inc.)
- Are You Cooperating Today? (IRI/Skylight Publishing, Inc.)

Logs
- The Thinking Log (IRI/Skylight Publishing, Inc.)
- The Thinking/Writing Connection (IRI/Skylight Publishing, Inc.)

Other Books from IRI/Skylight Publishing
- Building a Caring, Cooperative Classroom
- The Cooperative Think Tank
- The Cooperative Think Tank II
- Designs for Cooperative Interactions
- Tools for the Cooperative Classroom
- The Mindful School Series:
  - How to Assess Authentic Learning
  - How to Integrate the Curricula
  - The Portfolio Connection
  - How to Teach for Metacognitive Reflection
  - How to Teach for Transfer
- What to Do with the Kid Who. . .

Inservices/Trainings
- Call the Director of Client Services at 800-348-4474 or 708-991-6300 for information on regional teacher trainings.

Blueprints for Thinking in the Cooperative Classroom: Second Edition
Fifth Printing

Published by IRI/Skylight Publishing, Inc.
200 E. Wood Street, Suite 274, Palatine, Illinois 60067
Phone 800-348-4474, 708-991-6300
FAX 708-991-6420

Editing: Carla Bellanca Kahler, Sharon Nowakowski
Type Composition: Donna Ramirez, Ari Ohlson
Book Design and Typesetting: Bruce Leckie
Illustration: David Stockman

Printed in the United States of America
ISBN 0-932935-30-3
907B-8-94

ABSTRACT
Blueprints for Thinking in the Cooperative Classroom

Bellanca & Fogarty

Based on the most comprehensive and current research in the areas of cooperative learning and cognitive instruction, *Blueprints* presents the "best practices" for the K-12 classroom teacher. Beginning with the nitty-gritties of *forming* cooperative learning groups, *Blueprints* takes you step by step from the introductory phase to the subsequent phases of *norming, conforming, storming, performing* and *re-forming.* Each chapter is introduced with a background piece that defines and explains its basic concept. This descriptive section is followed by specific and necessary input for the three fully developed lessons—elementary, middle and high school models—featured in each chapter.

The lessons are filled with practical ideas and in-depth examples. For the novice or for the experienced teacher already using cooperative learning, *Blueprints* verbally and graphically displays the elements that promote high-content, high-support, high-challenge lessons for **all** students. To define high-content, high-support, high-challenge lessons, a quick analysis reveals the critical attributes: "High content" refers to the actual academic subject matter with conceptual learning as its base. "High support" targets positively structured peer interactions for intense student involvement. Higher-order thinking, the complexity of the task engaging students in thoughtful ways, fulfills the criteria for "high challenge."

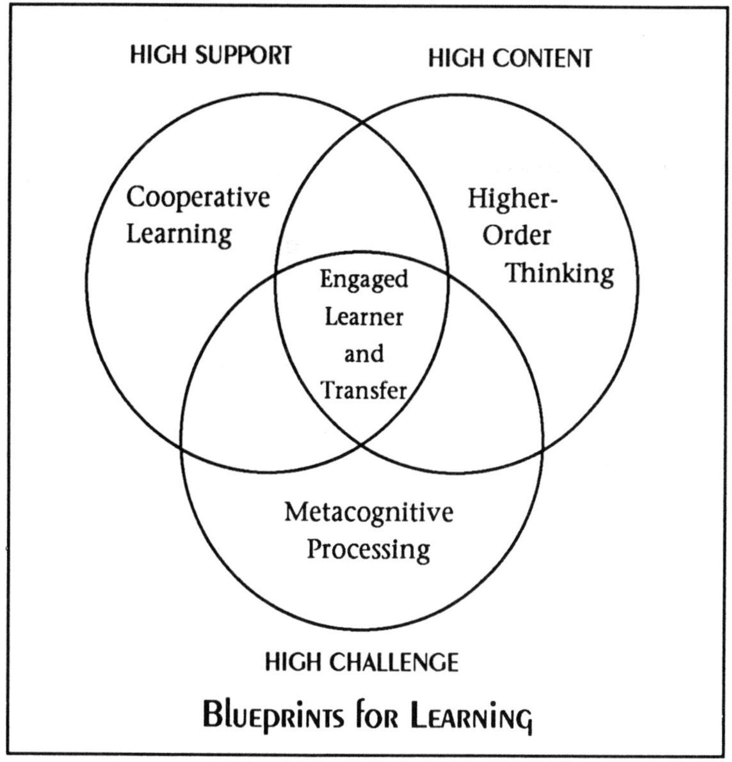

Acknowledgments

Our "blueprints for thinking" about this book, over the span of several years, were of course impacted by a myriad of sources. Within the walls of the IRI compound, special thanks go to the production and editorial staff of Bruce Leckie, Sharon Nowakowski, Ari Ohlson, Donna Ramirez and David Stockman for their "lost weekend" as we mounted a massive effort to go to press. Also, we are grateful to the IRI consultant team of David Lazear, Susan Archibald Marcus, Penny McDonald and Terry Stirling for their practical ideas and for their genuine feedback on *Blueprints* as a user-friendly text.

In addition to the IRI family of supporters who actually participated in the production of *Blueprints,* there are also a number of dedicated colleagues scattered across this country (and across the Canadian border) who sparked us with the inspiration, ideas and real-life illustrations to get us from thinking to inking. As noted within the pages of the book itself, the extensive work of David and Roger Johnson in the field of cooperative learning undergirds the entirety of *Blueprints.*

Paralleling the Johnsons' influence, Art Costa's work in cognitive instruction is evidenced throughout the book. In addition to these special educators, we'd like to acknowledge the work of Frank Lyman and Jay McTighe for their ideas on thinking tools; Beau Fly Jones for her work with cognitive organizers; Ann Brown, David Perkins and Robert Swartz for their extensions in understanding the metacognitive level of thinking; and David Perkins, Gavriel Salomon, and John Barell for their latest thoughts on transfer.

For fear of forgetting the "somebodies" who perhaps deserve our thanks most, we extend our heartfelt gratitude to the many school practitioners who led the way with us toward this rich synthesis of the best research and the best practice; your blueprints became our *Blueprints.*

Foreword

I can remember when I was young, my childhood chums, Charlie, Ronnie, Junior and I would work for days digging gigantic holes in a vacant field. We would construct a fort where we could hide from the world, fantasize about soldiers, cowboys and distant lands and do all those magical things little boys so fervently do. Now, if our mothers had *told* us to go outside and dig a hole that large, we would have resisted the task, resented having to do it and procrastinated as long as possible. Why is it that humans devote so much energy and time to enjoying a difficult task when we do it in reciprocity with others, but are reluctant to go it alone?

The answer probably lies in our human feelings of responsibility to others. Thus, as we manifest our sense of social obligation, we learn persistence. In addition, we learn a myriad of other intellectual skills—all through our interactions with other human beings.

Vygotsky lends psychological support for cooperative learning as a way of developing thinking skills. He states, "Every function in . . . cultural development appears twice: first on the social level, and later on the individual level; first between people and then inside." This applies equally to attention, to memory and to the formation of concepts. All the higher functions originate as actual relationships between individuals.

Indeed, Johnson and Johnson, Slavin, Kagan, Sharan and Sharan and others have repeatedly supported this principle with research. Their findings suggest that there is a strong positive relationship between the ability to think critically, to perform higher-order thinking and to think more creatively when learning occurs in group settings. These "higher" functions have been viewed as beneficial by-products of cooperative learning.

It is generally accepted that the acquisition of thinking abilities can best be experienced, practiced, analyzed and applied in cooperative settings. Higher-level thinking is enhanced when members of a group learn to listen, value each member's unique contribution, take another person's point of view, engage in a variety of group roles, achieve consensus and resolve conflicts.

As students perfect their performance in groups, they also develop operational indicators of what they do or say as they solve problems, reason and create. These indicators serve as criteria by which to evaluate their own and others' performances.

Thus, through this collaborative process, students develop a set of criteria, internalize those criteria, hold them in their head as they work together, and then rate their own and their group's performances. In addition, when these criteria are developed collaboratively, students derive a common definition and vision of what effective group problem-solving is and how it is enacted. In turn, the cooperative development of thinking—collaboratively developing concepts, visions and operational definitions—are used to guide, reflect upon and evaluate one's own performance while in groups or alone.

The teacher's role is a critical one as a stimulator and a mediator of this process. As the coach/facilitator, the teacher must structure the cooperative classroom, present problems to resolve, mediate each group's work with questions and non-judgmental feedback, monitor individual and group progress, and model thinking and cooperating in all they do.

In *Blueprints for Thinking in the Cooperative Classroom,* a wealth of student activities with explicit guidelines for teachers is presented, not because thinking is a mere by-product of cooperative learning, but rather because thinking is the intention, the goal and the desired outcome of the collaborative efforts of students and teachers. And, *Blueprints* goes several steps beyond. It gives the critical help for extending thinking into every corner of every classroom in a cooperative school. It guides the transfer of cooperating and thinking beyond the school walls and provides a blueprint for a new look at how teachers and students can benefit from a quality learning experience.

Art Costa
Sacramento, California
1990

Table of Contents

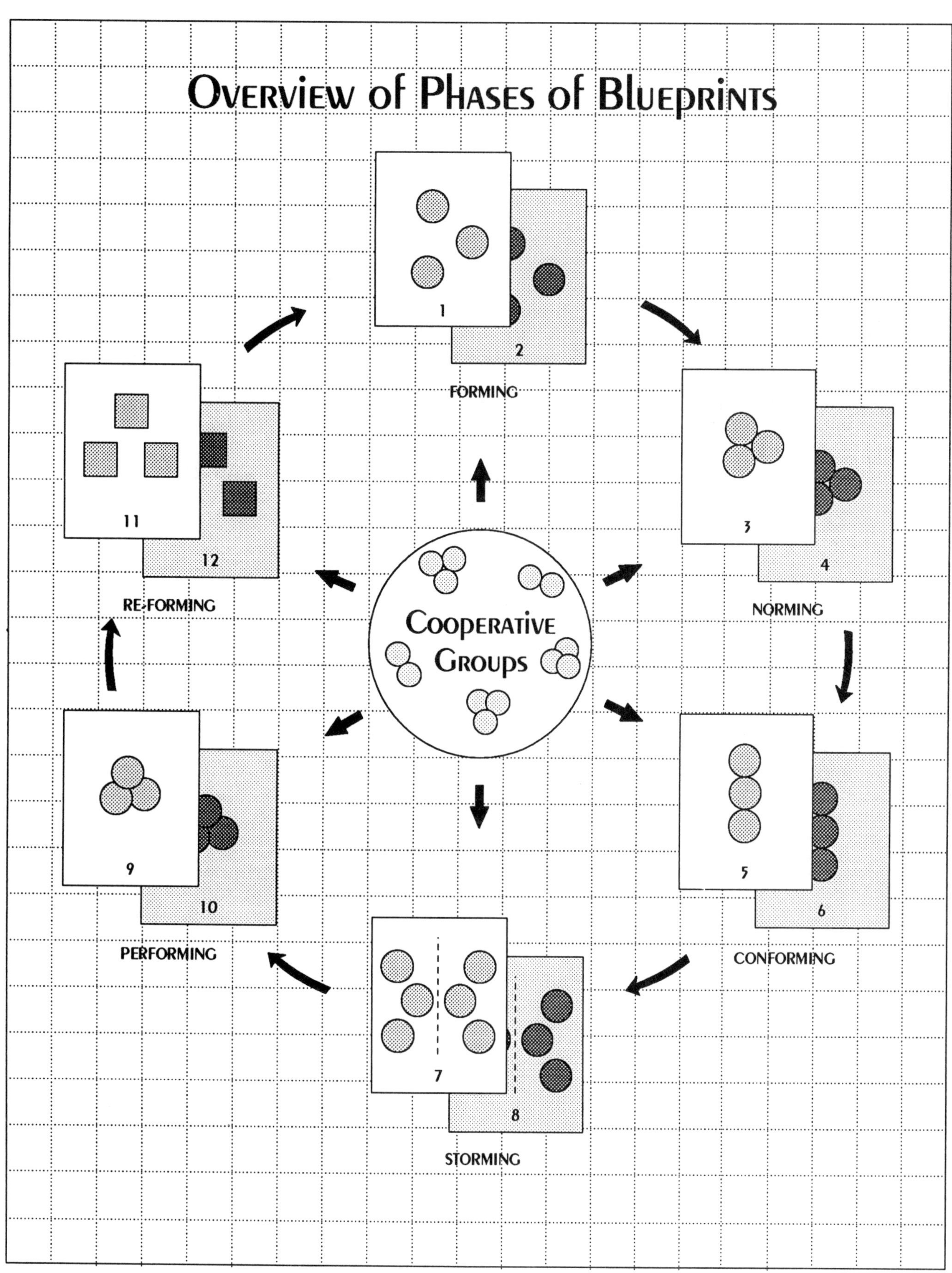
Overview of Phases of Blueprints
1
2
FORMING
3
4
NORMING
5
6
CONFORMING
7
8
STORMING
9
10
PERFORMING
11
12
RE-FORMING
Cooperative Groups

Each of us is the architect of our own future.
—Appius Claudius, 53 B.C.

INTRODUCTION

WHAT IT'S ALL ABOUT

Blueprints is more than just another book about cooperation in the classroom. It is a guide for those creative and seasoned teachers who see the cooperative classroom as a community of students eager to learn—not to learn for higher scores on standardized tests, but for transferring what they learn beyond the schoolhouse walls.

Blueprints is more than a metaphor for organizing this book. It is a metaphor selected to challenge the factory metaphor that dominates the all-American concept of schooling. For too many decades Henry Ford's factory has served as the structure for American education. The 1980s was the decade that epitomized the desire to make the assembly line work faster and better. The end result? Millions of students, the products of "teacher-proof" curriculum and instruction, were rolled off the assembly line. Supervisors newly trained with checklists watched each teacher follow step-by-step instruction. At the end of the line, the students were tested, checked and measured to ensure everyone met the minimal educational standards.

The Fords, Chryslers and GMs have discovered the limits of the assembly line. It is time for American schools to do the same. In the *Blueprints* precept, the schoolhouse is not a factory. It is an artisan's workshop in which the master nourishes and enriches the apprentices' talents. The apprentices learn not to be tested, but to develop knowledge, skill and talent that will serve them well when they step into their own world of work.

Blueprints advocates subtle shifts in the nature of school. In place of learning for a test, it advocates learning for life. In place of the teacher as assembler, it advocates the teacher as master artist. In place of the teacher as low-order mind stuffer, it advocates the teacher as champion of the intellect.

Such a shift sounds like an awesome task. In one sense it is; in the other, the shift allows teachers to do what most of them dreamed teaching would allow them to do—develop each child's capabilities to the fullest. It allows them not to develop copycat products, but rather creative talents ready and able to transfer learning to a multitude of changing challenges.

The shift has already begun in many classrooms. Aided by supportive professional development and encouraging supervisors, thousands of teachers are applying the tools of cooperative learning, thinking, whole language and mathematical problem-solving in their classrooms. National professional organizations such as the American Federation of Teachers, National Council of Mathematics Teachers, National Science Teachers, and the Association for Supervision and Curriculum Development are calling for major instructional reforms that utilize these methods.

The instructional tools are available to provide the shift from a recall curriculum to a transfer curriculum. At the first level, the cooperative learning approach provides the means for establishing positive, collaborative relationships among students and teachers. These relationships are essential building blocks in a community of learners with high-level cognitive goals. Instead of using coercive discipline practices, which highlight the external motivation tactics of behavior control, cooperative learning encourages internal motivation, which invites students and teachers to learn how to inquire together.

Given the development of students' willingness to learn together, teachers who are committed to learning for transfer have easily moved to the next level of instruction—teaching students how to think more creatively and critically. As students increase their abilities to reason, solve problems and make decisions, while utilizing the most important curricular content, the transfer teacher quickly perceives their readiness to look beyond the limits of any lesson.

Blueprints is organized to give teachers a framework that enables them to redirect their instructional goals from recall to transfer. It introduces practice steps for establishing the cooperative foundation, for initiating more skillful thinking and for preparing students for transfer.

The methods selected for this book are drawn from a variety of resources. The Johnsons' framework is the core; it is supplemented with more practical structures, strategies and curriculum models from Kagan, Sharan and Sharan, and Slavin, which experienced teachers have told us are the most workable and the most supportive of the transfer curriculum. Included are only those pieces that have passed the test of time in a variety of classrooms and have proven adaptable across the curriculum.

The criteria used for selecting cooperative strategies hold true for the selection of reasoning and transferring tools. If the methods didn't deeply engage students in the processes of thinking, problem solving, and transferring critical curricula *and* produce achievement results well beyond normal testing expectations, they are not included in this text. Furthermore, if the methods did not work as well in the high-risk classrooms as they worked in classrooms blessed with easily motivated students, they were also withheld.

The methods exist. But they will not succeed in transforming a classroom or a schoolhouse to transfer unless educational conditions encourage the changes *Blueprints* advocates. The secret of *Blueprints* is not in having one teacher try one or two cooperative methods (that's a start), but rather it is in spending the time and energy to make the whole school shift. That is why *Blueprints* was designed as a tool that encourages the faculty in a school to work together toward this goal, a complete shift.

Striving for the transfer transformation does not prevent utilization of cooperative learning or thinking in the cooperative classroom. You need only review the early research on cooperative learning to note its power in improving basic skill acquisition or other achievement goals. Once you have organized simple memory tasks for vocabulary, computation or math formulae, you will see how much more powerful the cooperative model is over other approaches. In the transfer school, short- and long-term memory enhancers will always have a place. But they won't be the *be-all* and *end-all* of daily lessons.

Whatever the reasons teachers have for adding cooperative learning to their instructional repertoires, we predict they and their students will benefit more than they expect. We only ask that as teachers start their journey they not ignore the possibilities outlined in *Blueprints*.

OVERVIEW

Just as the architect's blueprints provide an *overall* plan and specified *details* for every phase of the construction process, *Blueprints* also encompasses both the big picture on cooperative learning and detailed "specs" needed to begin, proceed and refine the most effective structure of interaction in the thinking classroom.

Based on the most comprehensive and current research in the areas of cooperative learning and cognitive instruction, *Blueprints* presents a synthesis of the best practices for K-12 classroom teachers. Six phases evidenced in the small-group process provide the undergirding framework for the book:

The Six Phases of the Small-Group Process

FORMING
How do I get started?
How do I build teams and trust?

NORMING
What social skills do they need?
What do I do with the kid who...?

CONFORMING
How do I get them thinking?
How do I make their thinking visible?

STORMING
How do I get them to be problem solvers?
What happens when they can't agree?

PERFORMING
What does the ultimate cooperative classroom look like?
How do I keep them thinking?

REFORMING
How do I restructure the school from the inside out?
What about grades & test scores?

HIGH CONTENT
HIGH SUPPORT
HIGH CHALLENGE

THE BOOK

Designing the classroom for high-content, high-cooperation and high-challenge learning requires blueprints and specifications that guide the various stages of the construction process. *Blueprints* designates two chapters to each of the six phases—forming, norming, conforming, storming, performing, and reforming. The first chapter in each set gives a survey or the "lay of the land." Basic concepts and strategies are described for the novice. In the subsequent chapter in each set, further depth and elaboration is given for the teacher who has more experience with the cooperative learning model.

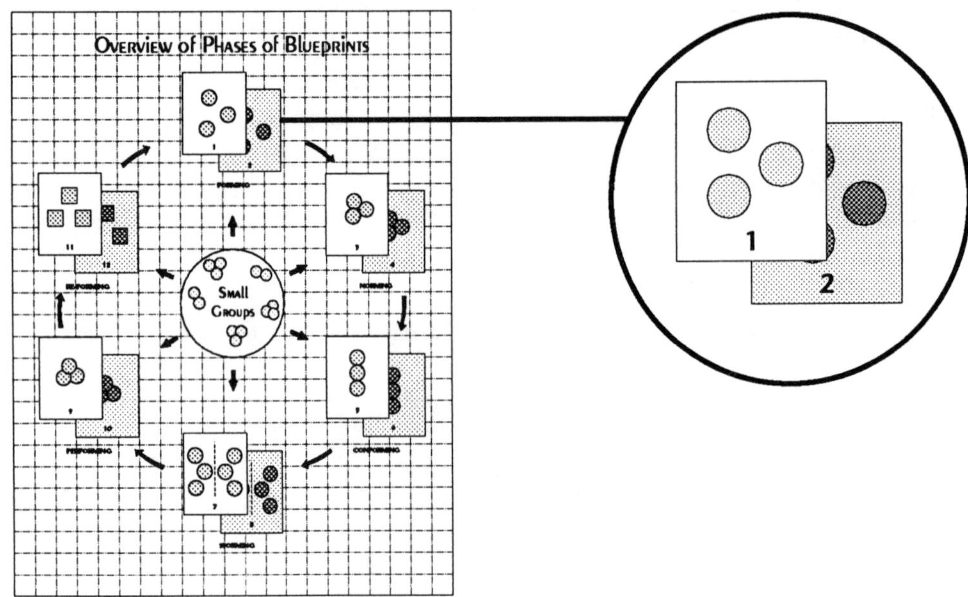

Although each chapter and the lesson within the chapters are ready to use in the classroom, please, adjust whatever is necessary to make the execution fit your particular situation and the needs of your students. Use the blueprints as guides, but adapt them as needed to personalize the design and make it work best for the students.

THE CHAPTER

THE DRAFT: In the Draft, the chapter's concept is developed with definitions, descriptions, explanations, rationale and research. The Draft section provides the background for the specific high-content, high-support and high-challenge elements designed into each lesson. By reading the Draft prior to using the lessons, teachers gain a grounding in the philosophy behind the lesson's strategy.

THE SPECS: As indicated in the heading, *specifications for the lessons* are given in this section. Input needed by students prior to the lesson, background material, tools, cooperative group structures, thinking skills focus and pertinent notes to the teacher are all found in the Specs.

THE BLUEPRINTS: Separate blueprints for elementary, middle and secondary levels appear in each chapter. Each model lesson is age- and content-appropriate to a specific grade level so teachers can readily see the adaptations needed to tailor their lessons to a relevant student focus.

THE BLUEPRINTS (THE LESSONS)

Again, for simplicity's sake and to further extend the blueprint metaphor, each blueprint/lesson is divided into three sections: Setting Up The Scaffolding, Working the Crew, Reflecting on the Design.

SETTING UP THE SCAFFOLDING: All preparation, input, handouts and materials needed *prior* to the activity are included in Setting Up The Scaffolding. Typical elements in this section might include a focus activity, instructions, identification of the cooperative social skill and targeted thinking skill.

WORKING THE CREW: This section of each lesson centers on the interactivity that occurs *during* the actual lesson. This is the activity that includes the cooperative interaction structure and/or the graphic organizer with which the students' work is outlined in practical, ready-to-use classroom procedures.

REFLECTING ON THE DESIGN: Focus in this section is on the processing procedures conducted *after* the cooperative thinking activity. Metacognitive discussion questions, log entries, follow-up strategies, practice, transfer and closure activities might be included in Reflecting on the Design.

THE APPENDIXES

Following the last chapter and lessons, additional references are provided for your convenience in Appendix A, B and C. **Appendix A** contains a glimpse of the research and findings on cooperative learning and cognitive instruction that undergird *Blueprints.* **Appendix B** provides professional blackline masters of information and tools used throughout the lessons to help you efficiently and effectively work with your class. The charts, quotes and other materials available in this appendix for class handouts and overheads are denoted with an asterisk (*) where they appear in the text. **Appendix C** answers educators' most frequently asked questions when learning *Blueprints* and cooperative learning.

CONNECTION WITH PRIOR KNOWLEDGE ON INSTRUCTION

How does *Blueprints* fit with what teachers have learned about the approaches to instruction? learning styles? Hunter? TESA? whole language? *Blueprints* operates on the assumption that good instruction is not limited to a single method or approach. That's why we have synthesized the best practices of cooperative learning from among the various "models." Careful study of *Blueprints* will show how we encourage you to integrate what you know about learning styles, especially the work of Bernice McCarthy's *4MAT*, the right-brain/left-brain methodologies and Howard Gardner's "multiple intelligences." From TESA we encourage those best practices of high expectations (wait time, equal distribution, etc.) especially important in the metacognitive process, which is essential to the principle of making sense. And don't ignore all that Hunter has taught about design, teacher decision-making and motivation, or all that Joyce has provided about multiple models of teaching and peer coaching. Use of prior knowledge on the best practices prepares the way for a classroom in which learning by every student is not limited to "one right way for everyone." Teachers are given the chance to select from a variety of learner-appropriate strategies to meet a wide array of learner styles.

In the past decade, research on effective instruction has provided a very usable "science of teaching." As the body of knowledge continues to expand, it has given seasoned teachers multiple choices for designing powerful learning situations. As teachers have increased their design skills, more and more students have blossomed as artists of learning—not only students who arrive in school ready and willing, but often those at-risk populations that benefit most from the highest quality of instruction. As research continues to ferret out the best practices, the future looks brighter and brighter for quality teaching and learning. The challenge to use these practices continues.

THE FIT WITH EFFECTIVE SCHOOLS

An effective school begins with agreement on the school's mission to promote learning for every child. Edmund's correlates spin from that belief as a framework to ensure the mission becomes practice. *Blueprints* celebrates the effective school and invites educators to go a step beyond. *Blueprints* invites teachers and administrators to utilize the best researched teaching strategies as the critical approach to attaining the school's mission goals. It encourages the school team to restructure the school from the inside out with absolute attention to learning as the central purity.

ONE FINAL WORD

While working through *Blueprints* it is important that teachers monitor, reflect upon and make sense of their learning. A beneficial way to keep track is by using a double-entry journal, which is similar to a regular journal, except instead of having another person respond to the entry, the writer reflects upon it. See the sample journal on the next page. The first column, "Initial Observations," is for listing concrete evidences, facts, thoughts and feelings; describing occurrences; noting changes in the classroom; and giving details of new experiences, including successful (and not so successful) ventures. The second column, "Upon reflection," is for looking over and reflecting upon the observations. Ask: So what? Now what? What worked? What didn't work? What should be changed? What resources are available to promote change? Which changes may be more difficult to execute? Finally, the observations need to be matched with personal expectations, goals and concerns. Teachers need to take time in the double-entry journal to examine their learning and beliefs about teaching.

SAMPLE DOUBLE-ENTRY JOURNAL	
Initial Observations	**Upon Reflection**
Date: 9/27 The Venn diagram is a helpful tool for teaching students how to compare and contrast. I am happy with our success. • Students seem to be enjoying using it as well. • Students weren't familiar with the Venn diagram at first, but successfully related it to familiar ideas/concepts (people wearing jeans/people wearing green) • We have been able to use it with more complex ideas.	Date: 10/4 There must be many, many, many applications of the Venn diagram that can help students compare and contrast patterns for thinking at any time. I think this tool will be a good one to continue to use; it helps students work together while organizing and visualizing their thinking. Also, the Venn diagram can be used in any subject—students can compare and contrast mathematical operations, characters in a story and countries in social studies.
Date: 10/4 BUILD represents the key elements that must be in my lessons. • The BUILD matrix for planning lessons is the biggest teaching treasure I've found yet. • It seems to be a bit complex, but I've easily created successful lessons with it. • Other teachers in our district also find it very helpful.	Date: 10/12 In using cooperative learning, BUILD gives me the key ingredients for maintaining successful cooperative learning lessons. In discussing the matrix with my colleagues, we were able to brainstorm many lessons in no time; in fact, I can apply many of my own strategies to this tool. By using it, I won't leave out pertinent elements, and I'll be better prepared to consistently teach my students cooperative-cognitive learning and transfer (that I hope will travel with them beyond the classroom!).

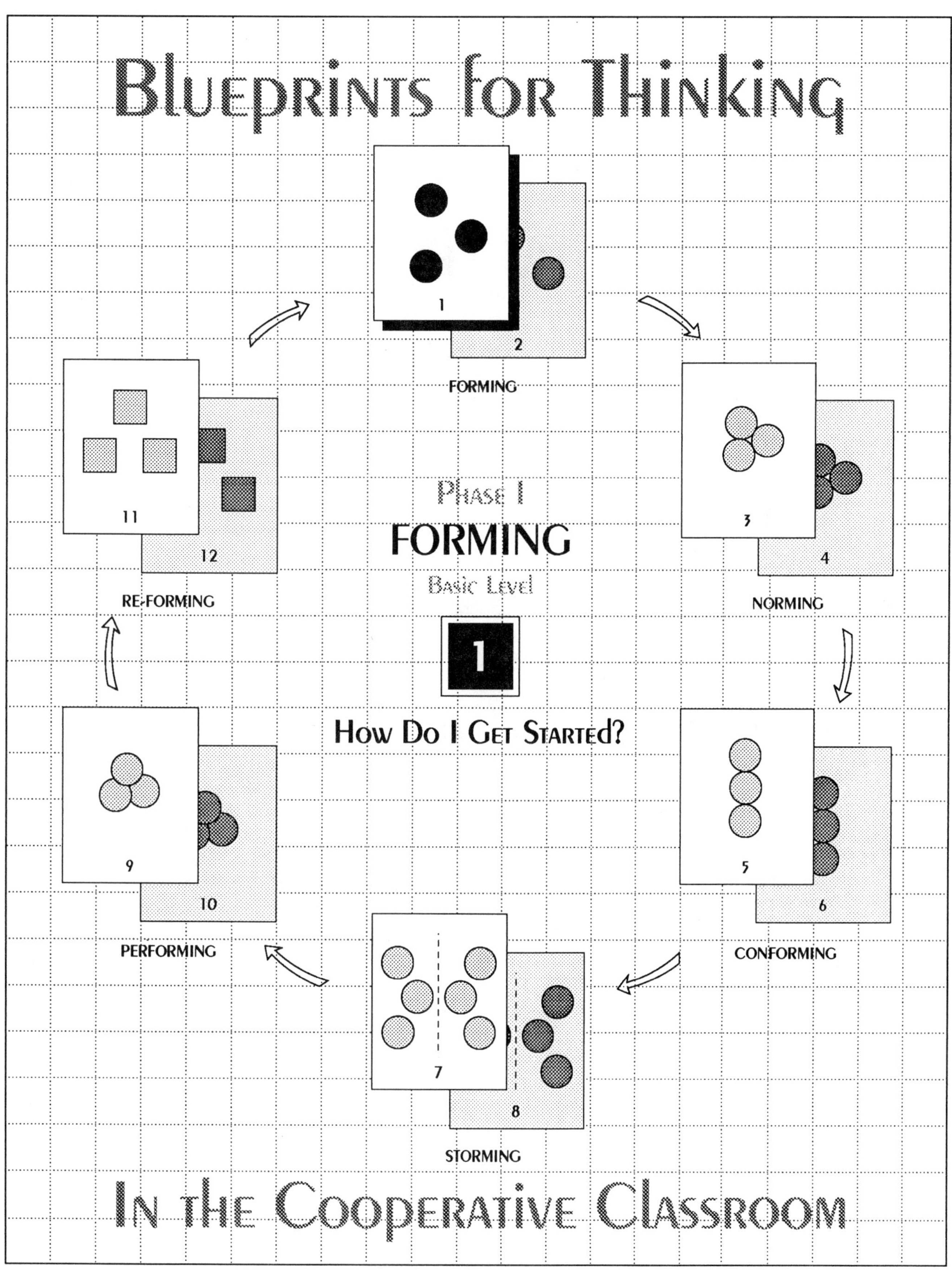

Blueprints for Thinking
1
2
FORMING
3
4
NORMING
5
6
CONFORMING
7
8
STORMING
9
10
PERFORMING
11
12
RE-FORMING
Phase I
FORMING
Basic Level
1
How Do I Get Started?
In the Cooperative Classroom

PHASE I:
FORMING
BASIC

HOW DO I GET STARTED?

The best things and the best people rise out of their seperateness; I'm against a homogenized society because I want the cream to rise.
—Robert Frost

DRAFT

"How do I get started?" is the most frequently asked question by novice teachers of cooperative learning and thinking who are in the forming phase. They know well that the first lessons in the first week of school set the tone for the year. The best starts are made *prior* to any formal introduction of cooperative learning, beginning with planning and preparing *what* and *how* to introduce a cooperative climate in the classroom.

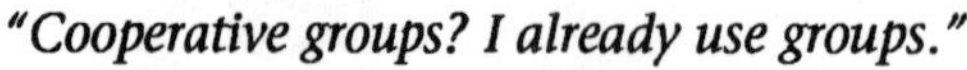

"Cooperative groups? I already use groups."
"I've tried groups. They didn't work then and they won't work now."
"Group work doesn't fit my style."

Such are some of the reactions when the concept of cooperative learning is introduced. When the discussion turns to thinking, the reactions can be even more resistive.

But reactions are not always so resistant. As pressure mounts for a major modification in teaching strategy, attention to the opportunities provided by cooperative learning and thinking in the cooperative classroom increases.

What is this thing called "cooperative learning"? How does it differ from traditional grouping procedures in the classroom? How does it change the teacher's role. Cooperative learning is an instructional strategy. It uses cooperative "groups" as a tool for creating a more cooperative classroom in which student achievement, self-esteem, responsibility, high-level thinking and favorable attitudes toward school increase dramatically.

Cooperative groups include two to five students of different ability, skill, motivation, sex or racial origin who work to achieve a single learning goal. In the cooperative classroom, the teacher uses a variety of structures and strategies to build on-task attention, trust and shared

?

What is a cooperative group?

- Two to five students
- Teacher-selected
- Members mixed by ability, motivation, sex, race
- Members with a shared academic goal
- A group with targeted social skills
- A group that focuses on processing

When do I start using cooperative groups?

Right away. Cooperative learning takes time to develop. The sooner you start, no matter how small a start, the better. See page 340 for details.

success. More than 500 research studies point out the benefits of the cooperative approach for *all* students.

Marcus and McDonald's acronym BUILD (1990) highlights the variables that produce the power in cooperative groups. For each variable, the teacher can select from dozens of strategies to design each cooperative thinking lesson. (As you read this material or participate in a training, use the BUILD matrix on page 331 to list a variety of useful strategies for each of the five variables.)

B = Build in higher-order thinking so students are challenged to think deeply and to transfer subject matter.

U = Unite the class so students form bonds of trust, which enable teamwork.

I = Individual learning: Each student is accountable to master all skills and knowledge. The groups are a means to facilitate mastery before the teacher checks each individual through quizzes, tests, essays or other more authentic assessment strategies.

L = Look back and debrief *what* and *how* students learned. Students are taught to "process" or "evaluate" their thinking, feelings and social skills. This emphasis on "taught" student evaluation shifts the responsibility for learning from the teacher to student.

D = Develop students' social skills. By providing explicit training in the social skills, the teacher helps students master cooperative abilities during cooperative work.

The teacher's role shifts dramatically in the cooperative classroom.

THE TEACHER'S ROLE

From the Traditional Classroom...	To the Cooperative, Thinking Classroom
...dispensing information	...planning dynamic lessons for transfer of learning
...performing for and entertaining passive students	...teaching students how to learn
...rewarding and punishing	...developing student responsibility
...preparing for standardized tests	...promoting active learning
...grading workbooks and tests for student recall	...facilitating student self-evaluation
...emphasizing teacher-student and student-material interactions	...encouraging and cheerleading mastery of skills and concepts
	...extending participation
	...motivating high-level thinking
	...building group skills
	...balancing teacher-to-student, student-to-material and student-to-student interactions

What kind of classroom interactions do we use?

Think about this . . .

To BUILD thinking in the cooperative classroom there are three types of interactions to consider:

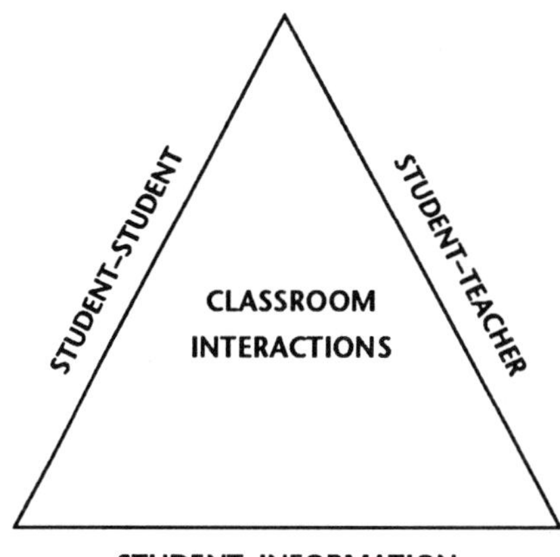

STUDENT–TEACHER = How teachers question and respond to students

STUDENT–STUDENT = How students talk and work with each other

STUDENT–INFORMATION = How students deal with the material

Will you model a lesson that illustrates B-U-I-L-D?

The portmanteaux lesson outlined on page 340 illustrates
- Building in higher thought
- Uniting teams
- Insuring accountability
- Looking over the work
- Development of social skills

The changed teacher role suggests the differences between traditional groups and cooperative groups in a thinking classroom.

How Cooperative Groups Differ

TRADITIONAL LEARNING GROUPS	COOPERATIVE LEARNING GROUPS
One goal/task, learned at a time	Higher-order thinking is woven into every lesson
Groups are done when product/task is done	Social skills are explicitly taught
Social skills are taken as a given	Teacher focuses on group interaction
One leader gets main role	Roles are shared and mixed
Evaluate group without looking at individual efforts	Individual contribution to group goal is evaluated
Teacher grades product	Group looks back and processes its interactions and group work
Homogeneous groups created	Students with different characteristics are mixed/matched
Students only responsible for themselves	Members share responsibility for group
Each student relies on him/herself	Students rely on each other

As the research of Slavin, Johnson and Johnson and other researchers of cooperative learning has shown, cooperative groups increase mastery of the basic skills. Reading and math scores go up, grades improve and students report how they prefer working together. But there is more, as Bruce Joyce reported in his meta-analysis of the effects of cooperative learning: *"Research on cooperative learning is overwhelmingly positive and the cooperative approaches are appropriate for all curriculum areas. The more complex the outcomes (higher-order processing of information, problem solving, social skills and attitudes), the greater are the effects."*

What Joyce points out is the most significant insight yet into the potential power of cooperative learning. As much as cooperative learning accomplishes when used as a single strategy, it provides a greater opportunity when combined with strategies that challenge students to think more skillfully, solve problems or generate new concepts. In essence, the combinations that Joyce noted provide windows of opportunity that have exponential effects on student learning. Where does it all start? A well-functioning cooperative classroom begins with careful preparation.

SPECS

☐ DESIGN THE BULLETIN BOARD

The bulletin board communicates to the class the spirit of cooperative learning as well as the key start-up logistics.

ELEMENTARY For younger students, cooperative story characters, cartoons or other illustrations of cooperation work well. Post the tasks for the major group roles (e.g., checker, encourager, reader, recorder). Add a list of

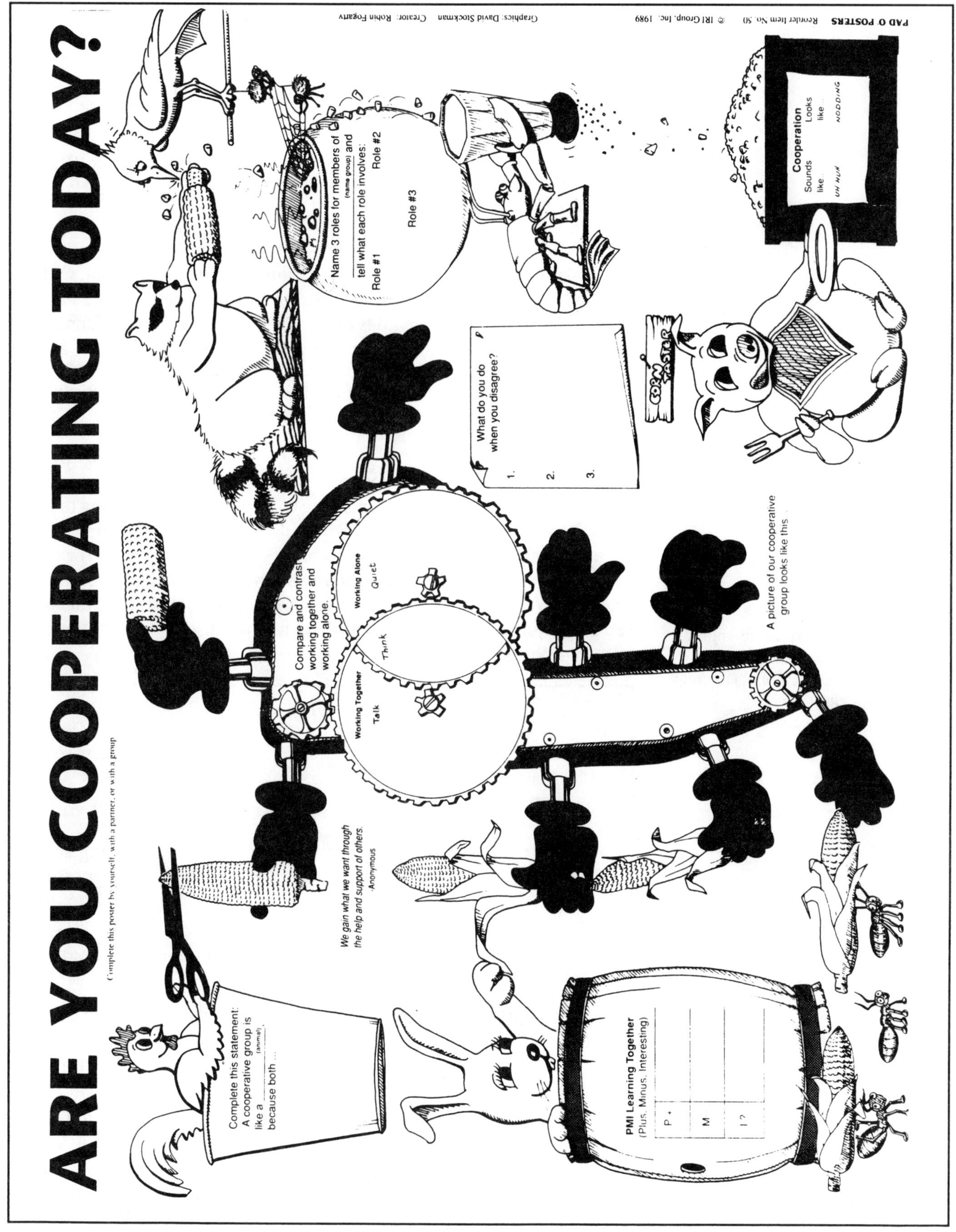
ARE YOU COOPERATING TODAY?
Complete this poster by yourself, with a partner, or with a group
Complete this statement:
A cooperative group is like a ______ (animal) because both ...
We gain what we want through the help and support of others.
-Anonymous
Compare and contrast working together and working alone.
Working Together
Talk
Think
Working Alone
Quiet
Name 3 roles for members of ______ (name group) and tell what each role involves:
Role #1
Role #2
Role #3
What do you do when you disagree?
1.
2.
3.
CORN TASTER
A picture of our cooperative group looks like this.
PMI Learning Together
(Plus, Minus, Interesting)
P+
M
I?
Cooperation
Sounds like...
Looks like...
UH HUH
NODDING
PAD O' POSTERS Reorder Item No. 50 © IRI Group, Inc. 1989
Graphics: David Stockman Creator: Robin Fogarty

the key "forming" social behaviors expected during group work (e.g., stay in seats; one person speaks at a time; encourage each other; speak in six-inch, quiet voices).

MIDDLE Build bulletin boards around sports figures and teamwork. Show samples of cooperative team play (e.g., football, basketball) and individualistic competition (e.g., tennis, swimming, golf). Discuss how they are alike (e.g., competition) and different (e.g., teams help each other, have roles, etc.).

SECONDARY For older students, pictures of cooperation in the workplace, the athletic field and intrapersonal relationships are appropriate. Quotes such as "All for one, one for all" or "We sink or swim together" add another dimension. If a bulletin board is not available, provide each student with a handout to keep in his/her handbook.

Be as graphic as possible. On the first days of class, use the bulletin board as a constant reference and reinforcer.

☐ MAKE ROLE CARDS

It's a good idea for students just starting with cooperative learning to have role cards or a printed worksheet of the various group roles and their duties. Each role card describes the responsibilities of one group role. For tasks, each member of the group is assigned a role and receives the corresponding role card. When using role cards, give each group one set so group members can rotate jobs. To help with group assignments, use matching numbers, letters or symbols for each set.

What are role cards?

Role cards explain members' responsibilities in the groups. See the sample blacklines on page 280.

Sample Role Cards*

Adapted from *Tools for the Cooperative Classroom* (1990) by Marcus and McDonald.

THE CHECKER This role may be the most critical to cooperative learning. When a group completes an assigned task, it is this member's task to check that *all* members of the group can do the task, explain each answer and tell why that answer was selected. When the checker does this job well, there is little need for more formal ways to gain *individual learning*. It is the teacher's job as the chief steward of learning to see that each group task is set up for easy checking. In task assignments, it's most helpful to structure discussion questions to support the checker's role. To help ease the checker's facilitation, consider the following *three-to-one technique*.

*Blackline master is available in Appendix B, page 280.

SAMPLE CHECK-UPS

Elementary Example (For students who read "Three Billy Goats Gruff")

- ✓ List three ways the billy goats might have crossed the stream without meeting the troll.
- ✓ Agree which was the safest way to cross.
- ✓ Explain why you think your group's choice was the best it could make.
- ✓ Be sure all members can explain the group's choice.

Middle School Example (From a unit on drug abuse)

- ✓ List three illegal drugs that are available in this town.
- ✓ Agree on which drug has the worst effect on students your age.
- ✓ Explain the reasons for your group's choice.
- ✓ Be sure all members can explain the group's choice.

Secondary School Example (From a math problem-solving sample)

- ✓ Describe at least three ways to solve this problem.
- ✓ Solve it each way.
- ✓ Agree on which was the easiest and most accurate method to use.
- ✓ Explain the reasons for your choice.
- ✓ Be sure each member can explain the reason for the group's choice.

Three-to-One Technique

- ✓ Ask questions that allow at least *three* possible answers. In a trio, each student gives one possible answer for the recorder to write.
- ✓ Ask a follow-up question that challenges the students to agree on the *one* best answer from the list. They can rank or combine ideas.
- ✓ The checker checks to see if (a) all members agree (members signal thumbs up), (b) each member can explain the selected answer, and (c) each member can tell why that answer was selected. Members should rehearse *b* and *c* before signing the group's worksheet to indicate "I agree," "I can explain," and "I can tell why we decided on this."

THE WORRIER The worrier has several responsibilities. First, the worrier checks with the group to be sure all members agree on the instructions that were given. If there is disagreement in the group, the worrier may ask for help. Second, the worrier sees that all members have an equal chance to participate. Third, the worrier keeps all members on task. In advanced groups, teach the worrier social skills for inviting on-task behavior.

THE RECORDER Cooperative groups work best when there is a single recorder. Although each member is encouraged to keep his/her own notes, the recorder writes the official answers for more complex discussions. It is important that the recorder be encouraged to check what he/she writes against what the speaker wants written. (The speaker has the last say.) The recorder's paper becomes the group's product, which is to be signed by each member and turned in to the teacher at the end of the lesson.

The use of one pen or marker and one sheet of paper contributes to *united teams*. This "work together" method enhances the feeling of "one for all and all for one." When the task is done and all agree on the answers, each member in the group signs the worksheet. A signature means "this is my best work."

How do I select the groups?

Random groups can be used to start cooperative learning. Then mixed ability and diverse groups can be arranged by the teacher. See page 343 for details.

Beyond the forming roles described here, a teacher can design roles specific to his/her subject matter. Here are samples:

MATH GROUP

Calculator: Checks work on calculator

Analyst: Analyzes strategies

Bookkeeper: Checks answers; records time

Inventory controller: Keeps inventory on materials; controls supplies

WRITER'S GROUP

Editor In Chief: Tracks progress; sets deadlines

Publisher: Sets guidelines

Scriber: Keeps notes

Author: Supplies materials

NOVEL GROUP (Becky Abraham)

Discussion leader: Prepares and leads questions

Vocabulary enricher: Selects enrichment questions

Literary illuminary: Reads favored passages

Agent: Gets materials

SOCIAL STUDIES GROUP

Presiding officer: Presides over the group

Parliamentarian: Observes group behavior

Secretary: Records information

Sergeant at arms: Keeps the time; gets materials

SCIENCE GROUP

Scientist: Observes progress; keeps time

Researcher: Provides guidelines to follow

Observer: Records information

Lab technician: Sets up materials and equipment

PRIMARY GROUP

Captain: Encourages group

Umpire: Observes and reports

Scorekeeper: Writes down information

Runner: Gets what is needed

THE MATERIALS MANAGER (In primary grades, "The Gopher") This person gets all materials, returns materials to the "bin" and sees that the group cleans up its area. The bin, located at the side or rear of the classroom, is where the necessary materials are placed for each assignment. Some teachers assign a storehouse manager to hand out sets of materials to each material's manager/gopher. During cooperative tasks, the gophers are instructed to move quietly to the bin and to get their groups' materials. A list on the blackboard or a paper posted over the bin should detail what items are needed for each group, for example:

TODAY'S LAB MATERIALS

Earth worms
1 dissecting kit
1 worm bottle
1 observation sheet
1 instruction sheet
1 pencil
2 sheets newsprint
1 cloth

THE ENCOURAGER The more competitive a school climate, the more the need to develop students' abilities to encourage. In the early grades, encouragement means a switch from "Dumbbell," "Stupid" and other put-downs to "I like your idea" and "Keep it up." In the upper grades the switch is from "Jerk" and "Nerd" to "That's a good idea," "You're really trying hard, " Great thinking," "Atta boy" and "Atta girl."

The encourager role develops this very important social skill among the students. A brief teaching of what encouraging looks like (smiles, pats on the back, high fives, etc.) and sounds like ("Great idea," "I like the energy you are using," "Keep at it," etc.), followed by all students practicing the specific behaviors in group work and receiving focused feedback on their practice, goes a long way toward developing a positive classroom climate that is filled with encouraging statements.

UNLIMITED ROLES In closing, there are many other roles possible for groups. Which roles are targeted in an activity depends on the task assigned. For example, in a reading task, have a reader role. In math, have a reader, calculator and recorder–checker. Combined roles are necessary in pairs and trios (e.g., recorder-checker). Pick and practice the roles that best fit the task and age levels of the students.

☐ INTRODUCE SOCIAL SKILLS

Select which basic cooperative **social skills** the students need to learn and predict which ones need emphasis during the first month or quarter. Post these on the bulletin board or give students a handout.

EXAMPLES OF FORMING BASIC SOCIAL SKILLS*

Elementary Example	Middle School Example	Secondary School Example
✓ Use 6" voices	✓ Use 6" voices	✓ Control your voice
✓ Listen to your neighbor	✓ It's OK to think	✓ Think for yourself
✓ Stay with the group	✓ Don't interrupt others	✓ Respect others' opinions
✓ Look at the speaker	✓ Help your neighbor	✓ Carry your weight
✓ Don't hurt feelings	✓ Know and do your job	✓ Help each other stay on task
	✓ Listen to all ideas	✓ Explore different points of view
	✓ Use encouraging words	✓ Include all members

For the first weeks of school, plan to use procedures that will structure "face-to-face prime-time interaction." Model and practice how the students should move desks in and out of groups, how students should sit close together in triangles or squares, and how to listen to the teacher as needed.

Later in the first year, use a T-chart to clarify such social skills as listening, encouraging, carrying your weight, respecting and including others. Before using each cooperative learning task, help the groups review the chart. After practicing the task, use the chart as a way to introduce simple processing: Which skills were practiced? Where was improvement?

☐ ARRANGE YOUR ROOM

Plan the classroom arrangement for face-to-face cooperative learning. Arrange the classroom furniture differently from the traditional rows. Try for a permanent desk arrangement that encourages *united groups in face-to-face* interaction.

As much as possible, provide aisles between student groups. This allows the teacher to move easily among groups to listen, help and monitor.

If the classroom can't be arranged into a permanent design, spend 20 minutes of the first week teaching students how to move the desks in and out of the arrangement. This is best done in conjunction with the first cooperative lesson. Insist upon keeping the room in order and quiet as students practice how to get in and out of groups.

*pages 281-283

Elementary Room Model

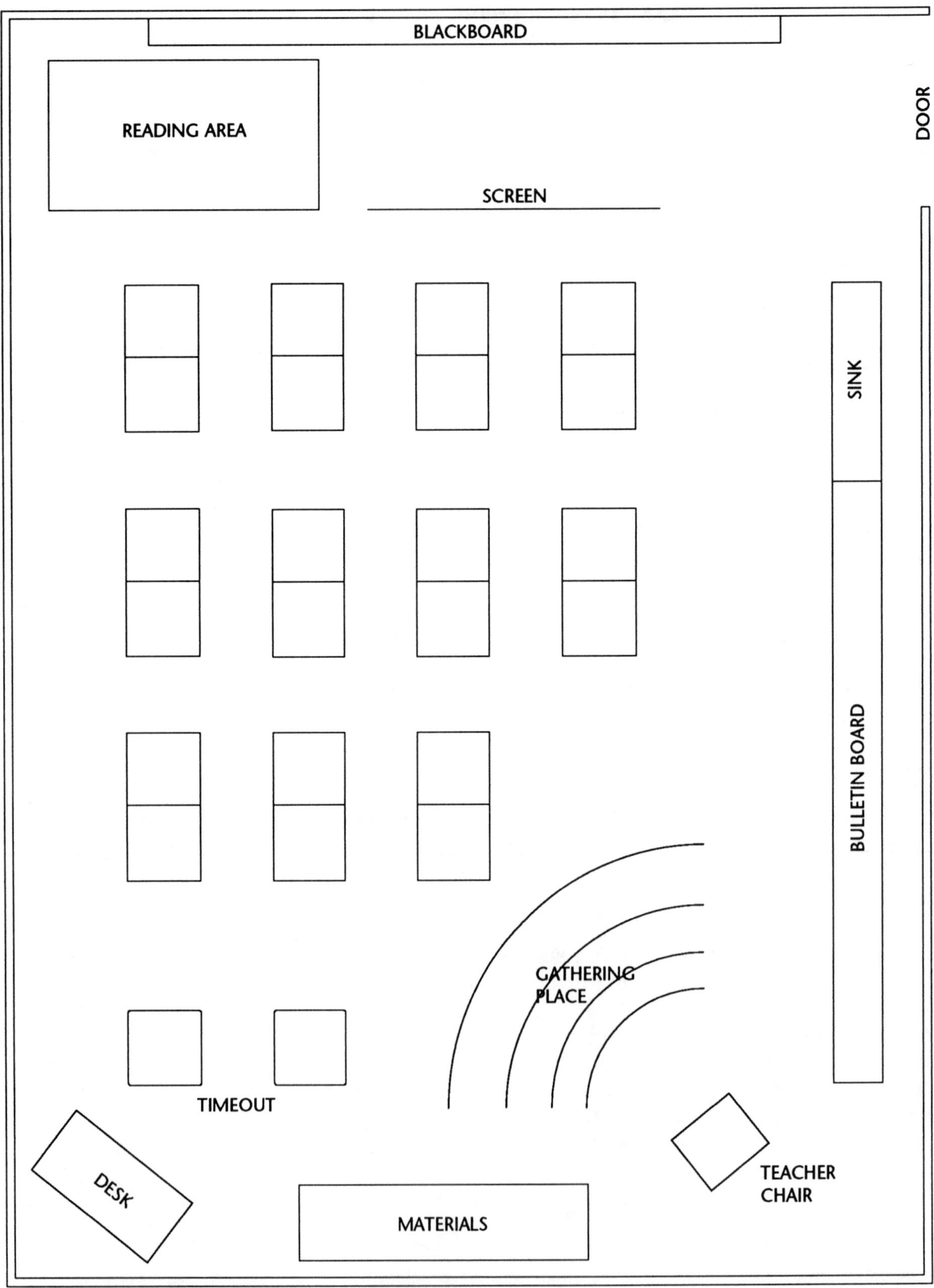

Elementary Room Model with Cooperative Learning Centers

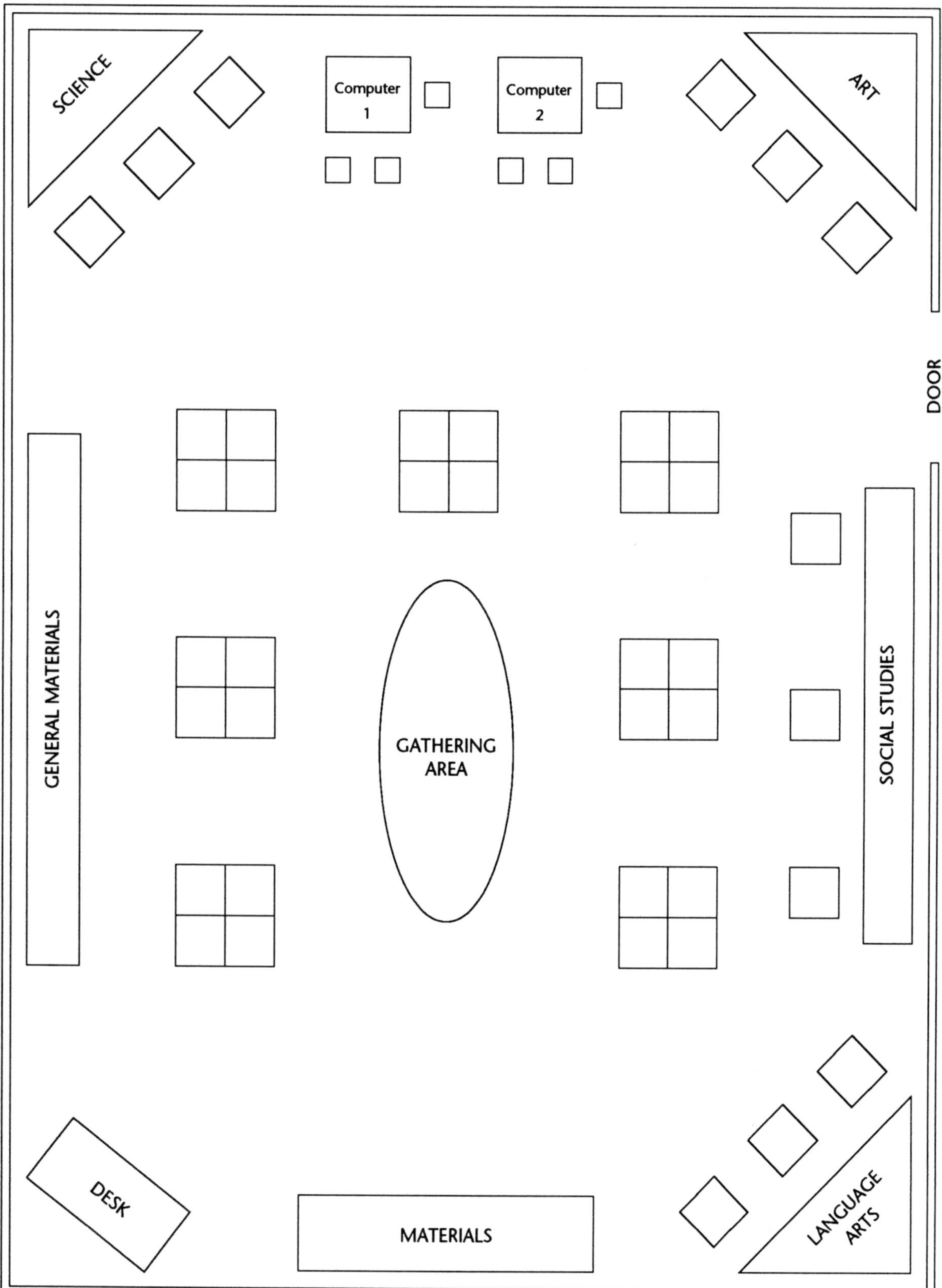

Middle School Lab

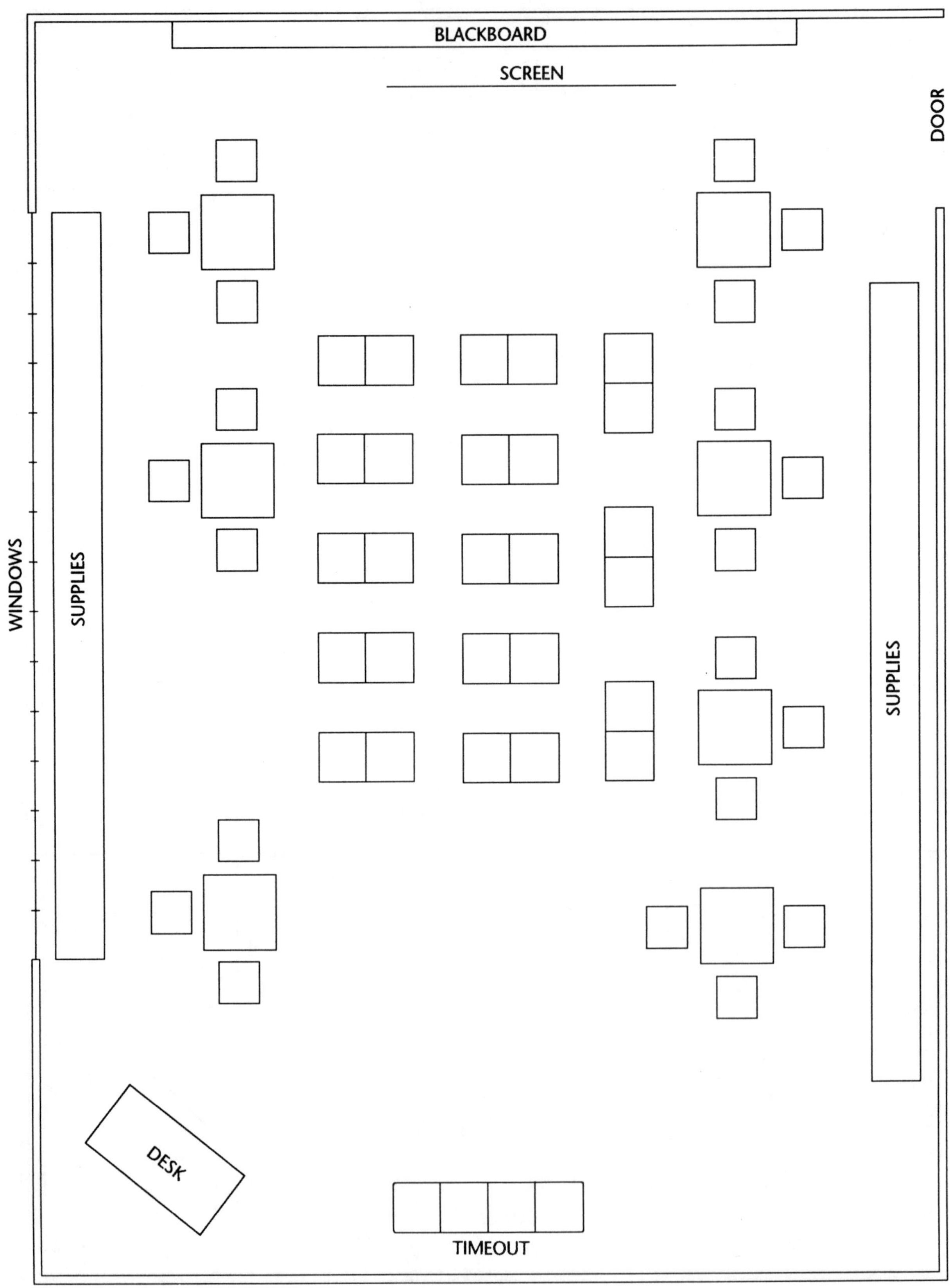

High School Classroom: Moveable Rows During Cooperative Task

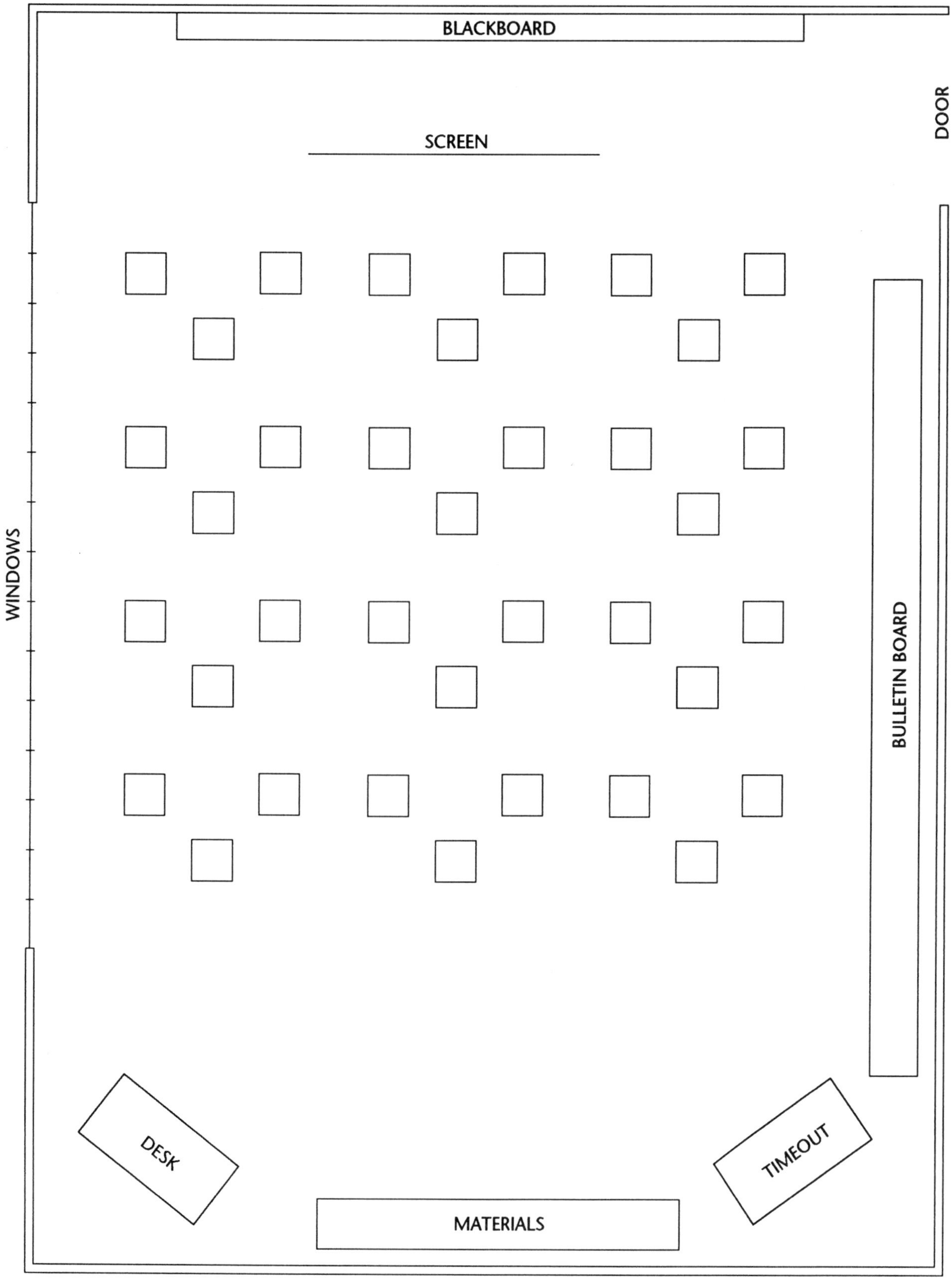

BLACKBOARD
DOOR
SCREEN
WINDOWS
BULLETIN BOARD
DESK
TIMEOUT
MATERIALS

High School Classroom: Moveable Rows During Lectures and Film

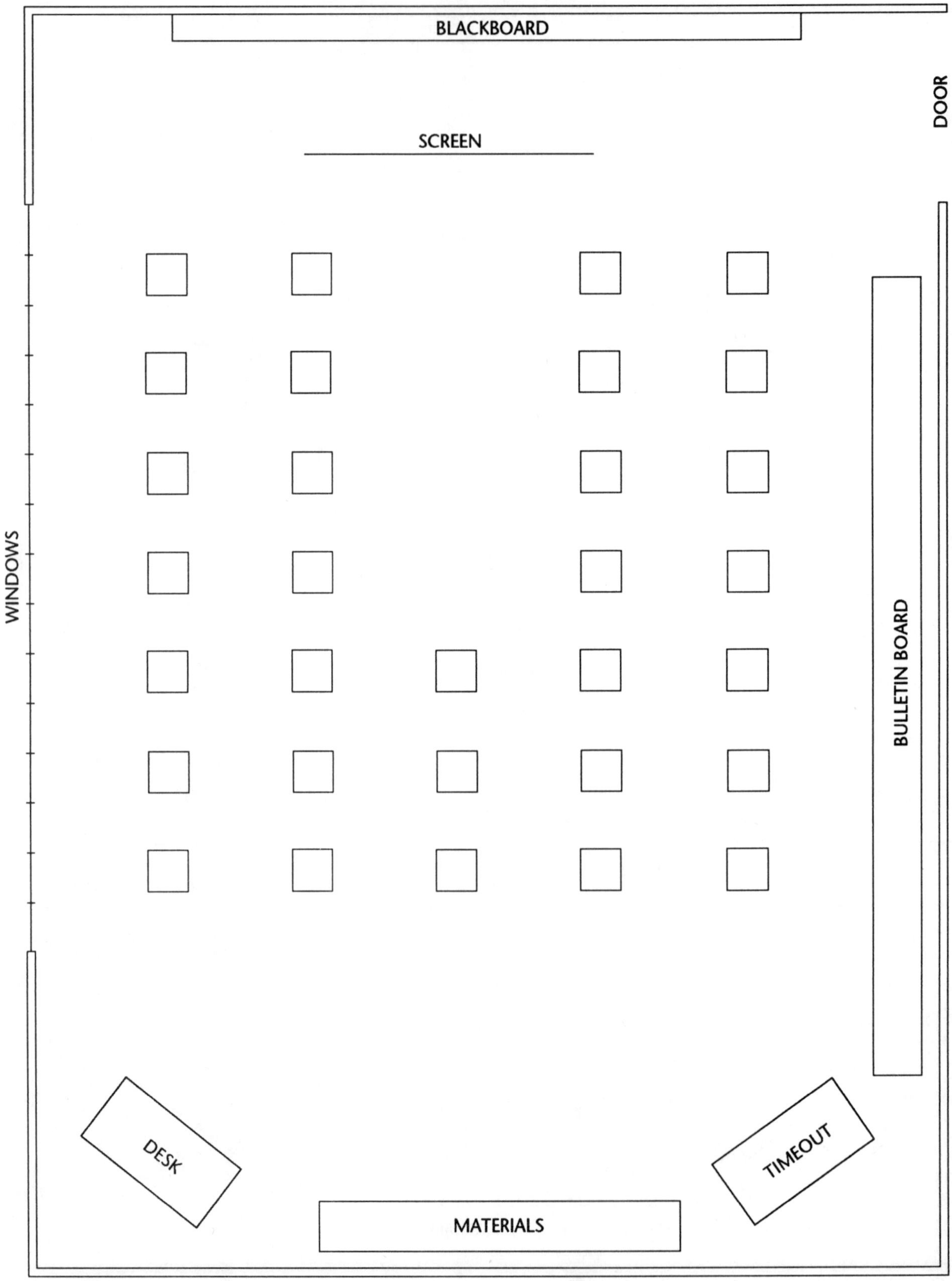

BLACKBOARD

DOOR

SCREEN

WINDOWS

BULLETIN BOARD

DESK

TIMEOUT

MATERIALS

☐ TEACH SIGNALS

Getting students into group tasks is easy. Getting them to stop is more difficult. Shouting above students' concentrated conversation turns any teacher's voice sour. Relying on a practiced signal is essential for the cooperative classroom.

For the most effective signal, use the well-proven "hands up." Introduced in the early 1900s by the Girl Scouts, this signal works with students of any age.

Introduce the signal by explaining what it is for, the class' attention.

"I'll hold up my hand

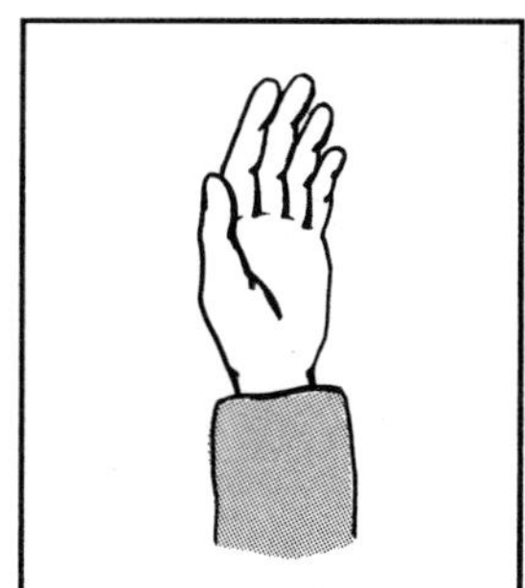

when I want everyone to stop talking and pay attention to me."

Let them know this signal alerts them to listen for the next set of instructions. Invite the students to do three things when they see the teacher's hand up: (1) complete their thoughts, (2) put up their hands, and (3) look at the teacher without talking. When all are silent, with pencils down and looking at the teacher, praise their attention ("I appreciate your prompt cooperation") and give the next instruction.

After demonstrating the signal, conduct a short practice. Use wait time and support it with eye contact. If some students are slower to respond, use "proximity"—Move next to the laggards and stand there with a raised hand.

After a week or two, some students may get sloppy. They do raise their hands when signaled, but forget to stop talking. To correct this, (1) plan to stand next to the offending group, (2) teach and repractice by having a strong group demonstrate the correct response and the others imitate, or (3) give stronger recognition to the most responsive students.

There are several appropriate times to use the signal. Essentially, to address the class, never begin talking until all students are looking at the teacher and not talking or working. Keep the hand up until that moment of absolute silence. Here are the three most common uses of the signal: (1) when giving class instructions, (2) when class talk becomes too loud and controlled voice levels (i.e, 3", 6", 12" voices) are needed, and (3) when a student or guest is to address the class.

Are there other signals?

For increasing student involvement, feel free to make your own signals to reinforce verbal answers. It also helps to put groups' task instructions on an overhead for students' easy reference. For example:

TODAY'S TASK

1. Meet with your partner.
2. Have one partner gather the materials. Have the other partner draw a Venn diagram for creative thinking and fishing.
3. Take turns listing similarities and differences.
4. When you are ready to share your diagram, hang it by your desk.

How do I evaluate learning in cooperative groups?

The same way you evaluate students now with individual and competitive learning. After working with groups for a year or so, other grading strategies can be used. See page 343 for details (see also chapter 12 on grades).

What do I do with students who won't cooperate?

Honor their right to work alone; motivate them to take advantage of the privilege to work together. See page 343 for more information.

The hands-up signal works in any class with any age of students, providing that the prompt response is consistently required. If all teachers in the school use the same signal, students benefit all the more.

It is not mandatory that every teacher use the same signal. Some prefer to flick the lights, ring a hotel bell or use the hand *T* to signal timeout. Any are fine as long as the signal is taught, practiced and used.

☐ PREPARE INCENTIVES

Prepare incentives for cooperative learning. A classroom of *internally* motivated students is every teacher's dream. The reality is that external motivators may be a prerequisite for many students. To develop *internal* motivation, some of the most fundamental tools are *external* incentives and rewards. It works best to have a variety of motivators which will help many different students. Following is a list of external motivators that experienced practitioners of cooperative learning have used. Note that the incentives are geared toward rewarding *the group* for accomplishments or rewarding individuals for contributions *to the group.*

GROUP REWARD Think about what to tell the students. Are the group rewards given to recognize the practice of specific social skills? How many times must the observer note each skill? Are groups expected to perform a fixed number of times? Is each group competing against itself to improve on its previous score? Or is this an intergroup competition?

Intergroup As long as students have the social skills to handle intergroup competition, consider giving the highest-scoring groups a group prize. For instance, if group 3 scores 79 on the task and groups 1 and 2 only score 65, then 79 wins. *If any member of the winning group makes negative remarks to the other groups, then his/her group may forfeit the prize.* Encourage all groups to celebrate the top-achieving group.

Intragroup A more appropriate form of recognition goes to groups that improve upon their previous performances in using social skills. To encourage cooperation within each group, use a group improvement score without singling out any one member.

Individual If individuals in the groups are identified, be sure the groups are not penalized. Focus on the team's improvement or give special recognition for individual improvement so the whole team benefits.

LOTTERY To avoid inappropriate competition among teams, give each team a fair chance to earn the reward. One of the best ways to do this is by having a lottery. In a given task, each team can earn so many tickets for a team prize (e.g., one ticket per 10 social skill points). Once a week have a drawing for a team prize that all members share. Here are some examples:

- ✓ 10 minutes of free time for each member
- ✓ a certificate for each team member to hang on the wall
- ✓ a certificate for each member to buy a paperback book
- ✓ a grab bag for each member

The grab bag can contain school supplies. Some schools draw points at the end of a quarter or semester, usually with every class in the school eligible to win. All classroom points are placed in the schoolwide draw, even if a team won in a classroom draw, and the prizes are more significant. In one school, the prize was a field trip for each grade's winning team, with lunch paid by the PTA. In another, individual students who earned team contribution points were eligible for a 10-speed bicycle. All students who earned 50 points a semester for team spirit received a special certificate. All 75-point earners received a plaque and a T-shirt.

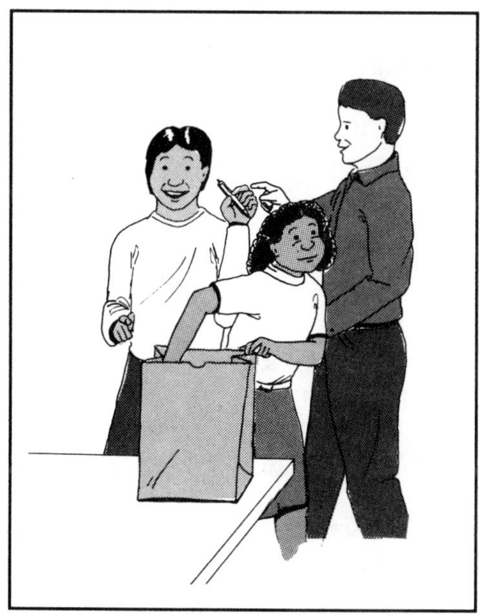

☐ PLAN YOUR INTRODUCTORY COOPERATIVE LESSON

There are a host of strategies that introduce the class to the purpose, methods and benefits of cooperative learning. Keep the first lesson short and simple (the KISS principle).

Following are some lesson blueprints for elementary, middle and secondary classrooms. They follow a three-part lesson design that extends the architectural metaphor of the *Blueprints* title.

Part I: Setting Up the Scaffolding
Part II: Working the Crew
Part III: Reflecting on the Design

Setting Up the Scaffolding, part I, describes all the preparation pieces, including input information, handouts and necessary materials needed *prior* to the lesson. The icon of the scaffold (at right) reflects the section content. Typically, this setting-up or "getting ready" section includes the anticipatory set or focus activity, the objective, the instructions, and identification of the cooperative and cognitive skills targeted in the lesson.

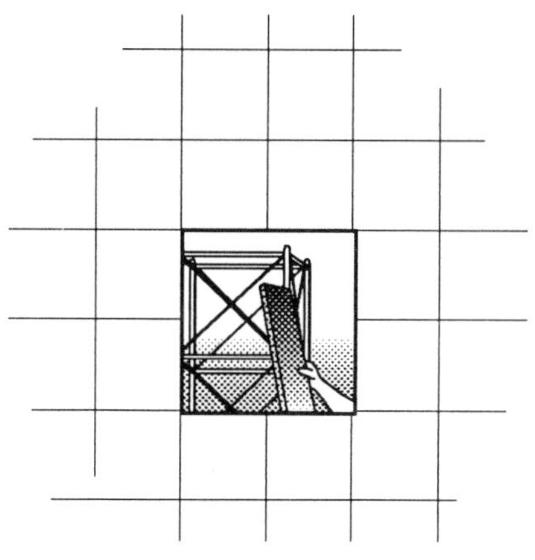

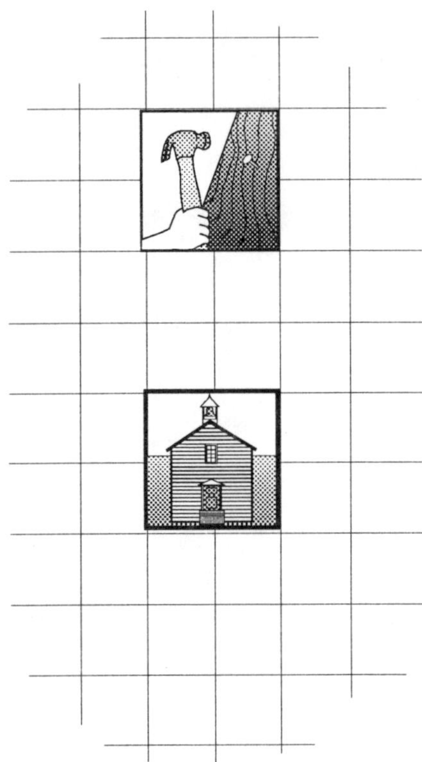

Use the key elements from the BUILD acronym as a tool in this preparation stage to help plan a high-support, high-content, high-challenge lesson.

Part II, **Working the Crew**, elaborates on the interactions that occur *during* the actual lesson. The hand-and-hammer icon (at left) indicates the activity orientation found in this section of the lesson. The activity includes the cooperative interaction structure and the graphic organizer with which the students work. This activity section includes all aspects of working the crew as students get intensely involved in the cooperative task.

The final section, **Reflecting on the Design**, presents the metacognitive discussion questions that require students to reflect and assess their behaviors, their learning and the lesson. The school icon (at left) is used. In this section, evaluation is focused on four distinct areas—the affective, the social, the cognitive and the metacognitive.

The *affective* processing focuses student thinking at the *feeling* level. Understanding how their feelings influence their learning is a key to increasing the students' learning process.

To process or talk about the *social skill,* highlight the expected cooperative behaviors. By targeting explicit social skills prior to the lesson and by discussing them immediately following the interaction, students can track their progress in developing the social skills necessary for group work.

Cognitive processing follows a learning situation and consists of a typical classroom discussion in which students' answers are sampled, evaluated and justified. This is "going-over-the-work" type processing that highlights *what* was learned.

The *metacognitive* processing involves reflective thinking that requires students not only to think about *what* they've been doing, but also *how* they've been doing it. This metacognitive processing involves planning, monitoring and evaluating one's thinking and behavior. It's like stepping outside the situation and looking in at what's going on. This stage of thinking also fosters the application and transfer of ideas as students reflect upon their thinking processes and their behavior in the groups.

The development of students' metacognitive dispositions starts with what the teacher does to structure each student's learning to think about thinking.

What does the teacher do? Essentially at the end of cooperative and thoughtful lessons, he/she structures thoughtful "look-backs" at the quality of thinking used in the lesson. There are a plethora of options available to the designer of cooperative and thoughtful lessons (see side box on opposite page).

The window of opportunity that cooperative lessons opens for thinking about thinking broadens when the teacher takes advantage of the following "It's better when..." guidelines provided by experienced process facilitators in the classroom. In processing, it is better when we...

✓ invite students to write or sketch individual responses before sharing in small groups.

✓ model sample responses.

✓ use wraparounds with the right to pass rather than open volunteer responses. To help students listen to others, signal that several students will be asked to summarize the wraparound.

✓ use "fat" prompts that allow multiple responses and extend them with, "Why do you think so?"

✓ model acceptance ("Thank you," eye contact, smiles), drawing out ("Tell me more," "Give us an example"), and encouragement ("Take your time," "You can do it," "Great idea").

✓ use wait time to encourage students to listen to each other.

✓ use all-class reports from two or three small groups and avoid round-robin reports from all groups on every task.

✓ post products that show students' thinking about thinking.

Because many students may lack strong social skills needed to do extended and whole-class processing, start with the KISS principle (keep it short and simple). Do the first processing in small groups only. When moving to whole-group processing, sample responses but don't ask every group to process. Later, as students learn to listen in a large group, extend the processing time.

Although all four levels of processing (affective, social skill, cognitive and metacognitive) are included in each lesson, discussion can focus with any one or any combination of the three levels. By talking about thinking the teacher takes advantage of the teachable moments and facilitates transfer.

There is no aspect of thinking in the cooperative classroom that is more difficult to do than inviting students "to look back" and review their learning. Nor is any element more important or more powerful. Skillful processing takes time, energy and commitment. Once a teacher provides the key to successful metacognition for each student, the results in learning and motivation are dramatic and powerful. As Ralph Waldo Emerson said, "What lies behind us and what lies before us are tiny matters compared to what lies within us."

□ □ □

Update your task sequence on page 348.

THOUGHTFUL LOOK-BACKS

Blueprints offers numerous ways of looking back at the quality of students' thinking:

- *Media*—Student logs, newsprint, 3"x5" cards, videotapes and art paper provide varied media on which students *do* their thinking.
- *Prompts*—Stem statements, PMI charts, Mrs. Potter's Questions, cartoon strips, "Make a sketch..." and other starter statements initiate students' "thinking about thinking."
- *Focus*—Individual responses, small-group wraparounds and whole-class reports provide a variety of focal points.
- *Means of Expression*—Students can share ideas, write, sketch and graph to express their multitude of ideas.
- *Extension*—Once students have initiated this processing, the teacher can use different strategies to extend thinking:
  a. Individual comments in a thinking log or journal.
  b. All-class discussion with a graphic organizer, wait time, equal responses, fat questions, reinforcement of skillful thinking and encouragement help students explore thinking patterns.

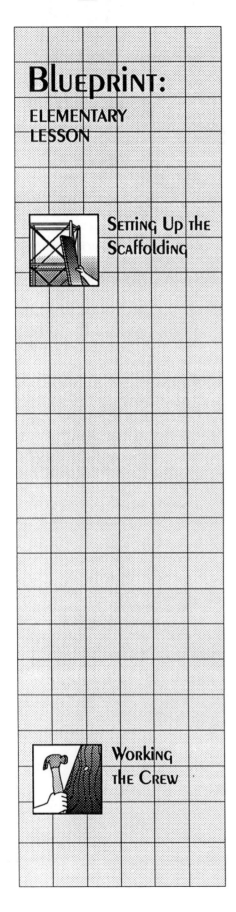

WHAT'S YOUR ROLE?

Roles are an important key to successful teamwork. They are a first step in preparing the students to bond by task, to be accountable for the whole group's work, and to assess the group's performance. This lesson not only *tells* the student about the roles, but gives an early, quick practice in the whole model. In checking for understanding, note for sure that everyone "knows" all the roles.

On the overhead, record the special jobs on a football team (e.g., end, tackle, halfback). Ask different students to tell what is special about two or three of those jobs. Ask the class to tell why is it important for each player to do his/her job. Ask what happens when one or two don't do their jobs. After this discussion, point out that the class is going to be organized into cooperative work teams and that each person on a team will have a role with a specific job to do.

On the overhead, show a picture of each role.

Reader: Reads the handout or material

Recorder: Keeps the group's official notes

Checker: Checks after the task

These are the key roles for all ages. Use age-appropriate cards that have each role's job outlined on a card. Review the roles with the class. Ask one student at random to paraphrase the review of each card.

Have three role cards for each group. Copy the ones from Appendix B or make some new ones.

Divide the class into groups of three by telling students, "Pick your partners." Or, give each student a card that has a number, a city name, 1/3 of a picture or something similar. Tell them to find the other two students who have the related or matching pieces.

Tell them to look for their assigned role on the back of the puzzle piece.

Leave the job descriptions for each role on the overhead.

Have one student review the recorder's role out loud to the class. Add to or correct as needed. Instruct the readers in each group to explain their role to their small groups. The other group members must agree on the role description. If any group cannot agree, only the checker may ask for help from the teacher. Allow two to three minutes for this.

Repeat this process for the other roles. Do one round at a time. At the end, have the checker recheck the group for agreement and understanding.

To process for the affective (or to quickly energize the class), show the class how to do a Eskimo "Hurrah!" Tell everyone to put two hands way up.

They are to wiggle their hands in the air. Model the hurrah and ask the whole class to practice. After the practice, tell them to each look at their small groups and give each member a hurrah for working well on the role task.

To process social skills, have students complete the following statement in a small-group round robin:

Having a "role to play" in the group is ______.

To process in a cognitive manner, ask students to suggest other *roles* that might be needed in future tasks. Keep a list.

To process for application and transfer, ask students to tell about a time when they may play several roles in a situation (e.g., speaker, listener, encourager).

□ □ □

Reflecting on the Design

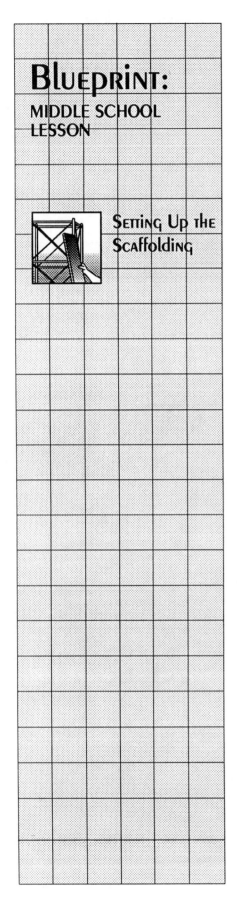

COOPERATIVE? COMPETITIVE? OR INDIVIDUALISTIC?

On the materials table place a pile of old magazines, one scissors for every three students, a pad of newsprint with crayons or markers and several rolls of masking tape. Tell the students that they are going to study three ways in which people work together. On the board, write the words *cooperative, competitive* and *individualistic.* Put a T-chart under each.

COOPERATIVE		COMPETITIVE		INDIVIDUALISTIC	
Looks Like	Sounds Like	Looks Like	Sounds Like	Looks Like	Sounds Like

Give a definition of each word. Write the definition under the word along with examples.

Cooperative: when two or more people work together toward a single goal (e.g., football players, airplane crew)

Competitive: when one or more persons work against each other toward a single goal (e.g., two football teams try to win the game, race car drivers try to win a race)

Individualistic: when one person works alone to reach a goal (e.g., a mountain climber, a house painter) according to a set criteria (80 percent etc.)

Ask members of the class to add other examples.

Working the Crew

Divide the class into teams of three. Have the students count off by threes. Tell them that each team is going to work together toward a single goal. Before they do the task, however, there are some things that need to be done to prepare the teams.

Give each trio one hanger, 24" of string, one 8" X 11" tagboard and one magazine. Assign the roles of *cutter* (cuts out selected pictures), *paster* (pastes on squares) and *arranger* (ties pictures to hanger). The cooperative goal is to make a mobile out of pictures that are glued to tagboard squares. The middle piece of each mobile has to have one of the following team words: *cooperation, competition, individualism.* Assign each group a theme and tell the groups that their pictures have to fit their assigned themes.

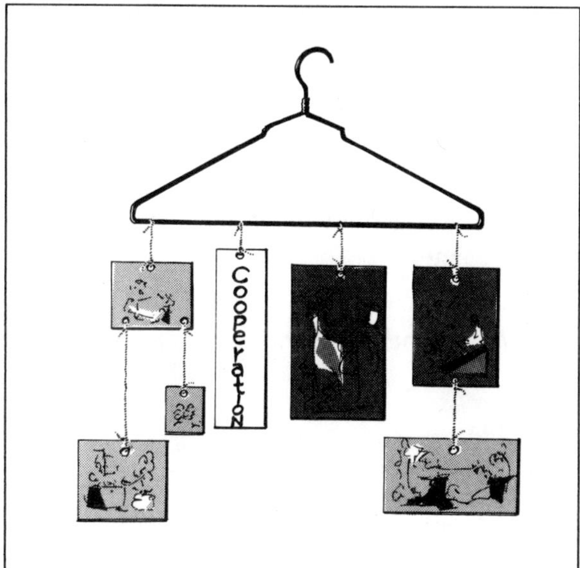

Allow 10 minutes for students to construct the mobiles and three minutes for groups to ensure that all members can explain the picture selections made for their theme. After all members have signed their finished mobiles, hang the mobiles throughout the room.

Reflecting on the Design

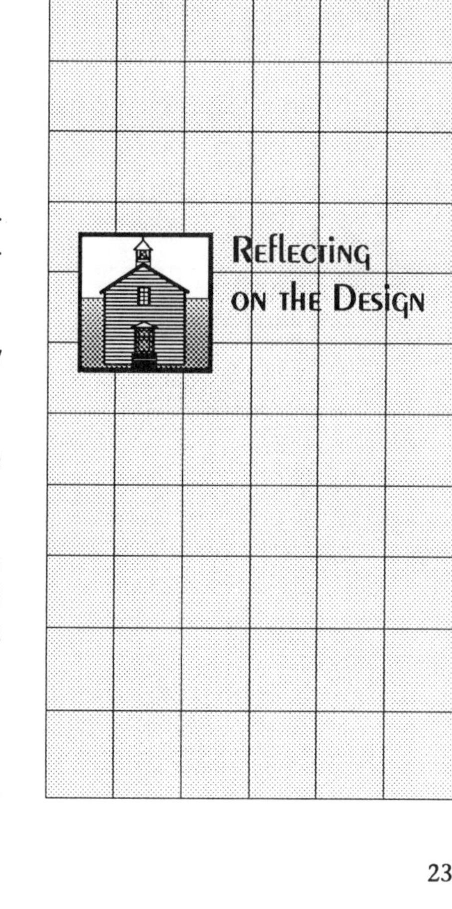

To explore how the students feel about the concepts of cooperation, competition and individualism, have them give examples of positive and negative feelings attached to each of the three ways to interact.

For social skill processing, ask students to describe a cooperating behavior they used today.

For cognitive processing, simply have students describe their products (the mobiles).

For metacognitive reflection, have groups talk about *how* they thought through the task. What did they do first? second? third? etc.? Reinforce that they will have many tasks to do this year in which they will work cooperatively to think critically and creatively.

□ □ □

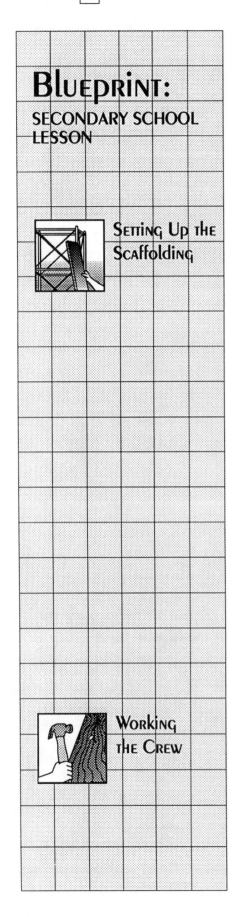

TORN CIRCLES

On the board or on a transparency, write the words that describe the three types of interaction.

> *Cooperative:* when two or more people work together toward a single goal (e.g., football players, airplane crew)
>
> *Competitive:* when one or more persons work against each other toward a single goal (e.g., two football teams try to win the game, race car drivers try to win a race)
>
> *Individualistic:* when one person works alone to reach a goal (e.g., a mountain climber, a house painter)

Elicit definitions of the words from students with sports examples of the three types of interactions:

> *Cooperation:* seesaw, leap frog
>
> *Competition:* Olympic, tug of war
>
> *Individualism:* swimming, tight-rope walking

Divide the class into teams of three and assign the roles:

Material's manager:	Gets the stuff
Reporter:	Gives report
Observer:	Talks about feelings

Explain that the Torn Circles activity is used as a quick, but graphically concrete example of the three types of social interactions. Suggest that as the students sample the three distinct interactions, they are to focus on how they *feel.*

Competitive Task

Instruct students to *each,* by themselves, take a sheet of scratch paper (gathered by the material's manager) and tear a circle. The goal is to tear the roundest circle in the group. Reiterate, "The winning circle will be judged by others for *roundness.*"

Once the individuals complete the task, instruct them to select the "best" circle in their groups of threes.

Once the "winner" from each group is selected, have each side of the room select the three roundest circles.

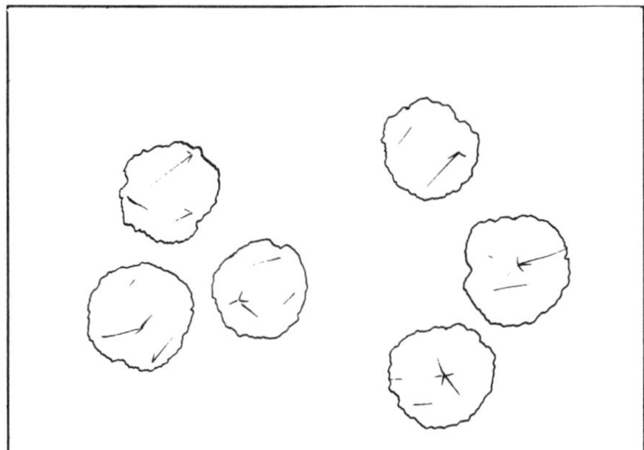

With the six finalists, have the students place their circles on the overhead projector and, using a pseudo "applause meter," judge the *best* circle in the room. (First-place, second-place and third-place winners may be picked.)

Once the competition is over, have students, in their groups of three, describe how they are feeling. Have the reporters sample the feelings experienced by the groups. Gather a list of words that describe their feelings on the competitive tasks. For example, competition makes one feel:

anxious

stupid

angry

nervous

Individualistic Task

Instruct students that again, they are to individually tear shapes. However, this time the torn circles must *meet this criteria*:

two straight sides

two curves

a hole

Any and all torn circles that meet the criteria earn a 100 percent grade for the participants.

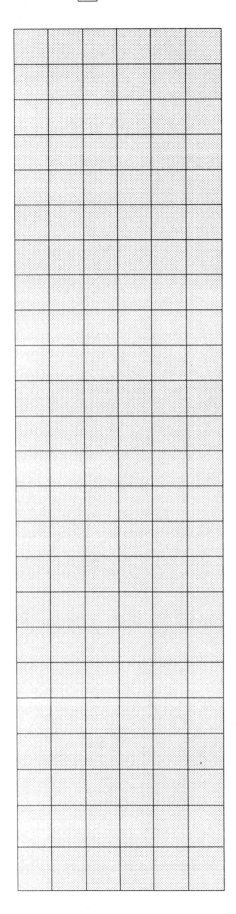

Torn circles for the individualistic task might include figures that look like this:

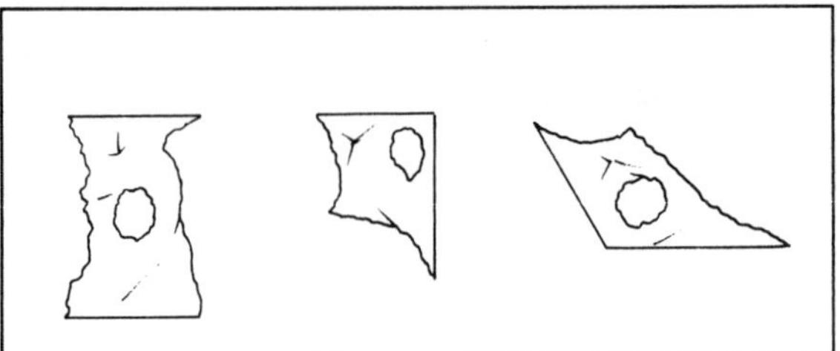

Again, talk about how students felt during this interaction. Gather words that describe their feelings when trying to meet individual *criteria* (e.g., successful, non-threatened, satisfied, a winner).

Cooperative task

Instruct students that in this last interaction they are to each contribute a piece for a final collage comprised of three pieces. The final collage design is to symbolize cooperation.

To reiterate, have each student trio design a collage that symbolizes cooperation using the group's three torn pieces.

Samples of Collage Designs: Cooperation

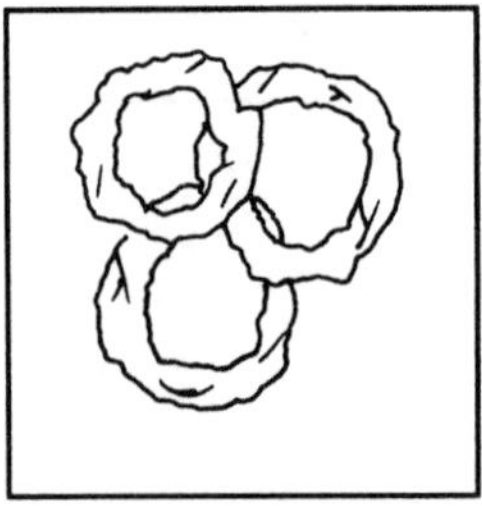

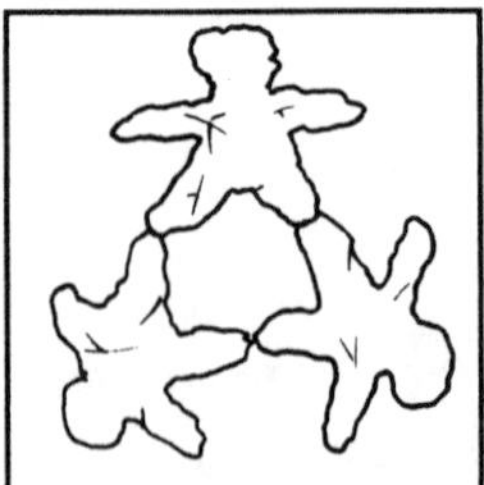

Again, process the feelings experienced by students as they cooperatively completed this "torn circles" task. Gather words that describe their feelings (e.g., supported, teamwork, pride, trust).

Through the interaction, the focus is on the affective or feelings level. Take time to compare and contrast the three lists of words describing the different feelings students had during the activities.

To process socially, ask students to describe a social situation in which someone acted inappropriately.

To process cognitively, check that students understand the three types of interactions. Ask students to role play in groups of six these three words: *competitive, individualistic, cooperative.*

Finally, to lead students to metacognitively transfer the concepts beyond this one situation, direct each student to make an entry in his/her log (the log is a notebook of ideas, thoughts, notes, etc. for them to refer to and add to throughout the year). Have them complete one of the following lead-ins:

Cooperation is like _____ because both _____.

Competition differs from cooperation because ______.

The hardest part about cooperating is ______.

□ □ □

REFLECTING ON THE DESIGN

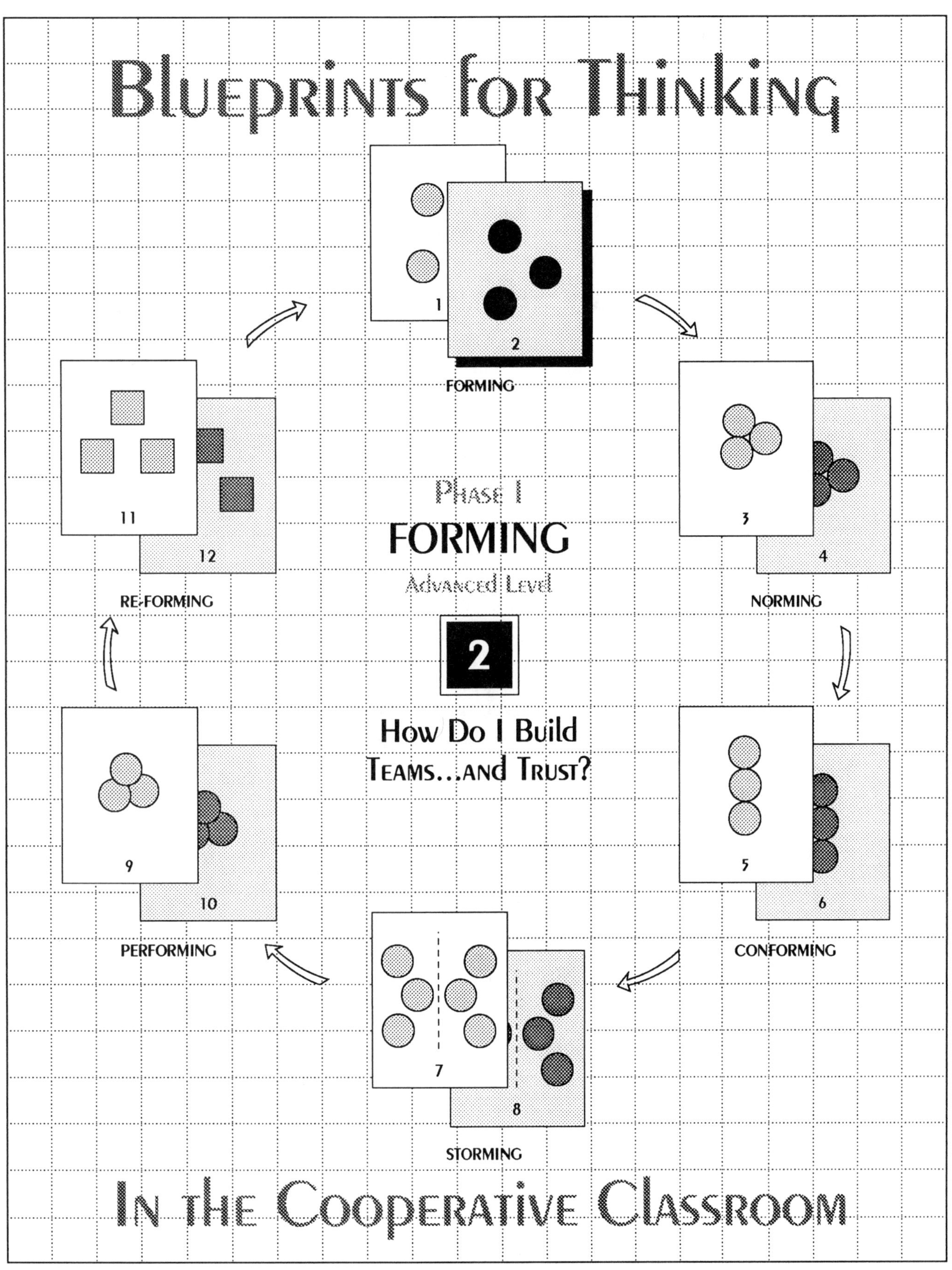
Blueprints for Thinking
1
2
FORMING
3
4
NORMING
5
6
CONFORMING
7
8
STORMING
9
10
PERFORMING
11
12
RE-FORMING
Phase I
FORMING
Advanced Level
2
How Do I Build
Teams...and Trust?
In the Cooperative Classroom

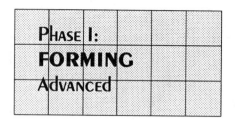

PHASE I:
FORMING
Advanced

How Do I Build Teams...and Trust?

Trust is the result of risk successfully survived.
—Jack Gibb

Draft

One of the most frequently asked questions about cooperative learning is, "How do I form groups?" The answer depends on the purpose for each group. However, the forming of the groups and building teams and/or trust is the next phase.

There are two types of cooperative learning groups: *task groups* and *base groups*. Use *task groups* for instruction. Some are *formal* and some *informal*. *Base groups* support the task groups; they provide students a main path toward *bonding* in the cooperative classroom (see summary chart of cooperative groups page 284).

Specs

☐ TASK GROUPS

The primary purpose of task groups is to promote students' cooperation in working to accomplish a common goal. Task groups, comprised of two to five students of different abilities, talents and motivation, provide the most powerful means for raising achievement, increasing positive attitudes toward school, developing skillful thinking and increasing self-esteem.

What is cognitive rehearsal?

Students' expressions of ideas or concepts. Cooperative learning and cognitive organizers are instructional models used to facilitate cognitive rehearsal.

INFORMAL TASK GROUPS *Informal Task Groups* are quick and easy tools for initiating *cognitive rehearsal* and *uniting group teams*.

Cognitive rehearsal refers to students' expressions of ideas or concepts. It is accomplished most easily when the teacher structures interaction between students for the discussion of a common topic. There are a number of easy methods to structure informal task groups for cognitive rehearsal, for example, cooperative learning and graphic organizers.

The strategies for promoting cognitive rehearsal don't require roles, guidelines and the other methods used in formal group tasks. While there are ways to heighten students' attention to each other (e.g., student A paraphrases B's ideas or A records all ideas), the following strategies take little more than two to five minutes of *face-to-face interaction.* Choose appropriate strategies from the following selections as opportunities occur.

INFORMAL TASK GROUP SAMPLES

Think-Pair-Share

The *Think-Pair-Share* rehearsal strategy can be used:

- ✓ after a lecture, to help students summarize key points,
- ✓ to begin a new topic or unit by having students discuss prior knowledge,
- ✓ to stimulate student thinking about an important piece of information,
- ✓ to check students' understanding of or insight into a topic,
- ✓ to bring closure to a lesson,
- ✓ to deepen students' short-term memories, or
- ✓ to promote student transfer of a concept.

With each of these uses of the think-pair-share strategy, give similar instructions:

Before the lecturette. "Today, I am going to describe (topic). After I define each term, I'm going to ask you to ________________ with a partner." To fill in the second blank in this statement, select one of the following: (a) summarize the key points, (b) tell what you already know about the topic, (c) pick one idea of importance to you and explain it, (d) tell how the information is important to you, or (e) tell something new you learned about the topic. After 10-120 seconds, sample student ideas for the whole class.

After the lecturette (or at appropriate times during a longer lecture). "Turn to the person on your (right/left side), and take turns (see a-e above). Allow about (two or three minutes) for each person to share."

Explain Why

Explain Why enables students to rehearse their reasons for selecting an answer. Before a lesson, ask students three to five multiple-choice questions. After each question is answered, invite several students to explain *why* they selected those answers. Solicit several answers to each question and write them on the board. Tell the class it will discover the correct answers as it studies the lesson.

Business Cards

Business Cards are motivational rehearsal tools that involve the entire class. Give each student a 3" x 5" index card. Explain the purpose of a business card—to greet other people, to tell about yourself.

Model the instructions on the overhead or board by giving sample answers to the following:

A. Write down your first name in the middle of the card using capital letters—TOM.

B. Write the name of your school beneath your name—e.g., ML King.

C. Write in one corner of the card a success you have had this week at school, home or play —e.g., made a friend, got a 95 on a quiz.

D. Write your learning *goal* for this week in another corner—e.g., improve vocabulary quiz score, finish a paper.

E. Write a *benefit* for doing your homework in yet another corner—e.g., higher grades.

F. Write down a *favorite* book title in the last corner—e.g., *Curious George, The Grapes of Wrath.*

G. Demonstrate your best cooperative skill—e.g., pat on the back, smiles or "Atta boy."

After all students have completed their cards, instruct everyone to find a partner. After the pairs settle, instruct them to focus on one of the corner topics (success, benefit, goal or favorite) and explain *why* that topic was selected. After one or two minutes, instruct students to switch partners. Continue switching until all four of the corner topics have been discussed.

*What We Know (KWL)**

What We Know is a cognitive rehearsal strategy that helps with pre-lesson diagnosis. Give each student a worksheet with these headings:

WHAT WE **KNOW**	WHAT WE **WANT** TO KNOW	

Give the unit or lesson title (e.g., safety, photosynthesis, *Moby Dick*, whole numbers). Invite pairs to list all they *know* about the topic in the first column. Second, have them list all they *want* to know about it in the second column. Match the pairs into foursomes so they can share their lists. After the unit, add a third column, What We **Learned**. Allow time for students to write what they *learned*. Discuss and share student lists from the third column.

*page 285

*Prediction Pairs**

Give each prediction pair of students a book or short story to read together. Let one partner read aloud while the other records the pair's predictions.

WHAT WILL HAPPEN NEXT	REASONS FROM READING

After each page, the recorder writes down the predictions both partners agree to in column I. Next, the recorder writes the reasons for the predictions in column II, listing supporting evidences from the pages. Invite one pair to share with another.

We Bags

Give each pair a paper bag. Invite the pairs to decorate them with their names, favorite books or foods, or names of places they have visited. Then have the groups fill their bags with objects that have special meaning to them. Students should prepare to introduce their partners by discussing each item that is in the bag. Match the pairs into foursomes to introduce their partners.

*I Learned Mail-Gram**

For rehearsal after a lesson, invite each student to complete an *I Learned Mail-Gram.* Pass out the cards with the "I learned..." stem. Have students fill in and sign the form. Next, match students into pairs to share the mail-grams. Rotate the pairs several times.

MAIL-GRAM

To: ____________

From: ____________

Message: **I learned...** ____________

____

____

Signed ____________

Pair Review

Pair Review works well as a closure task at the end of short lessons. Jigsaw the lesson's information. Ask each pair member to review one-half of the key information. Be explicit as to how each member should focus the review (e.g., pick out the three key ideas in the section; know the definitions of five vocabulary words; compare similarities of __________). Each member reviews the other's work. When doing review work, it's best that each member be asked to pick *X* number of ideas. After presenting each set, have each pair rank the most important words, ideas or concepts and list the reasons for their agreed upon rankings. This activity structures deeper processing and enables the students to strengthen their item or concept recall for both the short-term and the long-term memories. Encouraging students to use a graphic organizer such as a ladder or steps, further enhances students' recall. Use pair reviews for checking homework, reviewing pre-tests, recalling prior knowledge or renewing old acquaintances.

*pages 286 and 287

What are task groups?

Cooperative groups that are structured with:

- roles
- cooperative guidelines
- criteria for success
- a group goal
- a group processing strategy
- the ability to gather information, process concepts or make applications

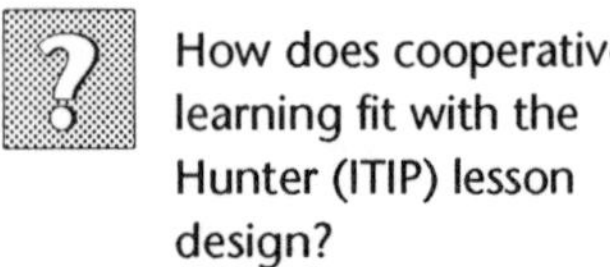

How does cooperative learning fit with the Hunter (ITIP) lesson design?

Very well when a direct instruction lesson is wanted. See page 344 for an example.

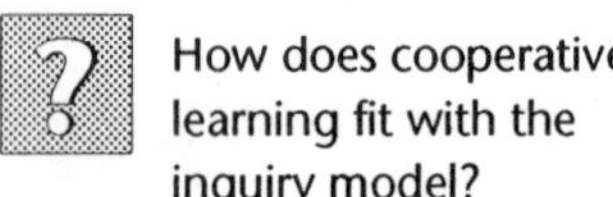

How does cooperative learning fit with the inquiry model?

Very well. See the sample lesson on page 344.

FORMAL TASK GROUPS *Formal Task Groups* can be used with any content lesson in the curriculum. Formal task groups are structured with roles, cooperative guidelines, criteria for success with a group goal, and a group processing strategy. In the direct instruction model, design formal cooperative task groups into the anticipatory set, input, guided practice or closure. In an inquiry lesson, design cooperation for gathering information, processing concepts or making applications. Tasks as simple as learning vocabulary and practicing computation, or as complex as contrasting two authors' styles or testing a hypothesis on physics, benefit from formal cooperative structures.

When students start in formal task groups it is helpful that they learn the procedures in a simple, fun way. Once they show a "working knowledge" of the procedures, it is possible to move into content. An easy place to start is vocabulary. Using fun new words made up of two words put together, try this sample hook lesson to demonstrate a round-robin jigsaw procedure with roles, guidelines and group processing. Keep the list of new words short so students can easily see and feel a "jigsaw" and learn the jigsaw procedures. In the processing, highlight the benefits of roles, guidelines and jigsaw pieces for learning the words. After the students demonstrate they know how to jigsaw, introduce the first formal vocabulary in the same model. Later, introduce the class to more complex jigsaws with portions of text chapters or characters in stories.

A Sample Starter: Jigsaw I

Select nine vocabulary words. Divide the class into trios. Give each group member three words and instruct him/her (a) to learn the definitions of the words, (b) to draw a sketch of each word's meaning, and (c) to use the sketch to teach the other group members in a round-robin teaching. In 15 minutes, all members must know the meaning of the words. To help, have the checker quiz the other group members after each round of three and for the total nine before you quiz each student.

Get Ready: Review your roles and the task.

Step 1: Learn the three words. Draw a picture of each word. (Use it to teach the other members).

Step 2: Conduct the first round of teaching and check. (Have each member review the definition.) Coach as needed.

Step 3: Second round of teaching and check.

Step 4: Third round of teaching and check.

Step 5: Groups double check.

Step 6: Quiz.

Step 7: Elicit a group list of learning strategies used. (check after each round; make and explain a sketch; give encouragement, etc.)

☐ BASE GROUPS

In task groups, the same students work together only for the duration of the task. That may be a five-minute pair-share or 40 minutes a day for 10 to 20 days. In base groups, the same students work together several times a week for at least a month and perhaps as much as a year.

COMPOSITION OF BASE GROUPS Base groups consist of three to five students randomly mixed to ensure heterogeneity of ability, motivation, social skills, sex, race and ethnic backgrounds. They are the classroom glue. In base groups, students develop their teamwork, build trust and solidify friendships.

Although it is not unusual for some teachers to form base groups in the opening week of school, it is better to hold off for at least a month. This gives the teacher the chance to observe each student in task groups. Who works well in a group? Who has difficulty? Who gets along with student A? Who doesn't?

BONDING OF BASE GROUPS The most effective way to help base groups bond is to structure activities that help the members develop a common identity. These activities include picking a group name, making a group motto and flag, writing an editorial to praise the group, creating a group logo on a T-shirt and setting group goals. After the groups have completed the identity task, have each group post the result and describe it. Encourage them to practice their roles and concentrate on encouraging, listening and helping each other.

10 Ways To Bond Cooperative Groups

- Use one worksheet and one marker or pencil per group.
- Design a group ad.
- Create a group song.
- Make a group motto.
- Make a group flag.
- Set group goals.
- Decide on a name for the group.
- List group accomplishments.
- Create group awards.
- Brainstorm similarities among the group members.

USES OF BASE GROUPS There are a variety of uses for the base groups. In addition to the team *bonding activities, social skill practice sessions* and *goal evaluations,* base groups serve as a place to *review the week's work, discuss current events, connect the themes and topics studied in various content areas,*

What are base groups?

- Three to five students mixed by the teacher
- Members who meet together regularly over a long period of time
- Members who build trust and develop social skills
- Members who complete special learning tasks such as unit reviews, goal setting and problem solving

When are the best times for base groups to meet?

- For self-contained class, as part of total group orientation
- For middle school class, as part of adviser/advisee period
- For high school class, as part of homeroom or in a study period

See page 345 for more information.

plan social events, *work out differences* and *solve problems*. In essence, they are a safe and secure home environment that encourages positive interactions, trust and friendship development. In base groups, "there are no strangers, only friends who have not met."

There are several guidelines that foster successful base groups:

✓ Emphasize to the students that the base group allows no separation.

✓ In the early weeks, keep the base groups simple and structured. Have a definite activity for the groups to perform. Reinforce the need to use roles, guidelines, group processing and social skills. Have a team product (e.g., an ad). Five to ten minutes per day is enough time at the start. Older students may be in base groups five minutes at the week's start and five at the end.

✓ Expand on the norming skills—Accept, draw out, acknowledge.

BASE GROUP SAMPLES

Group Goal Setting

At the beginning and ending of the week, have base groups take five to ten minutes to set up and evaluate learning goals for the week. After they have learned to ask goal clarifying questions (e.g., "How will that help you?" "What blocks will you face?"), have the groups take turns setting and clarifying a goal (e.g., "This week, I want to work on my spelling," "I'm going to reorganize my study space," "I'm going to practice problem solving"). At the end of the week, members of the base groups share what happened with their goals.

Previews

Have base groups jigsaw reading materials, notes and lab work prior to a quiz or exam.

Connections

Teach the students how to do cognitive mapping. Have the students map the various ideas learned during the week and identify related concepts.

Problem Solving

Teach base groups the problem-solving model. Once a week, take the course content and pose a problem (e.g., What would have happened if Washington had not crossed the Delaware?).

Homework Check

Use the jigsaw model to review students' homework. Each student in a base trio summarizes one-third of the assignment and teaches it to the others. The group checkers make sure all members "have it." (See portmanteaux lesson, page 340.)

Social Skill Practice

The more students practice and process social skills, the more they improve. Allow base groups to take advantage of down time in the classroom by using "sponge activities" at the beginning of a class or Friday afternoon to close the week. Practice can take little time since the base groups are preset. Keep practice instructions hanging in a favored spot on the blackboard. If a little more time is available, have base groups of three take three rounds, one for each member to play each role.

(Sample activity for middle school base groups to practice the storming skill of problem solving.)

BASE GROUPS APRIL 19-23

1. Rotate encourager, observer, problem solver each day.
2. Observer: Note problem-solving sequence.
3. Problem Solver: Talk aloud through problem from last night's homework. Pick your own.
4. Observer: Take last minute to report on the steps.
5. Start as soon as you get five extra minutes.

How often should I use cooperative groups?

More than 60 percent of students' learning time should be spent in cooperative groups, but students also need individual reflection time. See page 345 for details.

☐ ☐ ☐

Update your task sequence on page 348.

CALL IT

Ask students to watch as the teacher flips a coin. Ask one student to call "heads" or "tails" and mark it on a tally sheet on the board. Flip the coin several times and circle the tallies that are correct.

Explain that *predicting* is a thinking skill that requires them to use information they have to figure out what could happen in the future. Synonyms for *predicting* are *guessing* and *estimating*. Demonstrate prediction with additional coin flips.

Have students work together in pairs to make predictions about coins.

Each student gets a card that has either a red dot or blue dot. Red dots are the recorders. Blue dots are the coin flippers. Students predict what they think the coin flip will be—heads or tails—and the recorder marks the prediction on the chart. The recorder circles all predictions that are correct. Allow students to make many coin flips.

HEADS	TAILS
~~||||~~	|||

Review the guidelines for cooperation during group work.

- Use a 6″ voice.
- Stay with your group.
- Help your partner.
- Encourage each other.
- Keep your hands to yourself.

Explain the criteria for success by suggesting that students should use their 6″ voices and encouraging words. Let them know that as the teacher observes, a checklist of these behaviors will be used.

GROUP	6″ VOICES	ENCOURAGING WORDS
1		
2		
3		
4		
5		
6		
7		
8		
9		
10		
11		
12		
13		
14		

PERIOD ________________ DATE ________________

Reflecting on the Design

To process affectively, have students tell how they feel when they predict well.

To process the groups' cooperative skills, assemble the class into a large group. Ask volunteers to tell what they did well when working together. Take many answers before asking what they could do better. Emphasize students feelings.

To process cognitively, ask several recorders to tell how many predictions were correct. Ask the strongest predictors to explain why they think they did so well. How could they do better?

Finally, to facilitate reflective transfer, ask volunteers to tell other instances for making predictions (e.g., crossing the street, shooting baskets). Elicit life situations and other academic examples.

☐ ☐ ☐

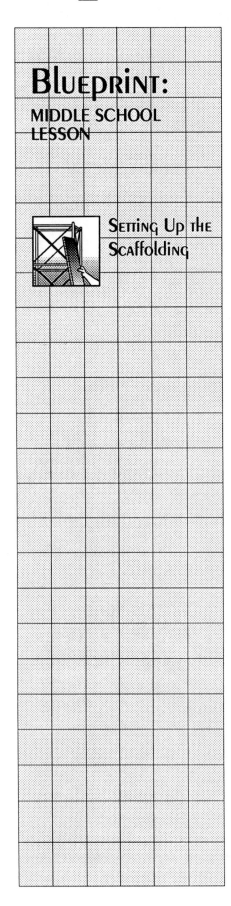

HOW THE ELEPHANT GOT HIS TRUNK

Find the fable "How the Elephant Got His Trunk" (obtainable from EBEC, see page ii) or a similar videotape to foster cooperation and thoughtfulness in the middle classroom. Tell students that they are to focus on two "big ideas":

1. the thinking skill called predicting, and
2. a cognitive organizer called the fat and skinny questions chart. Show them this graphic either on the board or on the overhead.

FAT AND SKINNY QUESTIONS*	
FAT Questions	SKINNY Questions
Before 1. 2.	Before 1. 2.
During 3. 4.	During 3. 4.
After 5. 6.	After 5. 6.

FAT QUESTIONS
Fat questions require lots of discussion and explanaton with interesting examples. Fat questions take time to think through and answer in depth.

SKINNY QUESTIONS
Skinny questions require simple yes/no/maybe or a one-word answer, or nod or shake of the head. They take up no space or time.

*page 288

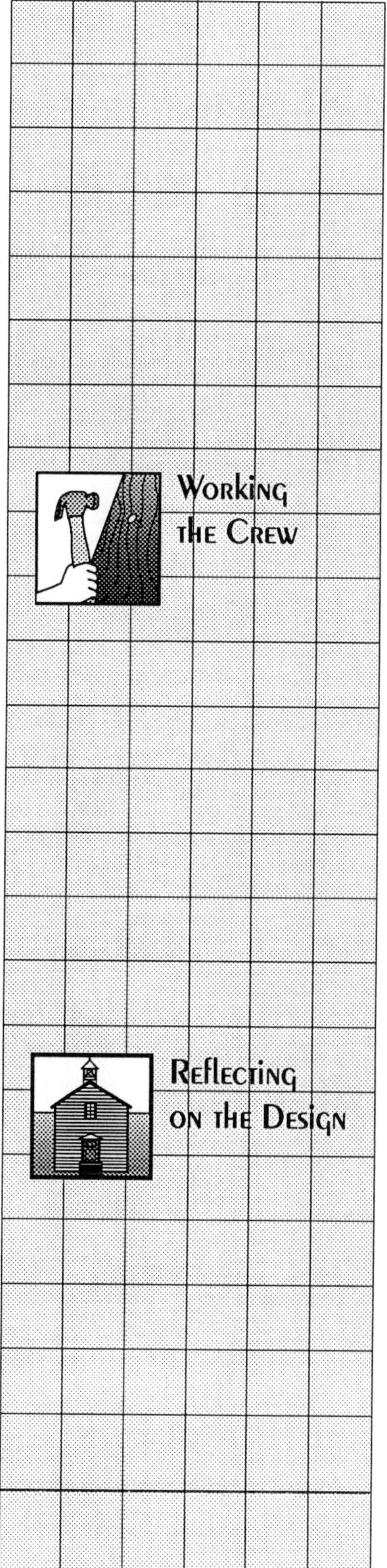

Using only the title "How the Elephant Got His Trunk," have students generate examples of fat and skinny questions. Do this as a total class to demonstrate what fat and skinny questions are.

Sample questions might be:

FAT	1. How do elephants use their trunks? 2. What if the animal had been a tiger?
SKINNY	1. Is the story true? 2. Are there other stories like this one?

Prepare the video for viewing.

Explain that in groups of two with assigned roles:
The *recorder* writes down questions.
The *reporter* tells questions to the class.

Tell the student teams they are about to view the video "How the Elephant Got His Trunk." Throughout the lesson they are to generate both fat and skinny questions.

Prior to viewing, they are to write two fat questions and two skinny questions that they have about the story.

During the video, they are again to write at least two fat questions and two skinny questions.

Then, after the video, they again jot down two fat and two skinny questions they have.

Have the partners star their best question from the collection.

To promote affective processing or talking about their feelings, ask students to tell their partners one thing about the activity they each liked and why.

To foster social skill development, ask students to describe how they behave when they are asked a difficult question.

For cognitive processing, sample the questions generated by the pairs. As these samplings are shared, talk about how to judge if the questions are fat or skinny.

For a metacognitive level of processing, have students discuss the following:
- Which type of question do you prefer, fat or skinny? Why?
- Do you prefer to *ask* fat or skinny questions?
- Do you prefer to *answer* fat or skinny questions?

□ □ □

ROBERT FROST'S POETRY

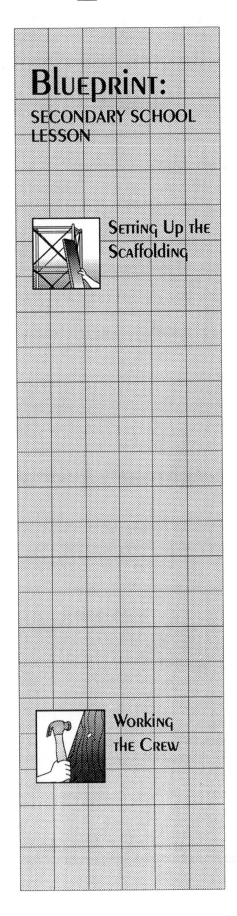

Use trios to review the characteristics of Robert Frost's poetry. Have each trio use a web (blank webs are available in Appendix B, page 289) to brainstorm all the characteristics they can recall about Frost's work.

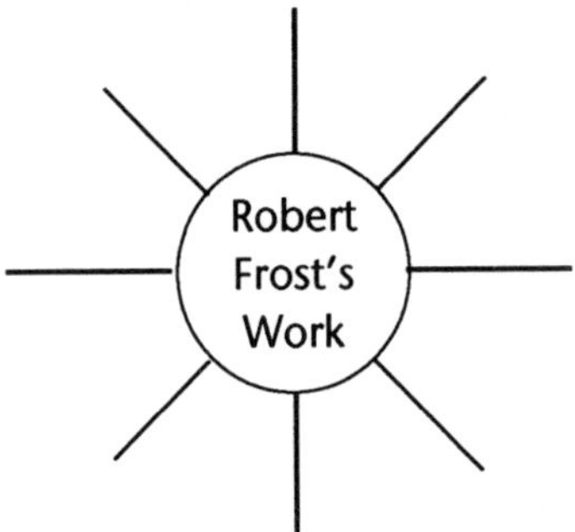

Next, have students select the three characteristics that make his work most unique.

Conduct an all-class discussion about Frost's writing characteristics. Underscore those characteristics they will search for in his poem "Stopping by the Woods." Each group needs the following materials:

- a copy of the poem
- individual notes
- worksheet/newsprint

Explain that students are to work in the same groups of three to analyze Frost's poem "Stopping By The Woods" to see how closely it matches the criteria selected from the webs.

Before beginning, rotate the three roles—checker, reader and recorder—and review the responsibilities of each.

In each group, have the checker review the cooperative guidelines.

Explain the criteria for success:

- Each group must have at least three arguments to defend its three selected characteristics.
- Each group member must be able to explain its group's choices.

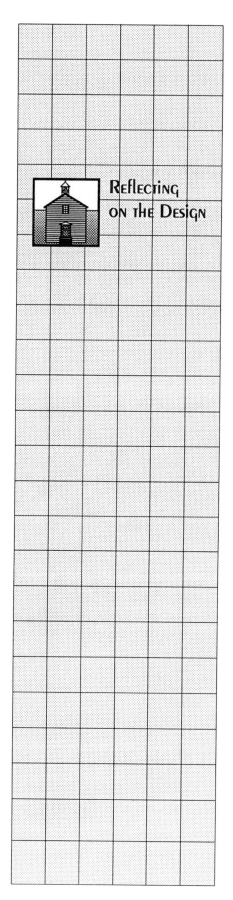

To process affectively, ask students to share how they felt during the activity.

To process the social skill of trust building, have the teams create an ad for their groups on the poster "How's Your Team Building Today?"

To process cognitively, have each person write a three-paragraph essay explaining how this poem reflects the major characteristics of Frost's other poetry.

To process metacognitively, ask each group to review Mrs. Potter's Questions:

MRS. POTTER'S QUESTIONS*

1. What were you supposed to do?
2. What did you do well?
3. What would you do differently next time?
4. Do you need any help?

☐ ☐ ☐

*page 290

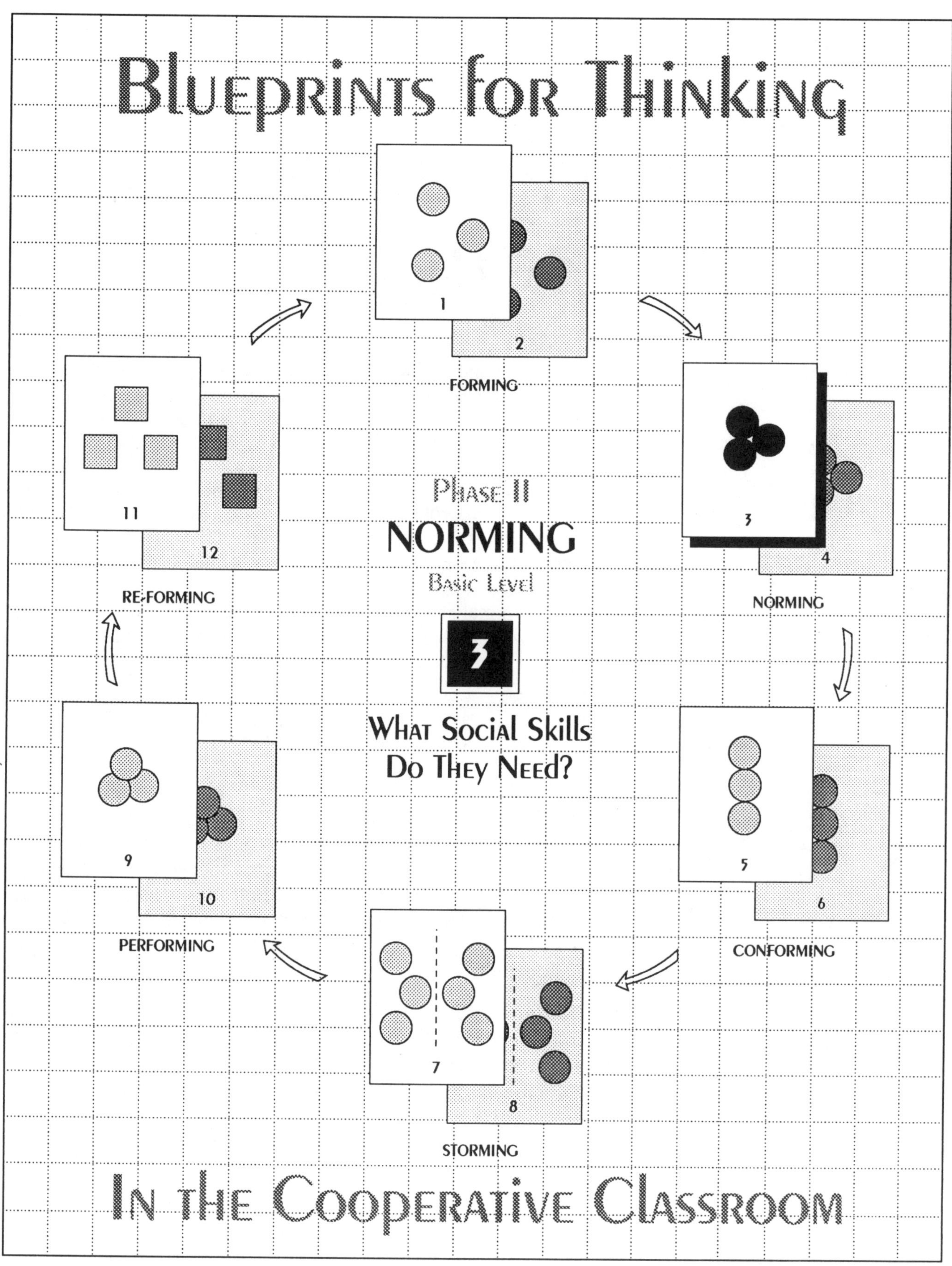
Blueprints for Thinking
1
2
FORMING
3
4
NORMING
5
6
CONFORMING
7
8
STORMING
9
10
PERFORMING
11
12
RE-FORMING
Phase II
NORMING
Basic Level
3
What Social Skills
Do They Need?
In the Cooperative Classroom

Phase II:
NORMING
Basic

What Social Skills Do They Need?

Lots of times you have to pretend to join a parade in which you are really not interested in order to get where you're going.
—Christopher Morley

Draft

Most students respond to the informal social skills woven into the classroom expectations, roles and guidelines. Many require more formal direction in acquiring the cooperative social skills. In the *norming* phase of group development are basic social skills ripe for formal instruction.

Give more formal attention to social skill instruction with younger students and with students in "low tracks." These are the students who can profit most with direct instruction, guided practice and constructive feedback.

Specs

DECIDING ON THE SOCIAL SKILLS How does a teacher decide which cooperative social skills to teach? Which ones are best done informally? The answers to these questions depend on the cooperative skill levels found in the classroom. Students who enter with strong cooperative skills, either because they developed those at home or in a previous class, need less time on the basics of forming and norming and can advance to the more sophisticated skills.

INFORMAL INSTRUCTION For the informal instruction in social skills, reinforce previously learned cooperative skills: roles (e.g., encourager, recorder) rules (e.g., 6" voices, one person talks), expectations (e.g., work on your attentive listening), processing (e.g., "Select a cooperative skill to practice and describe how you are improving"), and feedback (e.g., "I'm glad to see how quietly you moved into your teams"). Every activity, every lesson can be heightened by including informal, cooperative skill development within it.

FORMAL INSTRUCTION For the *formal instruction* of cooperative skills, it is important that students (a) understand the need and value of the skill,

(b) know the chief behavior indicators of the skill, (c) know when to use the skill, (d) practice the skill, and (e) persist in refining the skill until it is automatic.

☐ A FOCUS ON FORMING SKILLS

What Skills Are Best Taught? In the *forming* stage, individuals learn how to contribute to and benefit from teamwork. This stage includes learning (a) how to move into a group, (b) how to move out of a group, (c) who talks in a group, (d) who listens, (e) how to help the group, and (f) how to keep on task.

Assessing Your Class

THE FORMING SKILLS			
Skill	Needed	Have	Comments
Move into a group			
Move out of a group			
One person talks at a time			
Stay with group			
Control volume of talk (3", 6", 12")			
Practice all roles			
Keep hands and feet to self			

HOW TO MOVE INTO GROUPS With a permanent seating arrangement for the groups there is little to worry about in moving desks. If however, desks are moved in and out of rows, then teach, practice and reinforce the following model procedures:

1. "Pick up your books and set them against the wall. Sit down." (Do one row at a time.)
2. Give each student a group assignment.

   Who Is In Which Group? (Use cards with colored dots, group names or another group assignment method.)

   Who Has Which Role? (Assign roles appropriate for the lesson and the students: calculator, reader, encourager, etc.)
3. "Move your seats so you are sitting with your new group."

   Display the desired group pattern on the overhead or blackboard.

Invite the students to form their groups quietly. If the class is too noisy, *stop* the activity until all students are quiet; *reinforce* the class' quiet expectation and *begin again.*

4. Give positive reinforcement for a completed, quiet move and invite the students to gather their books or to get their work materials for today's task.
5. After the task is done, instruct students to put their materials back, to rearrange their desks (put diagram on overhead or blackboard), and to sit until they are dismissed.

☐ A FOCUS ON NORMING SKILLS

Every teacher deserves the norms of student-to-student interaction to be positive and encouraging. Unfortunately, the norms learned from TV's humor, sports figures and the playground may be negative and discouraging. To change the norms from negative put-downs and inattention to good social skills, explicit attention from the teacher is needed.

One forming skill most practical to initiate in any classroom is *encouraging.* In the TV-saturated world of students, the art of the comic put-down makes peer encouragement a highly needed "basic" skill for the classroom.

PREPARATION Solid formal instruction of a social skill requires the same careful preparation found in any procedural lesson. To teach a social skill, first use a T-chart. The T-chart, applicable to every cooperative social skill, helps students understand the specific behaviors that make up a chosen social skill. Instead of dealing with abstract words such as *encouragement* or *attentive listening,* the students work with specific behaviors. What does encouragement sound like? What does it look like?

T-Chart

ENCOURAGEMENT	
SOUNDS LIKE	LOOKS LIKE
"Keep at it."	thumbs up
"Atta girl," "Atta boy!"	pat on back
"Way to go!"	smile
"Here's another way to look at it ..."	head nodding
"Great idea."	beckoning hand
"Keep trying."	
"You're getting close."	

After thinking through the behavior lists, prepare a *display.* A large bulletin board celebrating *encouragement* with words and pictures, a model T-chart on the wall or a T-chart handout provides a daily reminder.

STAGES IN TEACHING SOCIAL SKILLS

Hook The hook lessons lay the groundwork. For the younger students and other students who lack the cooperative skills or thrive in a peer culture that reinforces negative social skills, more time and more energy on practice, reinforcement and recognition of the essential cooperative skills are necessary. All students need some form of encouragement to develop these skills.

Teach Use a T-chart or web with the students. This will enable them, after the hook lesson, to generate the specific behaviors of the social skill. Do charts for both the acceptable behaviors (i.e., listening) and for the non-acceptable behavior (i.e., non-listening). Add behaviors the students miss from your preparation charts. Post the charts on the bulletin board or provide a copy for each student's notebook.

Practice Guided skill practice, massed in short bursts, is a necessary step after presenting the hook and teaching the basics. For instance, active listening pairs can practice with each other in three- to five-minute segments. Student A listens as student B shares an idea, explains a selected concept or describes an event. After the practice, A self-evaluates his/her listening practice. On the next day, they reverse roles. As the pairs develop their listening skills, begin to focus more and more on using course content as the subject for practice.

Extended practices give students a chance to reinforce the listening skill. Build a listening component into each lesson. In the criteria for lesson success, tell the students what is expected with the skill: For example, "I want to see at least five listening behaviors from each group," or "On your group evaluation, I expect you to report five examples of active listening."

Observe As students practice the desired social skills, the teacher or designated student observers watch for examples. To help with the observations, some teachers keep a checklist. While the groups work on task, the teacher records samples of the specified social skills. After the groups process their work, the teacher recognizes the positive examples he or she observed and encourages continued practice of the skills by all students.

Practice should continue until the social skill becomes automatic. This takes time. When the skill is first introduced with the hook, the students enter the first stage of change: awareness. If the hook catches them, they will perceive the need for the skill and increase commitment to improvement. After positive feedback they refine and refine until the skill becomes automatic.

Reward In cooperative learning practice, it is best to use a group reward system (e.g., coupons, tokens or marbles dropped into a jar). Let the groups know they can earn rewards by using the social skill in each task; tell them how the reward system works. The rewards can add up to free time, reading time, or bonus points for grades or prizes.

To target the students' attention on the social skill, have a "hook," usually a role play, a structured group experience or a story that illustrates the social skill lesson (see the sample people search on page 291). From these examples, students can generate a T-chart with the behaviors and words common to the social skill (see chart at left).

Obviously, students who already have the forming and norming skills well in hand do not need to spend time on these basics of cooperation. Share the expectations and *unite the group teams* with them—they will be ready to wade into the course content and to learn the more advanced social skills.

☐ A FOCUS ON ADVANCED SOCIAL SKILLS

The forming and norming social skills are only the start. If students turn these skills into habits in a flash, as many do, they are ready to tackle the more advanced social skills. The higher the class goes, the more opportunities appear for infusion of these social skills into the lesson design. However, a precautionary word must be noted here: Always address social skills explicitly.

What social skill areas need to be addressed?

- Communication
- Trust
- Leadership
- Conflict resolution

  See page 347 for an explanation of each of these.

Social skills do not develop for the class as a whole without deliberate, specific and repeated attention to them. In the chart entitled "Phases of Introduction of Social Skills," the six phases of the small-group process are outlined. Coupled with each phase is a listing of suggested social skills appropriate for explicit attention during the instruction of that phase.

For example, it seems appropriate (and probably necessary) to talk about how to disagree with ideas, not people, as groups show evidence of *storming*. Similarly, as groups show signs of exquisite *performance* and become high-functioning teams, it is appropriate to target the more sophisticated skills of reaching consensus and dealing skillfully with controversy.

Although the charted skills are probably somewhat developmentally listed, individual situations dictate the depth and/or sequence of the actual teaching of social skills. Each teacher must decide on the final design of the social skill introductions. Reference to the chart is suggested only to help plan explicitly for the wide range of social skills needed.

As the social skill instruction develops throughout the year, inclusion of skills from each of the categories is important. Thus, when trying to choose which social skills to teach, how many skills to include and when to teach which skills, the categories may be helpful for picking the actual menu of items. The caveat to all: *Do not COVER social skills.* Each skill is meant to be modeled, practiced and used throughout the students' time in the classroom. One social skill mastered by the class each semester is more helpful than 20 "covered"! Less is more.

If teachers are under inordinant pressure to cover curriculum, it is difficult to see where social skills "fit." Let us say only this, whether a teacher takes the time to introduce the forming skills because those are needed for basic classroom management, or takes time to teach the more complex skills at the performing or norming stage, the pay off is always greater mastery of content. Sometimes it is necessary for a teacher to throw out miniscule facts in order to find the time. More likely, the improved social skills *enable* more on-task, on-focus, concentrated student effort. The results of such effort and such increased student responsibility to learning are obvious.

☐ ☐ ☐

Update your task sequence on page 348.

PHASES OF INTRODUCTION OF SOCIAL SKILLS*		
PHASE	SOCIAL SKILLS Communication (C), Trust (T), Leadership (L), Conflict Resolution (CR)	
Forming *to organize groups and establish behavior guidelines*	Use a 6" voice. (C) Listen to your neighbor. (C) Stay with the group. (C)	Heads together. (C) Do your job. (L) Help each other. (L)
Norming *to complete assigned tasks and build effective relationships*	Include all members. (L) Encourage others. (L) Listen with focus. (T)	Let all participate. (L) Respect each other's opinions. (T) Stay on task. (L)
Conforming *to promote critical thinking and maximize the learning of all*	Clarify. (C) Paraphrase ideas. (C) Give examples. (C)	Probe for differences. (CR) Generate alternatives. (CR) Seek consensus. (CR)
Storming *to function effectively and enable the work of the team*	Sense tone. (C) Disagree with idea not person. (CR) Keep an open mind. (T)	See all points of view. (CR) Try to agree. (CR) Contribute own ideas. (L)
Performing *to foster higher-level thinking skills, creativity and depth intuition*	Elaborate on ideas. (C) Integrate ideas. (L) Justify ideas. (CR)	Extend ideas. (C) Synthesize. (L) Reach consensus. (CR)
Re-forming *to apply across curriculum and transfer into life beyond the classroom*	Begin cycle of social skills again—each time: • New group is formed. • New member joins group. • Member is absent from group.	 • New task is given. • Long absenses occur.

THE LION AND THE MOUSE

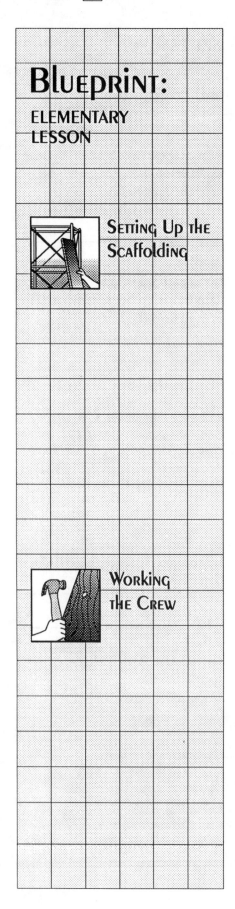

Ask students to raise their hands if they agree with the statement:

- "It feels nice when someone says nice things to you, like 'Way to go' or 'Good job.'"
- "It feels nice when someone helps you finish a difficult job."
- "It feels good when you help someone with a problem."
- "It feels bad when someone calls you a nasty name."
- "It feels good when you are left out from a game."

After the last vote, write the word *encourage* on the board. Help the class sound it out. Explain that the word means "to give courage." Next, tell the story of the cowardly lion from the *Wizard of Oz*. Explain how saying nice things or helping others gives people courage. Demonstrate some words that an encouraging person might use and write them on the board. For example, "Good job," "I like your work," etc.

Tell the class they are going to see a video. It is a fable, an animal story that teaches a lesson. Invite them to watch the "Lion and the Mouse" (obtainable from EBEC, see page ii) to see how encouragement can be helpful.

After the video is over, draw the class' attention to the blackboard.

ENCOURAGE

The Lion		The Mouse	
Did	Said	Did	Said

Ask the students to help fill in the chart with examples. After there are enough, ask students to tell how encouragement helped the lion escape and have them explain why it helped.

On the blackboard, make a list of discouraging words that the students heard in the video. What other words do they hear that they can add to the list? Make a permanent chart to post.

Group students in trios. Give the groups materials to water color (paint, paper, etc.) and have each group make a picture that shows "encouragement." Display the finished works.

To process affectively, ask students to turn to a partner to tell about a time when they were encouraged and how it felt.

For social skill processing, ask students to tell how they encouraged *or* discouraged a friend.

The cognitive focus, defining encouragement, can be checked with a quick stem activity— "Turn to your partner and define the word *encourage.*"

Conclude by asking students to discuss when it would be helpful to encourage each other in this class. This metacognitive reflection guides student transfer for future application.

☐ ☐ ☐

IALAC

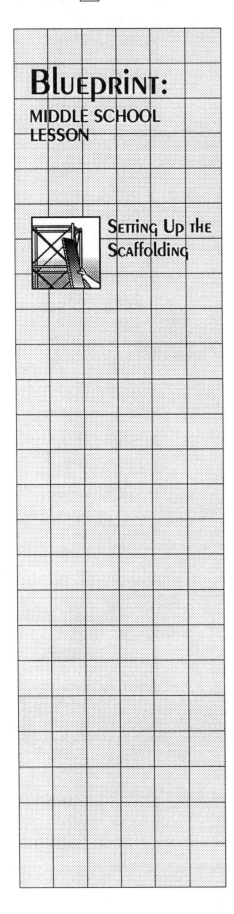

Use Sidney Simon's IALAC (I Am Lovable And Capable) strategy or tell the students a unique version of the IALAC story using the following sample. Hold the IALAC sign.*

(Name), age ________ , woke up one school morning looking at his/her pajama top. _______ saw a giant, neon sign. It flashed on and off, IALAC. ________ knew at once this meant "I Am Lovable And Capable." ________ dressed and ran quickly to the kitchen. ________ was very excited. Before ________ could speak, ________ sister said, "You pea-brain, (rip off a corner of the sign) what did you do with my new jacket?" "Nothing," ______ said. "Man," whined ________ sister, "________ is a jerk." (rip) "________," said ________ unhappy mother. "You oughta know better. Why can't you use your brain (rip) once in a while. Your big brother would never do nothing so stupid." (rip) "But Mom," ________ said, "I . . . ." "Don't sass me back," said ______ mother. "You are such a smart mouth." (rip) ________ saw ________ sister smurking. "Smart mouth, smart mouth." (rip, double rip)

By the time ________ left for the school bus, one-half of IALAC was ripped. On the school bus, George Burns said ________ was an idiot (rip), cry baby and jerk (rip). _______ sister laughed each time. (triple rip)

In the first class period, Mrs. Smartzolla asked to put _____ homework problem on the board. _______ forgot a (name item) in the formula. "________," she moaned, "how slow can you be? I've told you a thousand times." (rip)

In language arts, Mr. Thomas barked at _______ for getting the lowest score on the vocabulary quiz. (rip) He read how ________ had misspelled __________ to the whole class and said sarcastically, "I guess no one could ever accuse you of a gorgative brain." (rip) Everyone laughed. (rip)

By the end of the day, ________ went home with a very small IALAC sign. ________ was very upset.

*page 292

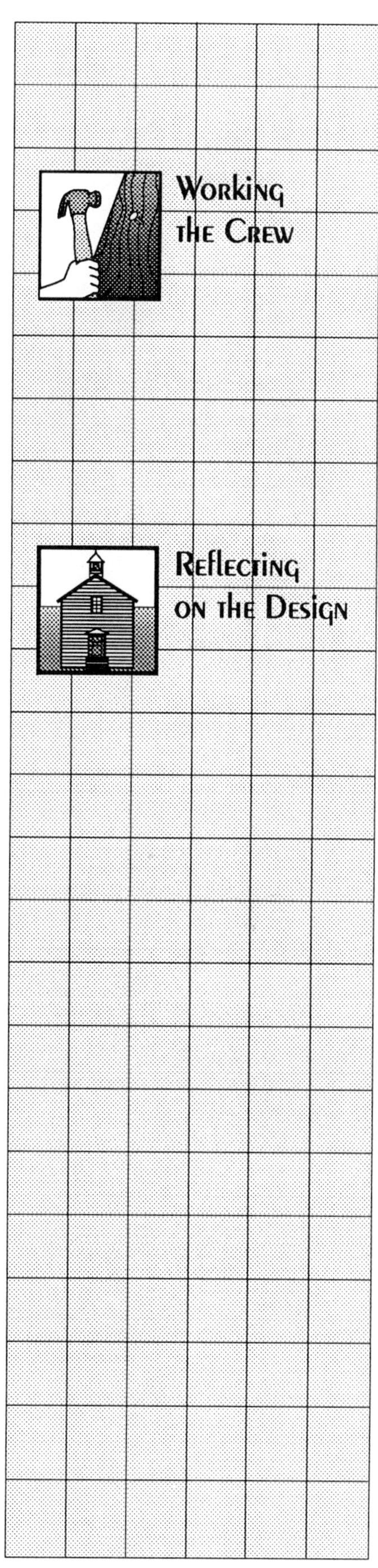

The next day, ________ woke to find IALAC on ________ pajamas, but very small. ________ hoped that today would be better. ________ wanted to keep his/her IALAC so much.

(Continue this story with additional IALAC demolition.)

After the story, place students into groups of five, each group with one piece of 3" x 5" newsprint and a marker. Appoint a recorder in each group to write down all the different ways they have their IALACs ripped. After five minutes, ask several recorders to share samples.

Instruct the groups to make a second list: What things can they do or say to increase people's IALACs? After five minutes, ask for samples.

Ask each group to pick the three best IALAC builders from its list. Make an unduplicated class list to hang in the classroom.

To process affectively, have students finish the following statement:
It feels good when . . . .

To process socially, ask students to take time today to use positive statements with a family member.

To process cognitively, post the encouragement T-chart and discuss how the class can use it to build each other's IALACs. On succeeding days, use these ideas for practice.

To process metacognitively, ask students to discuss:

what they did well in the groups, and

what they would do differently next time to help their groups.

TEAMWORK

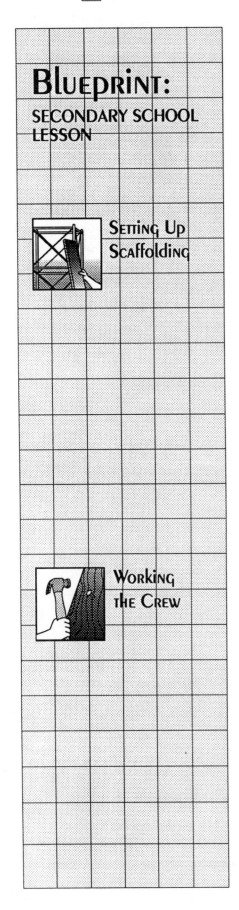

Introduce students to the teamwork norm for their classroom.

Ask the students to share examples of teamwork with which they are familiar (sports teams, business teams, etc.). Ask individuals to offer situations in which teamwork is beneficial.

On the board, sketch this double T-chart.

TEAMWORK		
LOOKS LIKE	SOUNDS LIKE	FEELS LIKE

Ask students to give specific examples for each column.

Assign students by number (count one through five) to small groups. Assign and review the five roles they'll be using. There are many roles to choose from and possibly combine.

- recorder
- worrier
- checker
- encourager
- reader
- observer

Give each team a copy of one story problem.* Either give every group the same story or select one story per group. Each team has five minutes to generate at least five solutions. Have teams use the following That's A Good Idea response-in-turn strategy to generate ideas. Then, have teams agree on the best solution to its story problem.

*page 293

THAT'S A GOOD IDEA*

1. Use DOVE guidelines:
   Defer judgment
   Opt for original
   Vast number of ideas are best
   Expand by piggybacking

2. Respond in turn with:
   a) "That's a good idea because..."
   b) Your idea

3. Allow students to say, "I pass."

4. Keep going around the circle until everyone has had a chance to respond.

5. Record all ideas and reasons on a chart.

Topic	
Idea	Reason
1.	1.
2.	2.
3.	3.

STORY ONE

The large plane carried a crew of seven people—pilot, co-pilot, navigator, head cabin manager, and three assistant cabin managers. One-half the way from New York to Chicago they ran into a heavy thunder storm. Lightning struck the plane and damaged the tail gears.

STORY TWO

The football team was playing for the league championship. At half time, seven members of the offense and both coaches became very ill. The team doctor said they could not return to the field.

*page 294

STORY THREE

On the way to a very important tennis match, the van with the girls' team was struck by a bus. No one was injured. However, all the racquets, except two were destroyed.

STORY FOUR

The students in Professor Swartz's law class had formed their own study groups. It was now time for the final exam. The last assignment was to review the second half of the textbook, including five chapters not covered in class. There were two days for the review.

STORY FIVE

The fire fighters in station 25 had worked together for 12 years. They were organized in five teams of seven. Due to retirements and reorganization of the department, there were five vacancies in the station. Two new workers are assigned to the station.

STORY SIX

The first pair of paramedics arrived at the accident at 6:10 p.m. It was already dark. Three adults were standing at the edge of the pond. Twenty-five feet out there was a hole in the ice. A young boy was in the water and holding onto a fallen tree. When the medics called for assistance, they were told everyone was at a fire across town. They could expect no backup for at least 15 minutes.

STORY SEVEN

The construction crew had two days to finish rebuilding the road before a "late fine" was imposed by the state highway department. The crew estimated that the job would take at least 20 hours with the equipment they had.

Review the T-chart for teamwork. Explain that each observer gets a checklist. Each time an encouraging behavior is observed, the observed team receives one point.

TEAM ____________ OBSERVER ____________

Add a check for each example.

	Behavior	Count
1	Smiling	✔ ✔
2	"Atta girl."	✔
3	Nod	
4	Pat on the back	
5	"That's a good idea."	✔
6		
7		
8		
9		
10		

TOTAL POINTS: ____________

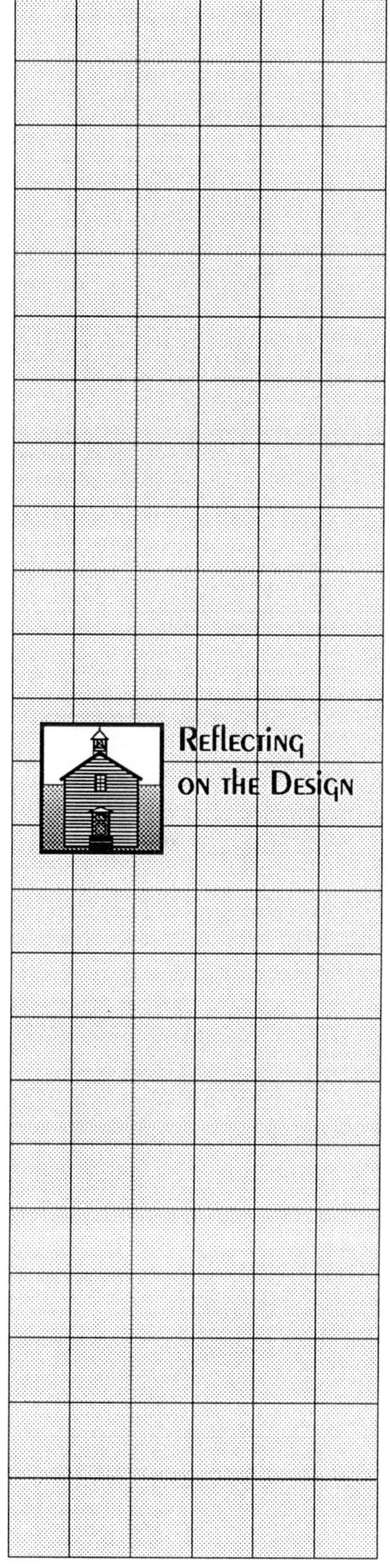

To process for feelings about teamwork, ask students to talk about an experience in which they wish there had been better teamwork.

To process the social skill of teamwork, have students recall a positive team experience in athletics or music or other social clubs.

Have students think about books and films that depict good teamwork as a cognitive processing task.

After teams have tabulated the total points, process metacognitively by asking the class to discuss how teamwork was beneficial. Make a "+/-" chart on the overhead or board to list the pluses and minuses of teamwork.

TEAMWORK

Plus +	Minus –

☐ ☐ ☐

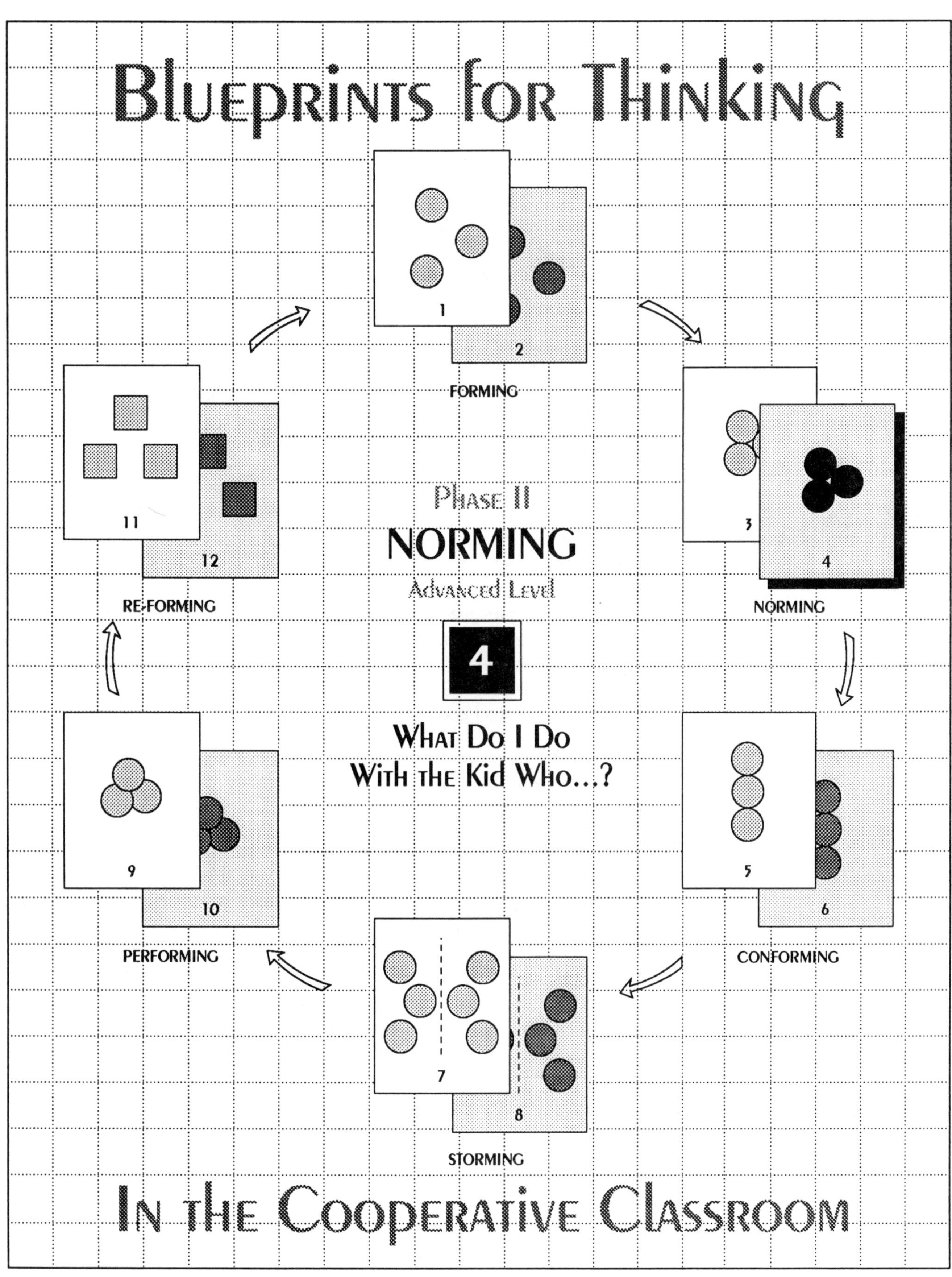
Blueprints for Thinking
1
2
FORMING
3
4
NORMING
5
6
CONFORMING
7
8
STORMING
9
10
PERFORMING
11
12
RE-FORMING
Phase II
NORMING
Advanced Level
4
What Do I Do
With the Kid Who...?
In the Cooperative Classroom

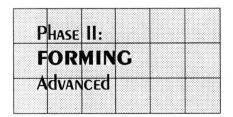

PHASE II:
FORMING
Advanced

WHAT DO I DO WITH THE KID WHO...?

Perhaps the most important single cause of a person's success or failure educationally has to do with the question of what he believes about himself.

—Arthur Combs

DRAFT

"What do I do with the kid who . . . ?" is a critical question of teachers starting cooperative learning. No matter how carefully the most skilled teacher prepares for the cooperative classroom, the realities of school-life dictate that there is no such place as the ideal classroom in which everything goes just right. In the next level of the norming phase, attention is given to the students who are most lacking in the social skills. Even if all the plans, strategies and structures from the previous chapters are in place, it is unrealistic to believe that every child, every day, and in every way can maintain perfect cooperation.

However, given that the classroom climate has been set for cooperative learning and that expectations for all students to develop their cooperative skills are in place, all teachers can prepare to manage those special and often irritating misbehavior problems that inevitably arise throughout the year.

Misbehavior in the cooperative classroom is often very different from that encountered in a competitive or individualistic classroom. It usually takes the form of a student who doesn't want to participate in a cooperative learning group. Sometimes the refusal is verbal: "I hate groups." "I want to work alone." "I can do better myself." "I don't want to work with ________." In other cases, it's subversive behavior in the form of goofing off, dominating other members, arguing or not doing the assigned role.

The primary means for resolving behavior difficulties is to teach students how to *apply* the social skills in new and different situations. It is important to encourage the students to use their new skills when problems arise in the groups. When all best efforts are to no avail, however, the teacher may have to intervene.

When intervention is needed, it is important to remember that the goal is to help the misbehavior get back on track with the least amount of task disruption. In some cases, *quick stop* and *timeout* options will do this. For the occasional student, a more complex strategy, *goal redirection*, may be needed. In all cases, it is best to remember that the goal is to help every child, *even the most difficult,* take responsibility for controlling his/her emotions.

□ QUICK STOP

SPECS

DEFINITION The earliest research on classroom management applies to the cooperative classroom. In fact, a teacher who does not use the basic quick-stop techniques for guiding on-task behavior will discover quickly that the cooperative classroom won't work very well. Following are the four quick-stop techniques.

PROXIMITY The TESA Project (Teacher Expectations and Student Achievement) demonstrated the power of proximity. When a student is "goofing off," the easiest steps are to stand next to the student, or move the student's desk or group to the front of the classroom where you can make quick eye contact with the offenders.

MOVEMENT In the classrooms mapped out (see pages 10-14) for cooperative work, the teacher has the opportunity to move easily from group to group. He/she can ask questions and lead discussions from different spots in the room and always keep the class on its toes. Unlike the teacher in Nick Nolte's movie *Teacher*, the "moving" teacher in the cooperative classroom will never die unnoticed behind the desk.

GUIDELINES AND RESPONSIBILITIES When the teacher sets up the guidelines for cooperation and teaches the roles (see pages 6-8) for group work, he/she has set the behavior expectations so critical to basic classroom management.

CATCHING THEM BEING GOOD The teacher who gives encouragement for positive behavior and offers specific feedback to celebrate students who "do good" is not only providing a "good feeling" for those who meet expectations, but also is pointing out samples of model behavior.

□ TIMEOUT

DEFINITION The most striking way to communicate the principle of self-responsibility to students in the cooperative classroom is to introduce and use timeout places. One timeout place is found in every cooperative classroom; a second may be found near the principal's office.

The timeout place is a physical spot in the room separate from all *group* activity. It is a place where a student who is unwilling or unable to work with a group may go or be sent. It is not a dunce's corner. It is an individual work station. At this station the student can do the assigned group tasks alone, read, study or reflect.

SELF-SELECT The timeout place works best if the teacher encourages students to elect their own timeouts. If for any reason, the student feels unready to work that day or do a task with the group, he/she may elect the timeout space. What the student does in that timeout depends on the situation. For instance, a student who comes to class upset from a previous class, peer disagreement or a family discord may want quiet time to gain composure. At other times during the class, a student may feel he/she is losing self-control in the group. In all cases, acknowledge that need to be alone and encourage the student to join the class activity when he/she feels ready.

Whatever the reason, the most important thing is to encourage students to make wise choices. In the beginning, the timeout space may be crowded. On most other days, however, the space is usually empty.

Students who elect timeout also elect "time-in" when they feel ready to rejoin the group. When there is concern about a student's self-selection of timeout, the teacher should take time to talk with and encourage the student to return. For the most part, it is important that the student recognizes that he/she is the decision maker in control of timeouts and time-ins.

To avoid students' misuse of self-selected timeouts, it's advisable to hold a classroom discussion early in the year. Talk about the timeout space, appropriate and inappropriate uses and the importance of self-selection. For younger students, a 15-minute time limit is appropriate; for older students, 40 minutes should suffice.

ELECTING TIMEOUT There are many instances when a student lacks the maturity or the self-confidence to self-select timeout. Instead, the student acts out by disrupting the group or by not contributing to the common goal. After it becomes obvious that the group cannot solve the problem or that proximity isn't an effective strategy, then the teacher or the group may elect timeout for the misbehaving student. For this, remember the axiom:

It is a right to learn alone. It is a privilege to learn in a group.

When a student is excluded from the group, two guidelines apply. First, the student is responsible to complete the task alone while the group reorganizes itself to work without the offender. Second, the student must convince the decider that he/she is ready to return to the group. That means, if the group votes the offender out, the offender must contract with the group for his/her return.

RETURNING TO GROUP For return to the group, several conditions must be met:

- ✓ The student must describe the misbehavior that lead to his/her timeout.
- ✓ The student must describe (preferably in writing) how he/she will behave differently, assuring positive contributions.

Unless the group is engaged in a multi-day task, it is best that the misbehaving student not return in mid-task. One of the consequences for disrupting the group is separation from the group; a second is having to complete the task without help.

TEACHER-SELECTED TIMEOUT To separate a student from a group, try to do so on teacher observation rather than a student's report. If students in a group complain about a member's disruptions, encourage them to resolve the issue, but keep a close eye. When it is decided that the misbehavior is beyond the group's ability to handle it, step in and address the situation.

Strategy #1—Tell Me

The *Tell Me* strategy is a helpful tool for addressing misbehaving students.

"(student's name), tell me what you are doing."

[There are a variety of answers possible—"Nothing." "They made me." or "I was ________." If the answer is "Nothing," try humor, "Only dead people do nothing. Are you dead?" or identify the behavior, "I saw you ____________. Was I seeing visions?"]

Next ask, "What is your role? In that role, what are you supposed to do?"

[If the teacher has set up the role carefully, the answer should be quick. If the student says, "I don't know," give him/her timeout to think it over, to read the role bulletin board or to ask someone else for help. The student must tell the teacher the expected job.]

Third, ask, "How do your actions help you do your assigned job?"

[This question may evoke silence or a creative answer with which you must disagree.]

Finally, ask the student to decide on a new behavior, "Are you ready to (expected behavior)?"

[If the answer is "No," give the student timeout to complete the group task alone. If the student says "Yes," then indicate that he/she may return to the group only if the new behavior is used. As soon as the misbehavior reoccurs, the student takes timeout. Outline the conditions for return: (a) "When we can agree how you will behave," and (b) "you show it."]

After the student returns from timeout to the group, keep a watch for the student's acceptable behavior. Give the student special recognition for the new positive behavior.

When a student is sent for timeout from the group, set the timeout conditions and determine a policy for return. As an alternative to working in the timeout space, allow the misbehaving student the option of being a classroom observer.

*Strategy #2—Observer's Checklist**

When a student disrupts a group, note which social skills he/she needs and prepare an observer's checklist.

DESIRED SOCIAL SKILL	GROUP A	GROUP B	GROUP C	GROUP D
1 Listening				
2 Encouraging				
3 Clarifying				
4 Summarizing				
DATE: ____________	OBSERVER: ____________			

For instance, to get the students to attend to social skills (e.g., letting one person talk at a time, encouraging participation) write these on the checklist. If the observer is to focus on checking or resolving conflict, write these down.

Next, review what the desired social skills *look like* and *sound like.* Check for understanding and then instruct the observer to spend 20 minutes observing in the classroom, recording instances of the desired behavior and then tabulating the results. Have the observer report on each group to the class or to the teacher. Conclude by asking the student to demonstrate the behaviors. Repeat this procedure until the student indicates a desire to return to his/her group and to use these social skills.

Tolerance and judgment determine how often the process is repeated so use another approach with continued misbehavior by a student. Whichever approach is taken, with the more serious and regular disruptions of a student it is important to look more intensely at the rationale for the continuation. One practical way to do this in a cooperative classroom is to examine the possible purposes for the continued misbehavior.

What do I do if there are many students not behaving after I have taught the social skills?

Work some more with the whole class. Refocus and reteach the social skills to all the students. See page 347 for more information.

☐ GOAL REDIRECTION

There is no perfect solution that guarantees cooperative behavior by each student. When "quick stop" and "timeout" don't work for a certain student, what is your next recourse?

DON'T PANIC Concentrate the bulk of the energy (80 percent) on improving the cooperative skills of the cooperative students. Out-of-control classrooms usually result when 80 percent of the teacher's energy is focused on the 5 percent to 8 percent of the students who try to disrupt any class.

*page 295

BE PERSISTENT The students who don't cooperate probably can't. It is not likely that behaviors or attitudes will change overnight. More likely, these students have had years of reinforcement for their misbehavior patterns. Solid doses of patience and persistence are needed to see even the first glimmer of change for that student who is having a difficult time.

Continued misbehavior *can* be controlled.

PLAN YOUR STRATEGY Behavior change takes time. Attitude change takes more time, and personal value change takes the most time. Reduce the time and increase the impact with a strategic plan to help the more reluctant student discover the personal benefits of cooperation.

There is no recipe for promoting change. However, knowing how to deal with the predictable possibilities for disruption before they happen, will help the success barometer rise.

CHARACTERISTICS OF PERSISTENT MISBEHAVIOR What are the common characteristics of the cooperative resister's chronic misbehavior?

- ✓ Is this a student who is extremely deficient in social skills? (This student may be very bright or very dull. The persistence is *not* tied to intelligence.)
- ✓ Is this a student who refuses to cooperate in a group for *power* reasons? ("You can't make me work with her!")
- ✓ Is this a student who refuses to cooperate in a group because he/she wants *attention*? ("Look at me!")
- ✓ Is this a student who refuses to cooperate in a group because he /she feels *inadequate* with the group? ("I can't do this.")
- ✓ Is this a student who refuses to cooperate in a group because of *revenge* motives. (I'll get you for that.")
- ✓ Is this a student who has major emotional, behavioral or social disturbances?

To answer these questions, step back from the misbehavior and look at the "big picture." Begin with a three-phase diagnosis of the problem.

Diagnostic Checklist

Diagnose the student's purpose for misbehaving. (Under each heading check all that apply.)

1. Lacks Social Skills

   ___ ______________________

   ___ ______________________

   ___ ______________________

2. Feels A Need For Power (Power Play)

   ___ over other students

   ___ over the teacher

   ___ over parents

3. Wants Attention (Attention Seeker)

   ___ from the teacher

   ___ from other students

   ___ from parents

   ___ other ____________

4. Feels Inadequate To Deal With (Inadequacy)

   ___ the teacher

   ___ a specific subject (e.g., math, reading)

   ___ peers

   ___ parents

   ___ the school system

5. Feels Hurt And Wants To Hurt Back (Revenge)

   ___ the teacher

   ___ parents

   ___ other students

   ___ "school"

   ___ other ____________

6. Extreme Disturbance (Mainstreamed or Disturbed)

   ___ social

   ___ emotional

   ___ behavioral

   ___ other ____________

T-CHART Make a T-chart, as modeled below, on the *behaviors* the student shows. Write each major misbehavior *purpose* (power, revenge, etc.) at the top of each T-chart.

______________ (Name) ______________ (Purpose) Target = ______________

LOOKS LIKE	SOUNDS LIKE

SAMPLE

Susan (Name) Attention (Purpose) Target = Teacher

LOOKS LIKE	SOUNDS LIKE
• leaves group	"Did I do it right?"
• interrupts students	"She's copying."
• taps on desk	"Isn't this OK?"
• waves hand even for a wrong answer	questions out of order
	"Do I have to?"

TEST YOUR REACTIONS The teacher should test his/her reactions to the student's misbehavior.

- ✓ "Am I annoyed?" "Irritated?" "Is this kid a royal pain?" "Is she funny, but never at the right time?" Yes to these questions means the teacher is probably dealing with an *attention seeker.*
- ✓ "Does this student make my blood boil?" "Is murder and mayhem what I want to do?" "Do I find myself blowing my cool with this student?" If so, then this student is probably working on a *power trap.*
- ✓ "Am I feeling hurt or betrayed by this student?" "Do I catch myself saying, "That ingrate, I'll fix her!" or "After all I've done, he goes and does this." If so, the teacher is a *revenge victim.*
- ✓ "If only I could help this child." "I feel so sorry for __________. Do you know all the hard times she's had?" "I just feel useless. Nothing I do seems to help." Yes to these responses suggests that the student has caught the teacher in the *inadequacy trap.*

Assuming that the student's parents or peers are the targets, switch the questions to their reactions. Does the parent say, "I just can't do anything with him; he rules the roost"? (power) "I just don't know what to do with her; I've tried everything"? (inadequacy)

Not all students have these self-destructive and antisocial goals. While some just lack the social skills, others suffer from severe and profound emotional, social problems that are more complicated to diagnose or change. Among the former are many very bright students who have the same sincere desires to belong that their peers have. For lots of reasons, including parental criticism, peer norms (to be "uncool," to be smart, etc.) and feelings of safety ("Am I doing it right?"), these students have not learned *how* to work or to relate with their peers. As with all normal students, there is the desire to be included, but the lack of "know-how."

TAKE ACTION Have a five-minute conference (during recess, before class, after class, etc.) to check out the data collected. In the conference, share the data to measure the *purpose* hypothesized. Watch the student's *reactions* and listen to the student's *responses*. (That's R and R!) Begin with this open-ended statement:

"(Name), . . . Could It Be . . . ?"

"I've noticed a number of times that you (list of observed behaviors)"

"I don't find these help you or your group's work. I wonder, could it be that you want (purpose)."

SAMPLES

"...could it be you want my *attention*?"

"...could it be you want your group to *notice you*?"

"...could it be you want to *lead* the group?"

"...could it be you think my class is run in a dumb way?"

...I'm Going To Tell You What I Think Your Purpose Is

Most times, the student responds to the teacher's on-target "could it be?" statement with a verbal or non-verbal yes. The student is more likely to agree if the teacher begins with some statements that are way off target. If the student does not offer a yes on the first round, do a second round, watching closely for behavior changes (delayed responses, blushing, eye blinks, etc.). Or take the next step. Either assertively say, "I'm going to tell you what I think your purpose is," or ask, "Would you like me to tell you what I think?" Again, watch how the student's non-verbal responses (eye glares, stares, looking away, clowning around etc.) and verbal messages ("So what?" etc.) indicate the student's misbehaving purpose. If this doesn't work, ask the student if he/she would mind an observation. The power youngster will refuse. Usually, the others will either love the attention or say they don't care. These are clues. If permission is given, give the hypothesized opinion.

...Could It Be . . . ? Revisited

Power and Revenge Students

Power and revenge students are often very direct with their answers, especially if "could it be" questions are put into a multiple-choice sequence. With some *power* students, using humorous and outlandish samples first will decrease the tension.

> "Could it be you were trying to fly to the moon?"
>
> "Could it be you wanted the week off?" (Obviously, you would ignore any smart-alecky "Yea, sure.")
>
> "Could it be you want to be the boss in your group?"
>
> "Could it be you could run your group better than anyone else?"

Notice how the last questions place the possible purpose into a phrase that may sound more positive to the student. This tactic gets the teacher closer to an honest response.

When diagnosing the likely *revenge* student, mix the "could it be" questions with other purposes.

> "Could it be you hate school and don't want to be here?" (inadequacy)
>
> "Could it be you could do a better job teaching the class?" (power)
>
> "Could it be you want me to give you special help?" (attention)
>
> "Could it be you want to get back at me for the *D* on your paper?" (revenge, teacher)
>
> "Could it be you want to get your friend in trouble?" (revenge, friend)
>
> "Could it be you want to make your mother feel bad?" (revenge, parent)

There is no certainty that the questions will elicit any information. The chances of successfully diagnosing rely upon (a) the teacher's ability to ask the question in an *encouraging* voice, (b) the teacher's ability to read the student's verbal and non-verbal responses and (c) the teacher's ability to connect (a) and (b) to the other diagnostic work—observed behavior and teacher's responses—without overreacting.

Attention Seekers and Students Who Feel Inadequate

Students who seek attention or who feel inadequate are the most difficult to diagnose with "could it be" questions. The *attention seekers* reveal their purpose by acting shy in the diagnostic session. If the teacher thinks he/she has an attention seeker, but the student increases his/her obnoxious or goofy behavior with just the teacher, chances are this is a power conflict working. If the student settles down, try the "could it be" questions with multiple-choice endings. End with, "Could it be you want me to pay more attention to you?"

With the student who feels *inadequate*, watch his/her body language. As this student is asked pressing questions, he/she tends to withdraw and avoid. The answer to the questions could appear in the student's closing-up behaviors such as lack of eye contact, tears, "I don't know" (whispered), etc.

Disturbed Students

The diagnostic conference is complicated when a student has mixed purposes or is extremely disturbed. When the student's misbehavior corroborates that the situation is more than a misbehavior pattern, it's time to consult with the principal, counselor or special education specialists to plan a more intensive intervention.

If a satisfactory response cannot be elicited to the "could it be" sequence, say to the student, "Would you mind if I told you what I think?" (power, revenge, attention) or "John, I'm going to tell you what I think is going on." (inadequacy) Again, watch non-verbals and listen to verbal responses. How the student responds may offer more insight than what he/she says.

...Other Strategies To Try

Once the teacher is satisfied with the student's answers (whether they are direct or indirect), it's time to develop a strategy. Following the directions outlined by Rudolph Dreikurs in his powerful but underused book *Maintaining Sanity in the Classroom*, put the following guidelines into practice:

Never reinforce the student's misbehavior purpose.

✓ Don't give attention to the attention seeker.

✓ Don't use power on the power seeker.

✓ Don't let an inadequate child withdraw.

✓ Don't "hurt" the revenge seeker.

Use logical consequences that fit the situation.

✓ Deprive the student of opportunities to achieve the misbehaving purpose (e.g., timeout isolation for the attention seeker).

✓ Recognize the student for the *positive* way he/she achieves the behavior purpose (e.g., public praise for "leadership" that keeps a group on task).

✓ Encourage, encourage, encourage! Switching from a misbehaving pattern to a positive behavior pattern is very difficult. The more deeply ingrained the misbehavior, the more encouragement the student needs to "do it right." The teacher's patience, persistence and encouragement are the keys to success.

Given these guidelines, there are a variety of practical, purpose-based strategies for changing a student's pattern of behavior.

STRATEGIES FOR RESISTANT MISBEHAVIORS

Attention

The greatest challenge with the attention seeker is changing the misbehavior by giving as little attention as possible. If the misbehavior can't be ignored, try these strategies:

- ✓ Highlight other students who are behaving appropriately. ("I'm pleased to see group A listening to each other.")
- ✓ Move the student out of the spotlight. ("John, I need you to take this message to the office.")
- ✓ Distract the student with a task question. ("Sue, I want you to explain the answers your group has collected so far.")
- ✓ Surprise the student with an unexpected response.("Ellen, let me tell you a story.")
- ✓ Attend to the attention seeker when he/she is on task.("Al, I'm glad to see you concentrating on your job.")

In small cooperative learning groups, it's unusual for the involved student to act out for attention. A powerful long-term strategy is to make attention a legitimate goal. Make this student the person who reports to the class. If the student likes to be a clown, coach the student on how to jazz up a report with well-timed humor and skillful acting.

Power

When working with the power-seeking student, above all else, keep it cool. The power student is well versed in starting arguments. Don't bite. Listen. Agree with every objection. "You are right, Mary."

After defusing the power surge, there are some key follow-ups:

- ✓ Say, "I see your point." Continue with, "Nonetheless . . ." or "Regardless . . ." and then state the rule that applies to all students. Follow with a choice statement, "At this point, you can either (follow the guideline) or (face the consequence)." For instance: "I understand that you hate the recorder role. Nonetheless, everyone in your group has done that job and it's your turn. At this point, I'm giving you the choice; either do the job without complaining or drop from the group and complete the lesson by yourself."

  After the student chooses, even if it's for timeout or another consequence, be sure the choice is completed.
- ✓ A second strategy to consider is to ask this power seeker, at an non-confrontational time, how he/she might handle a similar situation in a fair way. Contract to use the idea the next time this student grabs for power.
- ✓ Place the power seeker in a leadership role in the group or class. Set guidelines for appropriate "leadership" and review the results with the student.

  Reinforce the positive leadership.

Revenge

The revenge-driven youngster is very similar to the power seeker. Hurt by bad comments, verbal abuse or physical abuse, this student wants to strike back. Sometimes the strike is aimed at the perceived perpetrator. ("You flunked me, I'll get you.") Other times, the strike goes to an associate. ("You adults are all the same.")

The most effective strategy for the "hurt" child is to form a positive relationship. Cooperative trust-building strategies (e.g., think-pair-share) and creative problem-solving activities (e.g., That's a Good Idea) are a start.

Second, find ways to encourage the group members to show that they care for this youngster. Use an "includer" role to make sure the student has lots of invitations to participate.

Third, use cooperative activities that help the revenge student deal with his/her emotions. Magic circle activities (see Chase's *The Other Side of the Report Card*), self-concept activities (see Canfield's, *100 Ways to Improve Self-Esteem*) and base group activities that encourage the processing of feelings will assist (for example, "Today, I felt __________ in the group").

Inadequacy

The student who withdraws or feels inadequate aims to avoid failure. Ironically, this goal often appears as task avoidance. Rather than try to meet a challenge (social or academic) the withdrawer avoids whatever might end in failure. All too often, this child, who is seldom an overt classroom problem, melts into the woodwork, bothers no one and accomplishes the avoidance goal with ease.

When a student won't work in a group because he/she feels socially or academically inadequate, the last strategy is time-out. Other more effective strategies for this student are:

- ✓ Reduce the group size to two. Select a partner who is task-oriented and very empathetic.
- ✓ Lower the student's anxiety about mistakes.
- ✓ Build the student's confidence by breaking the group task into smaller chunks, which offer quicker successes.
- ✓ Remind the student of past successes. Ask what that student could do to ensure a repeat of that success.
- ✓ Use self-concept strategies (me bag or me collage) with the help of the group.
- ✓ Give *extra* recognition for individual contributions to group.
- ✓ Arrange for an academic tutor or a "playground buddy."

LOGICAL CONSEQUENCES

Logical consequences are an important ingredient in helping the student decide whether to continue or to break a misbehavior pattern. Logical consequences are not punishments. With a punishment, the student fosters resentment, espouses revenge, retreats or rebels further. Punishment reduces his/her self-esteem. On the other hand, with logical consequences the student sees the intervention as fair and earned by the misbehavior. This "seeing" is helped when the consequences are known before the next misbehavior. The student knows, "If I choose to do this specific act, I am also choosing this specific consequence."

The challenge of using logical consequences for the classroom is in gathering a list of effective consequences. Here is a list of consequences that have worked well:

- ✓ removal from the group activity
- ✓ loss or delay of a favorite activity for this child (e.g., recess, reading, singing, drawing, free time)
- ✓ loss or delay of using favorite equipment or objects (e.g., blocks, microscope), or having favorite group role
- ✓ loss or delay of access to favorite school areas (e.g., lounge, playground, reading chair, special corner)
- ✓ required meeting with parents and teacher and/or social worker
- ✓ repairing damages or paying for damages

All of these samples don't fit everyone's behavior. Be sure the consequence ties closely with (a) that which the student likes or wants, and (b) the misbehavior. For example, damaging property for revenge or attention merits repair or payment. Above all, avoid using as a consequence any act which (a) violates the law, (b) violates school policy, or (c) physically or psychologically harms the child.

STRATEGIES FOR CHANGING MISBEHAVIOR

Reinforcement

Regardless of the original misbehavior goal, when the student starts demonstrating the desired positive behaviors, recognition and reinforcement are critical for ensuring any permanent change. From the quick and clean to the intense and powerful, there are many reinforcement strategies available, whenever the student displays the new behaviors:

✓ Stickers, certificates, points and hurrahs accompanied by an overt connection to the accepted behavior.

"Marie, I'm giving you ________ because I'm pleased that you ____________."

✓ Special recognitions (e.g., student-of-the-day/week bulletin board specifying accomplishments, or good-news notes to send home).

✓ Catch them doing well with verbal and non-verbal encouragements.

"Jose, I'm pleased to see you (behavior)." "Donna, I like the way you are (behavior)."

"John, tell me what you are doing that I like." (You may have to coach the first time.) "Why do I like that?"

Use smiles, thumbs up, a pat on the back, head nods or a "secret" agreed upon signal.

✓ Contract special jobs in the classroom for special recognition (e.g., paper collector, messenger, leader of pledge, book distributor).

Logical Consequences

Backsliding will happen, especially with the students whose misbehavior goals are deeply entrenched. That is, some students will return to their misbehaviors. If a hand on the shoulder, a private signal, or an up-front seat ("proximity") doesn't work and the opportunity arises right away, return to the Tell-Me strategy:

"(Name), tell me what you are doing." If the student says "Nothing" or gives the look of innocent nothing, be more specific (e.g., "with your feet") or refer to past history (e.g., "What did we discuss not to do when we had our last conference?") In some cases it helps to go to multiple-choice questions (e.g., "Sue, were you standing on your head?" "No." "Were you building a house?" "No." "Were you bugging Mary?" "Yes.")

"Tell me what you are supposed to be doing." If the student avoids answering, start by (a) identifying his/her role in the group and have the student review that role, or (b) identify small-group behavior guidelines and have the student review the specific rule he/she broke, or (c) identify the T-chart and have the student review the appropriate behavior.

Ask the student to describe (a) why the misbehavior doesn't fit the expectation, and (b) when the expected behavior will be seen.

Ask the student to demonstrate the expected behavior.

Contract for the quantity and quality of that behavior and for an appropriate amount of time, with a logical consequence for any infractions during that period of time.

LAST RESORTS

The actions of last resort for continued misbehavior are (1) removal from the room, (2) principal involvement, and (3) special services involvement. The principal and/or special services (counselor, social worker, etc.) are most necessary whenever a student endangers himself, other students, or the teacher; violates major school policies on drugs, alcohol, property damage, etc.; or is not responding to in-class consultation. In such instances, it is possible to *plan* the student's removal from class so as to *avoid* a highly predictable confrontation. If removal from class is the decision, it is most important that the following be in place:

- ✓ adherence to school policy and procedures for protecting the student's rights
- ✓ a well-established alternative study room with a monitor who can supervise and assist the student in completion of all class assignments
- ✓ a scheduled parental conference with the teacher, the principal and the student (it is best for this conference to precede the student's return to class)
- ✓ an agreement on the conditions for return

All behavior breakdowns in the cooperative classroom are not likely to be individual. Some involve conflicts between students. Others, such as too much noise, may emerge from the students' enthusiasm.

TOTAL-GROUP MISBEHAVIORS

When problems involve all students in a group or class, do the most for developing their responsibility by involving them in real-world problem solving. William Glasser (*Control Theory in the Classroom*) has demonstrated the positive power of this model. If the problem is one group, only those group members need to work through the solutions. If the problem involves several groups, use a classroom circle and work through the steps by consensus (see chapter 8, 5-to-Fist consensus). The "noise" problem on the opposite page shows a good example of this approach.

☐ CONCLUSION

Cooperative learning does not cure poor classroom management. A teacher who has poor discipline will still have poor discipline with cooperative learning. Good classroom management, like mastery of the content, is a prerequisite to the cooperative classroom. On the other hand, the teacher who has good management skills can, with persistence and patience, take students to a higher level of cooperative behavior and learning in which they are the thinkers, the workers, the proud achievers.

The sample blueprints that follow demonstrate "what to do with the kid who..." as part of a social skill focus on active listening. An elementary school blueprint, middle school blueprint and secondary school blueprint are outlined.

☐ ☐ ☐

Update your task sequence on page 348.

CONTROLLING TOTAL-GROUP MISBEHAVIORS

THE NOISE PROBLEM

1. Review information about the problem.

✓ You have a 6" or "quiet voice" guideline.

✓ You have stopped the class at least twice to lower the volume.

✓ They say, "We forgot."

2. Make the challenge.

✓ As a class, identify at least three ways to ensure keeping the room quiet.

3. Brainstorm the options.

✓ Have a noise checker in each group.

✓ All whisper.

✓ One person speaks at a time in each group.

✓ Stop groups for the day.

✓ Have a roving noise monitor.

✓ Tape loud mouths shut.

✓ Ban loud mouths from the groups.

✓ Give a prize for the quietest voice each day.

✓ Use chips—two per person. No talking after you use your chips.

✓ Take away points from noisy groups.

✓ Put quiet signs on each desk.

4. Agree and act on the class' choices.

✓ One person speaks at a time in each group.

✓ Assign a noise checker to each group.

✓ Give points for the quietest voice each day.

The teacher of the class that gave these answers, an eighth-grade science class in Chicago, reported several results: (1) the problem-solving model became a weekly event, (2) the students' discussions became more and more involved as they realized they were "taking charge" of their own learning and being responsible, and (3) they policed their own decisions.

TELL / RETELL

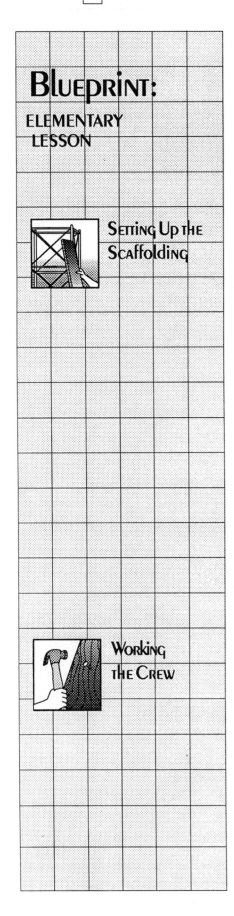

To teach about attentive listening, prepare a bulletin board with an attentive listening theme. Show pictures of (a) a class attending to the teacher, (b) group members attending to each other, (c) a class attending to a visitor, and (d) a class attending to a student speaker.

Make and display a T-chart on the bulletin board.

ATTENTIVE LISTENING

SOUNDS LIKE	LOOKS LIKE
1. "uh huh"	1. eyes alert and focused on talker
2. "I see."	2. mirroring emotions
3. clarifying questions	3. leaning forward or toward speaker
4. silence	4. head nods at right time
5. paraphrasing	5. taking notes
6.	6.
7.	7.
8.	8.

Gather students around and explain the bulletin board and chart. Ask volunteers to share how it feels to have someone's full attention. Solicit several answers. Demonstrate with the principal, another teacher or a volunteer what attentive listening looks and sounds like.

Divide students into pairs. Instruct one student to share a fun adventure. Instruct the other to attend closely so he/she can repeat the story. Walk among the pairs and give a thumbs-up to each child seen listening.

Use this monitoring time to be aware of misbehaving students, especially during these times when interpersonal skills and social behavior are the focus. Be aware of "the kid who..." seeks attention, feels inadequate, makes the power play, is looking for revenge or shows signs of emotional disturbances.

When a misbehaving student exhibits a deficit in a social skill, review the strategies presented earlier in this chapter and take time to address the social skill with clear, directed and effective action. Say, for example, in this "Tell/Retell" lesson, one student is causing lots of distraction during the partner interaction by clowning around and *seeking the attention* of the students around him/her. This is the teachable moment in which to address the question, **"What do you do with the kid who...*seeks attention*?"** Looking back at the suggested strategies to gradually extinguish this misbehavior, the teacher could begin with the strategy *recognizing a student who is modeling the proper behavior.* For example, standing near the attention seeker who is faking falling out of his chair to get attention from his partner and others, the teacher might say to a nearby pair: "I like the way you're positioned for good listening. Eye-to-eye, knee-to-knee is how attentive listening partners often sit."

By focusing on the desired modeled behavior and by telling explicitly what it looks like, the teacher cues the misbehaving student about two things: 1) modeling desired behavior gets the attention of the teacher, and 2) the desired behavior looks like this.

Although these actions seem like simple classroom management, by addressing the incident within the context of learning, the teacher adds power to the reinforcement strategy. Additionally, the teacher can talk about the incident or use the groups' reflection time to lead discussion on the idea of "seeking attention" as "clowning around."

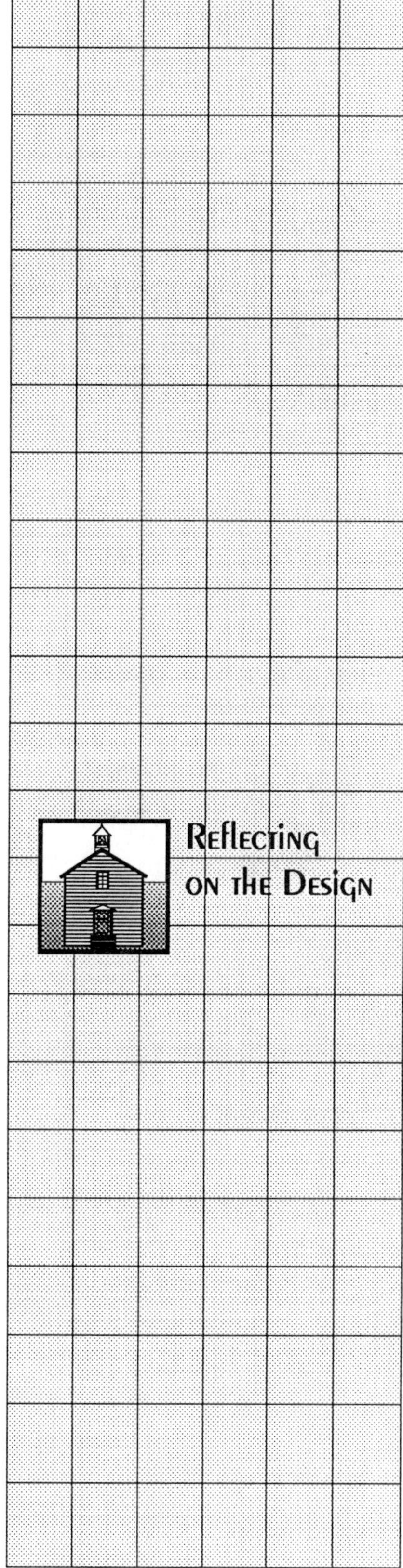

To process affectively, conduct a brief sharing, then let several listeners tell the class what they heard in their partner interactions. Praise them for good listening. Have them tell how it felt to have someone listen so carefully.

To process the social skill of active listening, ask students to tell about someone they think is a *good* listener.

To process cognitively, continue to practice on succeeding days. Begin each practice with a review of the T-chart. End it with praise to the attentive listeners.

After several short practices, have a discussion in which the class talks about (a) why listening attentively is a good idea, and (b) what times in class and at home are important for attentive listening. This metacognitive talk helps students transfer the social skill beyond the lesson.

□ □ □

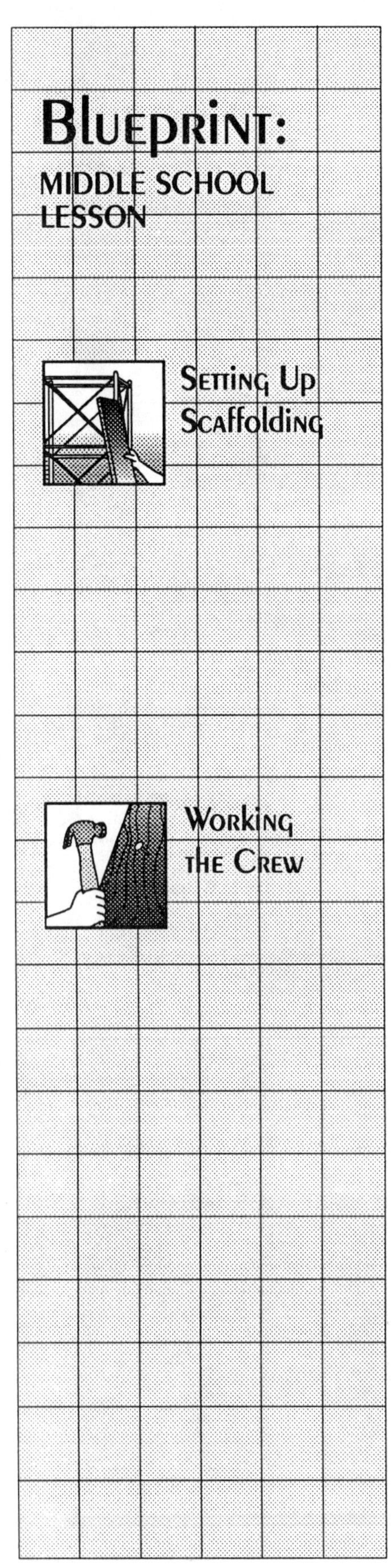

Blueprint:
Middle School Lesson
Setting Up Scaffolding
Working the Crew

THE NON-LISTENING ACTIVITY

Divide the class into pairs. Ask students to think of a recent time when someone important paid close attention to them. As they tell you how they knew they were getting attentive listening, make a T-chart for attentive listening.

ATTENTIVE LISTENING	
SOUNDS LIKE	LOOKS LIKE
1. "uh huh"	1. eyes alert and focused on talker
2. "I see."	2. mirroring emotions
3. clarifying questions	3. leaning forward/toward speaker
4. silence	4. head nods at right time
5. paraphrasing	5. taking notes

Identify the oldest student in each pair. Those students are A's. The younger student in each pair is B. Invite A to listen to the first instructions. Each A is to think of a time in the past year when someone did *not* listen. What happened? How did it feel? The A's are to prepare their stories while the B's are given instructions.

Invite the B's to review the T-chart. Now say, "Now that you have reviewed how to behave when you listen with attention, you are to do your 100 percent, absolute, total best NOT to listen to your partner's story! You are to model non-listening behaviors." Require these guidelines: (1) all must stay in the room, (2) speakers do your best to tell the story, (3) don't hurt each other, and (4) stop when the teacher gives the signal (e.g., lights off, hands up).

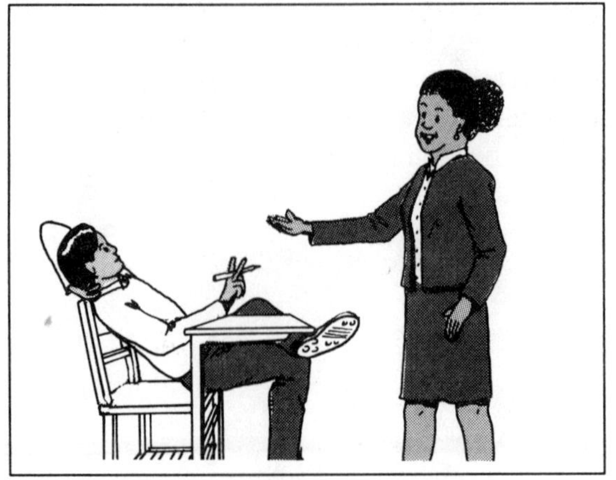

Move around the room and note the students' behavior. Be aware of genuine misbehavior in students, especially during these times in which interpersonal skills and social behavior are the focus. Be aware of "the kid who..." seeks attention, feels inadequate, makes the power play, is looking for revenge or shows signs of emotional disturbances. When a misbehaving student exhibits a deficit in a social skill, review the strategies presented earlier in this chapter and take time to address the social skill with clear, directed and effective action.

Even better, in the "Non-listening" lesson activity you have asked students to deliberately demonstrate poor listening skills. Now, take advantage of this activity. Find the student who takes over the partner interview as the dialogue becomes very one-sided. This is the teachable moment to address the question, **"What do you do with the kid who...*takes over*?"**

Looking back at the suggested strategies listed earlier in the chapter, *moving this student into a leadership role* seems to be an applicable strategy for this situation. For example, in the midst of this partner interaction, tell the class to "freeze frame." Suggest that to reinforce the roles of each partner, one pair will model or role play an interaction. Select the pair with the partner who has "taken over" and have them model the desired actions. Surprisingly, the misbehavior disappears instantly and the desired behavior is modeled in true leadership style. However, since the non-listening activity is intentionally set up to focus on misbehavior, this "power play" might be tried by others.

By designating a leadership role for the "offender" in front of the class, the "power play" in the small group is no longer as interesting to the misbehaving student. So be sure to highlight the reason the strategy of *giving a leadership role* works. In addition, this same student has actually modeled the very behavior he/she was lacking. Although this may be simple classroom management, by addressing this incident within the context of social skill instruction, the teacher adds power to the situation with positive reinforcement. She/he also can talk about the incident or use the groups' reflection time to lead discussion on the idea of power plays as taking over the group.

After two minutes, stop the activity. Have each pair shake hands, with the B's apologizing to the A's.

For affective processing, conclude with a discussion of the positive effects on a speaker and a listener when attention goes both ways.

To process the social skill of listening, have students describe a TV character who is a good listener.

To process cognitively, put a double T-chart for non-listening on the board. What did non-listening look like, sound like and feel like?

For metacognitve processing, discuss with the class instances when they may have experienced the same negative feelings caused by non-listening.

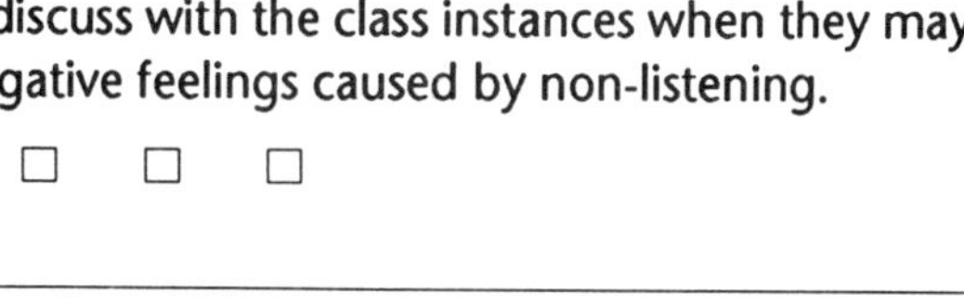

DRAW THIS

To focus on attentive listening, divide the class into group A and group B.

Give each A the following instruction sheet and a sketch of a figure.

> Your task is to describe the assigned figure to your partner. Your partner must sit back-to-back with you and may not (a) see your sketch, or (b) talk with you. Your partner must reproduce your sketch using your instructions. You will have five minutes.
>
> 
>
> Partner A-1*

Give each B the following instruction sheet.

> Your task is to sketch a figure as instructed by your partner. You may not talk to your partner or see the original. You will have five minutes.
>
> Partner B-1*

Match partners by counting off 1, 2, 1, 2 . . . .

Monitor the groups for five minutes. If more time is needed, give it.

Reverse the roles. Give the A's the instructions:

> You may not see the sketch. You may ask clarifying questions about the instructions and discuss how you are sketching.
>
> Partner A-2*

*pages 296-298

Give each B the new sketch and these instructions:

You may not show this sketch to your partner. You may answer your partner's questions about your instructions. You have five minutes.

Partner B-2*

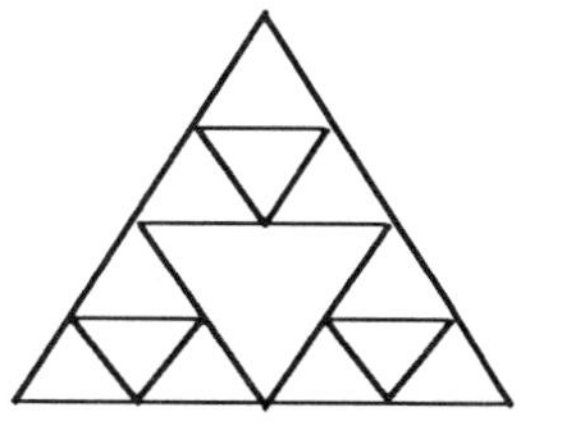

Be aware of all the students' social skills during this time in which interpersonal skills and social behavior are on focus. Be aware of "the kid who..." seeks attention, feels inadequate, makes the power play, is looking for revenge or shows signs of emotional disturbances. When a student exhibits a deficit in a social skill, review the strategies presented earlier in this chapter and take time to address the social skill with clear, directed and effective action. For example, if during the "Draw This" lesson, a student shows signs of *feeling inadequate*—lack of eye contact, fear, whispered "I don't know," "I can't," or other closing-up behaviors—take advantage of the moment to answer the question, **"What do you do with the kid who ...** *feels inadequate?*"

Looking back at the suggested strategies listed earlier in this chapter, *reminding the student of past successes and cueing for what can be done to ensure another success* seems like the most effective strategy to choose. For example, as the students proceed with their descriptions, one student drawer is making very tentative marks in response to the directions given. As facilitator, the teacher notices that the tentativeness is persisting throughout the interaction. The teacher moves near the student who is feeling inadequate and mentions a previous incident in which that student succeeded: "Remember how well you did when you had to memorize that poem? Think of what you did to remember it so accurately. Try to do those same things now as you try to reproduce the drawing being described. Keep in mind it's supposed to be fun. You will not be graded on the *drawing*. We're concentrating on *how to listen attentively*."

*page 299

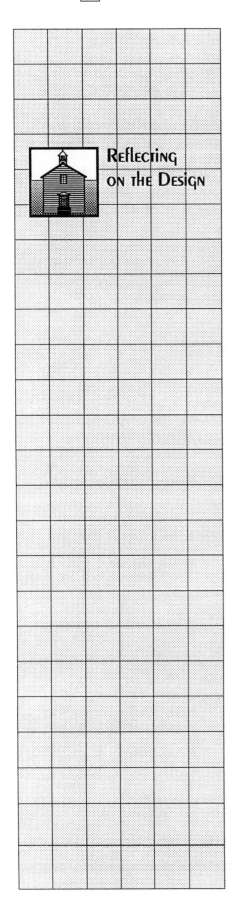

By reassuring the student who feels inadequate, the teacher successfully uses this opportunity to extend one student's confidence in a social situation. Success breeds success so the more frequently this student feels good about an achievement, the more likely he/she will develop socially.

For affective processing, ask students what they do when they are feeling unsure about things.

For social skill processing, have students describe an incident in which they paid the consequences for *not* listening.

For cognitive processing, list on the board or overhead students' ideas for (a) what was easy to do, and (b) what was difficult in the task.

For metacognitive processing, discuss with the class what they have learned from doing this task. Where could the use this information? How would it help?

☐ ☐ ☐

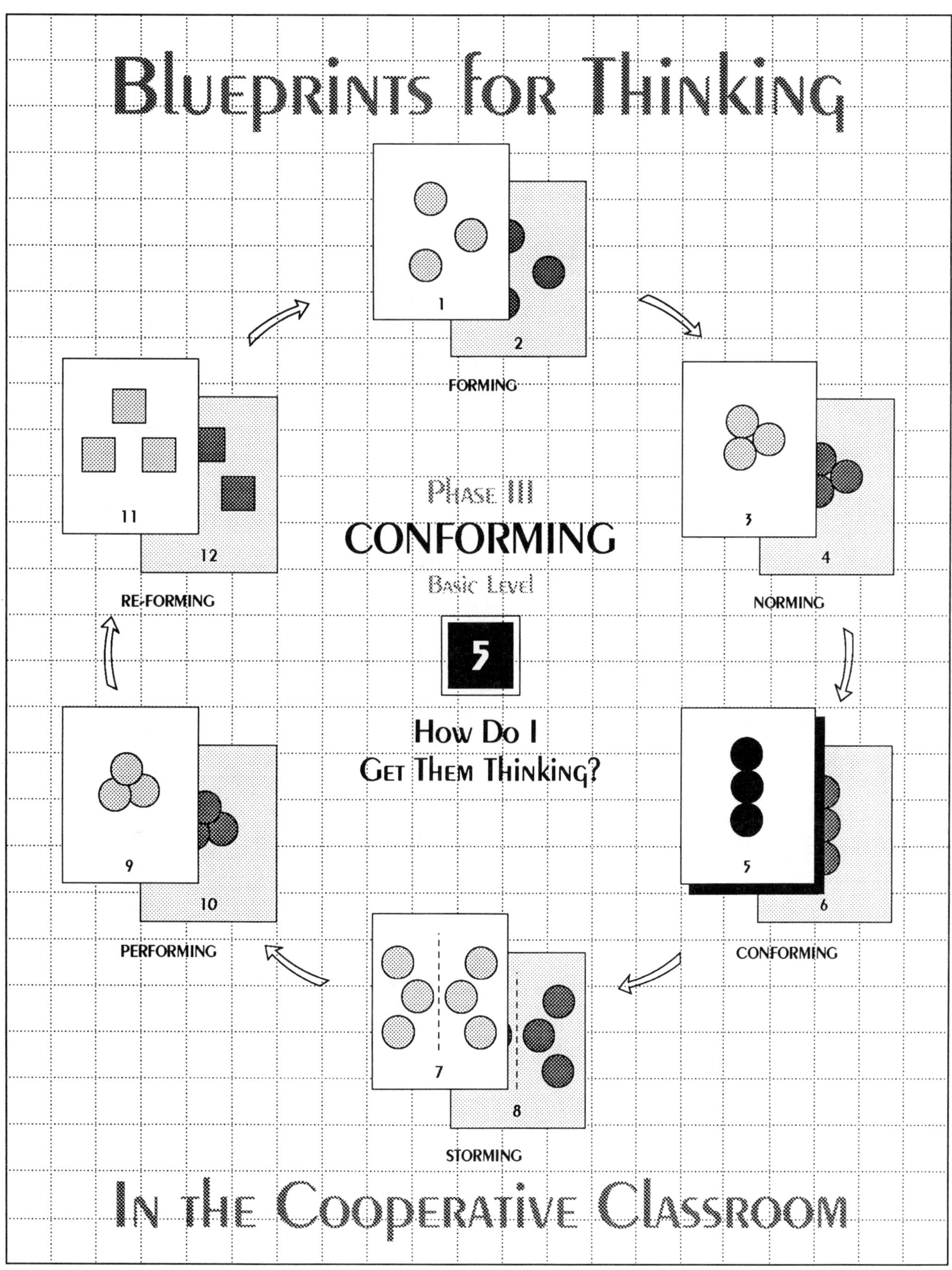
Blueprints for Thinking
1
2
FORMING
3
4
NORMING
5
6
CONFORMING
7
8
STORMING
9
10
PERFORMING
11
12
RE-FORMING
Phase III
CONFORMING
Basic Level
5
How Do I
Get Them Thinking?
In the Cooperative Classroom

PHASE III:
CONFORMING
BASIC

How Do I Get Them Thinking?

What spirit do we want our intelligence to have? Do we want children to be gifted and alienated? - literate and prejudiced? - brilliant and cynical? - intelligent and materialistic? - in need of help and ashamed? ... Unless we educate for wholeness in person and wholeness of our earth planet, we are not really intelligent ... The health and wholeness of our planet is not separable from health and wholeness of us as individuals.

—M.C. Richards

Draft

Once the basic skills of forming base groups and task groups are in place and the norms for expected social behaviors evolve in the classroom, it's time to examine the types of tasks the groups are assigned. At this point, the groups are entering into the conforming stage in which the cooperative tasks take on complexity and students' thinking becomes a focus.

Skilled cooperative learning groups work with a dual focus, with one eye on the academic goal and the other eye on the social skill goal. With the social skill goal moving into place, an important teacher decision at this time is how to set criteria for high-challenge academic work with the groups.

A basic step in motivating students to think in the high-challenge classroom is using teacher questions that promote more thinking—in quality and quantity. As the TESA (Teacher Expectations and Student Achievement) research shows, a predominance of "fat" questions at the upper two levels (processing and applying) engages students more deeply in a lesson's content. Add wait time (3 to 15 seconds of silence between questions), equal distribution of responses (a system that ensures low achievers get equal attention) and the other TESA variables, and student achievement goes up.

The second step, illustrated in the work of Beyer, includes explicit attention and direct instruction of the thinking skills in which students use the skills to question, process and organize the information. Consensus from the leading proponents in the thinking skills movement, (Feuerstein, Lipman, Marzano, McTighe, Costa, Jones, Palinscar, Fogarty and Bellanca, Perkins, Swartz, Barell and Brandt, among others) dictate explicit skill instruction to promote thinking for all students. While there is some disagreement as to whether or not the skills of thinking should be taught separately or infused in the content, the authors favor the infused model since it facilitates transfer for the student learner.

The third step, provided by the research of Jones, Lyman, McTighe and Bellanca, tells teachers about the importance of graphic organizers. These are visible renditions of the thinking process. As students learn how to use these cognitive patterns, they extend their ability to work with content in a thinking way. Concept maps, webs, matrices and more than two dozen other organizers provide a large number of options for classroom use.

The fourth step, shown by the research of Brown, Palincsar and others on "metacognition," indicates the necessity for students to learn how to ask higher-level questions about the subject they are studying. This research highlights the importance of students' learning to predict, summarize and develop hands-on questioning strategies that indicate they have "learned how to learn."

The latest research on metacognition is described by Swartz and Perkins as they peel away the layers of this type of thinking to reveal four distinctions in the metacognitive process. They cite tacit use of metacognition in which the learner regularly uses metacognitive thinking but is not fully aware of calling upon a strategy or technique. The researchers also suggest an aware user who consciously notes his/her strategic use of a behavior as contrasted with the strategic learner who deliberately selects a way to do a task and maps the transfer and application. Finally, at the highest level of metacognitive processing is the reflective user who questions at the planning stage, monitors during the activity and evaluates following a task. His/her own behavior is part of an ongoing process that exemplifies thoughtfulness and mindfulness.

As students learn how to use questioning strategies, explicit thinking skills, graphic organizers and metacognitive questions, they build a foundation of thinking skills for transfer into content and as ingredients for problem solving, decision making and creative ideation. Cooperative groups provide the best opportunity to practice the use of these "learning-to-think" strategies. The same groups provide the teacher with an opportunity to develop advanced content lessons in which students make regular, appropriate use of these thinking tools to "make sense" of the subject matter.

For all the benefits of these thinking strategies as "learning-to-think" techniques, nothing compares to the students' ability to extend the tools into learning to think.

Specs

To most easily set the criteria for high-content, high-challenge lessons, use the Three-Story Intellect model, which is especially helpful with complex thinking tasks. The conceptualization of the Three-Story Intellect is perhaps best presented in this inspirational piece by Oliver Wendell Holmes:

> There are one-story intellects, two-story intellects, and three-story intellects with skylights. All fact collectors, who have no aim beyond their facts, are one-story men. Two-story men *compare, reason, generalize,* using the labors of the fact collectors as well as their own. Three-story men *idealize, imagine, predict*—their best illumination comes from above, through the sky-light.*

To align this concept with the curriculum, visualize the three stories of the intellect combined with Costa's three-stage model of cognitive tasks (see opposite page).

☐ GATHERING INFORMATION

In the *gathering* stage, students are required to find the facts, acquire knowledge and understand the material. This first level of cognitive functioning engages the learners in typically schoolish tasks that direct them to *list, name, locate* and *describe*. To help students gather information, they often are asked to form questions about the topic under study. As the students are led toward generating questions that pull in lots of information and help them generalize about that information, it is helpful to distinguish between *fat* and *skinny* questions. Introduce the idea of fat and skinny questions to the students using the following definitions:

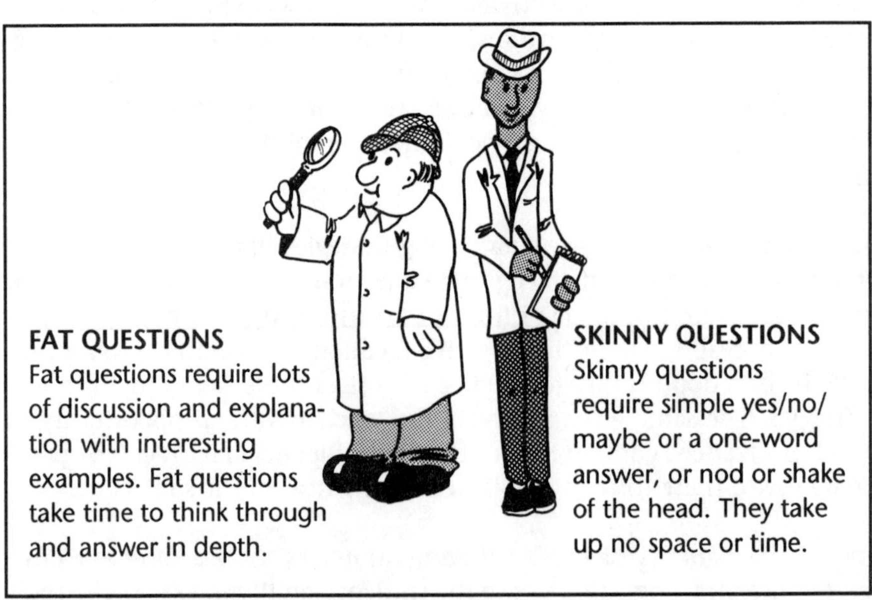

FAT QUESTIONS
Fat questions require lots of discussion and explanation with interesting examples. Fat questions take time to think through and answer in depth.

SKINNY QUESTIONS
Skinny questions require simple yes/no/maybe or a one-word answer, or nod or shake of the head. They take up no space or time.

Have them give some examples for each type of question. Remember to use both fat and skinny questions whenever students are researching or gathering information.

For example, cooperative learning groups might be assigned the task of gathering a compendium of information on the various geographic regions of the United States. To meet the academic goal, a checklist of requirements would act as a guide. A list of fat and skinny questions and a map depicting

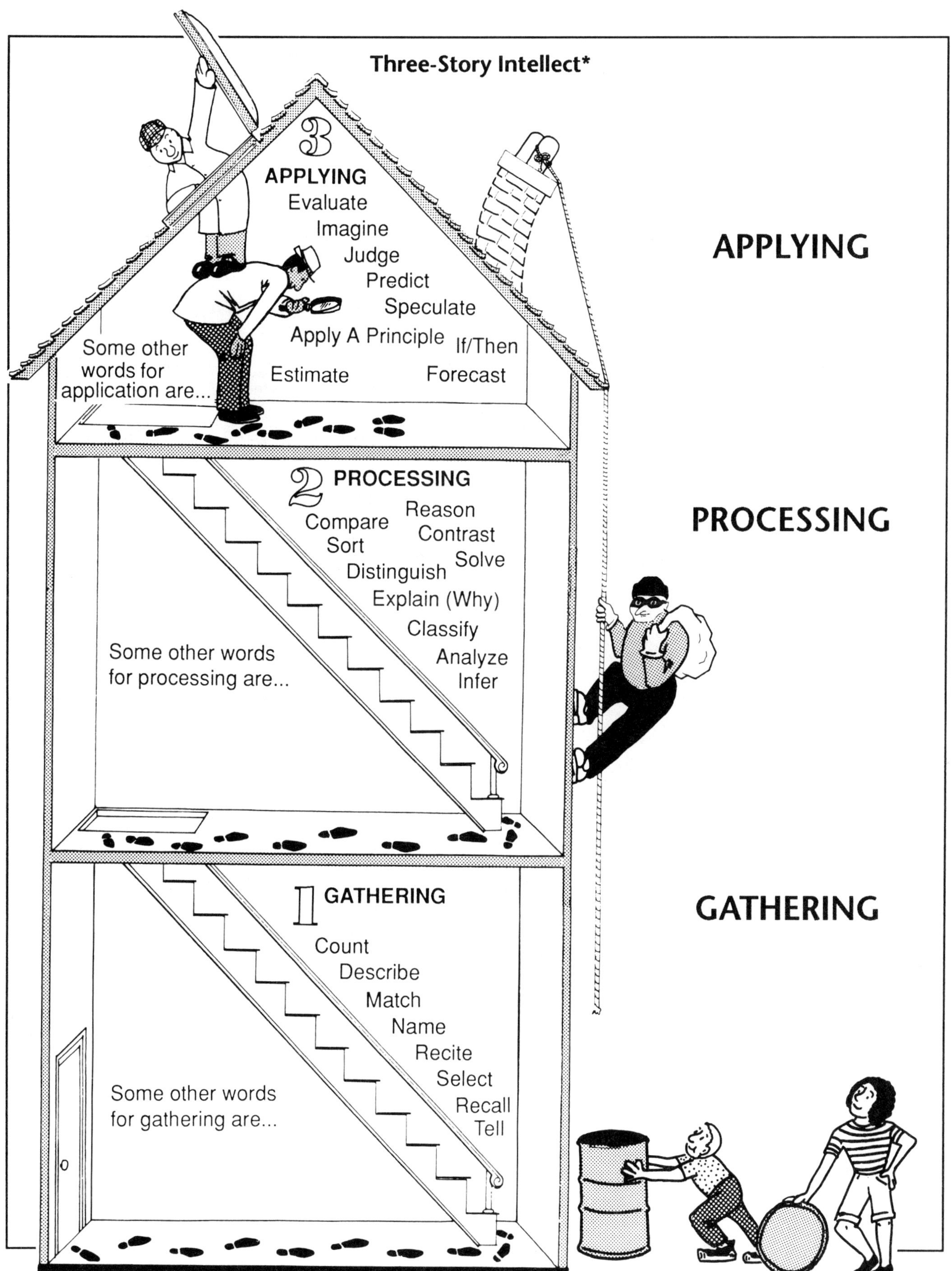
Three-Story Intellect*
3
APPLYING
Evaluate
Imagine
Judge
Predict
Speculate
Apply A Principle
If/Then
Estimate
Forecast
Some other words for application are...
2 PROCESSING
Compare
Reason
Contrast
Sort
Solve
Distinguish
Explain (Why)
Classify
Analyze
Infer
Some other words for processing are...
1 GATHERING
Count
Describe
Match
Name
Recite
Select
Recall
Tell
Some other words for gathering are...
APPLYING
PROCESSING
GATHERING

*page 300

the information might be the final products of this project by which group performance is judged. This is the first level, or "first story," of cognitive skills— gathering information.

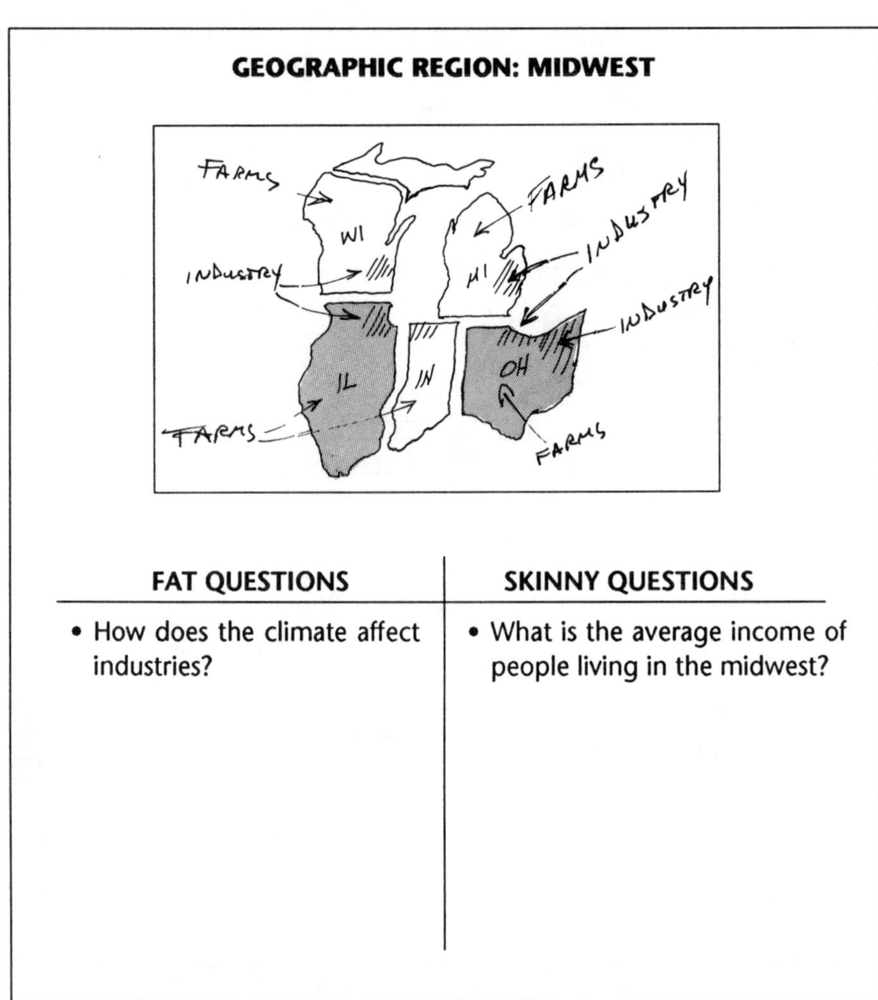

□ PROCESSING INFORMATION

While the first-story intellect involves the gathering of information, the second-story intellect coincides with Costa's next stage of cognitive behavior called *information processing*. Typically, second-story intellectual tasks engage students in *comparing and contrasting, classifying, determining cause and effect, prioritizing* and *analyzing activities*. It is in the "second story" of cognitive functioning that students are required to interact with the information in ways which help them to internalize it.

This second-story processing is not to be confused with the metacognitive processing section of each lesson in which student reflection is the goal. In the second-story processing stage, *students manipulate the new information, trying to make connections to prior knowledge, previous experience and/or developing concepts*. This is the *process* through which students grasp understanding of the content under scrutiny and make sense of things.

When learners manipulate knowledge and concepts, they anchor new ideas to personally relevant past experiences. It is through this second-story processing that individuals connect to prior knowledge and assimilate concepts and ideas in personally relevant ways.

Paralleling the first-story example in which students gathered information about various regions of the United States onto a map, the following second-story task involves deeper processing of the information. In essence, students "make sense" of the information for themselves by tying new facts and ideas to prior knowledge and experience.

For example, once groups display and discuss the maps of the different regions they can pair up with another group to compare their regions. This task involves students in finding similarities and differences between the two regions. They can use the Venn diagram to perform an analysis that will help make sense of the data. The final product can be a short homework essay in which each student compares his or her region to a similar region represented on a TV show.

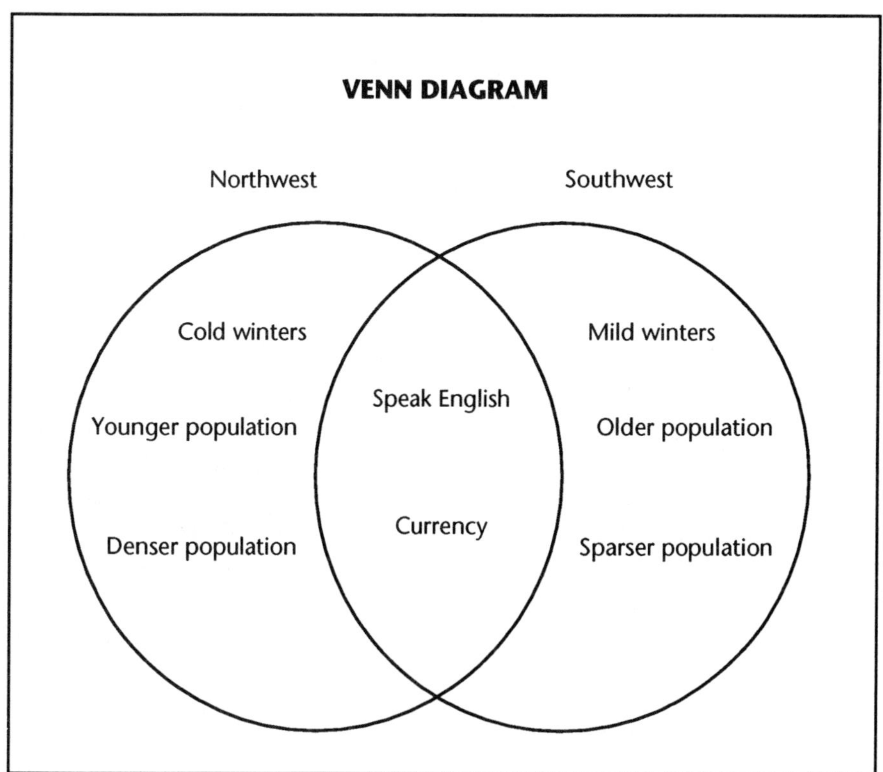

In both tasks, the group work in the classroom and the individual work at home, students are required to *do something* with the gathered facts. This analysis calls for a different type of thinking than in the first-story level of gathering facts.

☐ APPLYING INFORMATION

Beyond the cooperative tasks that reside in the first story and the second story is the highest level of cognitive performance, the third story. Third-story tasks engage students in the application of information that has been gathered and processed. It is in the third-story thinking that students *synthesize, predict, imagine, idealize* and begin to *use the new ideas in meaningful ways.*

Following the example of the social studies lesson in which students gather and compare data on regions of the United States, the third-story academic task now requires sophisticated use of the information as students select a "what if" question for the group to tackle.

WHAT IF . . . ?

Select one issue and prepare a brief paper stating your ideas.

Environment:

1. What if the *greenhouse effect* continues? How will this affect the various factors in the regions?

Demographics:

2. What if the *senior citizens' migration* to the South continues? How will that affect the region?

Economics:

3. What if the *recycling tax* goes into effect? How will that affect the region?

Inherent in the what-if speculations is an expectation that students know about current issues and can apply that knowledge to the lesson at hand. Expectations for immediate and relevant student use actually build the bridges for the transfer of learning. Without this application piece, lessons seem fragmented within the curriculum and bits of information seem isolated with little or no meaning in the context of students' lives beyond the classroom.

By structuring lessons that engage students in three-story intellectual tasks, cooperative learning groups take on an aura of the "corporate think tank." Group members begin to sense a synergy within the group tasks and the high-challenge approach creates not only a need, but also an appreciation of the team as a whole.

It's also appropriate at this point to differentiate between a smoothly functioning group engaged in high-level tasks and cooperative groups used for remedial work. To use cooperative learning groups for drill and practice work of remediation is to undermine the value of the groups for doing complex and challenging tasks. Remediation work calls for skillful reteaching that may not be appropriate in the group work.

Of course, leading students into three-story tasks takes development over time. To clarify and model this process in which student tasks are gradually elevated to second- and third-story thinking, complete sample lessons are outlined at the end of this chapter.

These specific blueprints for elementary, middle and high school students demonstrate how the academic tasks of *gathering*, *processing* and *applying* become integrated into lesson objectives. This hierarchy of thinking can be compacted into every lesson, no matter how brief or extensive. Look at how the lesson blueprints address these three distinct levels in subject matter lessons. Note that by building complexity into the academic task, the teacher automatically builds interdependence and a sense of "teamness" in the groups. Students need each other to get the task done well and they know it.

□ □ □

Update your sequence chart on page 348.

THREE AGREE

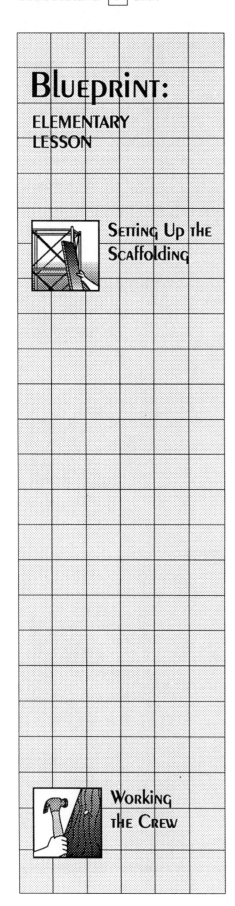

As schools have gradually accepted calculators into the classroom, teachers have struggled with how to use the calculators effectively and still keep the balance between the automated calculations and the traditional student-learned computational skills.

To help students through the Three-Story Intellect in gathering, processing and applying information about using the calculator, begin with this focus activity.

Ask students to draw and label, from memory or with a model the buttons on a pocket calculator.

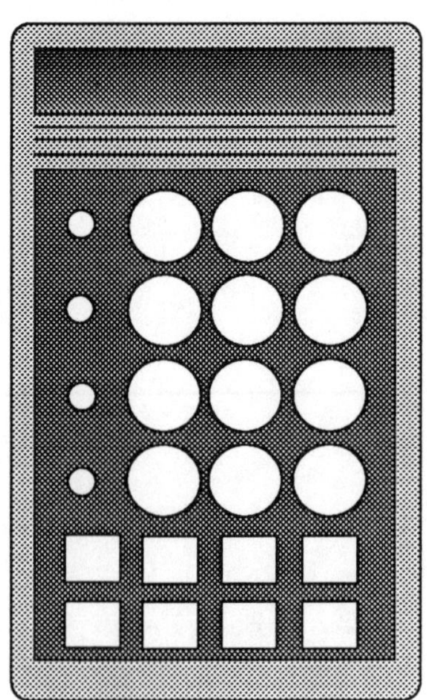

Sample Calculator*

Arrange students into groups of three. To begin role assignments, have them point to someone in their group on the count of three, "One! Two! Three!" Assign the person who is "it" the role of *bookkeeper*, the next as the *counter*, and the third as the *calculator*.

*page 301

ROLES

Bookkeeper: Reads the problems. Uses pictures or drawings to calculate the answers.
Counter: Checks the bookkeeper's answer by counting with beans or objects.
Calculator: Checks the answers using the pocket calculator.

To gather data, use a page from the math text, a blackline master or problems from the board. Have the students in each group compute the answers to the problems. Members are to use the calculating methods indicated by the roles. Each member is to use his/her own sheet of paper as a worksheet.

Bookkeeper: Draws sketches on a sheet and computes.
Counter: Uses beans to compute and mark a sheet.
Calculator: Uses the pocket calculator to compute answers.

To process the data after group members have completed calculations for all the problems, instruct the members to compare their answers using the agree/ disagree chart and tally marks.

PROBLEM	AGREE	DISAGREE
1	II	I
2	III	
3	I	II
4		
↓		

With the tallied charts, team members rework any problems for which there is lack of agreement. There is lack of agreement on a problem when there are not three tallies in the AGREE column next to each problem listed.

RULE: ALL THREE MUST AGREE!

To apply the information once agreement has been reached on all problems, the group members incorporate their individual answer sheets into a "Three-Agree design." For example, students can use the Three-Agree sheets to construct a snowman (see example below) since snowmen typically are made with three snowballs. Have construction paper, scissors and glue available for each group. Be sure to specify that all members' answer sheets must agree before the group can construct a design.

A snowman can be a Three-Agree design.

Other examples of threes are triangles, the three little pigs, the three billy goats gruff, the three bears, stoplights, tricycles, triathalons and pretzels. Let the students think of others.

Students can brainstorm other threes for designs.

Display the Three-Agree designs throughout the room.

For affective processing, refer to the displayed Three-Agree designs and ask students to write plus/minus statements on their feelings about the activity.

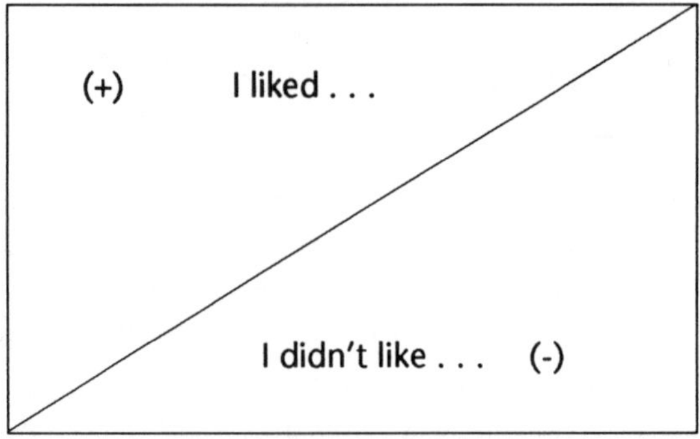

For social skill processing, have students talk about how they act when they disagree with someone. Give examples of situations in which people often disagree:

- Which TV show to watch
- Where to go for a vacation
- How to do something

For cognitive processing, take time to review the problems and sample some of the answers. Ask students to turn in their tally sheets.

For metacognitive processing, have students rank (1, 2, 3) the following according to their favorite method of problem solving:

___ drawing pictures

___ counting beans

___ pocket calculating

After ranking the items, students should turn to a friend and share why they ranked the items the way they did.

Encourage students to continue to bring calculators to the classroom for checking their other math computations.

□ □ □

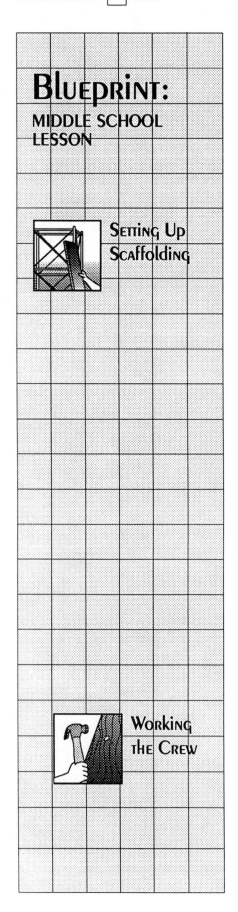

BED-TO-BED

Throughout the schooling years, and even beyond, the typical, overused and abused storytelling model takes on a narrative or "bed-to-bed" format. An illustration is the young student telling about a personal experience:

> "I got up (out of *bed*). I had breakfast. I went outside. I played with my dog. I had dinner. I watched TV and I went to *bed*."

That's a bed-to-bed format. Here's an older student's illustration that suggests a similar model used for a book report:

> "_________ was born in _____. He was educated at ___________. He became famous for ________________. He died in _____."

Both examples are simplified, but do suggest the bed-to-bed narrative that seems to dominate students' writing styles. As a quick focus activity, have students turn to a partner and tell a personal bed-to-bed story about a trip they recently took. Stress the bed-to-bed model that is to be followed.

> "We got up and got started at _____. We went to _____. Passed by _____. Arrived in _____ and went to bed."

After sufficient experimentation with the bed-to-bed model, tell students that the purpose of this lesson is to practice alternate formats for telling a story by using the Three-Story Intellect model. Explain that they are to interview someone to gather information. Then they are to process the information by charting, webbing, prioritizing or using whatever technique helps them focus the material. Finally, they are to tell about the person's life in a biography by applying the gathered and processed information. The biography must not fall into the bed-to-bed format. The students must explore fresh approaches to storytelling to complete this assignment.

To help students focus on interviewing techniques, especially the questioning strategies of a good interviewer, assign students the following task.

To gather information, have students select a TV interview show in which the host or hostess asks the guests questions. Brainstorm possibilities:

Johnny Carson   Arsenio Hall
Barbara Walters   David Letterman
Phil Donahue   Ted Koppel
Oprah Winfrey

Instruct students to view the selected show with pencil and paper in hand. Have them record the actual questions used by the interviewer. The next day, share the following definitions of fat and skinny questions with the students.

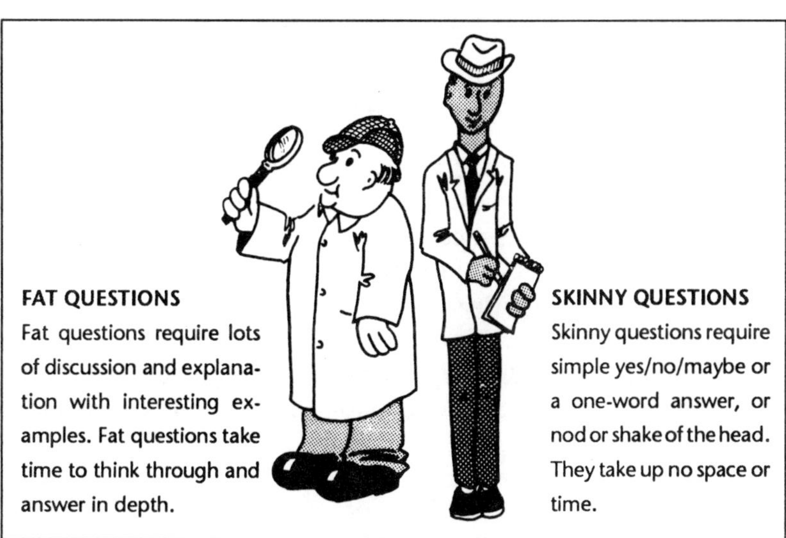

FAT QUESTIONS
Fat questions require lots of discussion and explanation with interesting examples. Fat questions take time to think through and answer in depth.

SKINNY QUESTIONS
Skinny questions require simple yes/no/maybe or a one-word answer, or nod or shake of the head. They take up no space or time.

Now, have students transfer their questions to a chart similar to the following. Have them rate each question.

FAT	SKINNY	QUESTIONS
	X	How old were you when . . .?
X		Would you rather . . .?
X		Who has influenced you and how?
	X	Have you always . . .?
X		What if you were to . . .?
	X	Has anyone ever suggested that . . .?

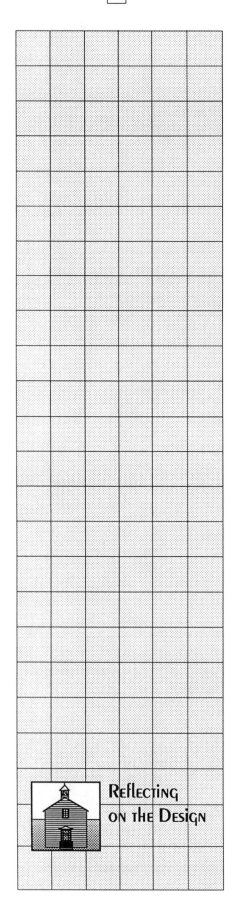

To process information with the fat and skinny questions as a guide, introduce students to the Three-Story Intellect diagram of verbs. Using both the Three-Story Intellect and the fat and skinny questions' rating sheet, have students write interview questions.

In groups of three, with a recorder, an observer and a reporter on each team, students should formulate a set of fat (and a few skinny) questions for an interview with a senior citizen. The completed sheet of questions will serve as the interview guide for the three group members when they actually interview their subjects.

Sample Interview Sheet

1. Tell me about a vivid childhood memory.
2. Compare yourself to a contemporary figure.
3.

To apply the information, use the completed interview sheets and have students conduct interviews at a local hospital or nursing home. (Relatives can become the interview subjects if a class excursion is not possible.) Suggest ways that they can "capture the interview"—for example, by taping the session or by jotting down notes during the interview.

Following the interviews, discuss how students can write their biographies without using the straight, narrative bed-to-bed format. Elicit ideas, including:

Quotes

A dialogue

A song

Poetry

Flashbacks

Episodes

A view from the eyes of a youngster (or another)

Once the final products are written, have students present the biographical pieces to their interview subjects as thanks for their cooperation.

For affective processing, complete a log entry using the following lead-in:

The thing I like most about this project is . . . .

For social skill processing, have students describe how they show appreciation to a favorite relative.

For cognitive processing, have students generate other uses for fat and skinny questions:

1.
2.
3.

For metacognitive processing, ask students to name, describe and justify a three-story intellect, a "thinker" they know:

____________ is a three-story intellect. She/he ______________. That is why I nominate him/her as a three-story intellect!

□ □ □

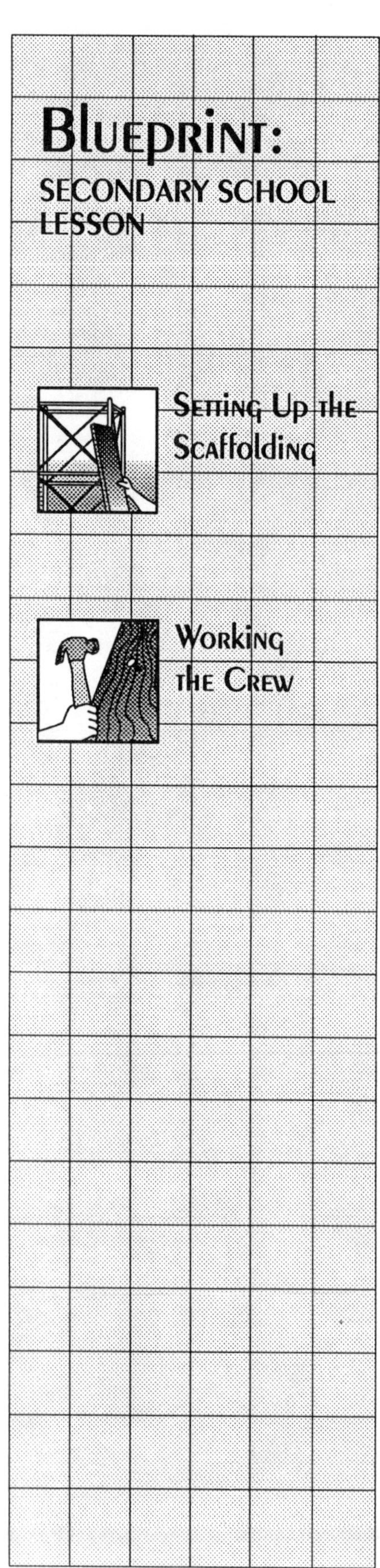

CREATE A CREATURE

Distribute a die to each lab group and tell the students that these will help them in today's lesson. Show the Three-Story Intellect model and explain that students will gather, process and apply information about classifying in a lab called "Create a Creature."

Using lab groups of three members each, assign and define the roles:

Researcher: Finds the information in the text.

Recorder: Charts the information.

Illustrator: Draws, diagrams and labels the creature with the designated attributes.

To gather information, distribute a copy of the blank Create-A-Creature matrix to each lab group. Using the text, have student groups complete the matrix by choosing possible variables. A completed one might look like this:

CREATE A CREATURE—CLASSIFICATION LAB *

	A	B	C	D	E	F
	BODY SYMMETRY	**SEGMENTATION**	**FORM OF LOCOMOTION**	**SENSORY ORGANS**	**SUPPORT STRUCTURES**	**BODY COVERING**
1	bi-lateral	none	none	eyes, ears & nostrils	bony skeleton	skin-hair
2	radial	2 body segments	2 or 4 walking legs	paired antennae	cartilaginous skeleton	scales
3	bi-lateral	3 body segments	legs & wings	compound eye & antennae	exoskeleton	skin-hair
4	bi-lateral	multiple segments	6 or 8 legs	tentacles	soft bodied	feathers
5	radial	2 body segments	fins	eyes, ears & nostrils	shell hinged	scales
6	bi-lateral	none	multiple walking legs	compound eye & antennae	shell carried	skin-hair

Lesson courtesy of Bob Kapheim, biology Teacher, York High School, Elmhurst, IL

*page 302

Once the grids are complete, have students roll the die. For each roll, have them circle the corresponding squares in each column of the grid. For example, for the first column the toss might be 4. Students would circle the fourth item in first column. For the second column, if the toss is 2, circle the second item.

CREATE A CREATURE—CLASSIFICATION LAB

	A	B	C	D	E	F
	BODY SYMMETRY	**SEGMENTATION**	**FORM OF LOCOMOTION**	**SENSORY ORGANS**	**SUPPORT STRUCTURES**	**BODY COVERING**
1	bi-lateral	none	none	eyes, ears & nostrils	bony skeleton	skin-hair
2	radial	2 body segments	2 or 4 walking legs	paired antennae	cartilaginous skeleton	scales
3	bi-lateral	3 body segments	legs & wings	compound eye & antennae	exoskeleton	skin-hair
4	bi-lateral	multiple segments	6 or 8 legs	tentacles	soft bodied	feathers
5	radial	2 body segments	fins	eyes, ears & nostrils	shell hinged	scales
6	bi-lateral	none	multiple walking legs	compound eye & antennae	shell carried	skin-hair

Continue with the tosses until all columns have a circled item.

To process the information, have students predict what they might do next. Invariably, students will figure out that the next step is to synthesize the various elements by creating a creature designed by the circled items.

CREATE A CREATURE

Directions:

1. Illustrate the new creature.
2. Label the diagram with all the designated attributes.
3. Name the creature appropriately.
4. Have all group members sign the sheet.
5. Display the creatures on the bulletin board.

To apply the information during the next lab period, have student groups select a creature other than their own. Using the labeled attributes on the diagram and referencing the text for the classification procedure, the lab groups should classify the creature according to formal scientific methodology. Once the creatures are classified in the appropriate manner, have the groups return the creature diagrams to the originators.

Reflecting on the Design

For affective processing, use a PMI to talk about the pluses and minuses they felt about the lesson.

What I liked [Pluses (+)]	
What I didn't like [Minuses (-)]	
Questions or thoughts [Intriguing (?)]	

For processing the social skills, have students complete the following stem:

> Taking turns is both good and bad because . . . .

For processing at the cognitive level, have students share their classifications.

For processing at the metacognitive level, have students complete a log entry on the lab technique using the following lead-in:

> What if . . . ?

□ □ □

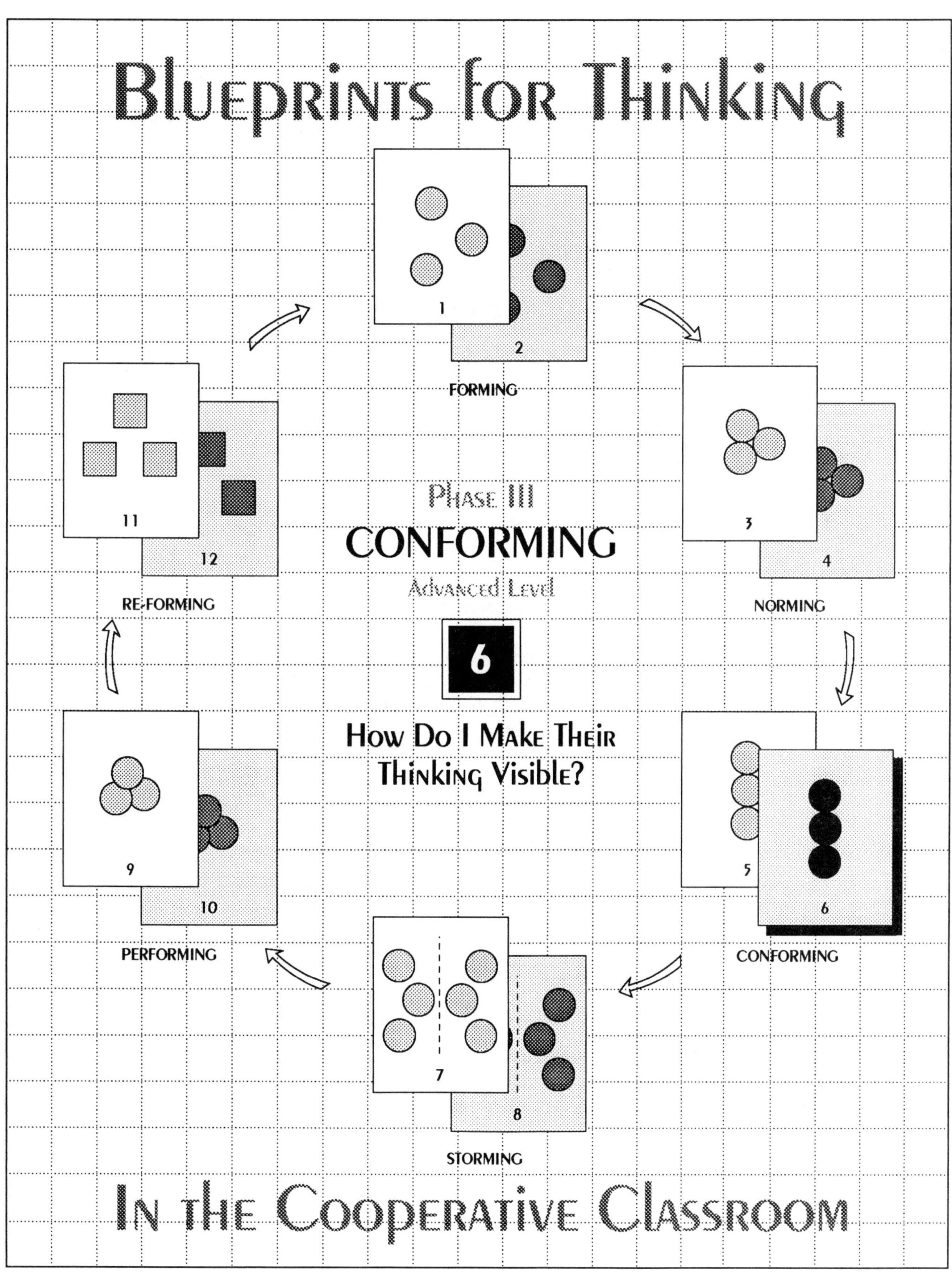
Blueprints for Thinking
1
2
FORMING
3
4
NORMING
5
6
CONFORMING
7
8
STORMING
9
10
PERFORMING
11
12
RE-FORMING
Phase III
CONFORMING
Advanced Level
6
How Do I Make Their
Thinking Visible?
In the Cooperative Classroom

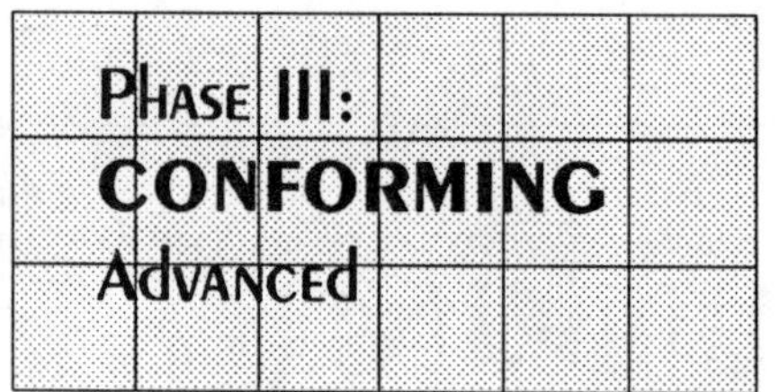

How Do I Make Their Thinking Visible?

The art of teaching is the art of assisting discovery.
—Mark Van Doran

Draft

As the small-group process continues, part of the comfort students feel in their groups is a result of the *conforming* behavior—both cooperative and cognitive—that they are sensing. Basic social skills and high-level thinking have been set as the expected behaviors. Students know the expectations and are more at ease in the interactions.

While targeting explicit thinking skills facilitates the intense involvement needed for "student-to-information" interactions, other critical elements are needed to help students process information in meaningful ways. These elements, commonly called *graphic organizers,* include webs, matrices and Venn diagrams.

These visual tools are also referred to as cognitive maps, visual displays and advance organizers. There is a saying that "thinking is invisible talk." These cognitive tools can be used to *see* what students are thinking and how they are thinking. The cognitive organizers provide visual representations that make the invisible talk visible. They help students organize, reorganize, revise and modify the connections they are making as they process information. Using graphic organizers, students learn how the concepts fit with their prior knowledge or background experience and how they will be used, applied and transferred in novel situations.

The cognitive organizers displayed on the chart on the opposite page help students manipulate information through a variety of thinking skills and strategies. For example, attribute webs are useful for analyzing traits; a listing is best for ranking ideas; and a Venn diagram can display the similarities and differences for comparing and contrasting.

By designing "student-to-student interactions" with cooperative learning and "student-to-information" interactions with cognitive organizers, there are greater effects in student achievement, retention and transfer.

☐ STUDENT-TO-INFORMATION MODELS

Combining the critical elements of the cooperative tasks with the critical elements of higher-order cognitive tasks is not as confusing or difficult as one might first suspect. For each cognitive map on the chart, an appropriate micro-skill for thinking is cited. These organizers/skills can be mixed and matched to fit specific instructional targets of a lesson. Explanations for the organizers can be found on the pages noted in the upper right corner of each box. In addition, blackline masters for each of the models appear on pages 303-314.

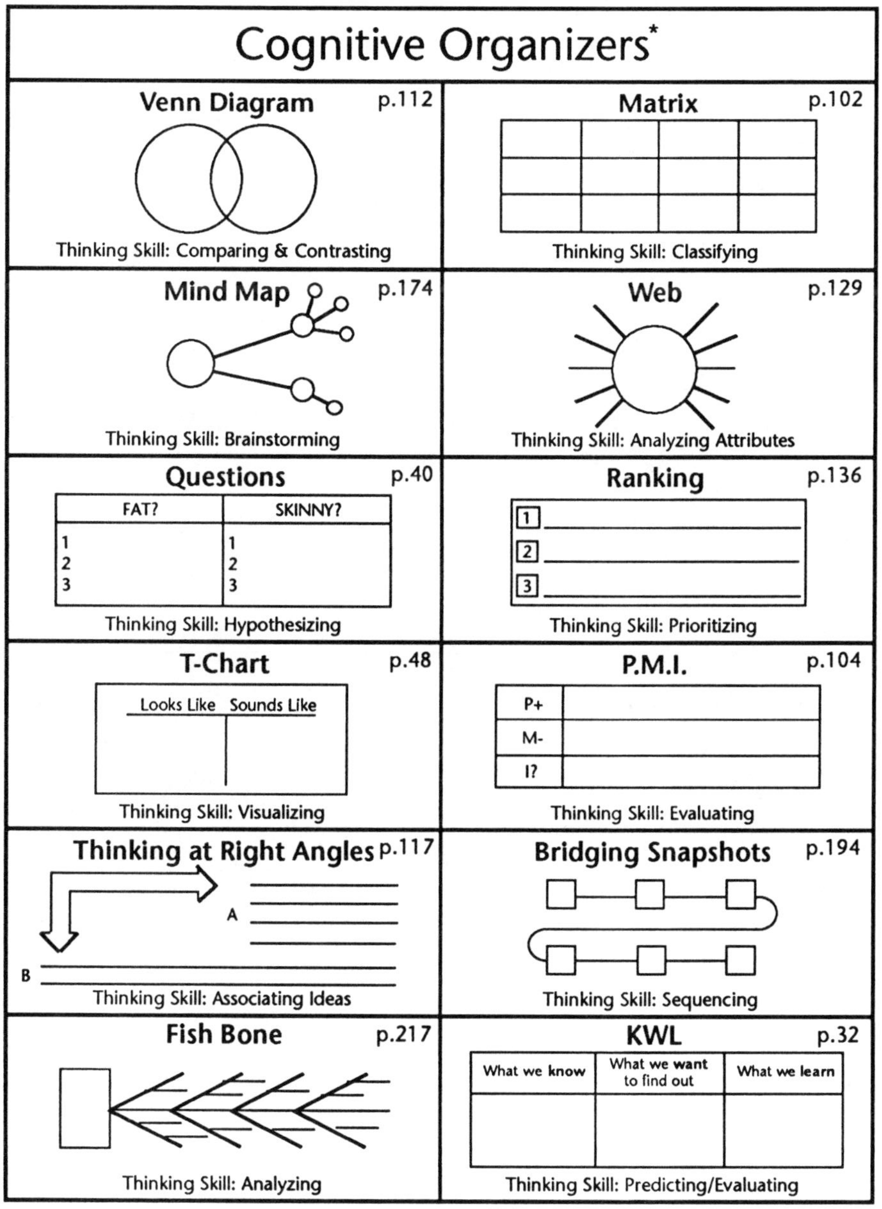

SPECS

Cognitive Organizers*

Venn Diagram p.112 Thinking Skill: Comparing & Contrasting	**Matrix** p.102 Thinking Skill: Classifying
Mind Map p.174 Thinking Skill: Brainstorming	**Web** p.129 Thinking Skill: Analyzing Attributes
Questions p.40 FAT? 1 2 3 / SKINNY? 1 2 3 Thinking Skill: Hypothesizing	**Ranking** p.136 1 2 3 Thinking Skill: Prioritizing
T-Chart p.48 Looks Like / Sounds Like Thinking Skill: Visualizing	**P.M.I.** p.104 P+ / M- / I? Thinking Skill: Evaluating
Thinking at Right Angles p.117 A / B Thinking Skill: Associating Ideas	**Bridging Snapshots** p.194 Thinking Skill: Sequencing
Fish Bone p.217 Thinking Skill: Analyzing	**KWL** p.32 What we know / What we want to find out / What we learn Thinking Skill: Predicting/Evaluating

* p. 303-314

Use this two-column, quick-reference chart to highlight the micro-thinking skill focus and a cognitive organizer for use in high-content, high-challenge tasks.

CHECKLIST FOR PLANNING A THINKING LESSON

THINKING MICRO-SKILLS	COGNITIVE ORGANIZERS
☐ Comparing & Contrasting	☐ Venn Diagram
☐ Brainstorming	☐ Mind Map
☐ Hypothesizing	☐ Fat & Skinny Questions
☐ Visualizing	☐ T-Chart
☐ Associating Ideas	☐ Thinking at Right Angles
☐ Classifying	☐ Matrix
☐ Analyzing Attributes	☐ Web
☐ Prioritizing	☐ Ranking
☐ Evaluating	☐ PMI
☐ Sequencing	☐ Bridging Snapshots
☐ Analyzing	☐ Fish Bone
☐ Predicting/Evaluating	☐ KWL

Over time and with explicit cueing and prompting by the facilitating teacher, students take over the decision-making role of selecting appropriate thinking skills and cognitive organizers. Part of every high-challenge task involves not only *doing* the task, but also deciding *how* to best attack the task. Leading students toward greater shared decision making that involves complete, holistic approaches and solutions to problems, is an overriding goal of the high-performance, high-challenge, cooperative classroom.

To set expectations for student involvement at the highest level is paramount to students' high performance in the ultimate cooperative classroom. To do this successfully, the master teacher, the architect of the intellect, must be secure and confident enough to relinquish more and more responsibility to the capable student apprentices. This is no easy mission for the dedicated teacher who feels an overwhelming responsibility and accountability for student learning. This shift in the teacher's role—from *conveyor of information* to *facilitator of learning*— evokes a very different picture of the modern teacher. In the traditional classroom, the teacher is "in front of the group," "in charge," "lecturing" or doing "stand-up teaching" in teacher-student, student-teacher interactions.

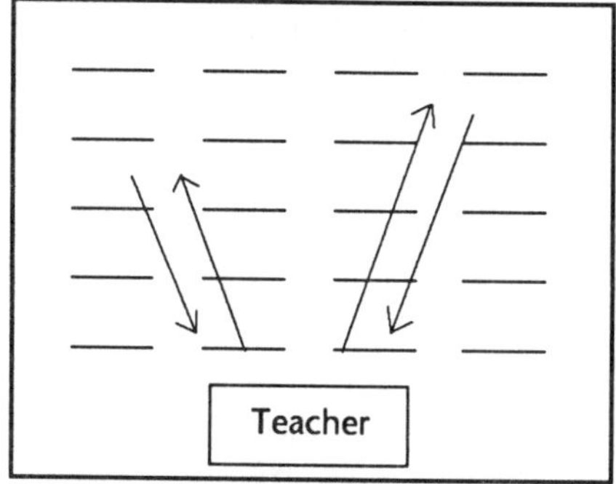

"TRADITIONAL STAND-UP TEACHER"

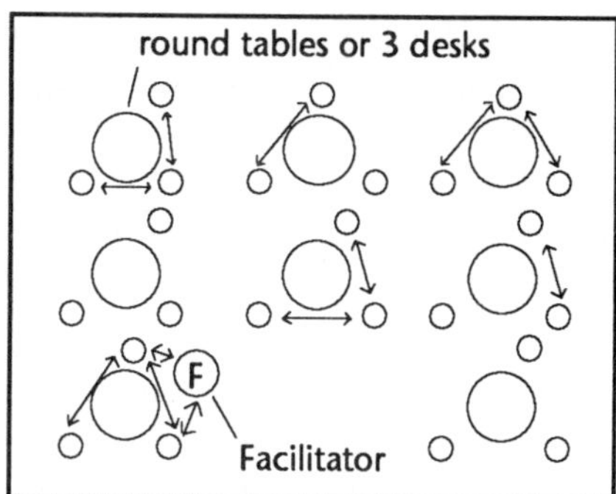

"HIGH-CHALLENGE FACILITATOR"

On the other hand, as facilitator in the high-challenge cooperative classroom, interactions are student-student, student-student, with occasional student-teacher or teacher-student interactions within the small-group setting. The facilitator role calls for a skillfully structured design, including *freedom of choice with the overriding structure.* So while the traditional teaching role appears to be more controlled and orderly, the order quickly breaks down in the absence of the teacher-enforcer. Yet, in the high-challenge cooperative classroom the facilitation role dictates student responsibility for control and order. Ironically, by relinquishing control, the control is expertly facilitated in the student groups as they take more and more responsibility for their own behavior. Control becomes intrinsically enforced rather than extrinsically enforced by the authority figure.

To demonstrate the use of the cognitive elements of an explicit thinking skill and the cognitive organizers, the following lesson blueprints for elementary, middle and secondary classrooms are modeled.

□ □ □

Update your task sequence on page 348.

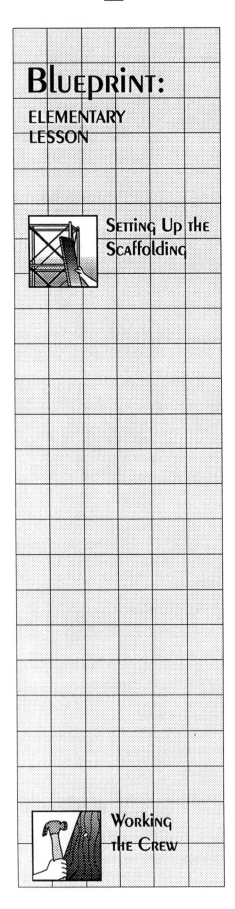

"ME-WE"

Have each student bring a stuffed animal from home. In groups of two, share the items and the significance of each item. Have students emphasize why they selected that particular item instead of others. What makes that stuffed animal special?

In the partner groups, students should talk about how their animals are alike and how they are different.

Discuss the sharings with the class and elicit student examples that illustrate how the animals are very different from each other. On the board or chart paper, have students do a PMI evaluation on the pluses and minuses of being different. Also, take time to note ideas that are neither a plus nor a minus, but just interesting thoughts about being different.

BEING DIFFERENT

P(+)	More interesting.
M(–)	Like different things.
I (?)	

Following the PMI, note that because *people* are different, sometimes we see things in different ways. Different things are important to each of us. Mention that these differences show up when we work in groups. We each think of the "me" and not the "we." In order to get along sometimes we have to combine our ideas into a "me-we." Let's see what that looks like.

In the same groups of two, have students create a "me-we" creature by combining drawings they do of the two animals. After these have been drawn, ask the pairs to name their "me-we" creature. For example, a lion and a teddy bear might be named Tedli.

Reflecting on the Design

To process affectively, have students talk about a time that it felt good to be different.

To process the social skills of teamwork, have students list things they can do in twos (seesaw, tennis, catch, etc.).

For cognitive processing, have students turn to their partners to tell one thing that is different about themselves.

For metacognitive processing, ask students to complete one of the following statements in a verbal wraparound:

I am special because . . . .

(my partner) is special because . . . .

Together we . . . .

☐ ☐ ☐

AFRICAN & ASIAN ELEPHANTS

Tell students to form groups of three with the following roles:

Recorder: Writes on chart.
Reporter: Reports results.
Leader: Talks about group.

Explain that this lesson has a double focus:

1. Learning how to compare and contrast, and
2. Using a Venn diagram as a graphic organizer to make thinking visible.

Show a Venn diagram model that illustrates the organizer's usefulness in listing similarities and differences.

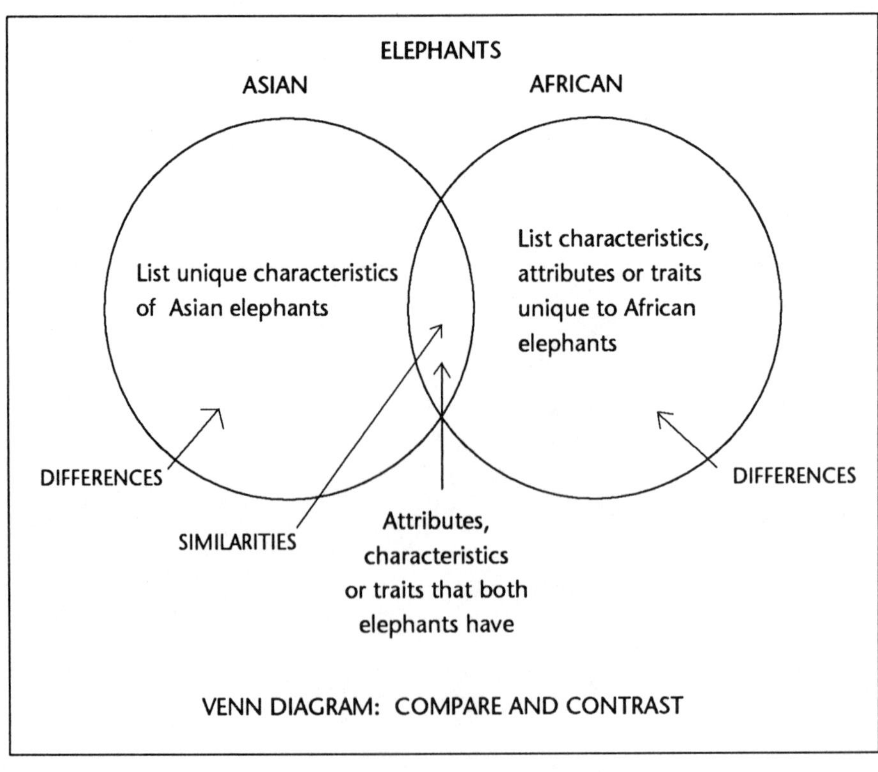

VENN DIAGRAM: COMPARE AND CONTRAST

Once students understand how to use the Venn diagram to delineate similarities and differences, have each reader get some large poster paper, a marking pen and a copy of the article "African & Asian Elephants."

AFRICAN & ASIAN ELEPHANTS*

Elephants are the largest of all land animals, and they are among the strangest-looking animals in the world, with their long trunks, big ears and pointed tusks. There are two basic kinds of elephants—African elephants and Asian (or Indian) elephants. It is rather easy to tell one kind from another.

Asian elephants have smaller ears than African elephants. They have a high forehead with two rather large "bumps" on it. The back of the Asian elephant bends up in the middle, and usually only the males have tusks.

African elephants have very large ears. Their foreheads don't have big bumps on them. The back of an African elephant bends down in the middle, and both the males and females have tusks.

African elephants are larger than Asian elephants, and the males of both kinds are larger than the females. The average Asian male is about 9 feet tall (2.74 meters) at the shoulder and weighs about 10,000 pounds (4,535 kilograms). African males average about 10 feet tall (3 meters) and weigh about 12,000 pounds (5,443 kilograms).

However, some elephants grow much larger than this. The largest African male on record was more than 12 1/2 feet tall (3.66 meters) and weighed about 22,000 (9,979 kilograms). The single elephant weighed as much as 150 average-sized people.

Male elephants are called bulls, and females are called cows. Young elephants are called calves. When an elephant calf is born, it is already a big animal. It is about three feet tall (1 meter) and weighs about 200 pounds (90 kilograms). Baby elephants are covered with hair, but as they grow they lose most of it.

Elephants can live a very long time. Asian elephants may live as along as 80 years, and African elephants may live for 60 years.

Instruct students to read the piece and have the recorders jot down the attributes of each type of elephant in the appropriate section of the Venn diagram.

*page 315

Once students have analyzed the characteristics, ask the groups to draw some conclusions about the likenesses and differences of the elephants. Sample the ideas as a class.

For affective processing, ask students to perform a PMI evaluation of the Venn diagram, telling what they like and what they don't like.

VENN DIAGRAMS

P (+)	
M (-)	
I (?)	

To process the social skills, have students compare good teamwork and poor teamwork.

To process at the cognitive level, have students use the completed Venn diagrams to formulate fat and skinny questions about other mammals.

FAT	Skinny
Write three FAT questions about ___ that will get FAT answers.	Write three SKINNY questions about ___ that will get SKINNY answers.
1.	1.
2.	2.
3.	3.
4.	4.
5.	5.

Finally, to help students metacognitively reflect on other uses of the Venn diagram, have students:

1. Make a human Venn diagram by having students actually move in and out of large Venn diagrams of yarn that are "drawn" on the floor.

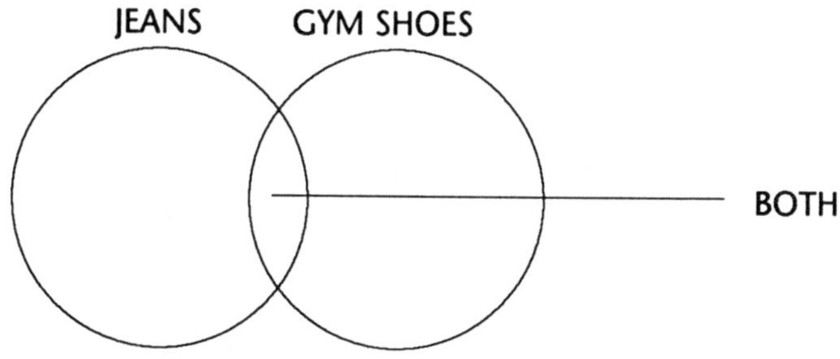

2. With a partner, design a use for Venn diagrams in math, science, literature and social studies.

SCIENCE: Energy/Growth Factors

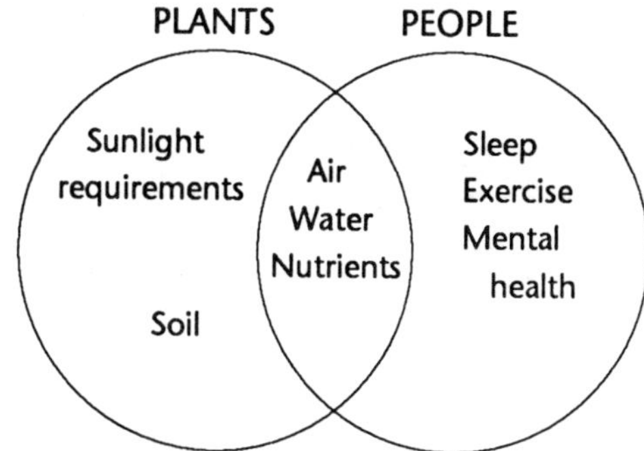

SOCIAL STUDIES: Civil War Unit

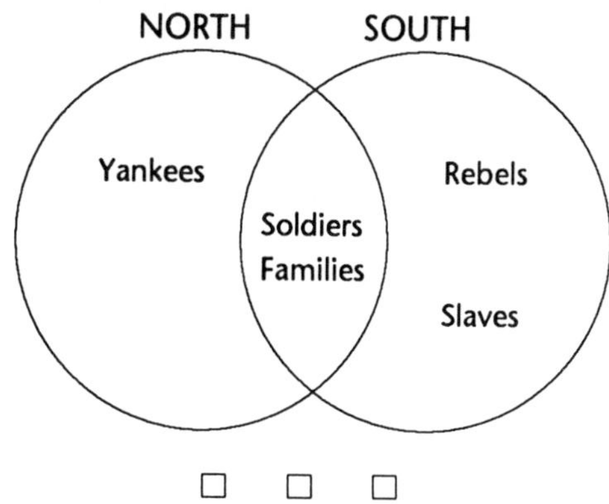

□ □ □

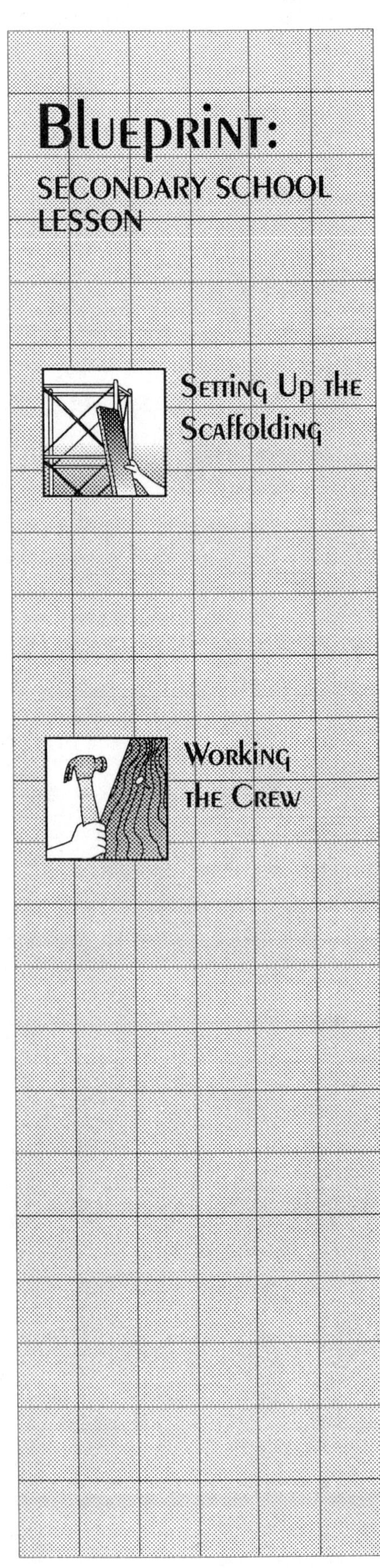

RIGHT-ANGLE THINKING

To introduce the thinking skill of associating ideas with the "thinking at right angles" cognitive organizer, divide students into partners. Explain that in this interaction the partners take turns being "on focus." Each partner takes on the roles of speaker and listener in rotation.

Discuss the thinking skill of *association*. Have students describe what connecting one idea to another is like by using the thought tree association techniques.

Have students draw this diagram:

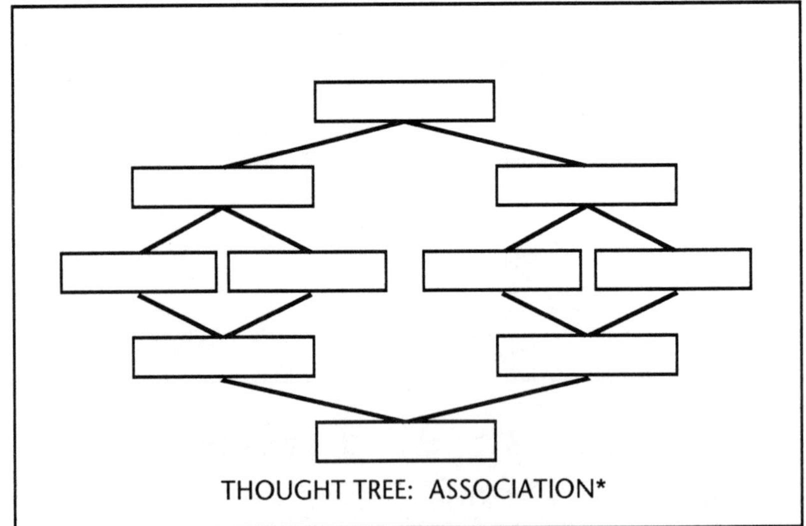

THOUGHT TREE: ASSOCIATION*

Now, ask students to individually complete the thought tree by associating ideas. Begin with the word *association* and think of two words related to it.

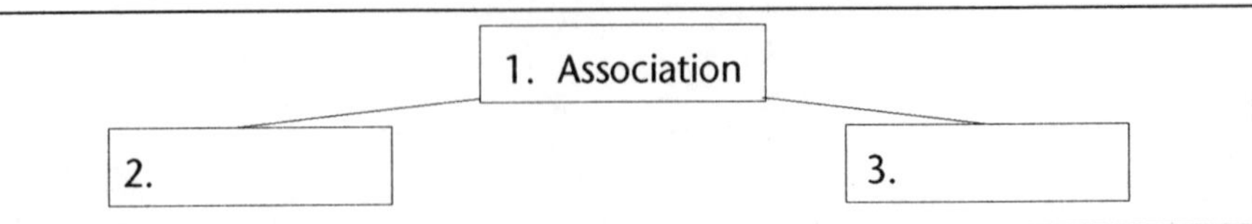

Following the hierarchy of the boxes on the diagram and using a stream of consciousness, students should move through the thought tree exercise as rapidly

*page 316

as possible. The more quickly the associations are made, the more candid the connections. Once the diagrams are completed, have each student complete the following lead-in using word #1 and word #10 from the tree.

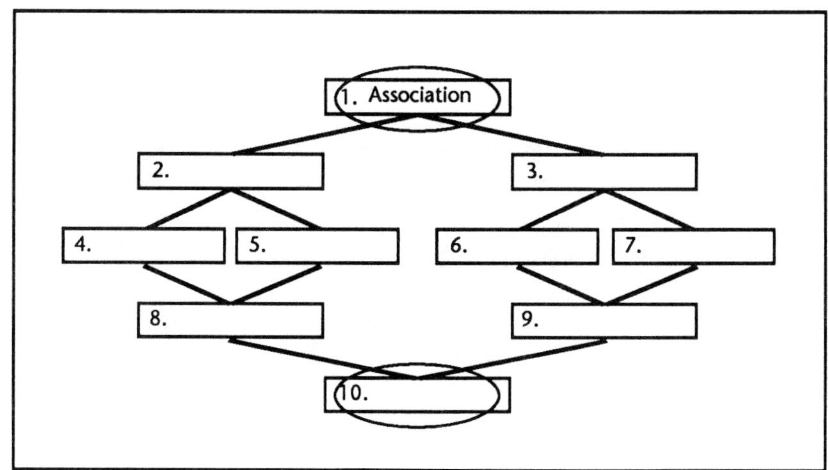

1ST CONNECTION: Word #1__________ is like word #10__________ because both a)____.

2ND CONNECTION (try again): Word #1__________ is like word #10 __________ because both b)____.

3RD CONNECTION (try just one more idea): Word #1__________ is like word #10__________ because both c)____.

Using this idea of association, explain that each partner takes on the role of speaker. The speaker begins discussing the biographical character he/she has been studying. As the speaker talks about the subject, the listening partner is to jot down interesting information on the right-angle chart (idea #1) and elaborate upon them in the space to the right of those ideas.

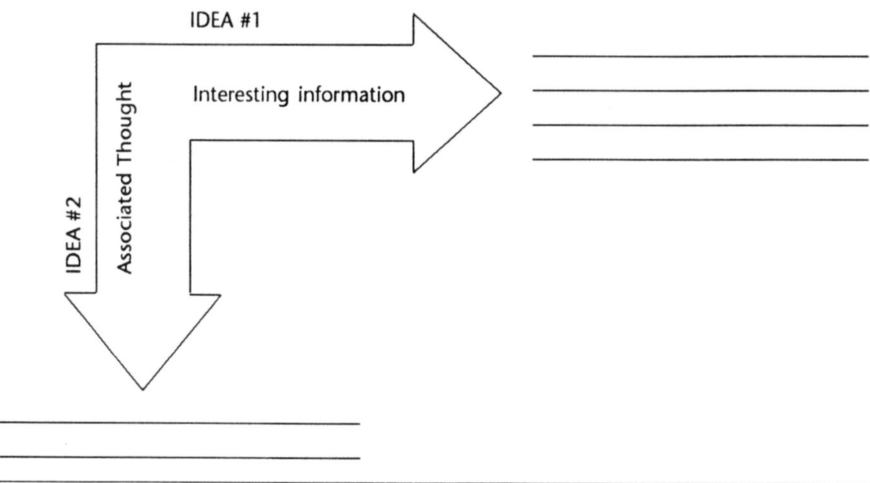

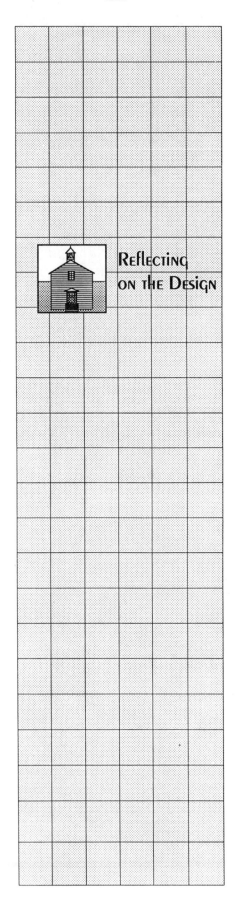

As the listener jots down this thought, he/she also notes any other ideas or thoughts he/she connects from personal experiences to the original idea. These associated ideas should be noted along the vertical arrow (idea #2) and elaborated upon in the extra space below that angle. Reverse the roles and try the same exercise again.

Talk about the importance of "capturing associated ideas" by eliciting examples of incidents of serendipitous discoveries, ideas that occur as someone looks for something else. Suggest that the right-angle organizer is a visual that illustrates how to deliberately "capture" the extraneous ideas or peripheral thoughts that naturally occur while focusing on something quite different. The learner is constantly making connections.

To engage students in affective processing, have partners share the feelings they had as they allowed their minds to follow the association and capture the "extra" thought.

To process social skills, have students recall:

A time I got a good idea from a friend . . . .

A time I got a bad idea from a friend . . . .

Process the cognitive content by asking the partners to compare the biographical characters they briefly discussed in the right-angle exercise.

Finally, to lead students toward metacognitive transfer, have them reflect on one of the following questions in a log entry:

Associating ideas is . . . .

Thinking at right angles might have helped me when . . . .

Biographies spark thinking because . . . .

☐ ☐ ☐

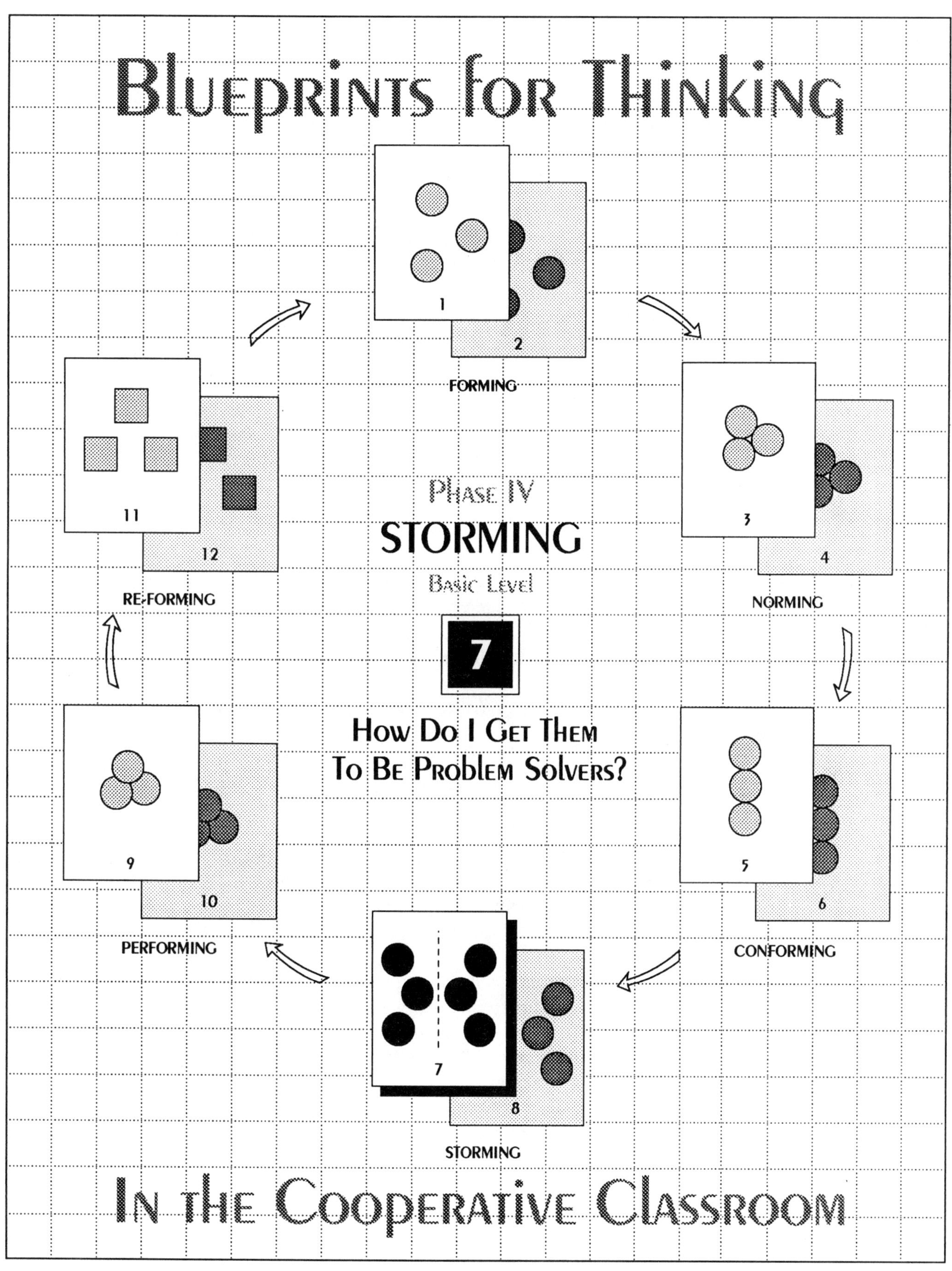
Blueprints for Thinking
1
2
FORMING
3
4
NORMING
5
6
CONFORMING
7
8
STORMING
9
10
PERFORMING
11
12
RE-FORMING
Phase IV
STORMING
Basic Level
7
How Do I Get Them
To Be Problem Solvers?
In the Cooperative Classroom

PHASE IV:
STORMING
BASIC

How Do I Get Them To Be Problem Solvers?

We must learn to explore all the options and possibilities that confront us in a complex and rapidly changing world. We must learn to welcome and not fear the voices of dissent.
—J.W. Fulbright

Draft

Question: *"Yes, but what do I do when . . .*
. . . one person in a group is totally apathetic and withdrawn?
. . . there is a big mouth hogging all the air time in a group?
. . . a group member is absent?
. . . fighting in a group stops all progress?
. . . no one wants this kid in the group?
. . . the students are not learning in the groups?
. . . the disruptive students act out?
. . . group members don't agree?
. . . hitchhikers appear in several groups?"

Answer: When the *storming* begins, celebrate! With the signs of *storming* in your cooperative learning groups come the signs of progress. Remember, small-group process seems to follow a predictable cycle or pattern: groups *form*, then *norm* and then *storm* as they mature into fully functioning groups.

It's important to know why they're storming. In the storming stage, group members are feeling the "groupness." In fact, the members are feeling a loss of identity and individuality. As groups enter into this phase of the small-group process cycle, group members often assert themselves, both positively and negatively, or they look for their niche in the group.

Some students, as discussed in earlier chapters, continually look for attention by clowning. Others withdraw their talents so the group misses them and realizes just how valuable a member he/she is. There are still others who play the devil's advocate as they assert their personal opinions and viewpoints.

Regardless of the form it takes, the storming stage is easily recognized by both the teacher and the students as group members search for their special identities. Note the informal, unclaimed role the students play. How they broadcast their individuality, their uniqueness, their signature piece to show other members that they are important.

Knowing all this, talk to the students about the storming stage. Let them know that storming means progress in cooperative groups. Help everyone recognize what's happening and celebrate. Celebrate the storming in public. Help them understand that storming presents volatile, visible signs that they are progressing normally.

In fact, until group members experience some of this storming, until individuals feel the need to "try their wings," groups are functioning at a somewhat superficial level. On the surface, everyone is polite and accommodating, much like we are with "company." It's much like the proverbial calm before the storm. As we get to know each other better, as we begin to sense viewpoints and motives and persuasions, we feel a need to assert ourselves as individuals within the group. Take and/or make time to talk about this group stage and celebrate as a class.

After the celebration—once the storming stage is publicly noted and properly celebrated through open discussion and appropriate action—take the second step toward harnessing the power of storming groups. The second step involves moving toward a dynamic model of interaction that propels groups to the performance stage of the small-group process cycle.

Step two in the storming stage is a giant step. In it, the teacher changes low-level fighting troops into high-level functioning groups. The teacher uses the very conflict the groups are experiencing as the platform for introducing problem solving, decision making and higher-order thinking strategies into the group tasks.

Interestingly, a significant outcome of this cognitive shift occurs in the *affective* domain. As students acquire the tools of critical and creative thinking and as they become more skilled in approaching problems and decisions, they in turn begin to feel good about themselves. They begin to see themselves as problem solvers and decision makers. They feel capable and confident that they can figure things out. With this emerging self-image they no longer feel enveloped by the groupness.

Feeling good about themselves, group members no longer need to "stand out" as the joker or "Peck's bad boy." They are recognized as valued members of the group through their empathetic intellect and skilled social behavior. Members are ready to consider others, including their feelings, concerns, viewpoints and suggestions.

Now, it's one thing to lecture about small-group cycles and postulate a Cinderella theory of the storming stage, but it's quite another endeavor to actually approach real-life groups of squawking, squirming kids with this highfalutin' notion.

For specific strategies to deal with the ever-present stream of concerns that are punctuated with the usual "What do you do with the kid who...?," refer to chapter 3, "Strategies." However, to go beyond the social skill development and to finesse these natural conflicts into structured controversies for the classroom, read on.

Specs

Help students learn how to solve academic problems and how to transfer the skill into solving problems within their groups.

Structuring controversy and conflict within the subject area content, as an outgrowth of the personal conflicts arising in the groups, is a natural extension for the skilled facilitator and is not difficult. In each of the four major disciplines on the opposite page, examples are plentiful. Have students give specific examples of each. Information can be gathered on the "Chart A Challenge" below.

Chart A Challenge*

Choose one problem area and create a problem scenario

1 SENSE THE PROBLEM	2 FIND THE PROBLEM	3 BRAINSTORM IDEAS	4 PRIORITIZE SOLUTIONS	5 SELL TO OTHERS	6 PLAN THE ACTION	7 FACE NEW CHALLENGES
Family						
Siblings						
Parents						
Car						
Appearance						
Grades						
Future						
Teachers						
Peers						
Self-Image						
	"Could it be...?"	"Ways out"	"Best one"	"Convincing others"	"First steps"	"Now what?" "What next?"

*page 317

Humanities

- ✓ Conflict in fictional pieces: man vs. man, man vs. nature
- ✓ Paradoxes
- ✓ Ambiguous statements
- ✓ Debate formats
- ✓ Persuasive essays
- ✓ Bias and point of view in commercials

Sciences

- ✓ Opposing forces: pendulum swings, gravity/levitation
- ✓ Creation vs. Evolution
- ✓ Medical mysteries
- ✓ Environmental issues
- ✓ Science vs. Ethics
- ✓ Nuclear power
- ✓ Genetic engineering

Fine Arts

- ✓ Art vs. Science
- ✓ Musical discord
- ✓ Synthesizers vs. Acoustics
- ✓ Traditional vs. Contemporary
- ✓ Aesthetic vs. Practical

Practical Arts

- ✓ Hi-tech vs. Hi-touch
- ✓ Automation vs. Craftsmanship
- ✓ Home vs. Career
- ✓ Equity issues
- ✓ Hardware vs. Software

☐ INTRODUCE THE CREATIVE PROBLEM-SOLVING MODEL

After exploring the natural controversies embedded within the context of our instructional materials and content, introduce students to the problem-solving model. Suggest that this problem-solving model offers a prototype with which to begin work.

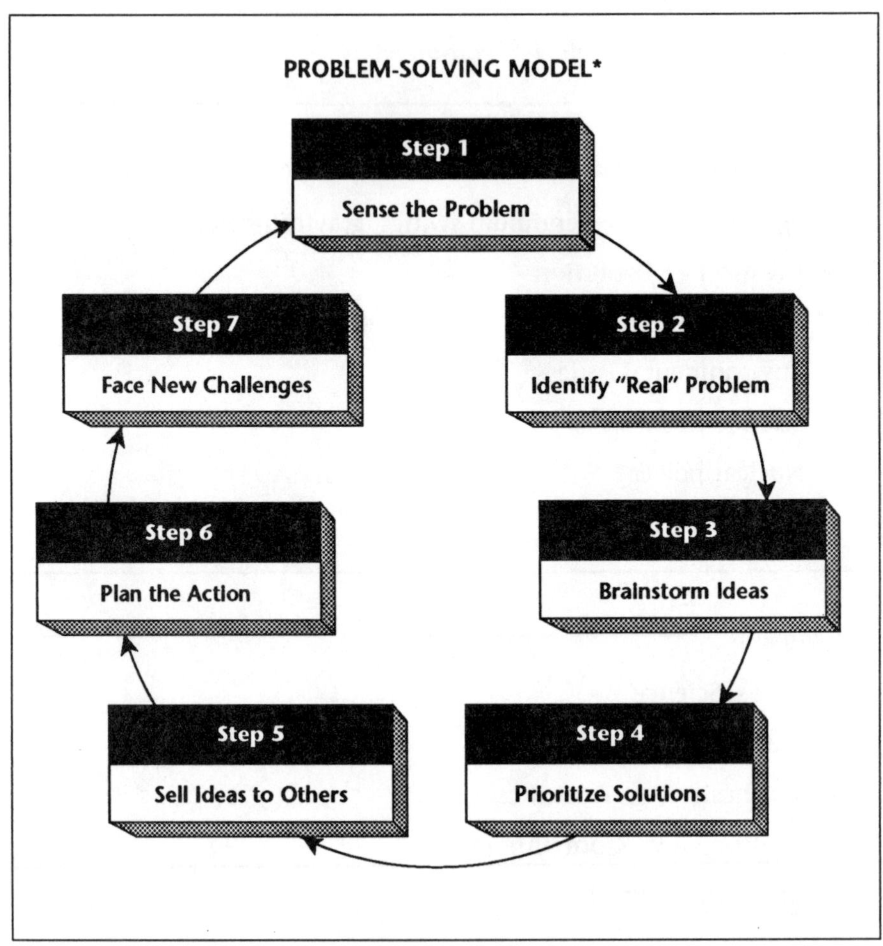

Take time to explain the steps of problem solving with the example on the next page.

After modeling the steps to problem solving with the whole class, post the steps on the board for quick reference. Discuss the micro-skills of *brainstorming, prioritizing, sequencing, evaluating, classifying,* and *comparing and contrasting ideas,* which all contribute to the macro-processes called problem solving and decision making.

To further assist the problem-solving process, use the chart on page 122 for gathering information. The Chart-A-Challenge matrix acts as a graphic organizer in slating all the needed information to solve a problem.

*page 318

Using the Problem-Solving Model

Subject: Social Studies—Cave Men

SENSE THE PROBLEM

Boulder has fallen in front of doorway to cave that has people inside

IDENTIFY "REAL" PROBLEM

Getting people out of cave—not moving boulder

BRAINSTORM IDEAS

Push it; use a lever to roll it; look for another way out; call for help; go to sleep and hope it moves by itself; or get someone from the outside to move it.

PRIORITIZE SOLUTIONS

	RANK
Use a lever to roll it	☐
Look for another way out	☐
Push it	☐
Call for help	☐

SELL IDEAS TO OTHERS

"Let's try to pry this log under the boulder and see if it will roll because that would be the quickest solution." (Notice criteria of quickest suggests expediency is a concern or value.) If the lever idea fails: "Let's try to find another way out. We're just not strong enough to move it by ourselves." (Notice here, the speaker analyzes the strengths and weaknesses of the situation and the people.)

PLAN THE ACTION

"Find a log. I'll pry it. You push and lift and roll. "

FACE NEW CHALLENGES

"Where do you think we can find a sturdy log?"
"How can I pry it when you're not budging the boulder?"

The secondary school blueprint on page 132, "Chart a Challenge," illustrates how this technique is used in problem solving.

After learning the "specs" on controversy and problem solving, students are ready to apply the problem-solving model. As Glasser has pointed out in his many works, the model can provide students with an "empowering" tool for resolving problems that emerge in the classroom, for taking a "problem-centered" approach to curriculum, and for facing problems outside the classroom.

☐ ☐ ☐

Update your task sequence on page 348.

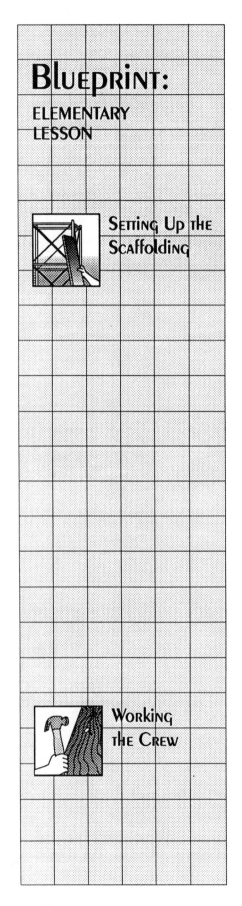

PICTURE PROBLEMS

Tell the students that they are to solve some problems today as presented in picture cards. Assign the following roles to partners:

Gopher: Goes for the materials.

Announcer: Tells the ideas following the task.

Present problematic situation to the student pairs by having each gopher select an illustrated card. Photocopy the samples in Appendix B or find others in workbooks, cartoons, magazines, etc. Try to find pictures that quickly present a problem situation.

cat stuck in tree

broken window

flat tire

dropped ice cream

kite on roof

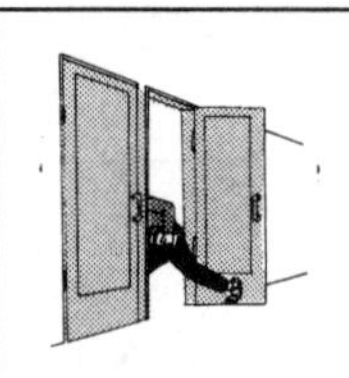
late for school

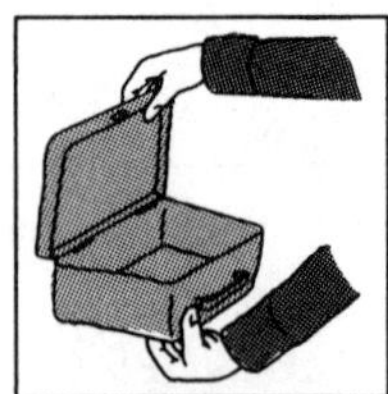
no lunch

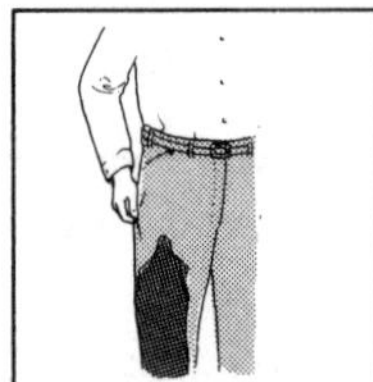
mud on clothes

Sample Picture Problems*

Have the partners talk about the first three steps to the problem-solving model.

PROBLEM-SOLVING STEPS (1-3)*

Step #1	What do you think the problem is? Why?
Step #2	What do you think you should do? List three ideas.
Step #3	Choose one idea. Tell why you chose it; explain your criteria.

*pages 319 and 320

Ask students to:

1. Find the Problem:

a. Look at the picture and take turns telling each other what you think the problem is.

b. Find agreement on the "real problem." Tell each other why it seems to be the real problem. Students must justify the answer for each other.

c. Tell the announcer in each group to explain to the class the problem in the picture and the group's reasoning for the explanation.

2. Find Ideas:

d. Now, list three ideas or solutions to the problem. Brainstorm more if you want to, but each group should be able to report at least three.

3. Find a Solution:

e. Now, select one idea—your best idea—for solving the problem. All partners need to talk about why it is their best idea.

f. Report to the class by having some of the announcers explain/justify their solutions.

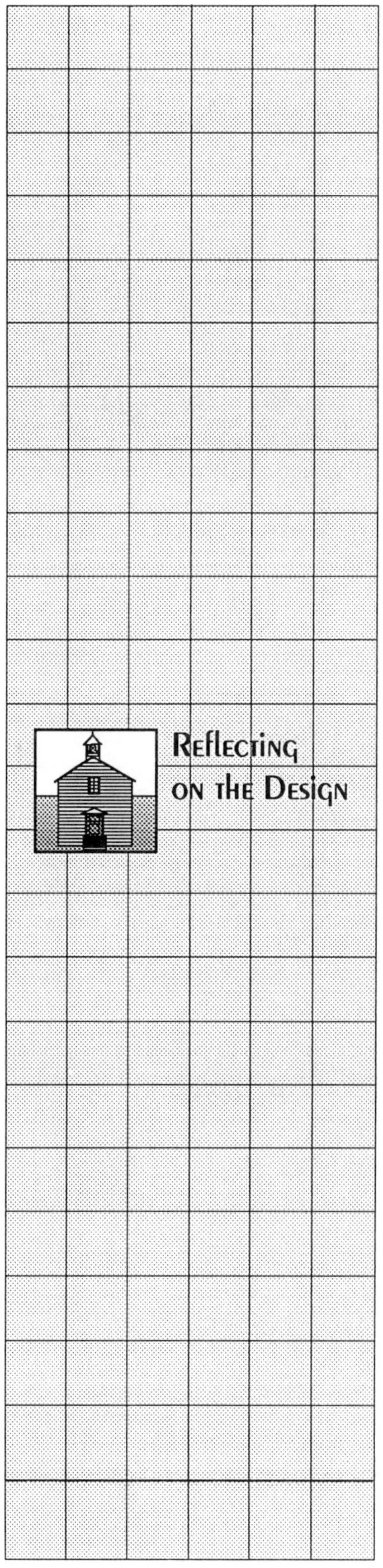

For affective processing, ask students to tell their partners:

"It feels like _______ when I have a problem because . . . ."

To process the social skill of team problem solving, have students share a school problem in which a friend helped.

For cognitive processing, asks students to repeat the three steps to problem-solving and to draw their steps.

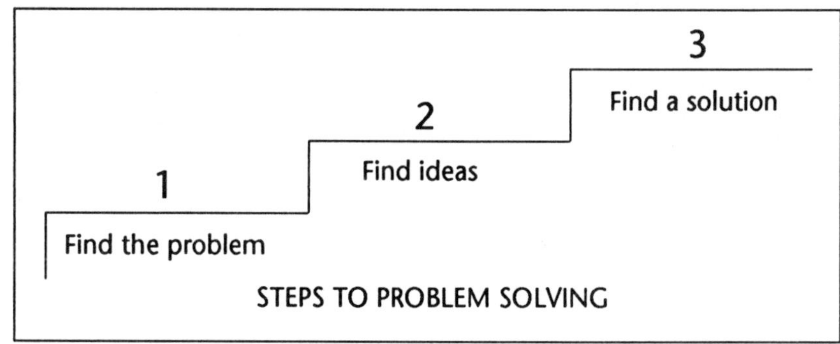

For a metacognitive piece, have student teams rate their teamwork as partners for the picture problems. Ask teams to report their findings to the class.

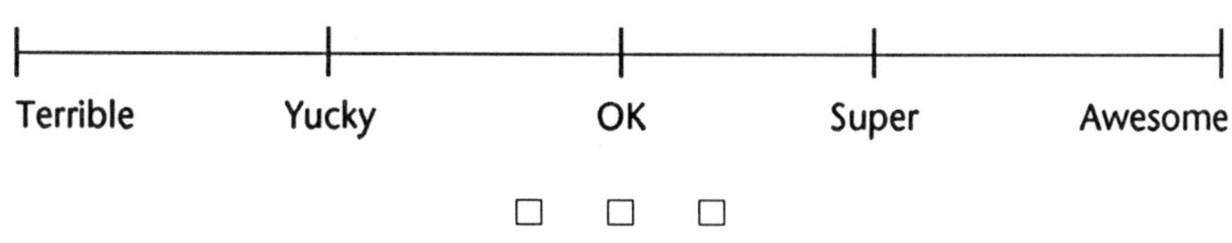

□ □ □

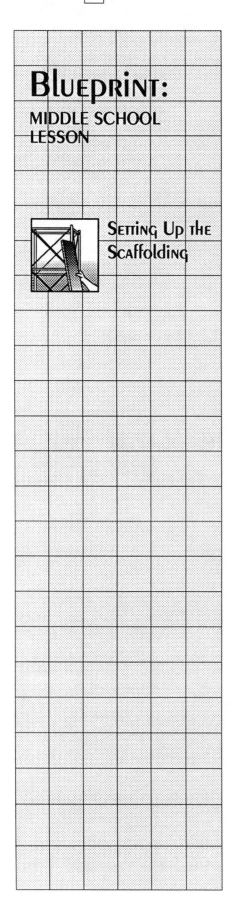

Blueprint:
MIDDLE SCHOOL LESSON

Setting Up the Scaffolding

NOTORIOUS WHAT-IFS

Middle grade youngsters seem to tackle an endless stream of challenges as they problem solve their way through the social maze seeking peer approval. By structuring constructive controversies within the context of subject matter learning, teens learn to turn peer pressure into peer power as they navigate the steps to problem solving together.

Please notice in the problem-solving lesson, the *explicit* thinking skills that are applied *and* the *implicit* skills needed to complete the task.

MICRO-SKILLS FOR THINKING = PROBLEM-SOLVING STRATEGIES

Explicit Skills	*Implicit Skills*
brainstorming	consensus seeking
evaluating	projecting
hypothesizing	summarizing
personifying	synthesizing
predicting outcomes	justifying
analyzing for attributes	composing text
prioritizing	

To set the stage for this problem-solving lesson that strings together a number of micro-skills for thinking, ask students to relate a personal vignette that illustrates this quote:

Trust is the result of a risk successfully survived!
—Jack R. Gibb*

After sufficient partner interaction, sample several volunteers for their renditions of their personal vignettes.

*page 321

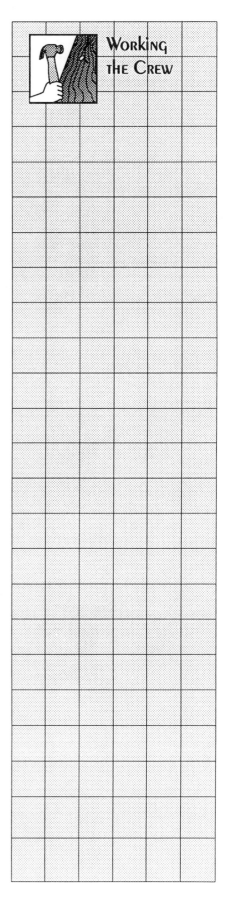

WORKING THE CREW

Using an integrated humanities context of history and literature, explain to students that they are to problem solve some of history's most notorious what-ifs. For example, what if . . . .

. . . the South had won?
. . . the Indians had kept their land?
. . . women could not vote?
. . . there had been no Berlin Wall?
. . . The Roman Empire had not fallen?

Have students form teams of three and assign the roles that are needed:

Scribe: Records information.

Orator: Is public speaker for group.

Historian: Gathers resources.

The first problem-solving task is to brainstorm a list of what-ifs from history while the historian in the group scans the history book and reviews notes from the semester.

WHAT IF . . .
1.
2.
3.
4.
↓

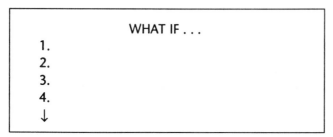

Once a master list is made in each group, have each team evaluate its ideas and select a favorite what-if to work with. Each group must have criteria for its final selection and be able to justify its choice.

Have students web possible outcomes to their what-ifs from history. Using responses in turn, each group should jot down 10 to 15 ideas.

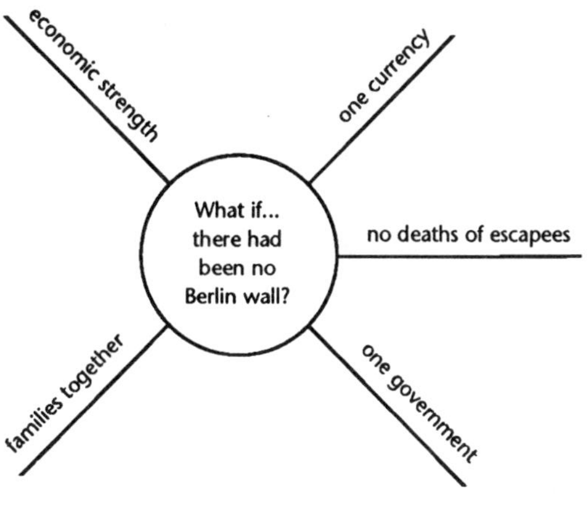

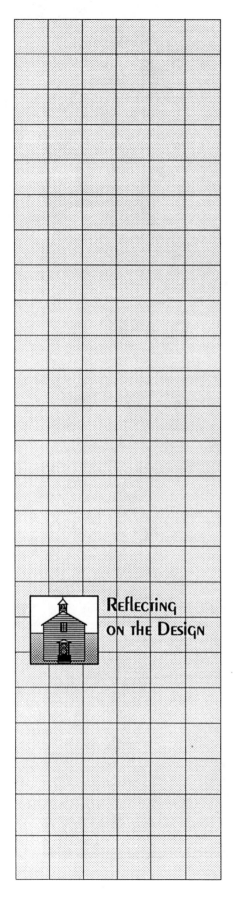

Using their selected scenarios of what-ifs, all students should write a brief essay. First, they should write from the eyes of a participant. That is, as a journal entry, rewrite the endings of the what-ifs as they might have been. They should personify with actions and feelings the words one may have written to describe the hypothesized outcomes of the what-ifs. Second, students should project the scenario into the present to describe how things would be if the what-if *had* occurred.

> NOTORIOUS WHAT-IFS...
> ASSIGNMENT
>
> 1. Rewrite history, through the eyes of a participant, as it might have been.
> 2. Project the scenario to present day and note how things would be if the what-if *had* happened.

After students have had sufficient opportunity to complete their individual assignments, have team members select an appropriate journal selection from their group that gives the audience the "revised" picture of history as presented in the what-if assignment.

Next, have the orators read the "capsules" of the personal journal entries to give the audience a flavor of how things would be different. This lesson may spill over into two days (or even more), depending on the purpose.

To process affectively, ask students to turn to their groups and discuss:

- how it feels to "walk in another's shoes," and
- some of the emotions they felt as they tried to think and behave as the other person.

To process the social skill of empathetic reaction, have students recall a time they needed understanding from someone.

To process cognitively, as a class discuss the what-ifs selected and try to decide which one would have caused the most dramatic difference today.

To process metacognitively, ask students to complete a PMI chart for the what-if strategy:

WHAT-IF STRATEGY

P PLUS	
M MINUS	
I INTERESTING	

Next, have students discuss some "what if" thinking in other contexts such as

LIFE: What if you want to change your hair style?

MATH: What if we all used the metric system?

SCIENCE: What if the ozone layer does disappear?

Finally, have students rate *what-iffing* as a problem-solving strategy.

RATING PROBLEM-SOLVING STRATEGIES*

____
Strategy Used

☐ Will never use
☐ Would like to try
☐ See definite possibilities
☐ Frequent use anticipated
☐ An all-time favorite...

I marked ______________________
because______________________
______________________.

☐ ☐ ☐

*page 322

Blueprint:
SECONDARY SCHOOL LESSON

CHART A CHALLENGE

Setting Up the Scaffolding

Discuss with the students the problem-solving model in which seven steps appear:

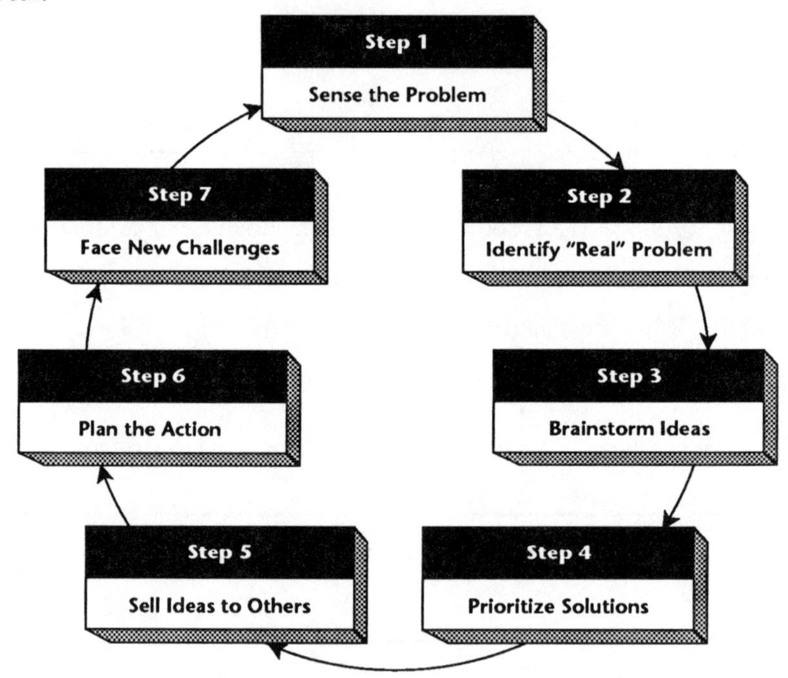

Working the Crew

Assign students to groups of three with a *reporter,* a *recorder* and an *observer.* Have each group choose a problem area from column one of the Chart-A-Challenge grid.

Chart A Challenge

Choose one problem area and create a problem scenario

1	2	3	4	5	6	7
SENSE THE PROBLEM	FIND THE PROBLEM	BRAINSTORM IDEAS	PRIORITIZE SOLUTIONS	SELL TO OTHERS	PLAN THE ACTION	FACE NEW CHALLENGES
Family						
Siblings						
Parents						
Car						
Appearance						
Grades						
Future						
Teachers						
Peers						
Self-Image						
	"Could it be...?"	*"Ways out"*	*"Best one"*	*"Convincing others"*	*"First steps"*	*"Now what?" "What next?"*

Students in one group select grades as a problem. This group writes a brief scenario about a problem with grades. (Other groups might select other problems. Each group writes a different scenario.)

Next, instruct the groups to create a possible scenario in that problem area. Be sure the groups write down their scenarios so the members can refer to it while filling in the chart-a-challenge grid.

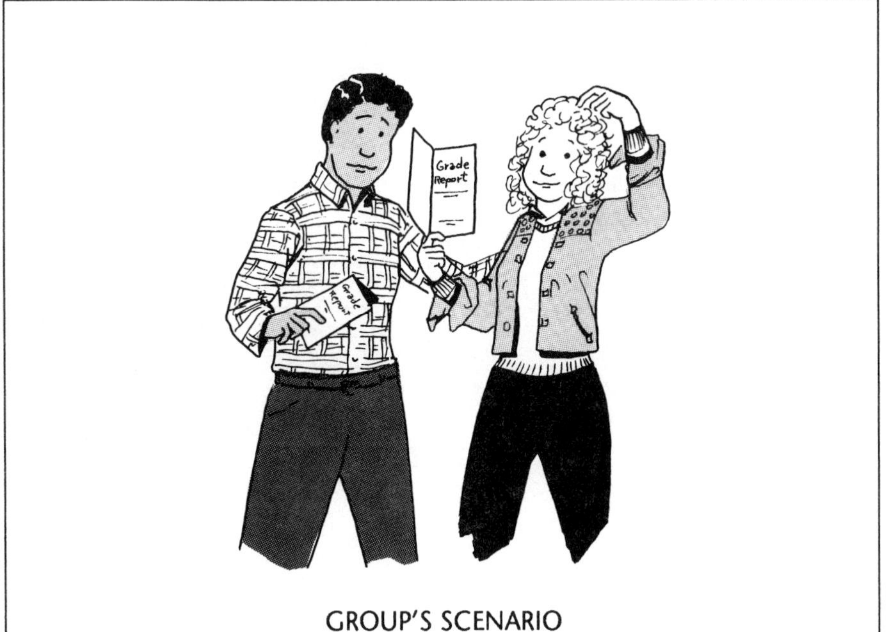

GROUP'S SCENARIO

Kitty and Juan typically get straight *A's*, but this quarter Kitty got a C in algebra. She asks Juan to help her figure out how to tell her parents.

After each group has written its scenario—in this case, on grades—the members move down each column to brainstorm all the possibilities for:

Column 2	• Finding the problem.	(Could it be . . . ?)
Column 3	• Brainstorming ideas.	(Ways out)
Column 4	• Prioritizing solutions.	(Best one)
Column 5	• Selling to others.	(Convincing others)
Column 6	• Planning the action.	(First steps)
Column 7	• Facing new challenges.	(What next?)

For example, to brainstorm for column 2, finding the problem about grades, the chart may look like this

1	2
SENSE THE PROBLEM	**FIND THE PROBLEM**
Family	How to tell parents?
Siblings	Who to tell?
Parents	When to tell?
Car	What to tell?
Appearance	How to change it?
Grades	Immediate consequences
Future	Complications from consequences
Teachers	How to appeal?
Peers	Next step?
Self-Image	How to validate?
	"Could it be...?"

Note that for each column, the brainstormed items are simply *possibilities*. In the second column, the possibilities concern identifying the real problem, which is "how to tell her parents."

In column 3, brainstorm ideas for solving the real problem. Look for and think about alternatives or "ways out" of the problem; find different approaches to the challenge. For example, an alternative might be to "face it head on immediately."

In column 4, prioritize the ideas from column 3 to find the best one. Set some criteria to help in the ranking process. For example, "hide it" (the report card) ranks 10 because it has to be signed and returned; it is not a practical solution.

Chart A Challenge

1	2	3	4	5	6	7
SENSE THE PROBLEM	FIND THE PROBLEM	BRAINSTORM IDEAS	PRIORITIZE SOLUTIONS	SELL TO OTHERS	PLAN THE ACTION	FACE NEW CHALLENGES
Family	How to tell parents?					rearrange schedule
Siblings		face it	1	research		
Parents						
Car						
Appearance						
Grades		hide it	10			
Future						
Teachers					go directly home	
Peers						
Self-Image						
	"Could it be...?"	"Ways out"	"Best one"	"Convincing others"	"First steps"	"Now what?" "What next?"

Choose one problem area and create a problem scenario

At this point, each group has completed the first four columns of the the chart. They have:

1. Stated the scenario selected in column 1.
2. Discussed the "real problem" by analyzing the ideas brainstormed.
3. Brainstormed possible solutions to the specific problem.
4. Prioritized the solutions by establishing criteria.

Now . . . tell the students to brainstorm ideas for the last three columns .

In column 5, brainstorm ideas for convincing others to agree upon your number-one solution. For example, you could "research it" to find what has worked with others.

In column 6, list all the possible first steps to achieve the top-ranking item in column 4. For example, if the solution is to "face it," the first step might be, "go directly home from school."

In column 7, anticipate new challenges based on the decisions made. For example, to "face it" and "go directly home" requires some "rearranging of a previous schedule." That's a new challenge.

Ask students to elaborate upon the ideas individually (or as a group):

5. Write a convincing, persuasive argument in favor of the number-one solution.
6. Develop an action plan for executing the "sold" idea.
7. Begin to anticipate the new challenges to overcome and the first steps necessary to solve them.

For affective processing, ask students to complete the following sentence:

My feelings range from _____ to _____ on ___________________.

To process for positive social behavior in constructive problem-solving, have students list encouraging statements:

I think that might work . . . .

What if . . . ?

For cognitive processing, have students, by consensus or agreement, rank the problem areas as stress producers for them as a small group.

PRIORITIZE PROBLEM AREAS

RANK	STRESS AREA
☐	Family
☐	Siblings
☐	Parents
☐	Car
☐	Appearance
☐	Grades
☐	Future
☐	Teachers
☐	Peers
☐	Self-image

For metacognitive processing, have students respond to all of the following:

- A way to use the Chart-A-Challenge idea would be . . . .
- The Chart-A-Challenge grid was most helpful because . . . .
- The problem-solving step that is
  - most helpful is___________________.
  - most confusing is ________________.

☐ ☐ ☐

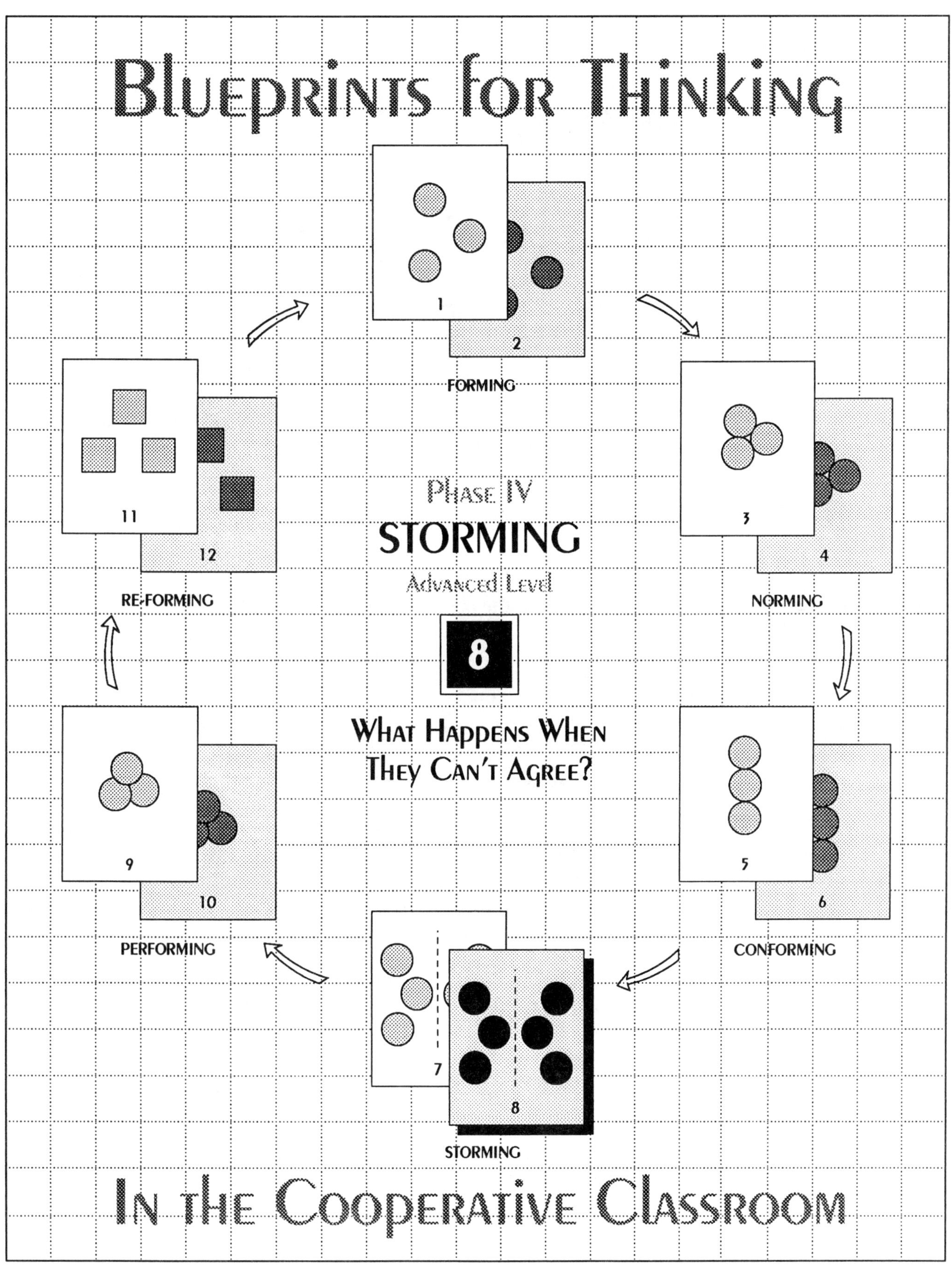
Blueprints for Thinking
1
2
FORMING
3
4
NORMING
5
6
CONFORMING
7
8
STORMING
9
10
PERFORMING
11
12
RE-FORMING
Phase IV
STORMING
Advanced Level
8
What Happens When
They Can't Agree?
In the Cooperative Classroom

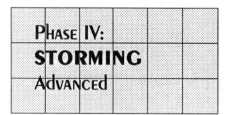

Phase IV:
STORMING
Advanced

What Happens When They Can't Agree?

> *'First of all,' he said, 'if you can learn a simple trick, Scout, you'll get along a lot better with all kinds of folks. You never really understand a person until you consider things from his point of view...'*
> *'Sir?'*
> *'...until you climb into his skin and walk around in it.'*
> —Harper Lee, *To Kill a Mockingbird*

Draft

As noted in the previous chapter, storming phases signal both *unrest* and *progress* in the small-group process. While the voices of individuals vying for position and recognition in the group seem to punctuate the storming phase, the rich opportunities for skill building cannot be overlooked.

Celebrating the storming phase by identifying it as such or by talking explicitly about the kinds of disagreements the groups are experiencing is the first tactic to explore. Second, one must provide complexity to the tasks so students sense an authentic "sink or swim" situation. The more difficult or complex the task, the more intense the interaction becomes. This intense involvement with each other in the small group, in turn, dictates more sophisticated levels of cooperative behavior. Student teams begin to engage in problem-solving and decision-making processes required to achieve the desired outcomes.

However, just as the intensity of interaction increases, so does the likelihood of conflicting situations. As these conflicts arise throughout the normal course of events in group work, the teacher needs to dictate explicit agreeing and disagreeing strategies if the groups are to experience growth and success.

Begin by giving students necessary information on the myriad formal and informal tactics used when people who disagree are trying to find ways to agree. Specific strategies to define and model for the students include arguing, persuading, giving in, avoiding, voting, compromising, mediating, delaying, arbitrating, reconceptualizing, negotiating, consensus seeking, ignoring and humoring.

By formally learning the strategies for reaching agreements, students begin to build their repertoire of social skills for conflict resolution. As they develop expertise in the different methods for dealing with controversy, they also begin to develop awareness and skill in knowing not only *how* to use the tactics, but also *when* to use each particular topic. Profiling this metacognitive aspect of using the strategies for agreeing and disagreeing provides lifelong transfer of the vital interpersonal skills. In this chapter, blueprints for decision making highlight the consensus-seeking model. However, cooperative classrooms need rehearsal in all 13 of the strategies listed to have students become skillful members of high-functioning teams.

Specs

Using the following checklist, give students time to understand the various strategies. Elicit definitions and examples of each.

WHAT DO YOU DO WHEN YOU DISAGREE?*

Instruct students to use this chart in a think-pair-share activity to assess their personal use of each strategy. Mark only the ones used.

- ☐ **Argue**—stand firm
- ☐ **Persuade**—justify, reason, appeal to
- ☐ **Vote**—majority rules
- ☐ **Compromise**—combine, modify
- ☐ **Mediate**—neutral party facilitator
- ☐ **Arbitrate**—agree to abide by decision of arbitrator
- ☐ **Delay**—table it, sleep on it, wait
- ☐ **Reconceptualize**—rethink, find new angles
- ☐ **Negotiate**—give and take
- ☐ **Give In**—give up, cave in, play martyr
- ☐ **Seek Consensus**—talk, cajole, juggle, adjust, modify
- ☐ **Humor**—veer away from confrontation
- ☐ **Avoid**—ignore or postpone indefinitely

A quick self-examination or think-pair-share interaction provides students assessments of their own use of the various techniques. Even a show of hands ("How many have ever argued? compromised? etc.") will activate prior knowledge or use of these strategies.

It's revealing as well as motivating for students to relate examples of their conflict resolution strategies. By beginning with student-initiated examples, the conflict resolution tactics can easily be extended to larger academic or social contexts.

*page 323

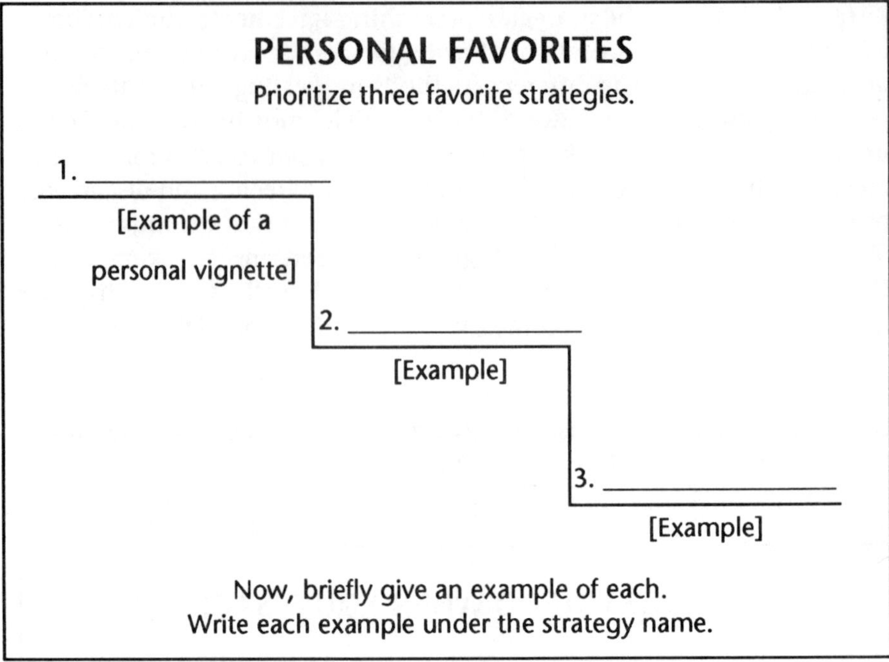

PERSONAL FAVORITES
Prioritize three favorite strategies.
1. ________________
[Example of a
personal vignette]
2. ________________
[Example]
3. ________________
[Example]
Now, briefly give an example of each.
Write each example under the strategy name.

Introduce and post the Tug O'War Thinking Creed.

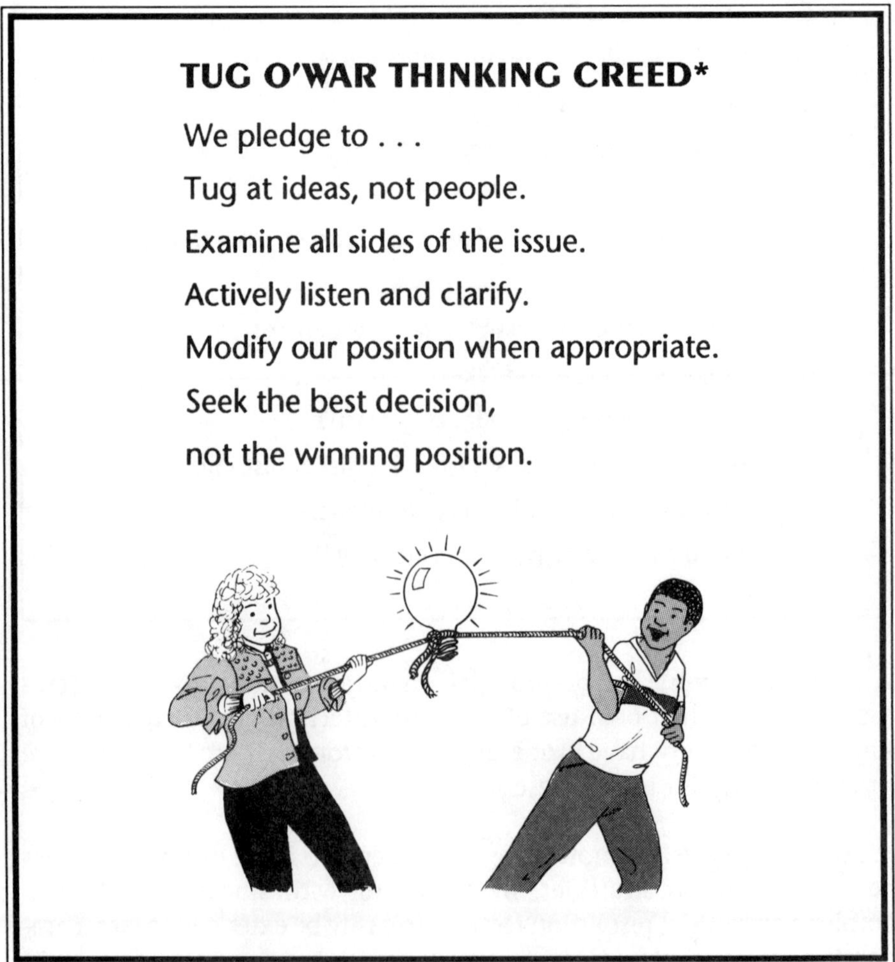

*page 324

The chart "What Do You Do When You Disagree?" lists thirteen different behaviors. At various points during the year, the teacher designing the cooperative classroom targets specific strategies for explicit attention. For example, students may be asked to practice the "art of persuasion" or to "negotiate" a position.

However, to show how a lesson targets a specific conflict resolution social skill, the following model lessons illustrate just *one* of the disagreeing strategies: seeking consensus. The other strategies also require teacher development as the opportunities for use occur.

After supplying this initial input to all levels of students, use the following blueprints for specific elementary, middle and secondary school lessons to introduce and practice the consensus-seeking technique. Please note that although a similar content is used for the three blueprints, "The Top ____," each one's strategies are specifically tailored to the appropriate student levels.

□ □ □

Update your task sequence on page 348.

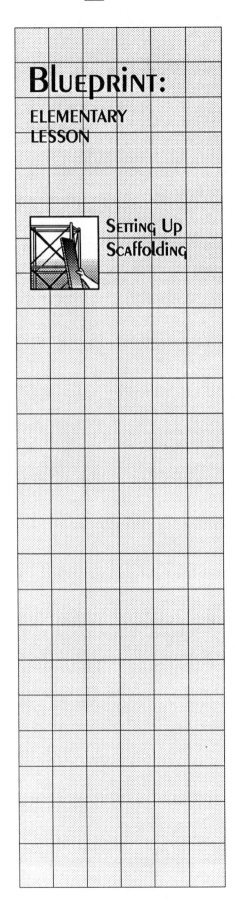

TOP THREE

Pass out one piece of a puzzle to each student, making sure the complete puzzle sets are distributed. (Each piece has a partner piece.) Instruct each student to find the partner with the piece that completes his/her puzzle.

CONFLICT RESOLUTION PUZZLES*

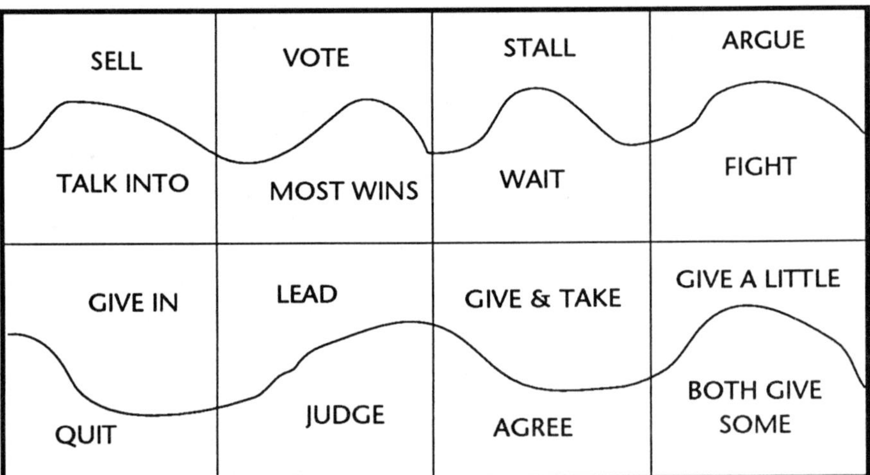

SELL
TALK INTO
VOTE
MOST WINS
STALL
WAIT
ARGUE
FIGHT
GIVE IN
QUIT
LEAD
JUDGE
GIVE & TAKE
AGREE
GIVE A LITTLE
BOTH GIVE SOME

After students have found their puzzle partners and discussed the words for agreeing and disagreeing that are on their puzzle pieces, talk to them about consensus. Introduce the word *consensus* and the rules for seeking consensus.

Consensus - group opinion or agreement

- Voting is outlawed.
- No horse-trading allowed.
- Don't give up.

Now show students the following consensus chart. Modeling with your hands, demonstrate how members signal the group (5 to Fist) as they call for a consensus reading.

*pages 325 and 330

CONSENSUS CHART			
5		(5 fingers)	All for it; top priority
4		(4 fingers)	Yes; high on my list
3		(3 fingers)	OK with me
2		(2 fingers)	Let's talk more
1		(1 finger)	Will trust group
FIST		(fist)	No! An alternative is ____.

Model the consensus-seeking process with a selected group of four. Tell them to rank the following three vegetables, from their most favorite to their least favorite: spinach, peas, broccoli.

Tell them to signal (5 to Fist) for each item when it is mentioned. Each student must give a signal for each item.

SPINACH

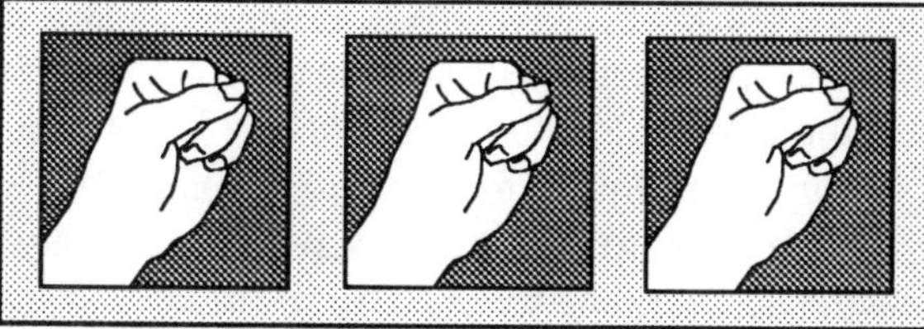

This first reading is easy. With three fists, consensus is reached, the alternative is "anything but spinach." Spinach is last.

PEAS

Talk about the fact that there must be one item that everyone agrees is their first choice. They must discuss the item until they can decide on the same reading.

PEAS

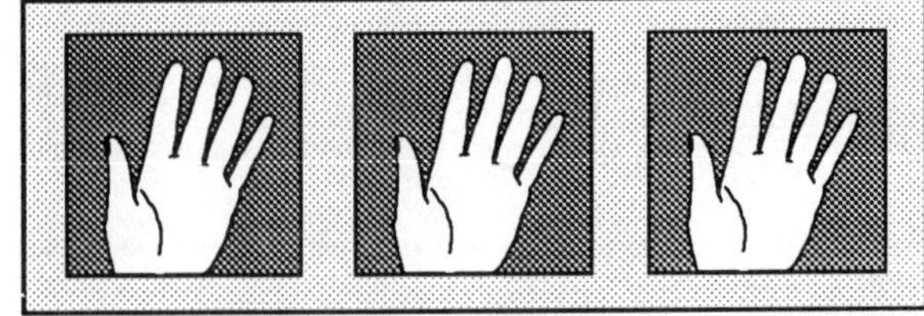

BROCCOLI

Rating

1	Peas	(5,5,5)
2	Broccoli	(3,2,1)
3	Spinach	(fist, fist, fist)

With the vegetable problem as a brief demonstration, students are now ready for a new problem—selecting the top three books for elementary students.

Tell the students that today they will make some important decisions as the "experts" for the elementary students in their school. Explain that their job is to select the best three books for students ages 5 to 11 throughout the United States. Elaborate on these instructions by explaining that they will make decisions about which three books they think every elementary student should read before leaving elementary school. These are the "must-read" books because they are the absolute best! Explain further that their decisions will be made into a list called "The Top Three," which will be posted in each classroom in the building for other students and teachers to consider.

Have the students get into groups of three and choose a:

Recorder—to write down ideas.
Researcher—to get resources needed.
Reporter—to tell the results of the task and teamwork.

Instruct groups to brainstorm books they think are possibilities for The Top Three list and write them on a large piece of paper. They are to try for 15 titles. They should include their favorite books and others they've heard of. Help with spelling as a facilitator.

POSSIBILITIES FOR "THE TOP THREE" LIST

1.________	6.________	11.________
2.________	7.________	12.________
3.________	8.________	13.________
4.________	9.________	14.________
5.________	10.________	15.________

Discuss the DOVE guidelines for brainstorming and accepting others' ideas.

DOVE*

Defer judgment; anything goes
Opt for original, different ideas
Vast numbers are needed
Expand the list by piggybacking on ideas

After brainstorming 15 must-reads for The Top Three list, review the consensus chart (5 to Fist) with the students. Explain that through discussion and use of the "5-to-Fist" consensus model they are to determine the top three books, naming book #1, book #2 and book #3. Allow time for discussion and the 5-to-Fist activity. Facilitate as needed. Collect the team ratings at the end of the session.

TOP THREE BOOKS

1.________

2.________

3.________

TEAM__________

GRADE____ DATE______

After reviewing the teams' rankings, compile the nominated book titles into a class list. Include all books listed by the teams.

Have each team review the class list and discuss the added book titles. The class goal is now to select, again by consensus, the top three books from the class list.

To encourage open discussion on all nominations, reorganize the students into new teams of three. Using discussion and the 5-to-Fist strategy, have student teams rank the top three.

*page 326

Reorganize teams again with all new members. Again, rank the top three books by team.

Reorganize! Rank the top three books by team. The continued reorganization of new threesomes and the subsequent new rankings eliminates the "ownership" issue in which students stay loyal to their own nominations. However, if the continued regrouping and re-ranking becomes tedious or too time consuming, this step needs to be modified accordingly.

But keep in mind that a group consensus needs to be reached in some manner. The specific design of that group consensus will vary.

After several group interactions, try a class ranking. Allow informal groups to *discuss, persuade* and *justify* as they seek class consensus. This may take more time than was planned. If this happens, there is no reason why they can't stop and continue at another time or on another day. It is not uncommon for committees to take several sessions to arrive at a consensus. If this is the case, talk to students about what's happening. Reassure them that reaching consensus requires time to talk, clarify and shift positions, and that making good decisions often takes quality time.

Once a class decision has been reached, post the results.

TOP THREE BOOKS
BY CONSENSUS
1.____________

2.____________

3.____________

________'s Class

Room ________

For affective processing, have students web the feelings they have when they are in conflict or disagree with another person.

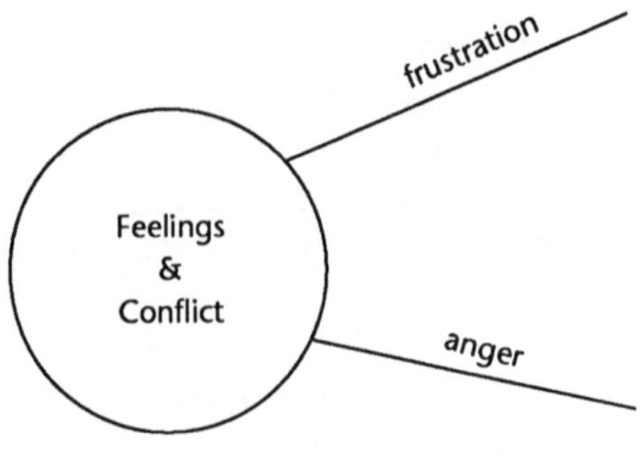

After webbing their feelings, students should complete this statement:

Conflict is like ___ because both _____.

For social skill processing, ask students to complete the stem:

Reaching consensus is good for our group work because . . . .

For cognitive processing, ask students to make decisions for each of the following statements by creating a human graph.

STATEMENT #1	STATEMENT #2
All students should read _____.	All students should not read _____.
Fiction is better than nonfiction.	Nonfiction is better than fiction.
A favorite author is _____.	A favorite author is not _____.
Books are better than TV.	TV is better than books.

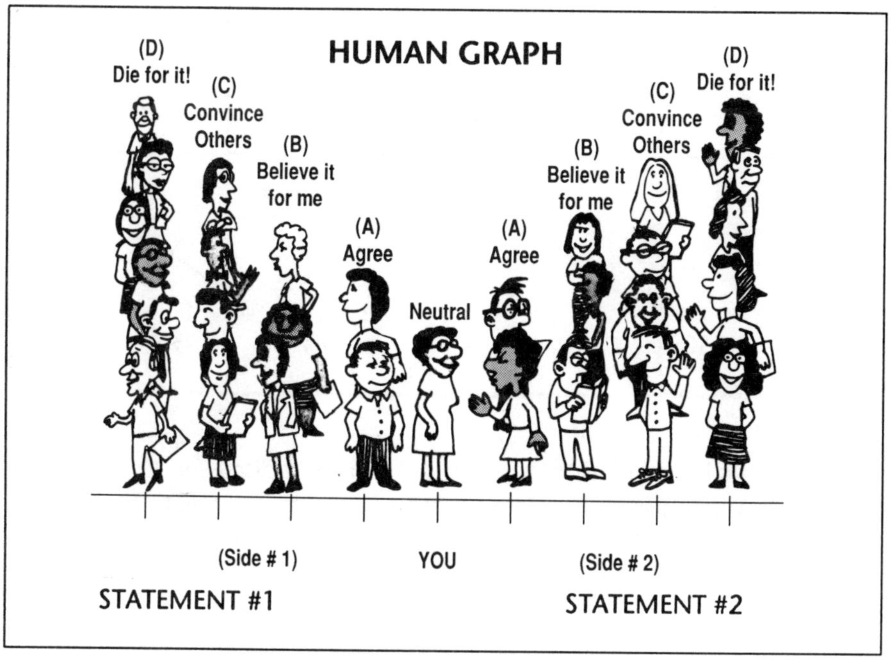

For metacognitive processing, have students complete these sentences:

The hardest part about reaching consensus is . . . .

The easiest part about reaching consensus is . . . .

Another opportunity to use the 5-to-Fist activity might be . . . .

☐ ☐ ☐

TOP FIVE

Pass out one puzzle piece to each student, making sure the complete sets are distributed. (Each piece has a partner piece.) Instruct each student to find the partner with the piece that completes his/her puzzle.

CONFLICT RESOLUTION PUZZLES*

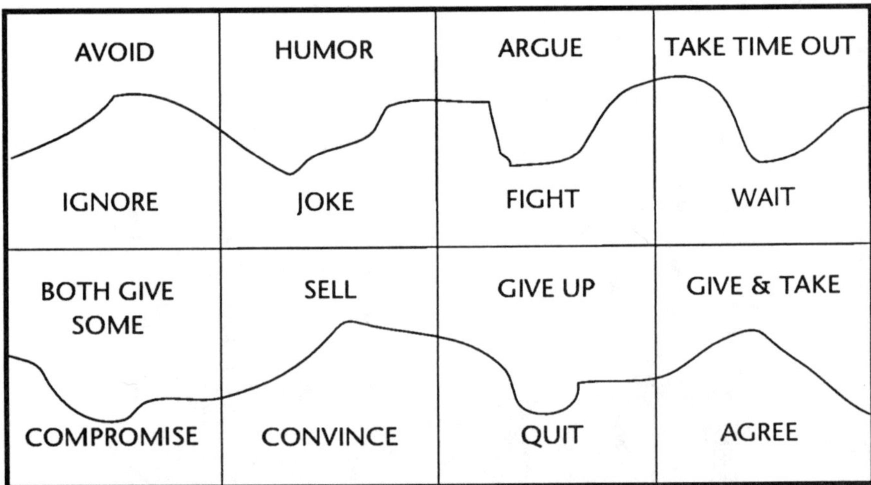

AVOID
IGNORE
HUMOR
JOKE
ARGUE
FIGHT
TAKE TIME OUT
WAIT
BOTH GIVE SOME
COMPROMISE
SELL
CONVINCE
GIVE UP
QUIT
GIVE & TAKE
AGREE

After students have found their puzzle partners and discussed the words for agreeing and disagreeing that are on their puzzle pieces, talk to them about consensus. Introduce the word *consensus* and the rules for seeking consensus:

> Consensus — Collective or group opinion or agreement
>
> ---
>
> Voting is outlawed.
> No horse-trading allowed.
> Don't give up.

Now show students the following consensus chart. Modeling with your hand, demonstrate how members should signal the group (5 to Fist) when they call for a consensus reading.

*pages 327, 328 and 330

CONSENSUS CHART			
5		(5 fingers)	All for it; top priority
4		(4 fingers)	Yes; high on my list
3		(3 fingers)	OK with me
2		(2 fingers)	Let's talk more
1		(1 finger)	Will trust group
FIST		(fist)	No! An alternative is ____.

Model the consensus-seeking process with a selected group of three or four. Tell this group to rank the following sports with their favorite one as number one:

- ☐ Baseball
- ☐ Basketball
- ☐ Football

They must signal with the 5-to-Fist strategy for each one as it is mentioned and discussed.

BASEBALL

No one wants baseball as first. They suggest that since all agree—make it number 3 or last.

BASKETBALL

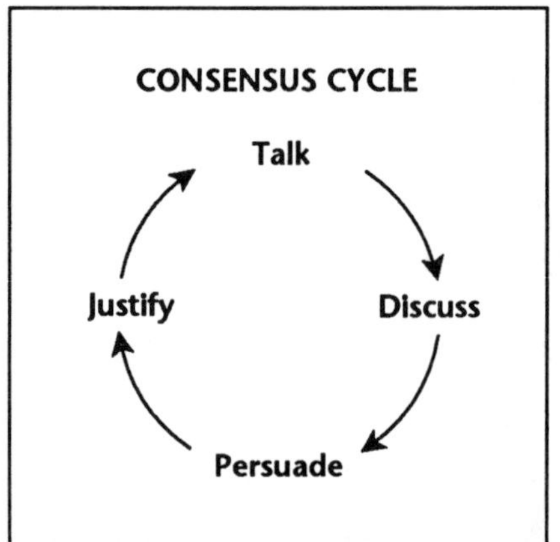

BASKETBALL

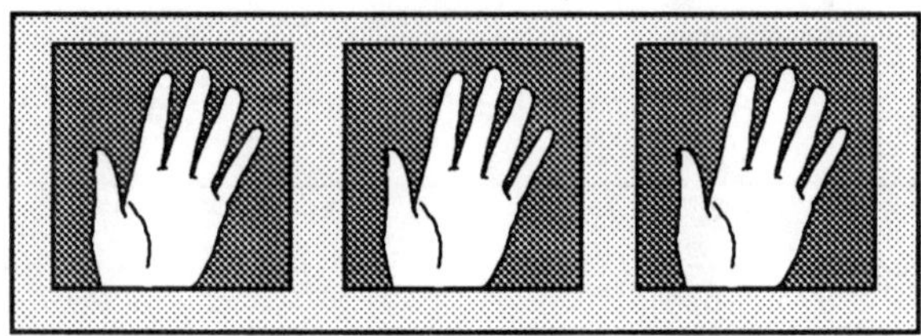

FOOTBALL

Ranking			
	1	Basketball	(5, 5, 5)
	2	Basketball	(3, 2, 1)
	3	Football	(fist, fist, fist)

Now, with the sports example in mind, give students the following task.

> By consensus of the class, select the top five, "must-read" books for all middle school students.

Tell the students that today they will make some important decisions as the "experts" for middle students in their school. Explain that their job is to select the top five books for students ages 10 to 13 throughout the United States. Elaborate on these instructions by explaining that they will make decisions about which five books they think every middle student should read before leaving middle school. These are the must-read books because they are the absolute best! Explain further that their decisions will be made into a list called "The Top Five," which will be posted in each classroom in the building for others to consider.

Arrange students into groups of three, with a:

Recorder— to write down ideas.

Researcher— to get resources.

Reporter— to tell results.

Instruct the groups to brainstorm books they think are possibilities for The Top Five list and write them on a large piece of paper. They are to try for 25 titles. They should include their favorite books and other books they've heard of.

Must-Reads

CONTENDERS FOR THE TOP FIVE

1.________	9.________	17.________
2.________	10.________	18.________
3.________	11.________	19.________
4.________	12.________	20.________
5.________	13.________	21.________
6.________	14.________	22.________
7.________	15.________	23.________
8.________	16.________	24.________
		25.________

Discuss the DOVE guidelines for brainstorming and accepting others' ideas.

DOVE*

Defer judgment; anything goes
Opt for original, different ideas
Vast numbers are needed
Expand the list by piggybacking on ideas

After brainstorming 25 book contenders for The Top Five list, review the 5-to-Fist consensus model with the students. Explain that through discussions and use of the 5-to-Fist consensus model, each team is to determine the top five books, naming book #1, book #2, book #3, book #4 and book #5. Collect the team rankings at the end of the session.

After reviewing the team rankings, compile the nominated book titles into a class list. Include all books listed by the teams. Have each team review the class list and discuss the additional book titles. The class goal now is to select by consensus the top five books from the class list.

To encourage open discussion on all nominations, reorganize the students into new teams of three. Using discussion and the 5-to-Fist strategy, have student teams rank the top five.

Reorganize teams again with all new members to rank the top five books.

*page 326

Reorganize! Rank the top five books by team. The continued reorganization of new threesomes and the subsequent new rankings eliminates the "ownership" issue in which students stay loyal to their own nominations. However, if the continued regrouping and re-ranking becomes tedious or too time consuming, this step needs to be modified accordingly. Keep in mind, a group consensus needs to be reached in some manner although the specific design of consensus will vary.

After several group interactions, try a class ranking. Allow informal groups to *discuss, persuade* and *justify* as they seek class consensus. This may take more time than was planned. If so, there is no reason why they can't stop and continue at another time or on another day. It is not uncommon for committees to take several sessions to arrive at a consensus. Talk to students about what's happening. Reassure them that reaching consensus requires time to talk, clarify and shift positions, and that making good decisions often takes quality time.

Once a class decision has been reached, post the results.

By Consensus,
TOP FIVE BOOKS
1.___________
2.___________
3.___________
4.___________
5.___________
CLASS______________
GRADE___ DATE______

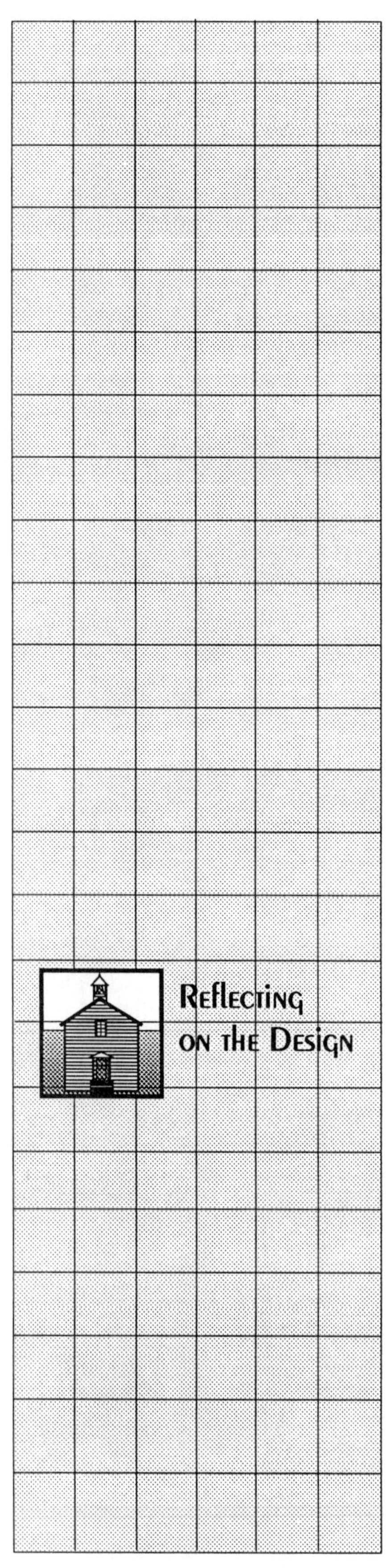

For affective processing, have students web the feelings they have when they are in conflict or disagree with another person.

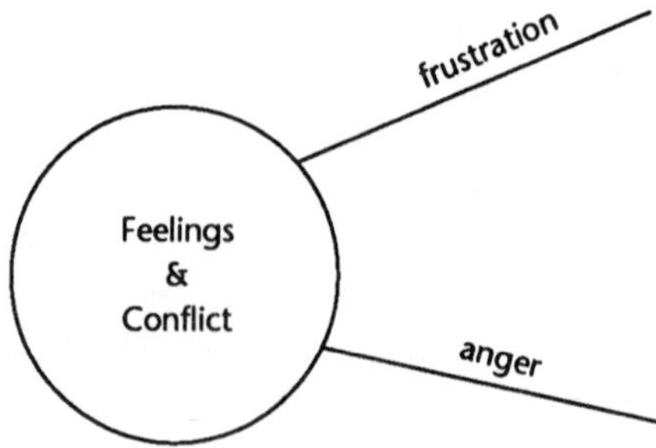

After webbing their feelings, students should complete this statement:

Conflict is like ___ because both _____.

For social processing, have students complete a PMI chart on consensus.

For cognitive processing. . .

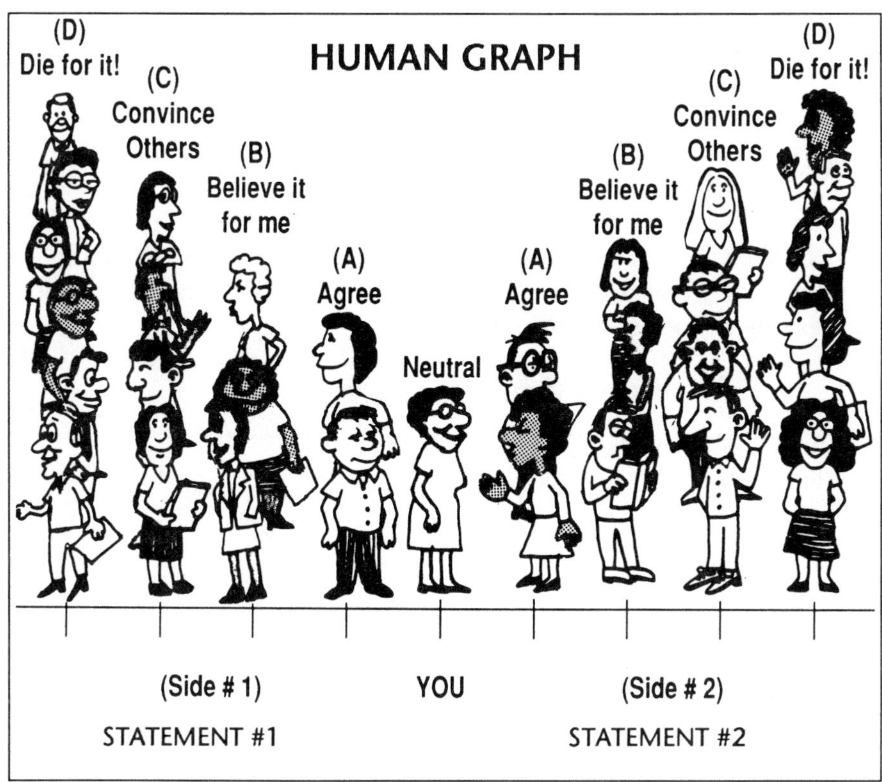

...ask students to make a human graph in the room and to move to the corresponding side of it for each of the following statements:

STATEMENT #1	STATEMENT #2
All students should read _____.	All students should not read _____.
Fiction is better than nonfiction.	Nonfiction is better than fiction.
A favorite author is _____.	A favorite author is not _____.
Books are better than TV.	TV is better than books.

For metacognitive processing, have students complete the following sentences:

The hardest part about reaching consensus is . . . .

The easiest part about reaching consensus is . . . .

Another opportunity to use the 5-to-Fist activity might be . . . .

□ □ □

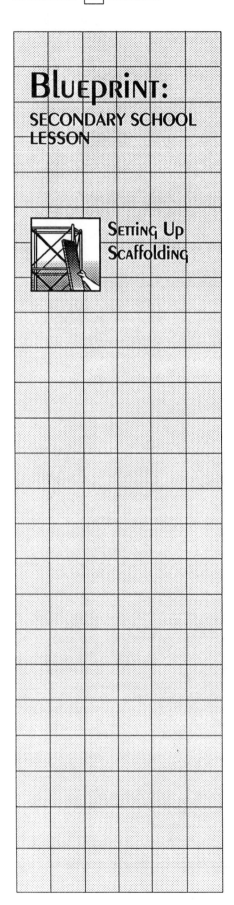

TOP TEN

Pass out one puzzle piece to each student, making sure the complete sets are distributed. (Each piece has a partner piece.) Instruct each student to find the partner with the piece that completes his/her puzzle.

CONFLICT RESOLUTION PUZZLES*

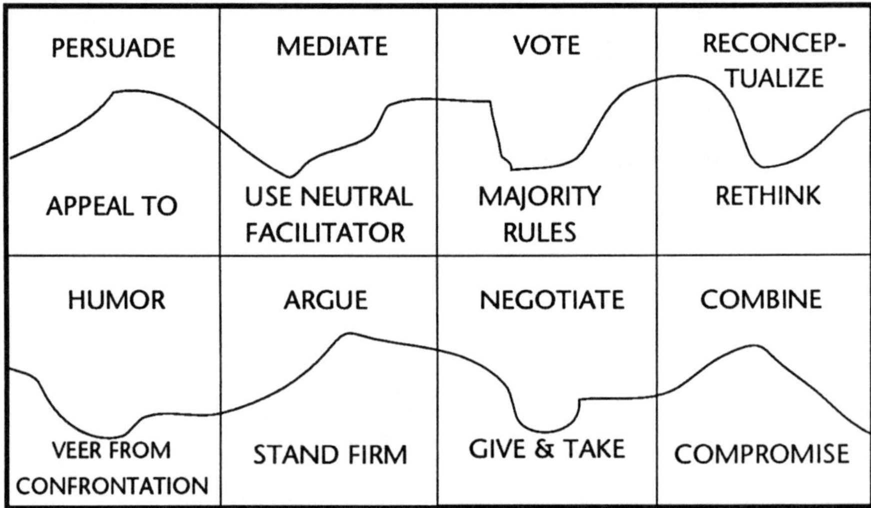

PERSUADE
APPEAL TO
MEDIATE
USE NEUTRAL FACILITATOR
VOTE
MAJORITY RULES
RECONCEPTUALIZE
RETHINK
HUMOR
VEER FROM CONFRONTATION
ARGUE
STAND FIRM
NEGOTIATE
GIVE & TAKE
COMBINE
COMPROMISE

After students have found their puzzle partners and discussed the words for agreeing and disagreeing that appear on the puzzle pieces, talk to them about consensus. Introduce the word *consensus* and the rules for seeking consensus:

> Consensus — collective opinion or agreement
>
> Voting is outlawed.
> No horse-trading allowed.
> Don't give up.

Now show students the following consensus chart. Modeling with your hand, demonstrate how members should signal the group (5 to Fist) when they call for a consensus reading.

*pages 328, 329 and 330

CONSENSUS CHART		
5	(5 fingers)	All for it; top priority
4	(4 fingers)	Yes; high on my list
3	(3 fingers)	OK with me
2	(2 fingers)	Let's talk more
1	(1 finger)	Will trust group
FIST	(fist)	No! An alternative is ____.

Model the consensus-seeking process with a selected group of four. Tell them to rank the following items according to personal preference:

- ☐ Albums
- ☐ Tapes
- ☐ CDs
- ☐ Videos

They must discuss and signal their ratings withthe 5-to-Fist strategy for each item until they see a decision they all can agree upon.

ALBUMS

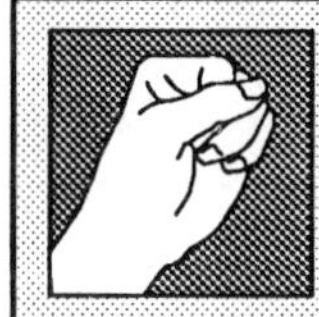
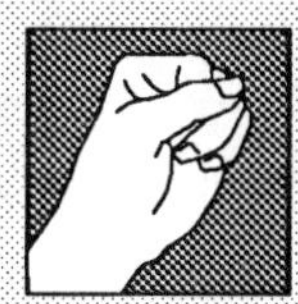

No one wants the albums first. They suggest a simple alternative. "Let's make this last on the ranking."

TAPES

TAPES

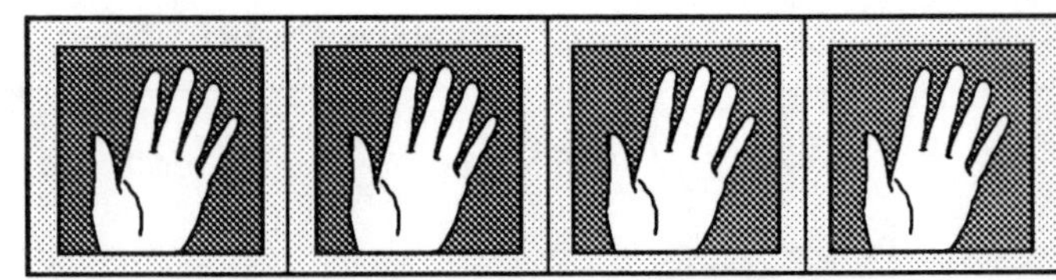

CDs

VIDEOS

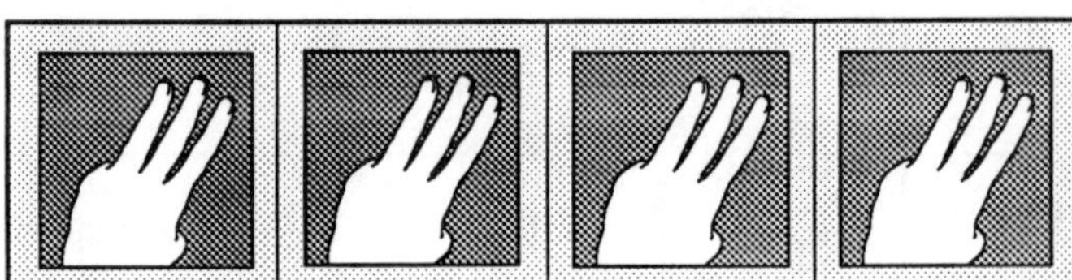

Ranking

1	Tapes	(5, 5, 5, 5)
2	Videos	(3, 3, 3, 3)
3	CDs	(3, 2, 2, 1)
4	Albums	(fist, fist, fist, fist)

Now, with the music example in mind, give the students the following problem:

> Select the top 10 books for secondary schoolers.

Tell the students that today they are going to make some important decisions as the "experts" for the secondary students in schools throughout the United States. Explain that their job is to select the top 10 books for secondary school students. Elaborate on these instructions by explaining that they will be making decisions about which 10 books they think every secondary student should read before leaving school. Further explain that these are the "must-read" books because they are the absolute best! Their decisions will be made into a list called "The Top 10," which will be posted throughout the school for others to consider.

Assign students to groups of three, with a:

Recorder—to write down ideas.

Researcher—to get resources needed.

Reporter—to tell the results of the task and teamwork.

Instruct groups to brainstorm books they think are possibilities for The Top 10 list and write them on a large piece of paper. They are to try for 25 titles. They should include their favorite books and other books they've heard of.

Must-Reads
CONTENDERS FOR THE TOP 10 BOOKS

1.________	9.________	17.________
2.________	10.________	18.________
3.________	11.________	19.________
4.________	12.________	20.________
5.________	13.________	21.________
6.________	14.________	22.________
7.________	15.________	23.________
8.________	16.________	24.________
		25.________

Discuss the DOVE guidelines for brainstorming and accepting others' ideas.

DOVE*

Defer judgment; anything goes
Opt for original, different ideas
Vast numbers are needed
Expand by piggybacking on other ideas

After brainstorming 25 must-reads for The Top 10 list, review the 5-to-Fist consensus model with the students. Explain that through discussions and use of this 5-to-Fist consensus model, they are to determine the top 10 books, naming book #1, book #2, book #3, etc. Collect these team rankings at the end of the session.

*p. 326

TOP 10 BOOKS

1.____________________
2.____________________
3.____________________
4.____________________
5.____________________
6.____________________
7.____________________
8.____________________
9.____________________
10.____________________

TEAM ________________

GRADE____ DATE_______

After reviewing the team rankings, compile the nominated book titles into a class list. Include all books listed on the teams.

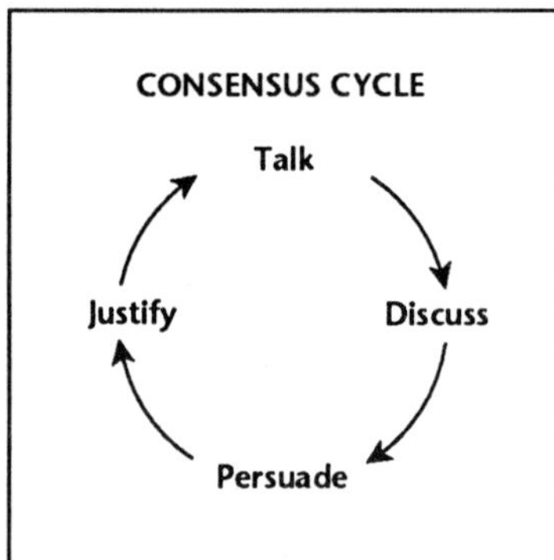

Have each team review the class list and discuss the additional book titles. The class goal is now to select, again by consensus, the top 10 books.

To encourage open discussion on all nominations, reorganize the students into new teams of four. Using discussion and the 5-to-Fist strategy, have student teams rank the top 10.

Reorganize teams again with all new members. Again, rank the top 10 books by team.

Reorganize! Rank the top 10 books by team. The continued reorganization of groups and the subsequent new rankings eliminates the "ownership" issue in which students stay loyal to their own nominations. However, if the continued regrouping and re-ranking becomes tedious or too time consuming, this step needs to be modified accordingly.

After several group interactions, try an all-class ranking. Allow informal groups to *discuss*, *persuade* and *justify* as they seek class consensus. This may take more time than was planned. If so, there is no reason why they can't stop and continue at another time or on another day. It is not uncommon for committees to take several sessions to arrive at a consensus. If this is the case, talk to students about what's happening. Reassure them that reaching consensus requires time to talk, clarify and shift positions, and that making good decisions often takes quality time.

For affective processing, have students web the feelings they have when they are in conflict or disagree with another person.

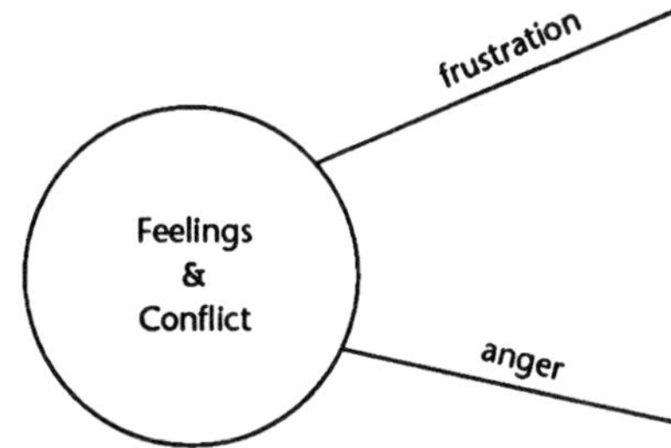

After webbing their feelings, students should complete this statement:

Conflict is like ___ because both _____.

For social skill processing, have students tell how they can facilitate reaching consensus.

For cognitive processing...

HUMAN GRAPH

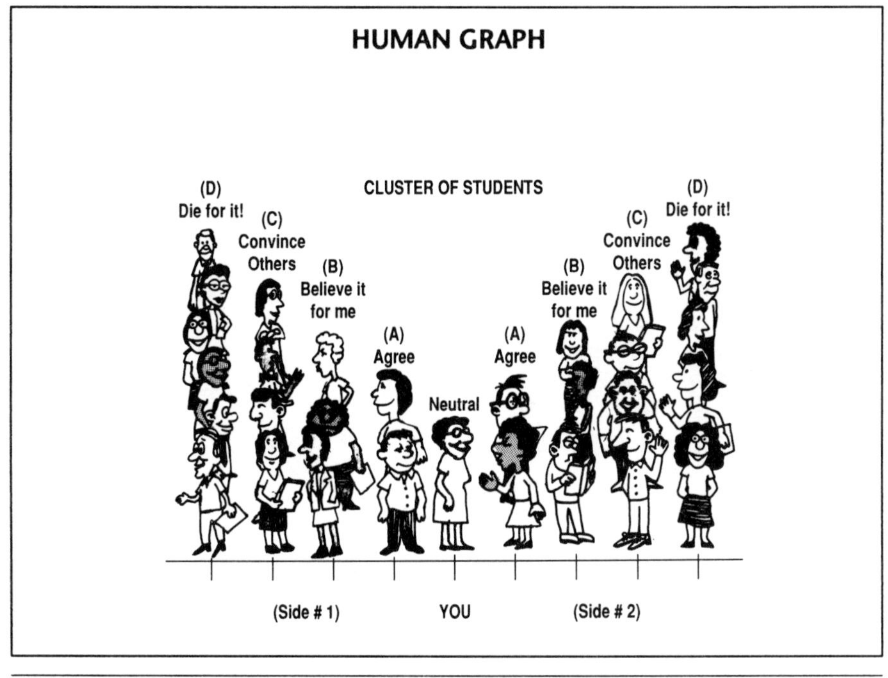

...ask students to move to the corresponding side of the graph for each of the following statements:

STATEMENT #1	STATEMENT #2
All students should read _____.	All students should not read _____.
Fiction is better than non-fiction.	Nonfiction is better than fiction.
A favorite author is _____.	A favorite author is not _____.
Books are better than TV.	TV is better than books.

For metacognitive processing, have students finish these sentences:

The hardest part about reaching consensus is . . . .

The easiest part about reaching consensus is . . . .

Another opportunity to use the 5-to-Fist activity might be . . . .

□ □ □

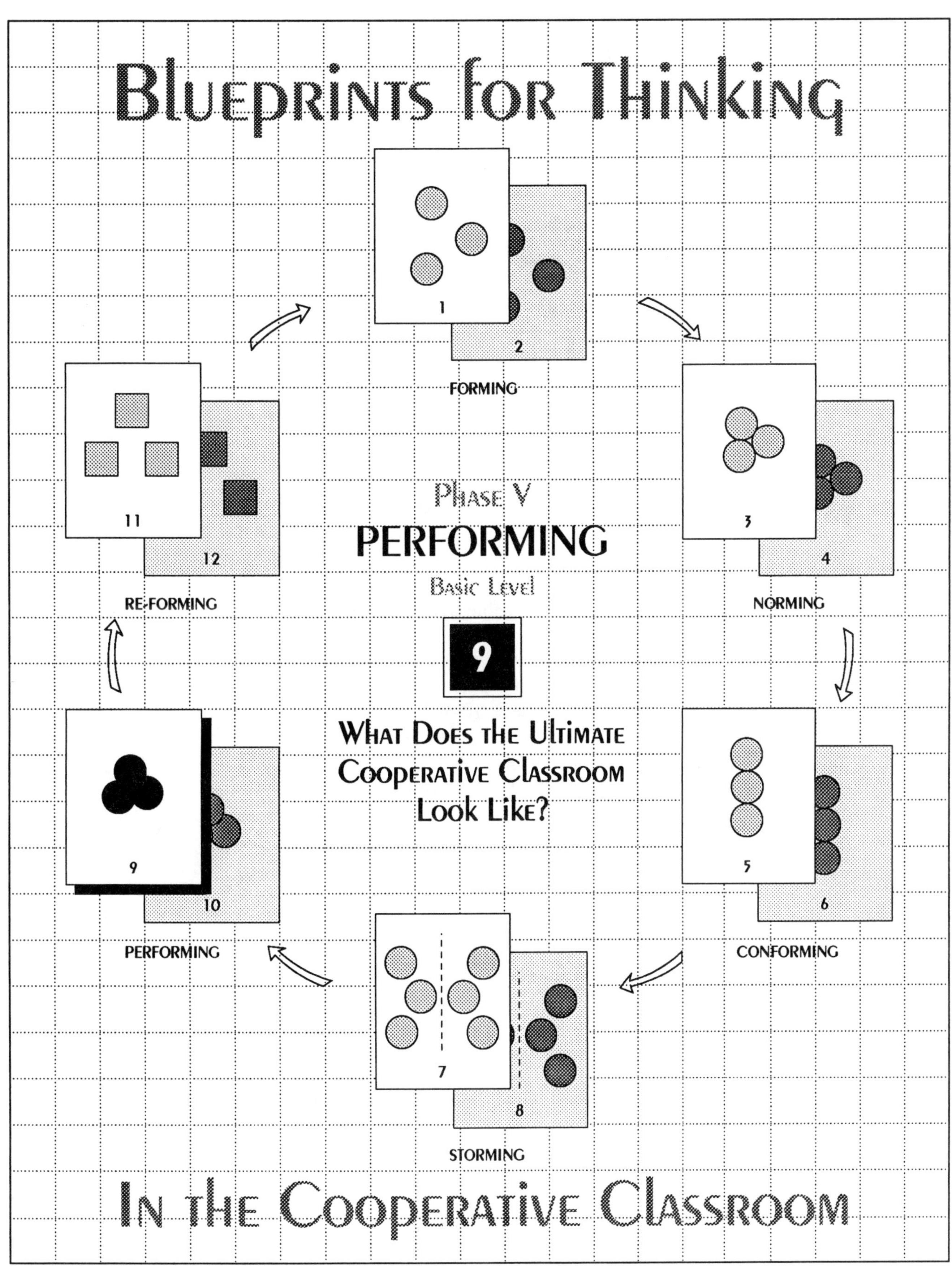

Blueprints for Thinking
1
2
FORMING
3
4
NORMING
5
6
CONFORMING
7
8
STORMING
9
10
PERFORMING
11
12
RE-FORMING
Phase V
PERFORMING
Basic Level
9
What Does the Ultimate Cooperative Classroom Look Like?
In the Cooperative Classroom

Phase V:
PERFORMING
Basic

What Does the Ultimate Cooperative Classroom Look Like?

Part of the teacher's art is to watch the balanced growth of their pupils.

—M.C. Richards

Draft

Progress through the various phases of the small-group process is usually punctuated by intermittent setbacks. An ebb and flow of movement in the desired direction of a smoothly functioning, high-challenge environment is the usual pattern of interrupted, but definite forward progress. Over time, the unmistakable signs of maturing group behavior are inevitable.

To visualize what a high-performing, high-challenge cooperative classroom looks like, a review of the following blueprint design for thinking and cooperating is needed. In this high-functioning instructional setting, a delicate balance between student interactions with each other in cooperative learning models and interaction with the material in information-processing models is demonstrated.

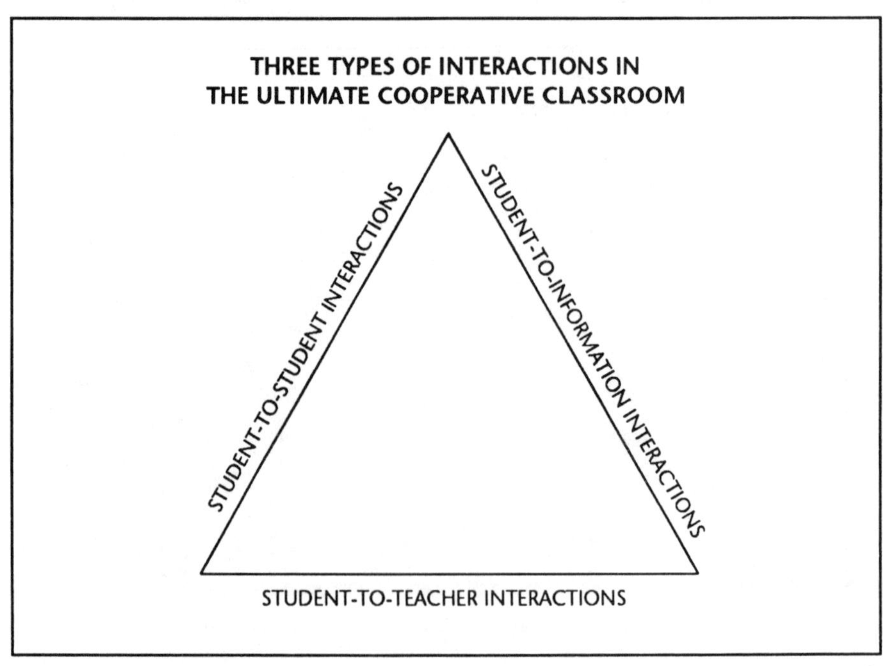

Elaborating on the dual interactions of student-to-student collaborations and student-to-information processing, this Venn diagram illustrates the ultimate high-performing instructional model. By placing students in informally structured cooperative groups, the ultimate instructional model dictates intense involvement by all students. The intensity of this student involvement is determined by certain critical elements.

Specs

Just to review briefly, with the cooperative learning model of student-to-student interaction one must BUILD in certain elements if the researched outcomes are desired. Using the acronym BUILD, as presented by Marcus and McDonald (1990), five key components comprise the effective cooperative model.

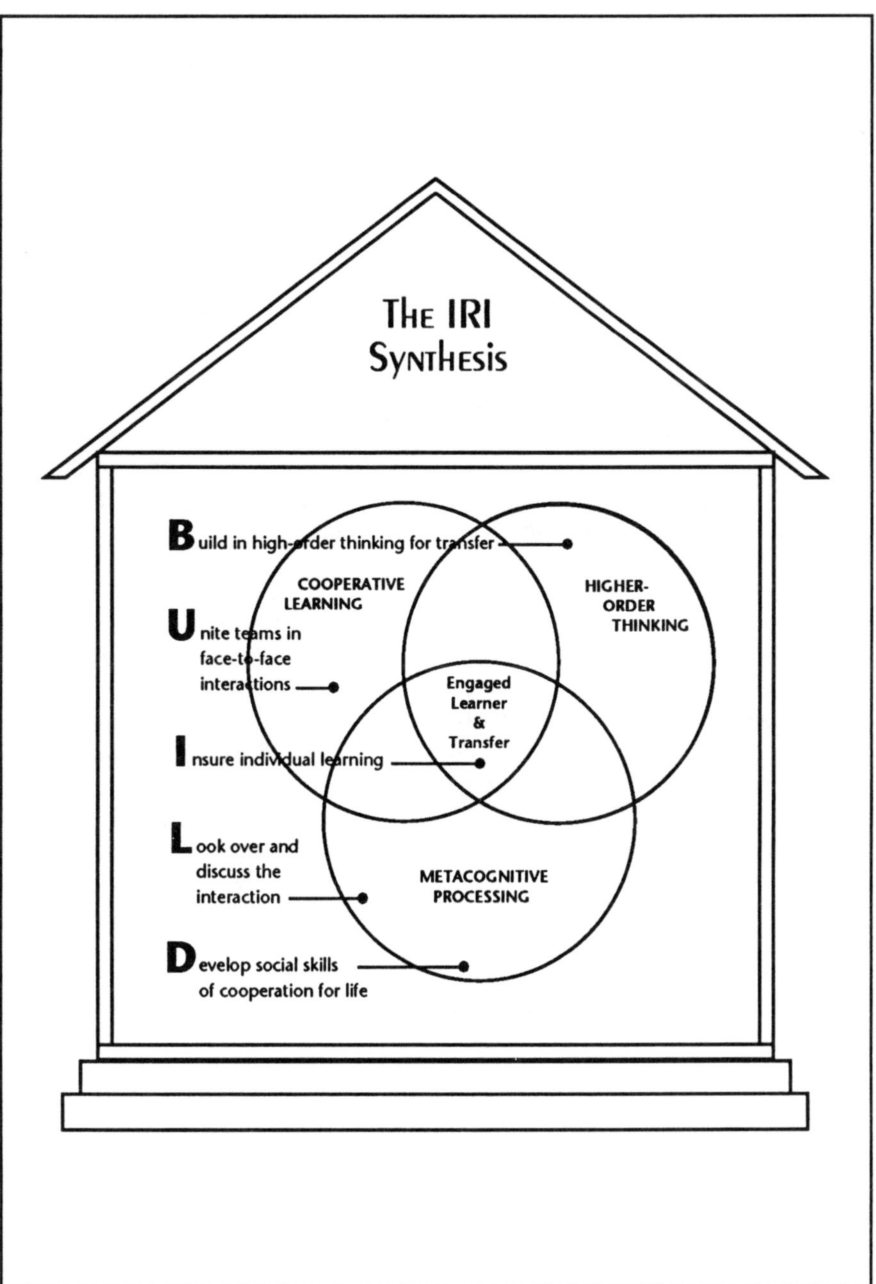
The IRI Synthesis
Build in high-order thinking for transfer
Unite teams in face-to-face interactions
Insure individual learning
Look over and discuss the interaction
Develop social skills of cooperation for life
COOPERATIVE LEARNING
HIGHER-ORDER THINKING
Engaged Learner & Transfer
METACOGNITIVE PROCESSING

THE ELEMENTS OF BUILD

B For achieving effectively functioning cooperative groups in which student learning, achievement and self-esteem are all increased significantly, the teacher-facilitator must build higher-level thinking into the tasks. By creating high challenges within the group assignment, cooperation automatically gets a boost because the members sense that they need the group to meet the challenge. Conversely, if the task is too easy, students feel, and rightly so, that they can do the task quicker, easier and better themselves. They don't think they really need the others. However, high challenge fosters high collaboration. In turn, the higher-level metacognitive discussion will promote the desired transfer.

U It follows then that by tailoring high-cognitive tasks a united group—a group with a "sink or swim together" posture—is formed by the members. When students know that they either all make it together or none of them makes it alone, the motivation to cooperate is naturally sparked. Helping create an interdependence in the groups to accomplish individual as well as group goals is an absolute key to the high-performance classroom.

I At the same time, another critical element is helping individual students learn in highly personal and relevant ways—ways that hold accountability and responsibility of each and every group member for achieving the task and learning the material in high regard. Often, students new to cooperative models are unskilled at learning *and* being accountable for the total picture at the same time. High-performing classrooms, on the other hand, have taken deliberate, visible and gradually more sophisticated steps to insure individual learning. These graduated moves range from quick, individual quizzes to more elaborate, independent and appropriate applications.

L Taking time to look over what the group has done—to plan, monitor and evaluate both the academic task and the cooperative task—is another critical element in the high-performing classroom. The metacognitive model, which promotes further application and transfer from the lesson, also fosters critiquing among the group members. Without the group processing time, without the group processing formats, little, if any transfer is likely to take place. Yet, by simply addressing the group behaviors and task results students exhibit noticeable tendencies toward meaningful transfer.

Just think for a minute about the number of times a person disagrees among a small group of friends or colleagues. How often or how many people take the time to think about "what we do when we disagree"? And yet, by asking students to discuss just that (What do you do when you disagree?) a skilled facilitator can almost guarantee that a few "what-to-do-when-you-disagree strategies" will filter out into other situations those students encounter. The processing time, the time it takes to guide that kind of metacognitive reflection, is critical to continued high-performing collaborative classrooms.

D A final element for the high-functioning cooperative learning teams, of course, is the explicit attention to developing social skills, which are needed for communicating, building trust, promoting leadership and re-solving conflicts. The structured cooperative-learning models target specific social skills that help students develop into valuable, contributing and empathetic members of groups. Social skills targeted for explicit attention might include the *active listening* behaviors of *paraphrasing, affirming* and *clarifying* or the *leadership* skill of *encouraging* others. Further along the social skill continuum are the *conflict resolution* skills of *disagreeing with ideas and not people*, listening to *others' points of view* and *seeking consensus.*

Without the deliberate teaching of the social skill, the cooperative learning groups simply function as task groups focused on the final product. However, by putting an emphasis on the spectrum of social skills, co-operative groups develop social behaviors that facilitate collaborative efforts at all levels of the social spectrum.

QUICK REFERENCE: SAMPLE COOPERATIVE LESSON PLANNER*

	B	U	I	L	D	
	Build in High-Order Thinking	**U**nite Teams	**I**nsure Individual Learning	**L**ook Over & Discuss	**D**evelop Social Skills	
	Problem Solving Decision Making Creative Ideation	*Build Trust & Teamwork*	*Insure Individual Learning & Responsibility*	*Plan, Monitor & Evaluate*	*Communication Leadership Conflict Resolution*	
1	Critical and creative thinking *p. 182*	Bonding and group identity *p. 35*	Assigned roles *p. 6*	Goal setting *p. 36*	Paraphrase *p. 78*	I hear I see...
2	3-to-1 technique *p. 7*	Shared materials *p. 8*	Quiz *p. 228*	P.M.I. *p. 131*	Affirm *p. 57*	That's a good idea
3	Problem solving *p. 122*	Single product *p. 7*	Random responses *p. 233*	Human graph *p. 147*	Clarify *p. 82*	Tell me more!
4	Decision making *p. 147*	Jigsaw *p. 34*	Individual application *p. 234*	Teacher observation sheet *p. 66*	Test options *p. 50*	What else?
5	Fat & skinny questions *p. 88*	Lottery *p. 16*	Individual grades *p. 230*	Student observer feedback *p. 49*	Sense tone *p. 80*	That feels___
6	Application *p. 92*	Bonus points *p. 231*	Signature. I agree! I understand! *p. 7*	Success award *p. 16*	Encourage others *p. 57*	No put-downs!
7	Transfer within/across/into *p. 268*	Group grade *p. 231*	Round robin (Wraparound) *p. 234*	Log entry *p. 228*	Accept others' ideas *p. 145*	Set DOVE guidelines
8	Graphic organizers *p. 107*	Group reward *p. 49*	Homework *p. 37*	Individual transfer or application *p. 233*	T-chart *p. 48*	Looks like Sounds like
9	Metacognitive exercises *p. 264*	Consensus *p. 142*	Bonus points *p. 231*	Team ad *p. 228*	Disagree with ideas not people *p. 140*	Other point of view
10	Making metaphors *p. 195*	Extended projects *p. 228*	Expert jigsaw *p. 234*	Mrs. Potter's questions *p. 43*	Reach consensus *p. 142*	5 to fist

*blank BUILD grid available on page 331

The morphological grid, which uses the critical elements of BUILD as the organizing headings, charts myriad cooperative skills and strategies for fostering its "framing" elements. For example, strategies to "look over and talk about the group work" are Mrs. Potter's Questions, a thinking log, an observation sheet and a PMI chart. Methods for "uniting the team" in a sink-or-swim-together attitude include a single product, shared materials, a jigsaw approach and bonus points.

As the teacher of the high-performing classroom plans ongoing lessons, this quick reference serves as a guide to ensure that the critical elements of high-challenge cooperative group lessons are included. By plotting a lesson that has an element from each column, the teacher readily puts together a success-oriented, high-contact, high-content cooperative lesson.

For instance, plotting one element in each column might look like this:

B	U	I	L	D
Creative Skill				
	Shared Materials			
		Quiz		
			Mrs. Potter's Questions	
				DOVE Guidelines

In working with a math class on problem solving, this teacher might use the elements designated above to design the following lesson:

Building in higher-order thinking: the students will *predict* or *estimate* (creative thinking) a reasonable answer.

Uniting the group: students will solve their problems on large poster paper and list their strategies using the same materials.

Insuring individual learning: one student will be selected from each group for a quiz on the problem types.

Looking over what was done: students will review Mrs. Potter's Questions in their small groups and samples will be reported to the class.

- What were we supposed to do?
- What did we do well?
- What would we do differently?
- Do we need any help?

Developing a social skill: the DOVE guidelines will be part of the instructional input before the group approaches the task.

Defer judgment on ideas
Opt for original ideas or strategies
Vast numbers of ideas are needed
Expand by piggybacking on another's idea

However, the student-to-student interaction that results in intense learner involvement is only half the interaction model for the high-performing classroom. The other part of the interactive model includes student-to-information interactions. When processing information in an interactive classroom, the student becomes intensely involved with the information under study.

Couple every cooperative task in the classroom with a complex cognitive task. Explicitly build higher-order thinking processes into high-challenge lessons. Target specific micro-skills for thinking or string several thinking skills together into a macro-process approach to complex thinking. Using BUILD and the thinking skills and thinking processes ensures a high-challenge activity.

MICRO-SKILLS

CRITICAL THINKING SKILLS	CREATIVE THINKING SKILLS
1. Attributing	1. Brainstorming
2. Comparing/Contrasting	2. Visualizing
3. Classifying	3. Personifying
4. Sequencing	4. Inventing
5. Prioritizing	5. Associating Relationships
6. Drawing Conclusions	6. Inferring
7. Determining Cause/Effect	7. Generalizing
8. Analyzing for Bias	8. Predicting
9. Analyzing for Assumptions	9. Hypothesizing
10. Solving for Analogies	10. Making Analogies
11. Evaluating	11. Dealing with Ambiguity & Paradox
12. Decision Making	12. Problem Solving

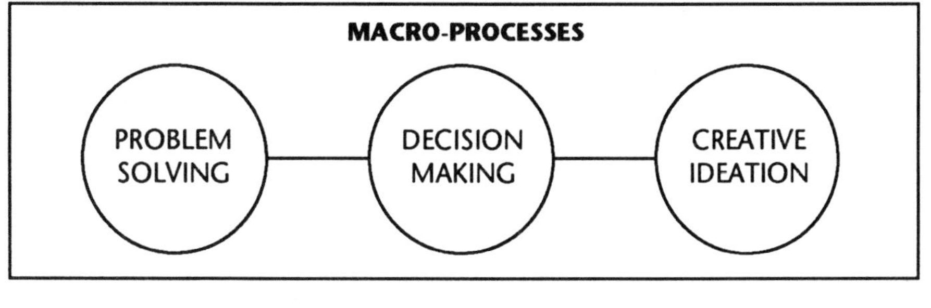

□ □ □

Update your task sequence on page 348.

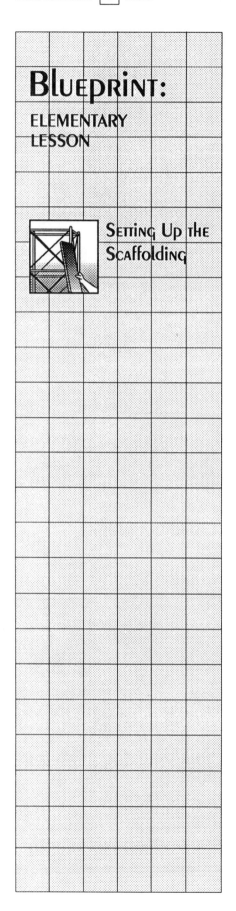

MAMMAL MANIA

Using a completed BUILD chart of the cooperative learning elements, scan and select key elements for the envisioned lesson "Mammal Mania." By using the BUILD chart, the teacher automatically includes the critical elements of a higher-order thinking/cooperative lesson. For example, a teacher may create the following BUILD chart and choose the circled items to create a cooperative lesson.

SAMPLE COOPERATIVE LESSON PLANNER

	B	U	I	L	D	
	Build in High-Order Thinking	**U**nite Teams	**I**nsure Individual Learning	**L**ook Over & Discuss	**D**evelop Social Skills	
	Problem Solving Decision Making Creative Ideation	*Build Trust & Teamwork*	*Insure Individual Learning & Responsibility*	*Plan, Monitor & Evaluate*	*Communication Leadership Conflict Resolution*	
1	Critical and creative thinking	Bonding and group identity	Assigned roles	Goal setting	Paraphrase	I hear I see...
2	3-to-1 questions	Shared materials	Quiz	P.M.I.	Affirm	That's a good idea
3	Problem solving	Single product	Random responses	Human graph	Clarify	Tell me more!
4	Decision making	Jigsaw	Personal application	Teacher observation sheet	Test options	What else?
5	Fat & skinny questions	Lottery	Individual criteria	Student observer feedback	Sense tone	That feels___
6	Application	Bonus points	Signature. I agree! I understand!	Success award	Encourage others	No put-downs!
7	Transfer within/across/into	Group grade	Round robin (Wraparound)	Log entry	Accept others' ideas	Set DOVE guidelines
8	Graphic organizers	Group reward	Homework	Individual transfer or application	T-chart	Looks like Sounds like
9	Metacognitive exercises	Consensus	Bonus points	Team ad	Disagree with ideas not people	Other point of view
10	Making metaphors	Extended projects	Expert jigsaw	Mrs. Potter's questions	Reach consensus	5 to fist

B - Requiring critical and creative thinking (brainstorming, inventing, performing) stretches the mind.

U - Establishing a group identity unites each team.

I - Assigned roles keep members accountable for tasks and learning.

L - Mrs. Potter's questions structure quality review.

D - Setting guidelines for students to accept others' ideas enforces social skills.

Next, using the list of micro-skills for thinking as a reference, select an appropriate thinking skill(s) for the lesson.

MICRO-SKILLS

CRITICAL THINKING SKILLS	CREATIVE THINKING SKILLS
1. Attributing	1. Brainstorming
2. Comparing/Contrasting	2. Visualizing
3. Classifying	3. Personifying
4. Sequencing	4. Inventing
5. Prioritizing	5. Associating Relationships
6. Drawing Conclusions	6. Inferring
7. Determining Cause/Effect	7. Generalizing
8. Analyzing for Bias	8. Predicting
9. Analyzing for Assumptions	9. Hypothesizing
10. Solving for Analogies	10. Making Analogies
11. Evaluating	11. Dealing with Amiguity & Paradox
12. Decision Making	12. Problem Solving

Using all of the chosen elements as a guide for designing the lesson, incorporate the specific components into the plan. For example, in preparation for a spring field trip to the zoo, which is a culminating activity for the mammal unit in science, the following lesson has been created using the selected elements.

Have students **brainstorm**, as a class, a web of mammals.

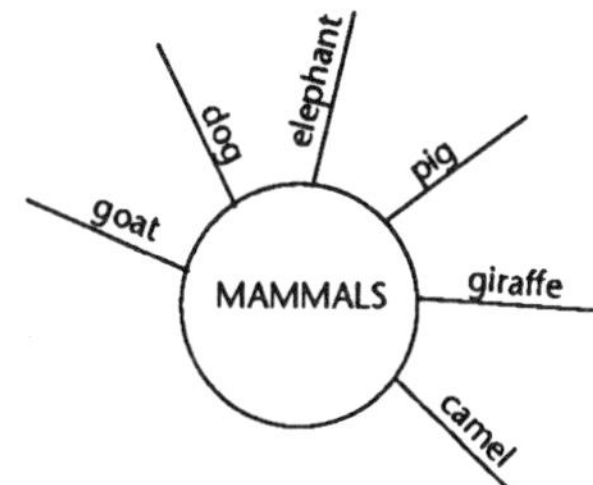

Ask students to turn to a partner and recall the critical attributes of mammals. Instruct them to check that all listed animals fit the definition.

Next, arrange students into groups of three and assign the roles of: *recorder/illustrator, animal trainer, actor.*

Explain to the groups that their first task is to select an animal from the unit and to **invent** a name for their teams that signify their mammal selections. A **group name** creates a **group identity**. For example, their group name might be the Elephant Explorers.

Instruct students that they are going to use a strategy called **That's A Good Idea (cooperative skill: accepting others' ideas)** to create an animal that can talk and behave like a person (**creative thinking skill: personifying**). Explain and model how to perform responses in turn, the That's A Good Idea process. Begin by having students list human characteristics and behaviors for a mammal.

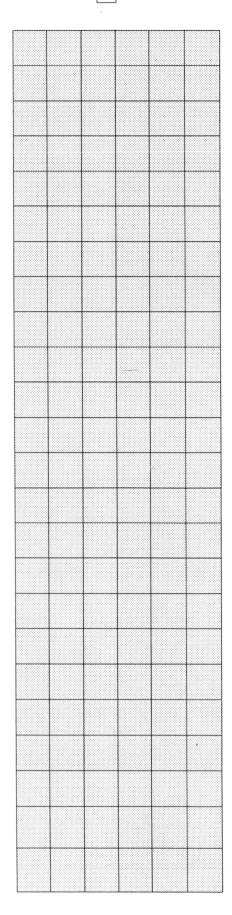

For example, the *first* person personifies by giving a human trait to the elephant ("He can ride a bike").

The *second* person tells why that trait is a good idea ("That's a good idea because he can get around faster") and then gives another trait for the elephant ("He can also talk").

The *third* person tells why the last trait given is a good idea ("That's a good idea because he can communicate with others") and then gives another idea ("He flies kites too").

Continue around the group until all members have praised another's idea *and* added a trait to the animal. (Let students know they may pass but they cannot say, "The same thing he said.") As the traits and praises are stated, have the recorder write them on a group chart.

Tell students the goal is to create a fictional character (an animal) out of their mammal that can behave in human ways. They must brainstorm at least six improvements to add to their mammal. Once the recorder has listed everyone's improvements on a large sheet, have the illustrator draw the animal in a way that shows the personified characteristics.

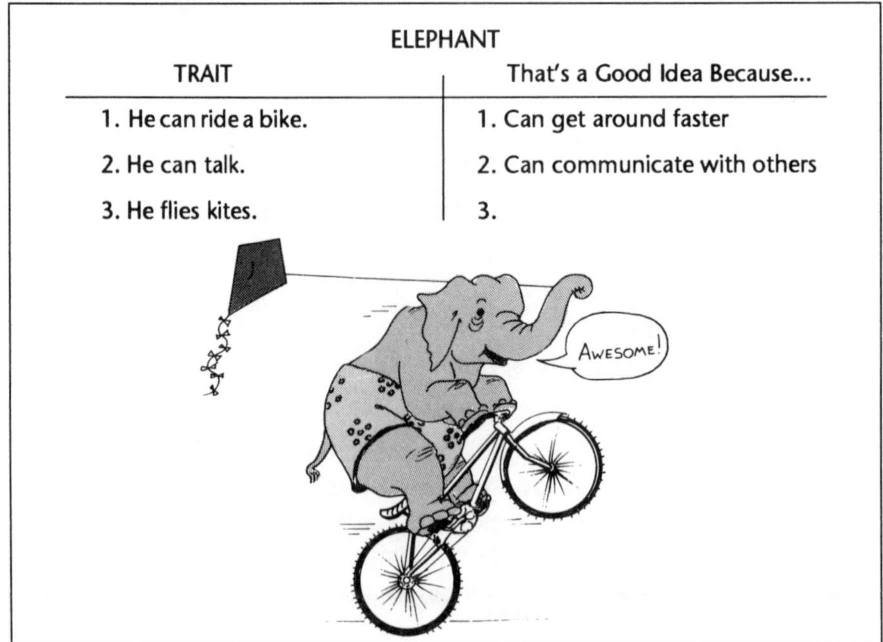

ELEPHANT

TRAIT	That's a Good Idea Because...
1. He can ride a bike.	1. Can get around faster
2. He can talk.	2. Can communicate with others
3. He flies kites.	3.

The final task requires the animal trainer and the animal actor to **perform** a brief skit incorporating the various human characteristics. These performances can be done for another small group or for the whole class.

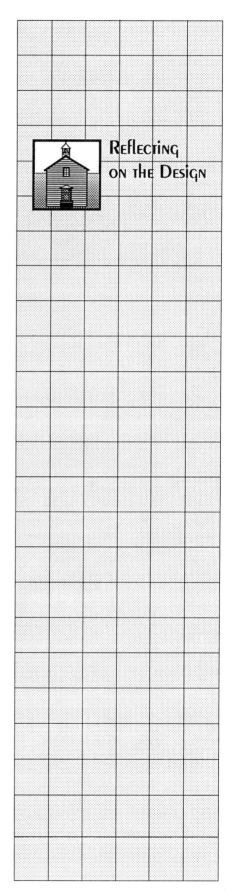

For affective processing, ask students to "become the animal." Ask them to imagine the actions and feelings of the mammal. Then, in their groups of three, have them finish this statement:

I want to be more like ___________ because . . . .
(animal)

For social skill processing, have students discuss why it is important to add ideas to the group and to accept others' ideas.

For cognitive processing, have students talk about the thinking skill personifying and answer these questions:

What was difficult about trying to change the animal into a human-like character?

Why is using That's A Good Idea (responses in turn) a good idea?

For metacognitive processing, have the groups talk through **Mrs. Potter's Questions:**

What were we supposed to do?

What did we do well?

What should we do differently?

Do we need any help?

☐ ☐ ☐

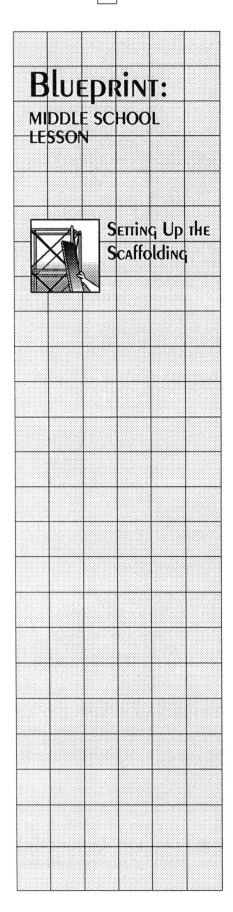

METRIC MATTERS

Using a completed BUILD chart of the cooperative learning elements, scan and select key elements for the envisioned lesson "Metric Matters."

For example, thinking about the purpose of the lesson, which is to force application of the metric model into various subject contents, a teacher could select the following elements to create a cooperative lesson. By using the BUILD chart, the teacher automatically includes the critical elements of a higher-order thinking/cooperative lesson.

SAMPLE COOPERATIVE LESSON PLANNER

	B	U	I	L	D	
	Build In High-Order Thinking	**Unite Teams**	**Insure Individual Learning**	**Look Over & Discuss**	**Develop Social Skills**	
	Problem Solving Decision Making Creative Ideation	*Build Trust & Teamwork*	*Insure Individual Learning & Responsibility*	*Plan, Monitor & Evaluate*	*Communication Leadership Conflict Resolution*	
1	Critical and creative thinking	Bonding and group identity	Assigned roles	Goal setting	Paraphrase	I hear I see...
2	3-to-1 questions	Shared materials	Quiz	P.M.I.	Affirm	That's a good idea
3	Problem solving	Single product	Random responses	What? So what? Now what?	Clarify	Tell me more!
4	Decision making	Jigsaw	Personal application	Teacher observation sheet	Test options	What else?
5	Fat & skinny questions	Lottery	Individual criteria	Student observer feedback	Sense tone	That feels...
6	Application	Bonus points	Signature. I agree! I understand!	Success award	Encourage others	No put-downs!
7	Transfer within/across/into	Group grade	Round robin (Wraparound)	Log entry	Accept others' ideas	Set DOVE guidelines
8	Graphic organizers	Group reward	Homework	Individual transfer or application	T-chart	Looks like Sounds like
9	Metacognitive exercises	Consensus	Bonus points	Team ad	Disagree with ideas not people	Other point of view
10	Making metaphors	Extended projects	Expert jigsaw	Mrs. Potter's questions	Reach consensus	5 to fist

B - A graphic organizer creates a higher-order thinking lesson.
U - Bonus points in groups unite the teams.
I - A wraparound ensures the individual learning process.
L - Answering What? So what? Now what? forces students to look back on the lesson.
D - Encouragement is targeted for social skill building.

Next, select appropriate micro-skills for thinking from the list.

MICRO-SKILLS

CRITICAL THINKING SKILLS	CREATIVE THINKING SKILLS
1. Attributing	1. Brainstorming
2. Comparing/Contrasting	2. Visualizing
3. Classifying	3. Personifying
4. Sequencing	4. Inventing
5. Prioritizing	5. Associating Relationships
6. Drawing Conclusions	6. Inferring
7. Determining Cause/Effect	7. Generalizing
8. Analyzing for Bias	8. Predicting
9. Analyzing for Assumptions	9. Hypothesizing
10. Solving for Analogies	10. Making Analogies
11. Evaluating	11. Dealing with Ambiguity & Paradox
12. Decision Making	12. Problem Solving

The following lesson is described—using the selected elements—as it might occur based on the Sharan and Sharan Group Investigation Model.

SHARAN & SHARAN GROUP INVESTIGATION MODEL

Stage 1:	Posing the big question and forming groups by interest
Stage 2:	Identifying the inquiry problem and planning how to research
Stage 3:	Dividing up the work and gathering information
Stage 4:	Synthesizing, summarizing and writing the report
Stage 5:	Presenting by groups and evaluating

Give the following input:

Academic Task:	Use the metric system in two subject areas.
Cooperative Task Focus:	Encouraging others
Thinking Task Focus:	Brainstorming, prioritizing, problem solving, transferring

Through discussion with the class, fill in a graphic organizer (such as a mind map) with various aspects of metric matters that groups may want to investigate. Allow students to **brainstorm** many ideas.

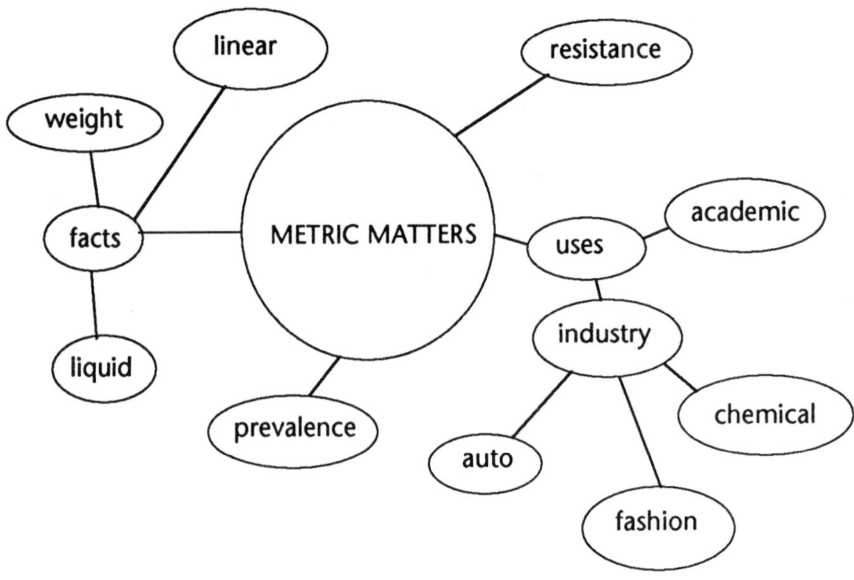

Group Investigation Step I: *Pose the Big Question and Form Groups by Topics of Interest*

Once the general topic has been properly explored, ask students to rearrange themselves according to their specific topics of interest. Require no more than three students to a group in the early attempts of the Group Investigation Model.

Group Investigation Step II: *Identify the Inquiry Problem and Plan How to Research*

Instruct groups to discuss ways to gather information for the initial research needed. Suggest library resources, primary resources such as interviews and other media possibilities. Also, suggest the librarian as a quick resource.

Group Investigation Step III: *Divide the Work and Gather Information*

a. Specify the jigsaw model in which each member is responsible for a piece of the completed puzzle.

b. Have groups set a time/date to reconvene with their completed parts.

c. Specify a checker to see that all members contribute.

Group Investigation Step IV: *Synthesize, Summarize and Prepare the Presentation*

Instruct students in the refinements of the jigsaw model. That is, as each member contributes to the whole, the members must have definite ways to "teach each other" about their particular parts as they prioritize, share, synthesize and summarize information. Without a thorough understanding of each separate piece, the synthesis will be fragmented and superficial. When group investigation is working well with a high-performing group, a synergy occurs in which the final piece is far richer than any work done by a single student.

WAYS TO TEACH ANOTHER*

- Tell
- Model
- Demonstrate
- Draw
- Give Examples
- Use Visuals
- Make Analogies
- Quiz

Group Investigation Step V: *a) Present the Information*

The groups **problem solve** a final presentation that fulfills the task requirements. Student teams demonstrate how the metric matters they investigated can be applied across at least two content lessons. This can be presented to one other group or to the whole class. **Bonus points** are given to each group member who actually applies the idea in another class. Proof from the other teacher is required.

REFLECTING ON THE DESIGN

Group Investigation Step V: *b) Evaluate*

For affective processing, ask students to discuss their feelings about the group investigation jigsaw. Do a quick **wraparound** with the stem "I felt...."

For social skill processing, have students talk about how they **encouraged** each other.

For cognitive processing, have students discuss the pros and cons of the group investigation process that they just used.

For metacognitive processing, ask students to discuss the **"So what?"** aspects of group investigation. How can they parlay this model into other situations—**"Now what"?**

□ □ □

*page 332

IN DEFENSE OF HUMAN RIGHTS

Using a completed BUILD chart of the cooperative learning elements, scan and select key elements for the envisioned lesson "In Defense of Human Rights: Small-Group Investigation" (based on the Sharan and Sharan model). By using the BUILD chart, the teacher automatically includes the critical elements of a higher-order thinking/cooperative lesson.

SAMPLE COOPERATIVE LESSON PLANNER

	B	U	I	L	D	
	Build in High-Order Thinking	**Unite Teams**	**Insure Individual Learning**	**Look Over & Discuss**	**Develop Social Skills**	
	Problem Solving Decision Making Creative Ideation	*Build Trust & Teamwork*	*Insure Individual Learning & Responsibility*	*Plan, Monitor & Evaluate*	*Communication Leadership Conflict Resolution*	
1	Critical and creative thinking	Bonding and group identity	Assigned roles	Goal setting	Paraphrase	I hear I see...
2	3-to-1 questions	Shared materials	Quiz	P.M.I.	Affirm	That's a good idea
3	Problem solving	Single product	Random responses	Human graph	Clarify	Tell me more!
4	Decision making	Jigsaw	Personal application	Teacher observation sheet	Test options	What else?
5	Fat & skinny questions	Lottery	Individual criteria	Student observer feedback	Sense tone	That feels___
6	Application	Bonus points	Signature I agree! I understand!	Success award	Encourage others	No put-downs!
7	Transfer within/across/into	Group grade	Round robin (Wraparound)	Log entry	Accept others' ideas	Set DOVE guidelines
8	Graphic organizers	Group reward	Homework	Individual transfer or application	T-chart	Looks like Sounds like
9	Metacognitive exercises	Consensus	Bonus points	Team ad	Disagree with ideas not people	Other point of view
10	Making metaphors	Extended projects	Expert jigsaw	Mrs. Potter's questions	Reach consensus	5 to fist

B - Application of the group investigation information builds in higher-order thinking.
U - The jigsaw unites the members as they rely on each other to help complete the assignment.
I - Individual criteria insures individual learning by forcing students to state their reasoning.
L - P.M.I. allows time to look over and discuss all aspects of the lesson.
D - Reaching consensus gives students practice in using their social skills.

Next, select appropriate strategies from the list of micro-skills for thinking.

MICRO-SKILLS

CRITICAL THINKING SKILLS	CREATIVE THINKING SKILLS
1. Attributing	1. Brainstorming
2. Comparing/Contrasting	2. Visualizing
3. Classifying	3. Personifying
4. Sequencing	4. Inventing
5. Prioritizing	5. Associating Relationships
6. Drawing Conclusions	6. Inferring
7. Determining Cause/Effect	7. Generalizing
8. Analyzing for Bias	8. Predicting
9. Analyzing for Assumptions	9. Hypothesizing
10. Solving for Analogies	10. Making Analogies
11. Evaluating	11. Dealing with Ambiguity & Paradox
12. Decision Making	12. Problem Solving

With the cooperative elements in mind, explain the project to the students. In small-group investigation they will explore the topic "In Defense of Human Rights," and with their groups they will present a five-minute snippet to the class. The purpose of each presentation is to delineate a particular right of human beings that has been abused throughout history. The scenarios should project an empathetic viewpoint. Humor may be used. Good taste and appropriateness should be part of the grading criteria.

After the presentations, each student is responsible for **applying** information presented into a paper on a human rights position other than the one researched by his/her group. In other words, they must gather information from the other groups' presentations in order to formulate their individual positions on human rights issues.

As a class, **brainstorm** a number of human rights issues (e.g., our own bill of rights, right to bear children, choose own spouse, hostages, treatment of mentally ill, censorship, POWs, homelessness, free speech, citizenship, assembly, discrimination, free elections).

Group Investigation Step I: *Pose the Big Question and Form Groups by Topics of Interest*

> Instruct students to form their small groups according to topics of interest. Limit the groups to three or four students each. Suggest that each team create a group name to designate its topic.

Group Investigation Step II: *Identify the Inquiry Problem and Plan How to Research*

Using the **jigsaw** model for group investigation, have the teams discuss and plan their research procedures. Be sure the groups include a variety of sources for gathering information and **visualizing** past abuses of human rights.

Group Investigation Step III: *Divide up the Work and Gather Information*

Have group members take individual responsibility for specific pieces of the whole project. Have group checkers collect completed assignments and data from the various members. Have groups set a date, time and place to share their various segments.

Group Investigation Step IV: *Synthesize, Summarize and Prepare a Report*

Proceeding with the Sharan and Sharan Group Investigation Model, have student teams reassemble with their respective pieces of information. In the jigsaw format, as each person shares his/her "piece," care is taken in *how* that sharing is done. This is really the "teachable moment," when each member teaches the other members of the group. Remind students that each member is responsible for learning *all* the pieces of information as they fit them together into a total picture, their presentations.

Group Investigation Step V: *a) Present by Groups*

After reaching **consensus** on a format for presenting, have student groups present their "In Defense of Human Rights" pieces to the class.

Require students to fill in observation sheets to use as reference prompters when evaluating the information and writing their papers. Or you may want to videotape the presentations.

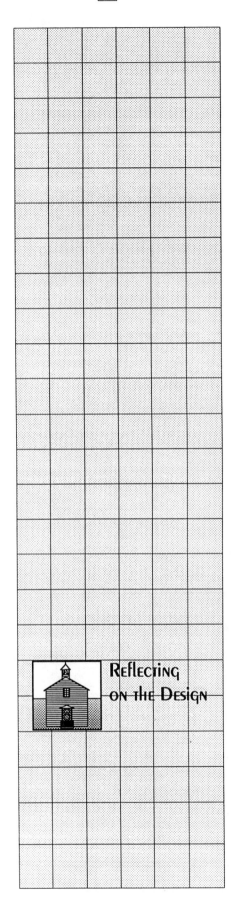

Reflecting on the Design

Group Investigation Step V: *b) Evaluate*

For affective processing, discuss the following question within the small groups:

How did your feelings influence your performance?

To process the social skills, have students describe an instance when their behavior infringed on someone else's rights.

For cognitive processing, use the human graph to take readings on the issues discussed in this lesson. Have students display their intensity of feelings using the ratings *agree, believe it, convince others, die for it,* as they **evaluate** their thinking by stating their **individual criteria for their decisions**.

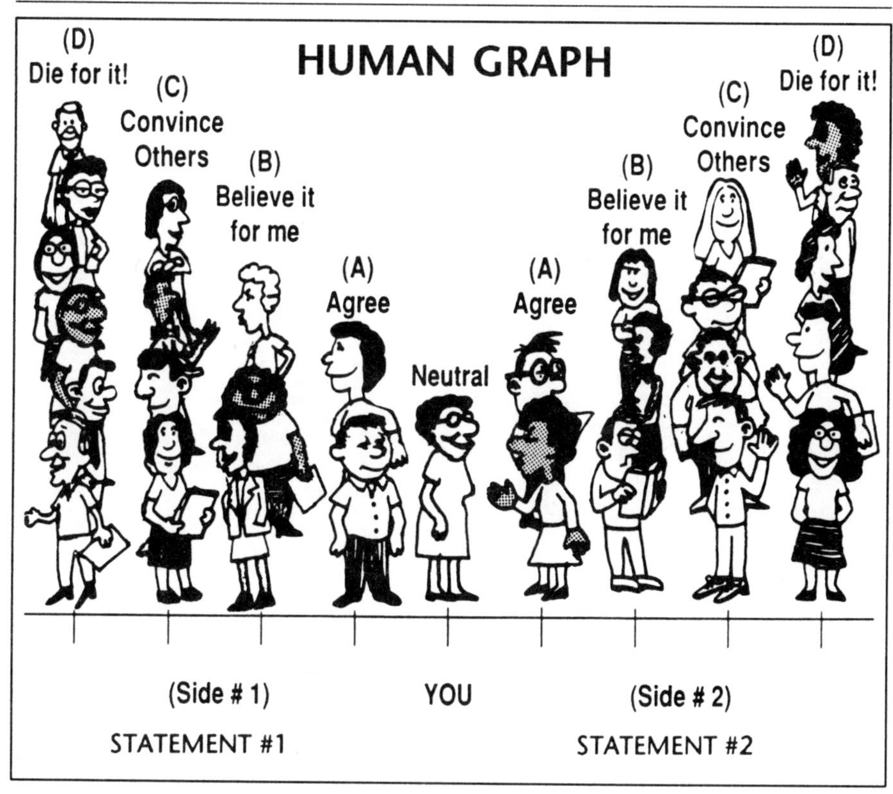

ISSUES

1. hostages
2. homelessness
3. mentally ill
4. POWs
5. free speech
6. free elections
7. citizenship
8. censorship

(Elaborate on the topics)

For metacognitive processing, evaluate Sharan and Sharan's Group Investigation Model with a **PMI** chart:

GROUP INVESTIGATION	
PLUS (+)	
MINUS (-)	
INTERESTING (?)	

☐ ☐ ☐

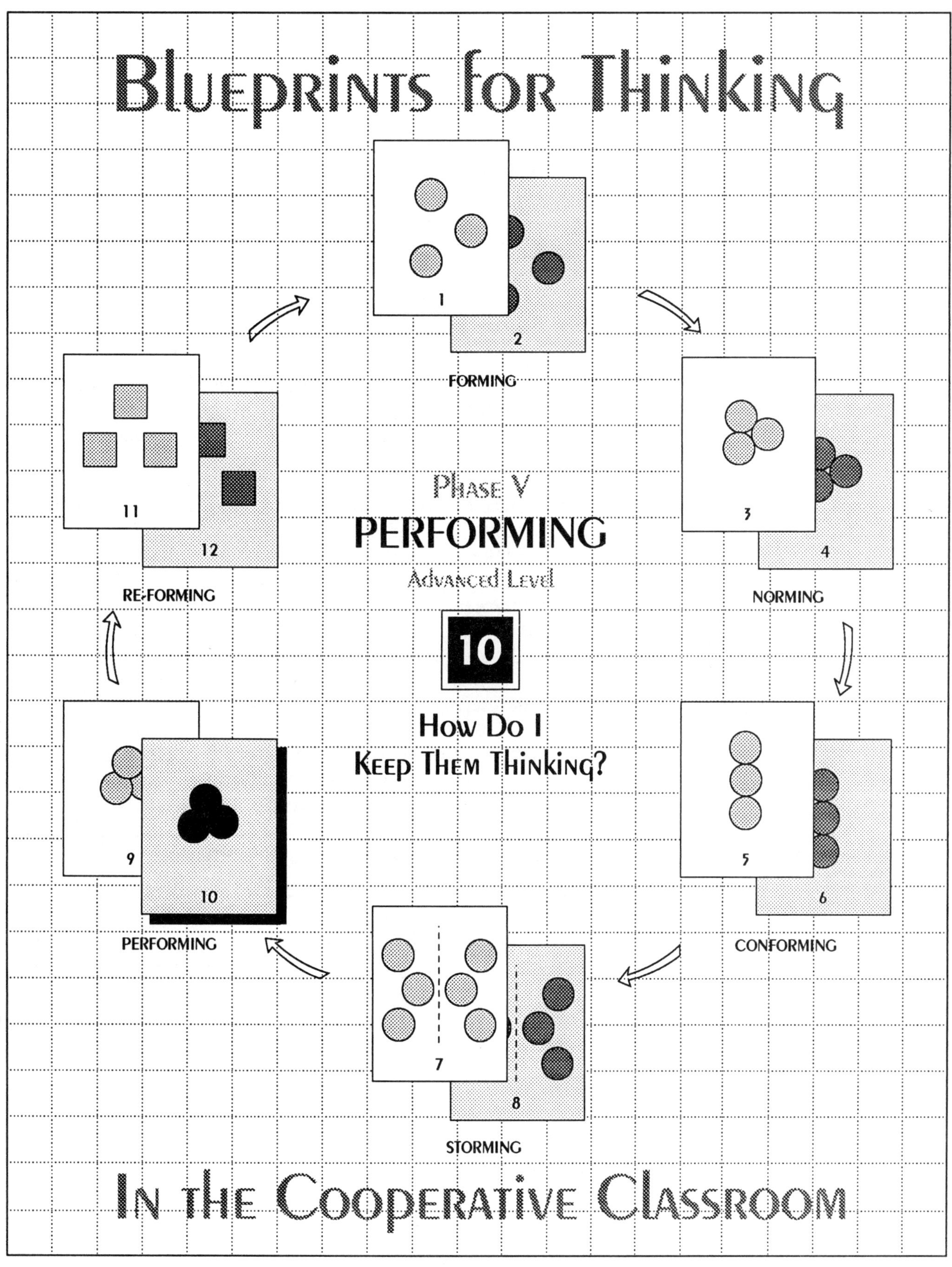
Blueprints for Thinking
1
2
FORMING
3
4
NORMING
5
6
CONFORMING
7
8
STORMING
9
10
PERFORMING
11
12
RE-FORMING
Phase V
PERFORMING
Advanced Level
10
How Do I
Keep Them Thinking?
In the Cooperative Classroom

Phase V:
PERFORMING
Advanced

How Do I Keep Them Thinking?

We have in our thinkery, a well-experienced power to think ourselves out of trials and difficulties.
—F.R. Feland

Draft

Once students are familiar with the Three-Story Intellect model for gathering, processing and applying information, the groundwork is laid for infusing complexity into the group tasks.

In the *performing* phase, as part of the small-group process cycle, students are performing to high expectations in the high-challenge classroom. Group members work to meet the explicit and implicit expectations. They accept the challenges. In fact, students know when rigor is required in their thinking and they relish it.

As students accept the Three-Story Intellect of high expectations, a hierarchy of complex thinking behaviors is introduced and practiced as the various opportunities for group work occur. This hierarchy (or taxonomy) of cognitive behavior begins with micro-skills, compounds into macro-processes and moves toward metacognitive behavior.

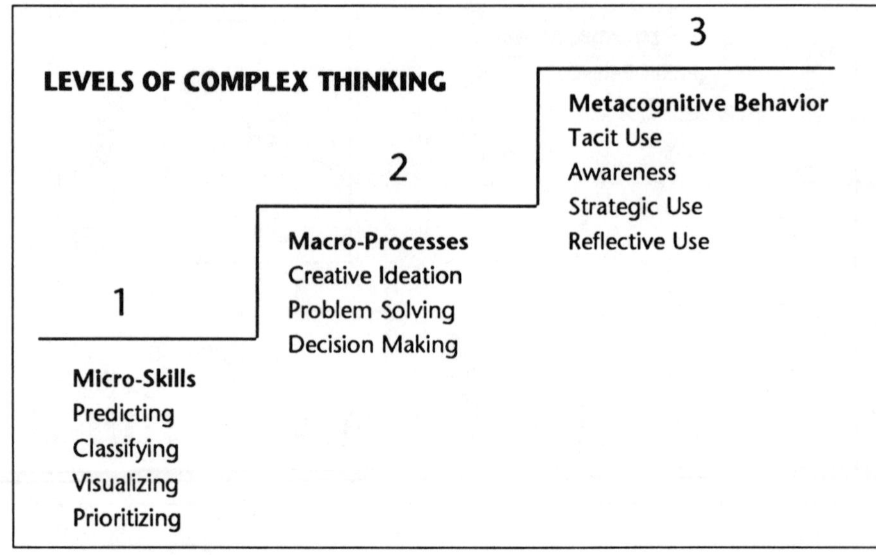

Paralleling the Three-Story Intellect, micro-skills, macro-processes and metacognitive behavior provide a broader frame to the instructional design.

To keep groups working well, set expectations for all students to achieve success with high-level thinking tasks. Do this consistently in the classroom to move groups toward higher-order thinking in all tasks. They conform to expectations, so set them high. Begin with the micro-skills in manageable chunks, but proceed to the problem-solving processes as rapidly as possible. It is at this level, when students are calling upon their micro-skills, that mental processing reaches the complex level. It is also at this problem-solving stage that the group's cooperation reaches new heights. The group members *need* each other to succeed with complex thinking tasks and the "sink or swim together" attitude sets in naturally. They become high-functioning, smoothly performing groups.

As the move toward the macro-processes of problem solving elevates student motivation for cooperative involvement, the metacognitive stage guarantees future application and transfer of these dispositions. For it is at the metacognitive level of thinking that the mental procedures which are there for use across content and into life situations are explicitly brought forward.

All three levels of higher-order thinking are needed if groups are to continue successfully in the classroom. The complex tasks command a "think tank" attitude by all participants.

□ MICRO-SKILLS

Specs

Micro-skills, in the cognitive hierarchy, encompass a spectrum of explicit thinking skills. Frequently, these micro-skills are labeled either critical thinking skills or creative thinking skills.

Micro-skills labeled as *critical thinking* require mental processing that is *analytical and/or evaluative in nature.* Micro-skills labeled as *creative* trigger mental processing that is *generative or productive* in nature. Both types of mental processes are needed to problem solve and make decisions. A more extensive list of typical micro-skills, critical and creative, are shown below.

MICRO-SKILLS			
CRITICAL THINKING SKILLS		CREATIVE THINKING SKILLS	
Attributing	Determining Cause/Effect	Brainstorming	Generalizing
Comparing/Contrasting	Analyzing for Bias	Visualizing	Predicting
Classifying	Analyzing for Assumptions	Personifying	Hypothesizing
Sequencing	Solving for Analogies	Inventing	Making Analogies
Prioritizing	Evaluating	Associating Relationships	Dealing with Ambiguity and Paradox
Drawing Conclusions		Inferring	

Explicit instruction in the micro-skills helps students build a repertoire for *selective* use when groups attack the tasks assigned in their course work.

□ MACRO-PROCESSES

It is unlikely that the mind defines micro-skills as separate and disparate procedures. This distinction is made only to discuss the skills in a magnified manner as they are taught explicitly to students. Later, when student proficiency is developed with the micro-skills, various combinations are processed simultaneously as skilled thinkers navigate a particular situation or problem. For example, a thinker may brainstorm and prioritize simultaneously.

When the micro-skills are strung together in a series or simultaneous networking system, students enter the next hierarchical level of thinking, *macro-processes*. It is in this stage that students critically analyze the problem, brainstorm to generate alternatives, set criteria and evaluate the choices to make a final decision.

This stringing together of the micro-skills for thinking is how we parlay discrete and separate mental procedures into more complex cognitive networks—the macro-processes needed for problem solving. In the Venn diagram on the opposite page, the micro-skills of creative and critical thinking are used in clusters for problem solving and decision making.

□ METACOGNITIVE BEHAVIOR

At the highest level of the cognitive hierarchy, in fact "beyond" the cognitive in its purest sense, is metacognitive behavior. *Meta*cognitive, meaning beyond the cognitive, implies that at this level one is not thinking about the problem itself, but rather about how to solve the problem or how the problem has been approached. More clearly, when students engage in metacognitive behavior, they focus on thinking *about* their thinking and not so much on the problem itself. This is the "ah ha" processing that helps students talk about and "make sense" of their learning and behavior *(see "ah ha" processing map for making sense, page 333).

For example, when a person recites a memorized piece, he/she is demonstrating cognitive processing. However, when that person begins to explain *how* he/she learned the piece by rote, metacognitive thinking takes over. This metacognitive level promotes transfer through awareness and discussion of use. A helpful tool for distinguishing the various types of reflective processing is the "Are you cooperating, today?" poster (chapter 1, page 5).

The following blueprints model the *micro*, *macro* and *meta* components of complex thinking tasks designed for lessons in the elementary, middle and secondary classrooms. These are prototypes to follow when planning additional thinking tasks (see how micro-skills are clustered in macro-processes on opposite page).

□ □ □

Update your task sequence on page 348.

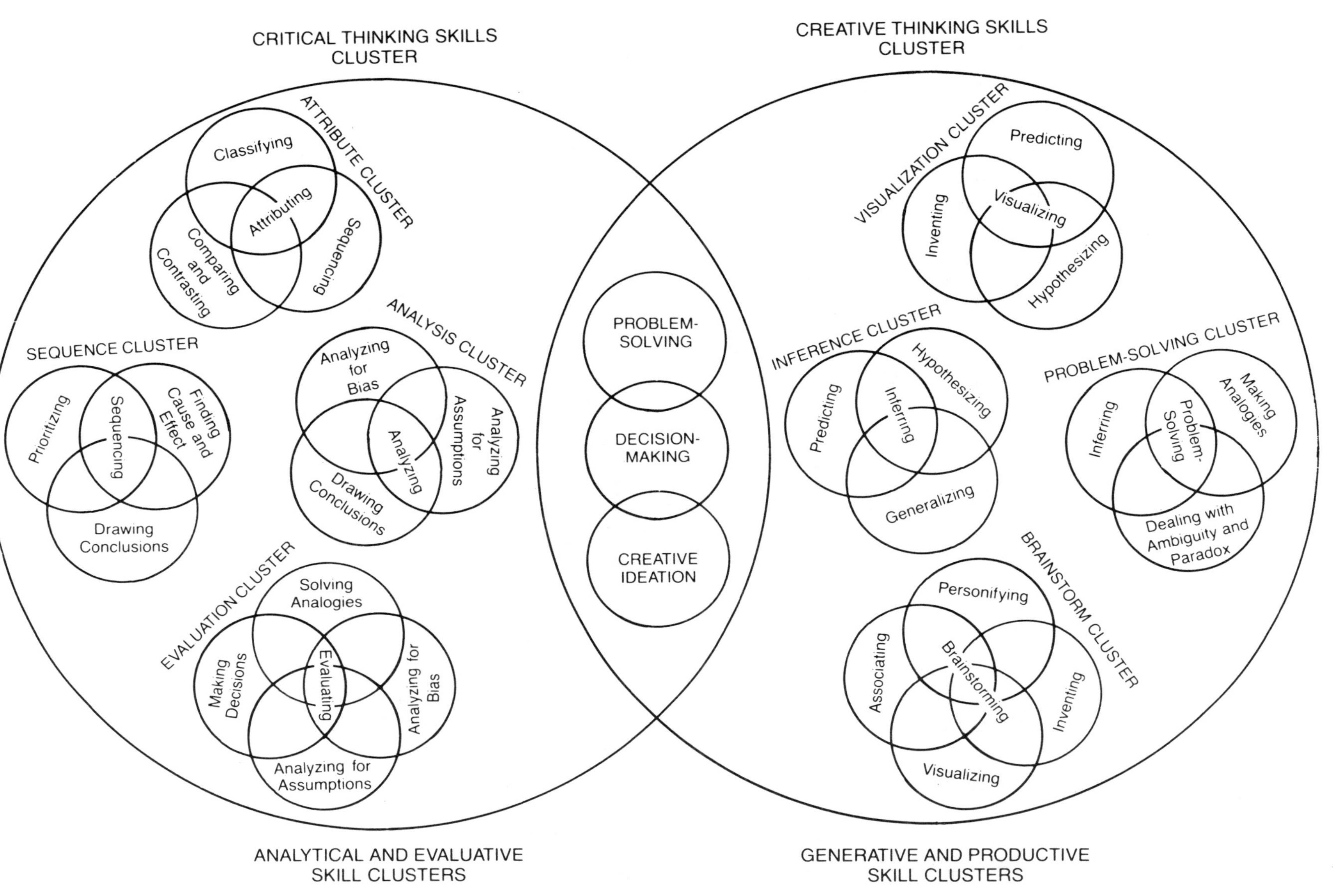
THE CLUSTER CURRICULUM
CRITICAL THINKING SKILLS CLUSTER
CREATIVE THINKING SKILLS CLUSTER
ATTRIBUTE CLUSTER
Classifying
Attributing
Comparing and Contrasting
Sequencing
SEQUENCE CLUSTER
Prioritizing
Sequencing
Finding Cause and Effect
Drawing Conclusions
ANALYSIS CLUSTER
Analyzing for Bias
Analyzing
Analyzing for Assumptions
Drawing Conclusions
EVALUATION CLUSTER
Solving Analogies
Making Decisions
Evaluating
Analyzing for Bias
Analyzing for Assumptions
PROBLEM-SOLVING
DECISION-MAKING
CREATIVE IDEATION
VISUALIZATION CLUSTER
Predicting
Inventing
Visualizing
Hypothesizing
INFERENCE CLUSTER
Predicting
Inferring
Hypothesizing
Generalizing
PROBLEM-SOLVING CLUSTER
Inferring
Problem-Solving
Making Analogies
Dealing with Ambiguity and Paradox
BRAINSTORM CLUSTER
Personifying
Associating
Brainstorming
Inventing
Visualizing
ANALYTICAL AND EVALUATIVE SKILL CLUSTERS
GENERATIVE AND PRODUCTIVE SKILL CLUSTERS

MEETING MAGNETS

In the *micro-skills* phase of the introductory lesson on magnets and their characteristics, use this letter to gather objects and items for experimenting.

> Dear Parents,
>
> Please help us gather objects from around the house, garage and attic that will help us in our science experiments with magnets.
>
> Send small items that we can keep in our lab (nuts, bolts, screws, nails, bottle caps, corks, clothespins, etc.)
>
> Thank you,
> Grade 1

Have students *predict* which items are likely to be attracted to the magnets and why. Next, experiment with the assorted items to find out which *are* attracted to the magnets and which *are not*. Record the results on the tally sheet next to the appropriate item (word or picture).

Draw items and indicate YES if attracted to magnets or NO if not attracted to magnets.		
1 YES NO	2 YES NO	3 YES NO
4 YES NO	5 YES NO	6 YES NO
7 YES NO	8 YES NO	9 YES NO
10 YES NO	11 YES NO	12 YES NO

In the *macro-processing* phase, to *synthesize* and *analyze,* have students discuss with a partner some rules about magnets. Then have them compare the rules with other partners (using *metacognitive processing*). Rewrite, revise and evaluate the results as a class.

To process for the affective, have students tell:

What was hardest to do . . . .

What was easiest to do . . . .

To process the social skills, have students talk about how they helped each other during the task.

To process the cognitive, have students discuss the predictions they had prior to the experiment and if they were good ones or not.

For *metacognitive processing,* have students talk about a "something" they learned in this lesson that they can use somewhere else.

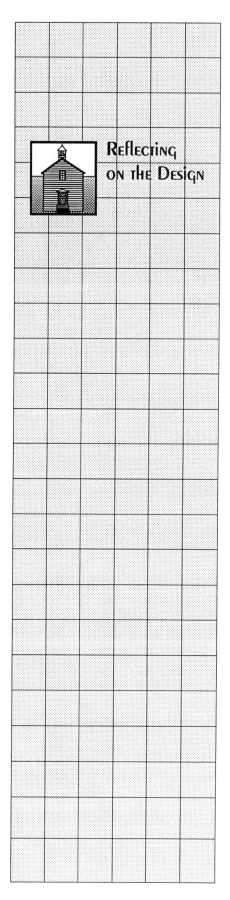

☐ ☐ ☐

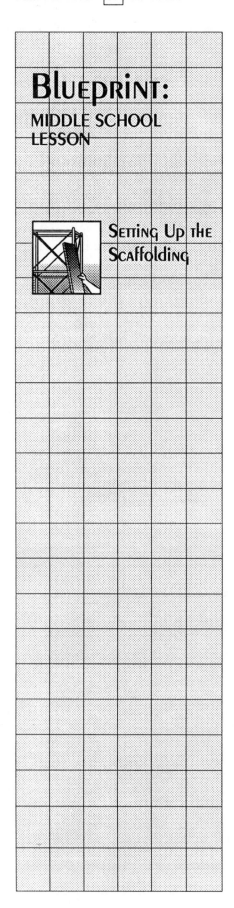

THE GOOD, GOOD STORY

In working with the *micro-skills,* use the "Good, Good Story" to focus on the skills of *brainstorming* and *analyzing* for precision of language. Read the story and discuss the overuse of the word *good.*

THE GOOD, GOOD STORY

The GOOD boy got a GOOD grade on his GOOD report. However, his GOOD friend did not feel very GOOD that day. So when the GOOD boy told his GOOD friend about his GOOD report, his GOOD friend did not reply in a GOOD manner.

Instead, his usually GOOD mood was not so GOOD and his reply was not as GOOD as expected. Luckily, the GOOD boy, who was always GOOD, just used his GOOD sense and took the not-so-GOOD remark in GOOD humor.

It was a GOOD thing too because just as the GOOD boy broke into a GOOD smile, the GOOD principal of the GOOD school appeared. He nodded hello as all GOOD principals do and went about his GOOD tasks.

Needless to say, the GOOD boy had a GOOD day and his GOOD friend had a GOOD lesson that day. Be GOOD to your GOOD friends and they will be GOOD to you. And in the end, that will be GOOD for all.

Working the Crew

In cooperative groups of three, have students assign the roles recorder, reporter and observer. Responding in turn, students should use the micro-skill of brainstorming to list overused words. These should include words that appear frequently in their own writing. To prime the pump, suggest words such as *nice, said, a lot, like* and *then.*

OVERUSED WORDS	
LIST	RANKING
nice	
said	
a lot	
like	
then	
also	
everybody	
always	

After compiling the list of words, ask students in each group to use the micro-skill of *prioritizing* to rank them from the *most* overused to the *least* overused (in their opinion). Note, this ranking is based on their use and overuse of the words and is a somewhat subjective ranking. Next, have groups select one word to slot into a story similar to the "Good, Good Story."

Notice that the micro-skills used in this first part of the lesson involve brainstorming, which is a creative, generative skill, and prioritizing, which is an analytical and evaluative critical thinking skill.

Now, to take the micro-skills into a problematic situation in which students are required to process the information as they interact with it, the *macro-processing* stage of cognitive instruction begins.

Remaining with their original task groups of three, have each group write a progressive story or tale in the style of the "Good, Good Story." Instruct students to:

1. Select an overused word to use for slotting into their writing of the "Good, Good Story."
2. Use an ABC order to structure sentences, having the recorder begin with *A.* He/she uses the selected word at least three times in a sentence that begins with the letter *A.*
3. The recorder passes the paper to the next group member who must now start a sentence with the letter *B* and include the overused word at least three times.

4. At this point, the story might look like this:

Selected Word – Nice
Although a nice man in a nice brown suit was having a nice breakfast in a nice diner, a not-so-nice event occurred.
Before the nice man could think of a nice way to help the victim who seemed so nice, a nice young man appeared with a nice fresh roll.
Calling his nice name...

5. Continue the procedure until each group member has had a least two turns and until the story is complete.
6. Note that students must piece a number of micro-skills together in this macro-process stage as they synthesize elements. Each student must brainstorm with fluency and demonstrate flexibility in shifting thoughts as the story line shifts with each member's added sentence. *Analysis* is required as each "author" evaluates which letter to use and whether or not the sentence makes sense.

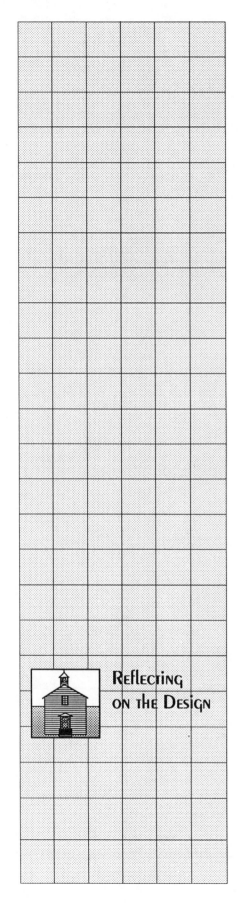

Reflecting on the Design

To sample students' feelings about the task use a PMI chart to talk about what they liked and didn't like, or comments or questions they have.

PRECISION OF LANGUAGE

P(+)	
M(–)	
I(?)	

To process the social skills, have students discuss a point where they got "stuck" in the task and how they got "unstuck" with someone's help.

Using a continuum to process the cognitive content, have students quickly brainstorm words to slot in for each extreme; focus on the concept of precision of language.

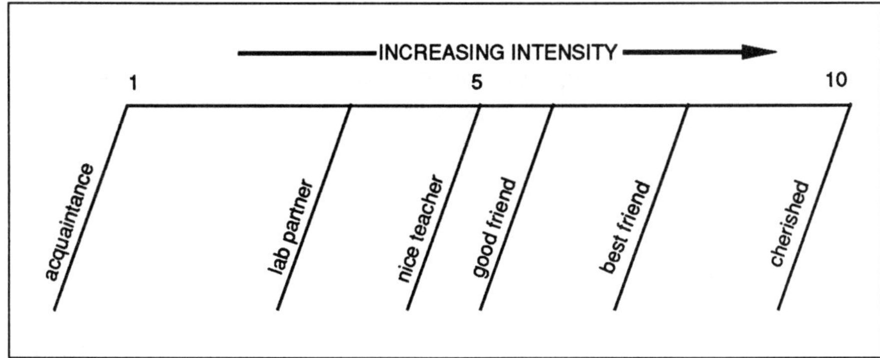

To process metacognitively, ask students to agree or disagree with the following statement:

Not being precise with language can get you into trouble.

Next, have them do a log entry with this lead-in:

By stringing several thinking skills together I _______________.

☐ ☐ ☐

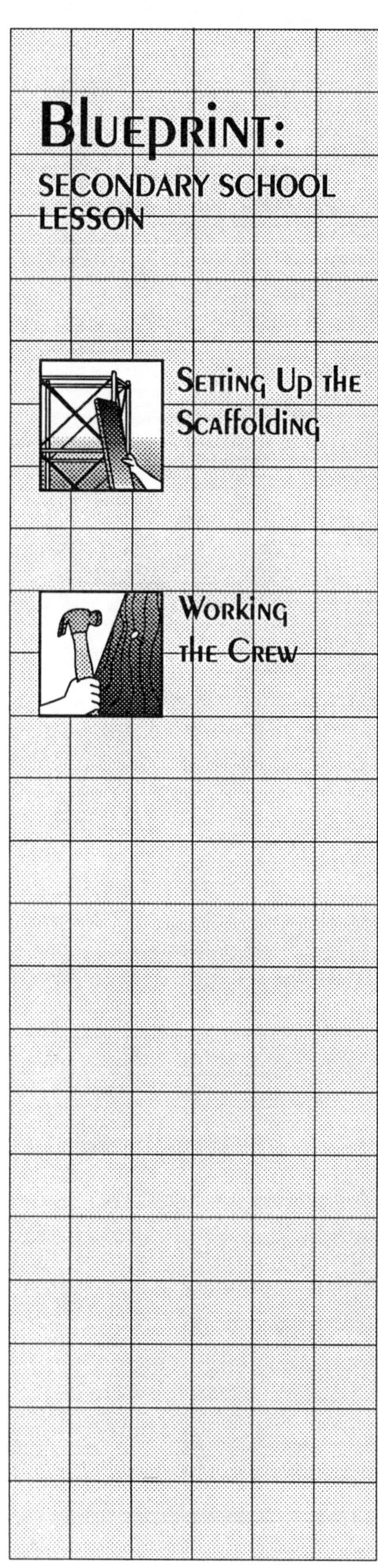

DESIGN A DECADE

As a culminating unit in contemporary American history, tell the students they have to prepare a metaphorical presentation of a decade for review. Place students in groups of three with the following roles:

Scribe: Keeps records.
Historian: Seeks resources.
Orator: Reports findings.

Using the *micro-skill* of *brainstorming*, have each group of three complete the following chart by generating three words they associate with each decade. This is an initial focus activity to prime the pump, but books and other resources may be used.

LIST THREE WORDS FOR EACH DECADE.*				RANK
1900-09	__________,	__________,	__________	______
1910s	__________,	__________,	__________	______
1920s	__________,	__________,	__________	______
1930s	__________,	__________,	__________	______
1940s	__________,	__________,	__________	______
1950s	__________,	__________,	__________	______
1960s	__________,	__________,	__________	______
1970s	__________,	__________,	__________	______
1980s	__________,	__________,	__________	______
1990s	__________,	__________,	__________	______
2000-09	__________,	__________,	__________	______

*page 334

Following the brainstorming and upon completing the chart, each group should *prioritize* the decades according to their favorites (ranking the list).

Using the group rankings, assign or have students select a decade for their design project. Next, have students quickly select an identifying name for their group that indicates their chosen decade.

DECADE	GROUP NAME
1900-1909	________________
1910s	________________
1920s	________________
1930s	________________
1940s	________________
1950s	________________
1960s	________________
1970s	________________
1980s	________________
1990s	________________
2000-2009	________________

Using the *macro-processing* skill of *problem solving,* students should use any and all resources necessary to research, gather and review information about their decades. Instruct students to select 10 to 12 "snapshots" or key elements from their decades.

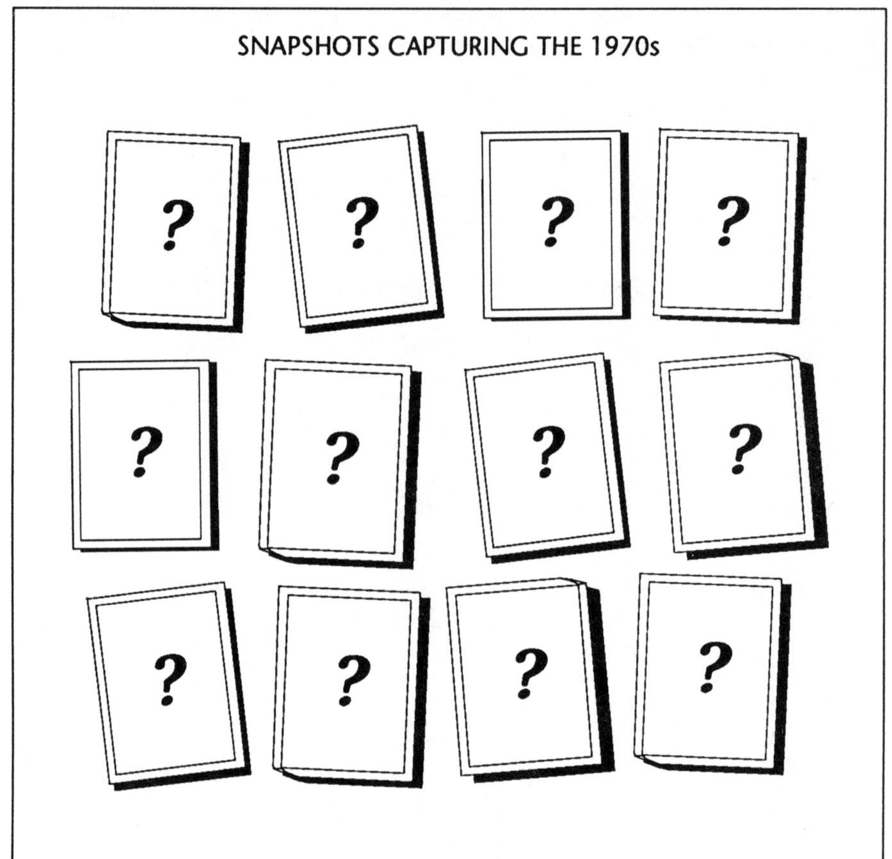

Now, after groups have decided on 10 to 12 snapshots that depict the significant events or moments of their decades, ask the team members to "bridge" the snapshots by providing connectors between them. For example:

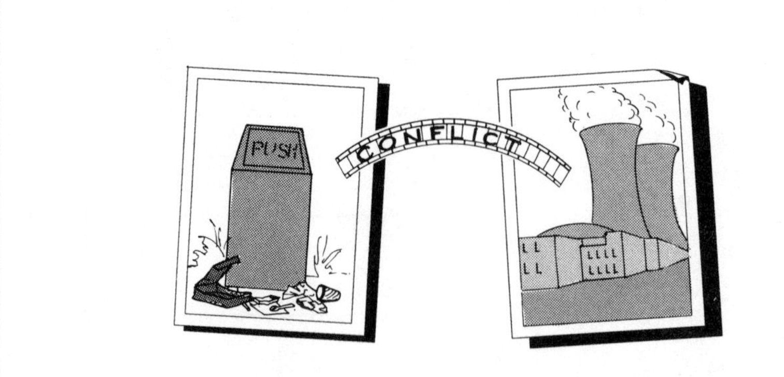

In the 1970s, environmental issues such as litterbugs were a major focus. Nuclear power plants were also springing up amidst major controversies. A bridge or connector between these two might be the idea of conflict or opposing ideas.

Bridges provide a synthesizing process to the snapshot activity. Instead of having 10 or 12 isolated snapshots "floating" around, bridges allow teams to find relationships between seemingly disparate ideas. In bridging the snapshots, students begin to see patterns or overriding themes that emerge.

After bridging their snapshots, teams are able to sift out key attributes of their decades. These key attributes help members create extended metaphors for their decades (using the *metacognitive processing* stage) when they prepare to present their decades to the class.

After processing and analyzing the critical attributes of a decade through the bridging snapshots activity, have each team use the key components to create an extended metaphor representing its decade.

For example, the decade of the 1930s might be compared to a roller coaster ride that has gotten out of control. Just as the stock market climbed precariously to the top and then suddenly crashed, so too could a roller coaster.

Once student teams have created their metaphors, instruct each team to:

1. Use its metaphor and develop comparisons for each snapshot.
2. Illustrate the metaphor on large paper with appropriately labeled parts.
3. Prepare to present the metaphor to the class.

For example, if the decade is compared to a parade, then the various elements depicting the significant events of the decade can be matched to the standard components of a parade. The metaphor model can be virtually anything that is a concrete, tangible concept that lends itself to easy comparison.

For affective processing, have each student team create a song that reflects how the members feel about their decade.

To process the social skills, ask students to describe how they helped each other make "bridges" as they tried to finish the task.

For cognitive processing, have students take their 10 to 12 snapshots and write an "equation" that includes all of the elements depicted in the snapshots.

For metacognitive processing, ask students to reflect on how they used the following skills and processes in completing their projects:

- Micro-skills of thinking were used . . . .
- Macro-processes of problem solving and decision making were required . . . .
- Transfer of ideas occurred . . . .

□ □ □

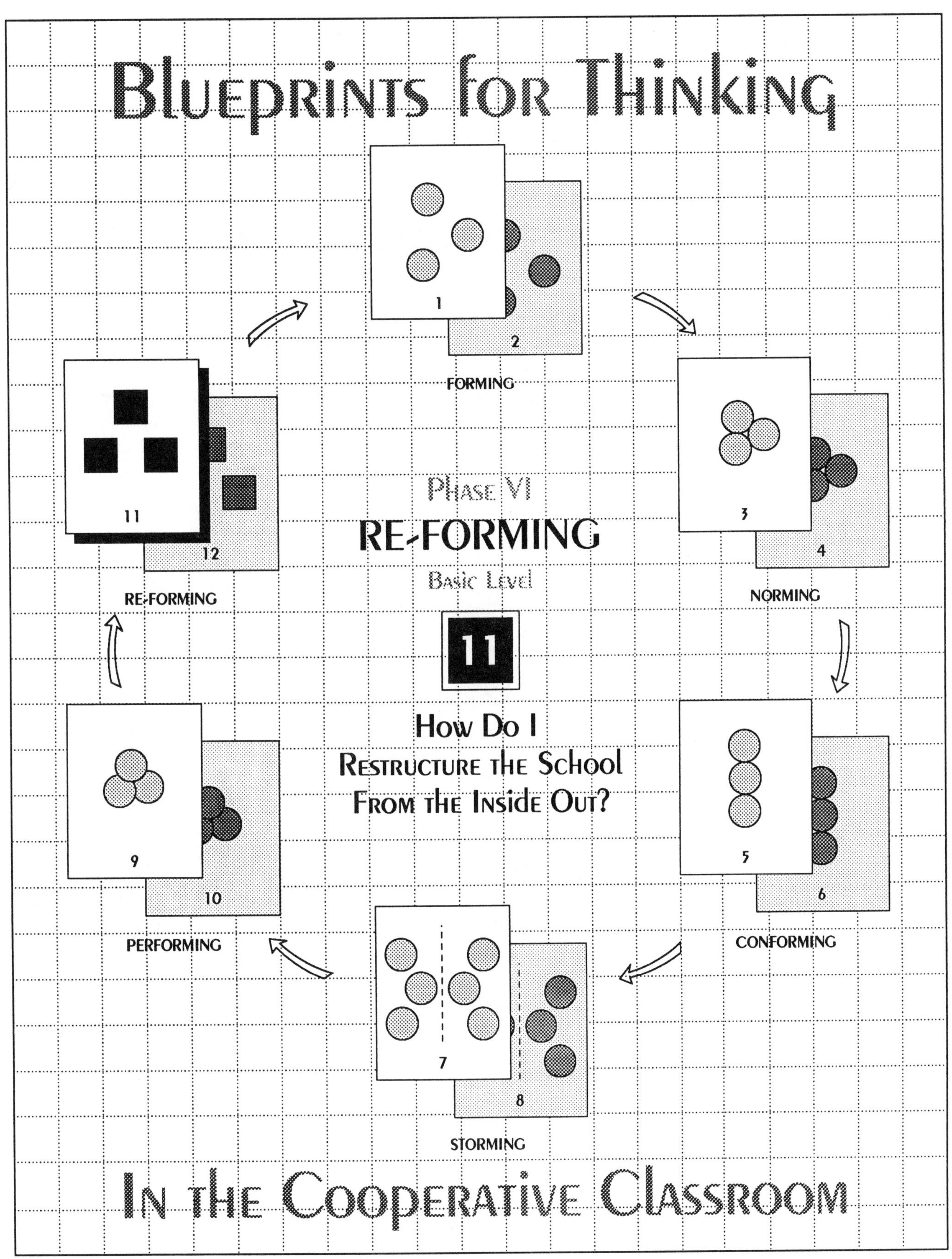
Blueprints for Thinking
1
2
FORMING
3
4
NORMING
5
6
CONFORMING
7
8
STORMING
9
10
PERFORMING
11
12
RE-FORMING
Phase VI
RE-FORMING
Basic Level
11
How Do I
Restructure the School
From the Inside Out?
In the Cooperative Classroom

PHASE VI:
RE-FORMING
BASIC

How Do I Restructure the School From the Inside Out?

Ours is a time of pioneering . . . The foundations of the new building of humankind are deepening . . . The vitality of youth and the inspiration of teachers will help to create educational forms for public service. —M.C. Richards

Draft

Every decade is marked by failed attempts to force change on American schools from the outside in. Failing to learn from history, the well-meaning reformers pressed one idea after another onto the people in the schoolhouse. Each time the people in the schoolhouse fought off the great ideas and continued as they did before.

Specs

☐ THE '60s: THE ROMANTIC REVOLUTION

The 1960s might be best characterized as a romantic revolution in American education. Disenchanted with what Carl Rogers labeled the "pour and store" approach to instruction (pour in the information until every head is full), Postman, Weingartner, Kozol and others attacked the rigid formalism that trapped youngsters in a boring lock-step sequence of fact-filled learning. Building on the British Infant School model, the 1960s' advocates of reform designed open classrooms in which young learners could feel free to explore, to inquire and to experiment. Most of all, children could be free to follow their natural instincts for learning, unfettered by the chains of letter grades, dull textbooks or even the confinement of walls. Teachers, who were freed from the constraints of bells, curricula guides and attendance books, would facilitate learning and encourage students to follow their natural predispositions to learn and grow.

Down came the walls! Out went letter grades! In came activity learning, self-concept programs with values clarification and affective education. Whatever *stimulated* children to learn was good. Whatever held back their learning was bad. The Romantics were alive and well!

☐ THE '70s: BACK TO BASICS

As with most revolutions, especially of the romantic variety, excess became a troublesome problem. And there were excesses. So mad was the desire to abandon any method or approach that might hamper a child's natural instincts to learn, that some teachers lost all sight of the need for students to have reading instruction or to follow a set curriculum in math or writing. If the child felt like sleeping all day, that was *OK*. If a high schooler wanted to put 100 percent of his time into making a film about beach balls, that was fine. In these scenarios, how a student felt became the all-out rallying cry. The affective focus monopolized the educational lens and the mind was relegated to the peripherals.

In the late 1970s the reaction set in. Concerned with declining test scores, increased drop-out rates and illiteracy, the voices for accountability began to speak out. First came minimal competency tests, to ensure that the basics of reading and writing were taught. Research on direct instruction became a prize for those who wanted to increase accountability through teacher evaluation. Hunter's interpretation of direct instruction became almost a natural model on the "right way" to teach. Instead of the dynamic prototype for instruction in which the teacher led the way toward excellence through skillful decision-making and skilled technique in the science of teaching, a simplistic recipe, "Seven Steps (To Heaven)," became a bastardized evaluation checksheet—all in the name of accountability.

☐ THE '80s: TOP-DOWN REFORM

By the 1980s, accountability was in full swing. Early in the decade, led by the report "A Nation At Risk," there were 32 calls for reform from educational policy makers throughout the country. Bolstered by research on effective schools, legislators added laws that set standards for student-learner outcomes and required district "report cards" to measure learners' objectives in reading, math, science and social studies. Public reporting by districts kept school personnel hopping in attempts to exceed the standards and to publicly "shine." Mandates from the state level dictated policy to districts, with accountability built in for teacher training. Teachers, colleges and departments of education were burdened with evaluating the basic skills of teachers and teacher-trainees. Districts were required to file fully-developed, long-term staff development plans. District funding, tied directly to the acceptance of the plan by the state, once again amplified the top-down reform and played havoc with district resources in their attempts to meet the state demands. Top-down reform became known as "Band-Aid reform" in which nothing of essence really changed; the sores of education were simply covered. On the surface, they looked better. Educators at every level scurried to make visible changes in schools so that the nation would no longer be "at risk."

☐ THE '90s: DECADE OF DÉJÀ VU /DARING DESIGNS

In response to the top-down reforms of the 1980s, the decade of the 1990s is sensing a grassroots movement, a bubbling up from the rank and file, as the inevitable Arthur Schlesinger's-prophesized-30-year cycle suggests an unmistakable sense of a déjà vu:

> *déjà vu: the illusion of having previously experienced something actually being encountered for the first time*

To call the '90s the Decade of Déjà Vu may seem discouraging or a bit stagnating by some. But, indeed, just the opposite seems to be true. The Decade of Déjà Vu seems to suggest three exciting possibilities.

The first and inherently obvious implication of the déjà vu experience is the *revisiting* of some things previously entertained; in this case, it means revisiting almost every aspect of the educational scene, but in the very best sense of a return visit. As one views the curricula, the classroom, the school calendar, the daily school schedule, teacher preparation, school personnel, evaluation results and even the physical structure of the school itself, one senses the freshness of the air as from an opened window. This déjà vu carries the scent of spring-like newness with it.

The second implication noticed in the 1990s' Decade of Déjà Vu is the indelible mark of daring designs. While *restructuring* is a term ushered in from the late 1980s in *restructuring* versus *reform*—with restructure as a more powerful concept—the restructured school of the 1990s reflects daring designs. The schools of the '90s are restructured not by outside sources with well-intentioned mandates, but by *insiders*.

Finally, a third implication of the Decade of Déjà Vu is in the *renewal* of both skills and spirit. Following the "Back to Basics" and the "Top-Down Reform" years in which the scientific, technical side of teaching was heralded, the fresh breeze of the '90s brings a déja vu of the other side of teaching. The '90s reinforce that teaching is not only a science, but also an art. With this notion, the rawness of the scientific model is softened and parents, teachers and youngsters feel renewed, not only in the skills of parenting, teaching and learning, but also in spirit.

From each of the previously mandated efforts has come a clear message: the inside of our schools are peopled by the most knowledgeable, best- trained group of educators in the history of the world. In spite of outside interference from state and national officials, university professors, and other political pushers who know little about the practicalities of classroom life, these professionals have survived. They have done this by selective, common-sense decisions on what is best for students. They have done it in spite of the tremendous barriers and obstacles thrown up by the theoretical outsiders whose major driving concept has been the factory's assembly-line model of education.

If there will be any substantive change that provides the radical shift from the factory curriculum to the transfer curriculum, then it will come by honoring the professionals who people our classrooms.

FOUR DECADES OF EDUCATION REFORM	
The 1960s The Romantic Revolution	• Open classrooms • No grades • No walls • Team Teaching • Values Clarification • Humanistic Education • Student Exploration and Inquiry
The 1970s Back To Basics	• Reactionary Stance • Minimal Competency Tests • Public Law #94-142 • Effective Teaching Model (Hunter's Seven-Step Lesson Design) • Effective Schools Research • Accountability
The 1980s Top-Down Reform	• Student-Learner Objectives • State Mandated Tests • Outcomes-Based Educational Objectives • Teacher Evaluation • Public Reporting of Scores • State Reform (Band-Aid Reform)
The 1990s Decade of Déjà Vu and/or Daring Designs	• Déja Vu: Revisit, Restructure, Renew • Diversity, Collaborations, Partnerships • Integrated Curriculum • Shared Decision-Making • Lifelong Learning • Technology Comes of Age • Restructuring From the Inside Out

☐ TO REVISIT AND RESTRUCTURE

While the 1990s may be the Decade of Déjà Vu, it is also the Decade of Daring Designs as the school restructuring process bubbles up from the inside out. An illustration of this somewhat mixed metaphor provides a clear look at how the educational déjà vu gives at once the illusion of having previously experienced something in the traditional sense and yet at the same time, daring designs of something being encountered for the first time.

By comparing and contrasting the two ideas, déjà vu and daring designs, in reference to the 1990s, key attributes provide an easy analysis. To revisit education, one must look at:

The Structure: Architectural buildings and facilities
The School Calendar and Schedule: Calendar year as well as daily schedule
The Classroom: Groupings of students
The Curricula: Goals, organization, content and evaluation
The Personnel: Staff, students and community support
The Teacher Training: Preservice and inservice
The Results: Assessments and outcomes
Beyond the School Years: Lifelong learning

As depicted on the Venn diagram on the opposite page, revisiting the educational scene releases a spectrum of déjà vu visions.

To revisit . . .
. . . the *structure* of the school, the concept of a single building or one structure, is to shift to the 1990s' vision of the community as the school—businesses sharing their computer labs, their expertise and their high-tech training centers as well as providing funding for special-interest programs.
. . . the hub of the school system is to see a giant communications center with technological networks monopolizing the very heart of the building and large, adaptable areas filled with flexible furniture arrangements and hi-tech equipment.
. . . the neighborhood school is to consider the values system, where parents select appropriately from schools of real choice.

To revisit . . .
. . . *the school calendar* is to see the 45-15 Plan give way to a year-round calendar in which students and teachers have one extended vacation, a month off. Students gain the advantage of more time in class (like the Japanese model), and teachers have a month for in-depth professional development either at an on-site training facility or through professional channels of their choice.
. . . split-day sessions of years ago is to see *the daily schedule* shift to larger blocks of time to accommodate long-term, extended project work and cognitive/cooperative models in which students need time to think and solve problems. While the day begins earlier, with the pre-school accommodating working parents and setting the standard for the early starts, it also ends later.

To revisit . . .
. . . *the classroom* is to shift from graded classrooms to family clusters of primaries (ages 4 to 8), middle schoolers (ages 9 to 14) and secondaries (ages 15 to 18) as alternatives to instructional tracking.
. . . the mainstreamed classroom is to see heterogeneous groupings of students, with great diversity of the student populations in each room.

To revisit . . .
. . . *the curricula* is to see the shift from units of study to an integrated curriculum.

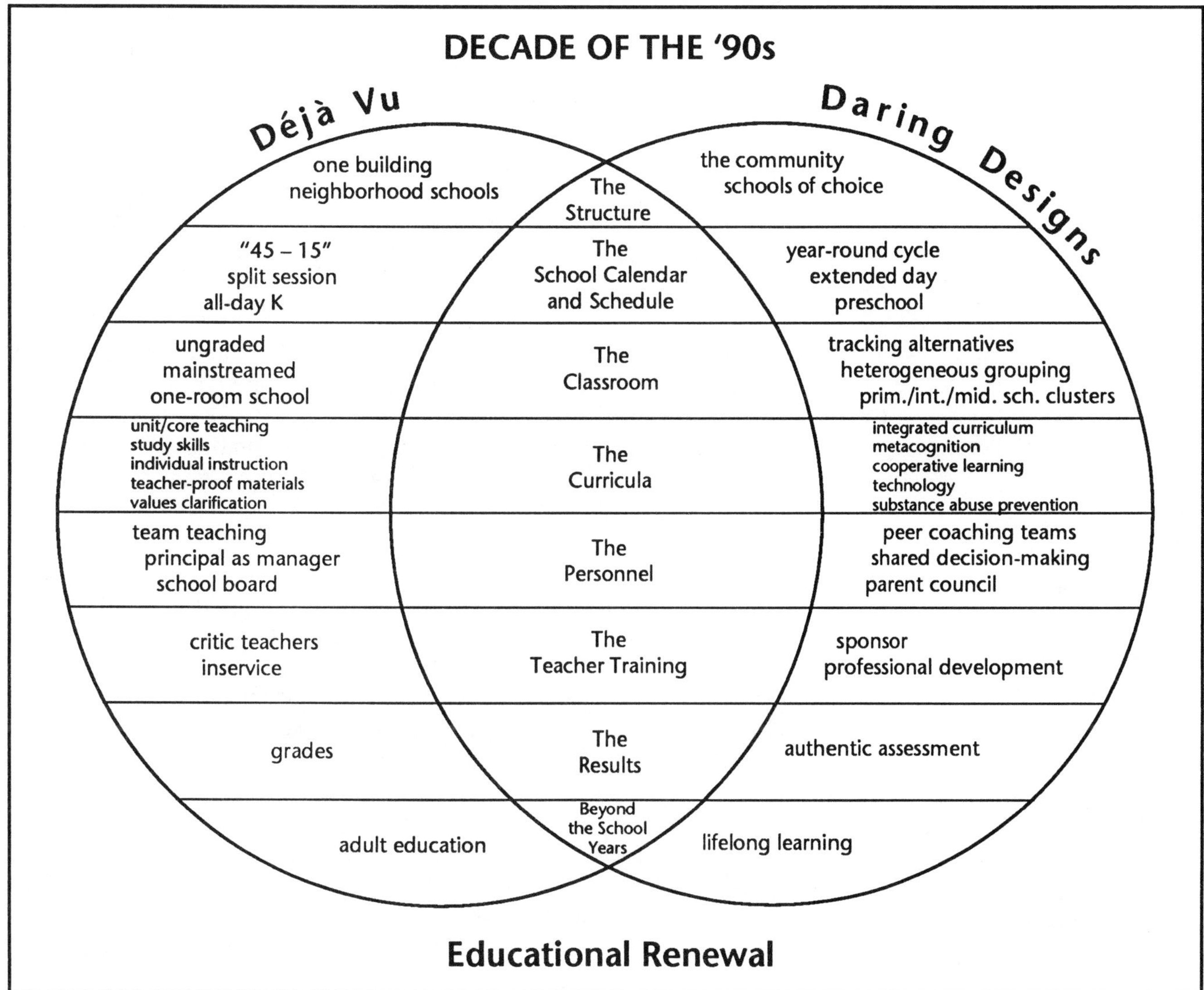

. . . study skills is to shift to the contemporary version called metacognitive processing.
. . . individualized instruction for meeting individual student needs is to shift to cooperative learning models that also meet individual needs.
. . . teacher-proof materials, disdained by all, is to see high-tech materials that provide instant feedback to both students and teacher-management systems.
. . . values clarification and humanistic education is to hear terms like self-esteem, decision making and choices.
. . . the curricula itself, is to shift from minute, specialized little boxes of information that overload the system to more encompassing disciplines: humanities, science, practical arts and fine arts. These broad umbrellas provide fertile ground for an integrative curricula approach.

To revisit . . .
. . . *the personnel* of the school, what was called team teaching with an emphasis on shared instructional loads, is to see a shift to peer coaching

with emphasis on supportive planning, observation and feedback among colleagues.
. . . the call for principals as instructional leaders is to shift toward a policy of shared decision-making at the building level.
. . . the school boards is to see them take on either the staidness of royal heads of states or shift toward the role of a more participatory parent council model. No longer do board members endorse recommendations from central office administrators. Now, the board members or council members "dig out" the data and make the decisions themselves.

To revisit . . .
. . . *the teacher training* is to shift subtly in practice, from the teacher as critic to the sponsor or mentor teacher in student teaching— new teacher induction models.
. . . scanty one-shot inservice days is to shift to comprehensive staff and professional development models that range from graduate courses to in-depth residency training seminars.

To revisit . . .
. . . *the results* of our efforts in the educational arena, static test scores, grades and standardized norms is to shift toward a more dynamic model of student evaluation in the concept of authentic assessment. Genuine analysis of student progress suggests that portfolios of work, response journals, thinking logs, artifacts and test scores all contribute to the emerging picture of student achievement.

And finally, to revisit . . .
. . . *the years beyond,* prior to and following the school years K-12, is to shift away from the 5-year-old entrance and capsulized model of adult education to a dynamic model of lifelong learning, with the pre-school years and the post-school years permeated by a never-ceasing learning environment.

Decade of Déjà Vu and/or Decade of Daring Designs? Both! Yes, definitely both! To revisit is to have the illusion of previously experiencing the educational phenomena, but somehow the designs seem more daring as something being encountered for the first time.

Perhaps that is because these are exciting times in education: tremendous bodies of research in the social models and in cognitive techniques are confirming and extending our effectiveness with learners. To be involved, intensely involved in the Decade of Déjà Vu—or as Yogi Berra says, "Déjà vu, all over again!"—is to *revisit, restructure* and *renew.*

☐ TO RESTRUCTURE AND RENEW . . .

To restructure from the *inside out,* to effect change from within the system, is the grassroots movement shuffling restlessly among the school ranks. To restructure from the inside out means change, either drastic or subtle, but real change at the classroom level. This change, even if in a single classroom, means curricular changes with a focus on the learner, the learning and the subsequent transfer of learning.

When focus is on the learner and the professionals who school the learner, there is, in fact, a redefinition of the restructuring process—change in schooling is not from the top down, not from the outside in, but from the inside out.

A single classroom may model a transfer curriculum, but that does not create a transfer culture in the school. By itself the classroom model has little chance to transform the school's culture from recall to transfer. The overwhelming array of mandated tests, fact-laden textbooks, repetitious seatwork assignments, homogeneous skill groups, tracked classes, minimal competency objectives and checklist performance evaluations that are characteristic of the recall curriculum make it difficult for the single teacher to imitate, let alone sustain any substantive change.

School leaders are finally learning John Goodlad's unsung song—the school, not the district, is the place of change. Ironically, though, the fastest track for substantive school change is the slow track.

While there are many ways to start, there are only a few keys needed for successful transition from recall to transfer in curriculum and instruction:

- ✓ A pre-structured peer and administrative support program.
- ✓ A volunteer instructional improvement program.
- ✓ A teacher-directed curriculum renewal project.
- ✓ A mentor program.
- ✓ A strategic plan for total transformation from the inside out.

A PRE-STRUCTURED PEER AND ADMINISTRATIVE PROGRAM The pre-structured program with peer and administrative support elements is the first component for success. In this concept, two to five teachers, working as a seed team in a school, commit to an application-based program in cooperative learning. Each teacher commits not only to participate in a minimum of 30 classroom hours, but also to develop the needed classroom start-up materials (role cards, bulletin boards, T-charts, etc.); to teach at least one cooperative lesson per day; to keep a daily progress log; to collect a portfolio of student products; and to meet at least one hour per week with participant peers who co-plan lessons, co-observe with feedback, evaluate lesson results and solve application problems together.

When possible, the principal or department chair participates as a member of this first team by teaching lessons and sharing results. At a minimum, the principal also schedules opportunities for team members to meet each week, arranges substitutes and divergence from the daily schedule, encourages risk-taking with daily lessons, supports team effort and above all, celebrates a teacher's willingness to innovate as more valuable than a teacher's adherence to 20-year-old lesson plans. Until the start-up group of five becomes a critical mass, "trying out" the first steps requires 110 percent of the instructional leader's blessing.

The more intense the applications over the first six months, and the more regular and supportive the peer assistance meetings, the more deeply the roots of cooperative learning sink into these first classrooms. Every act of encouragement the innovators learn in the classroom sessions applies doubly to their own application work. More importantly, the feelings of support generated by administrative assurance that the meeting logistics, substitutes and other support details are in place before the program starts, motivate more active involvement by each team member.

A VOLUNTEER INSTRUCTIONAL IMPROVEMENT PROGRAM Teachers, like other self-directed adult learners, feel their professionalism is encouraged when they choose how and what they learn. Mandated cooperative learning will succeed no better than mandated lesson designs, mandated assertive discipline or mandated anything. In fact, given the vision of the transfer school, it is all the more essential that each individual volunteers to enter cooperative learning. That will hold true not only for the first-wave participants, but even more so for all those who follow.

The easiest way to solicit volunteers is to expose teachers to cooperative learning. By inviting a major speaker to provide a one-day awareness program for all staff, the seeds become sown. If the awareness session provides the most interested teachers the opportunity to engage in a basic cooperative learning program that has built in application work, there will be little difficulty in forming the first team in a school.

After the first volunteer team has completed its application trial, still only volunteers will be accepted, right down to the 10 percent of the faculty who would die rather than change their practice. Concentration on those teachers who elect cooperative learning at their own pace is more important than making martyrs of the resistors.

A TEACHER-DIRECTED CURRICULUM RENEWAL PROJECT Over a three- to five-year period, the peer support systems expand to form a critical mass of teachers who engage in cooperative learning more than 50 percent of the instructional day. At this point, teachers can predict major discomfort with time and the curriculum.

The time-curriculum crunch created by a cooperative and cognitive approach to learning is more than the superficial "concern" identified in the "concern model" of staff development. Time is a real and descriptive barrier caused by the conflict between "content coverage" and "quality inquiry."

For the past two decades, curricula has become the overstuffed sausage ready to burst. Zealous legislators who are promoting their special interests intensify the information explosion by adding more and more topics to, and seldom subtracting anything from, the 185-day school year. The only choice open to the serious teacher who is pressed by standardized tests and superficial evaluation methods, is to cover more topics faster and with less depth and quality in the same given time. Without the authority to remove outdated and often erroneous information, or to prioritize concepts or topics, teachers end up trying to "cover" everything—garbage as well as gold. As a consequence, both garbage and gold are hidden from the students' view; teachers rightly see little time to build cooperative inquiry, to teach students the processes of learning and thinking, or to guide serious problem-solving explorations.

In order to dump the trash in the curriculum, teachers who are prepared for thinking in the cooperative classroom need the opportunity and support for "selective abandonment," as Costa says. At its best, this clean-up empowers groups of teachers to fashion higher-level objectives than are found at the core of most standardized tests. In place of naming, recalling and picking facts, these objectives must focus—as do the Illinois and Michigan reading assessments—on such key higher-level thinking skills as predicting, inferring and summarizing.

There are two curriculum renewal approaches that have proven successful in practice. The first focuses on the identification of thinking skills implicit in quality curricula. In this approach, the macro-processes of gathering, processing and applying information build the teamwork; the micro-skills in each process become explicit goals for students to master and use across the curriculum.

The second approach, championed by Costa, focuses on the identification of desired student characteristics:

- ✓ Fluency
- ✓ Flexibility

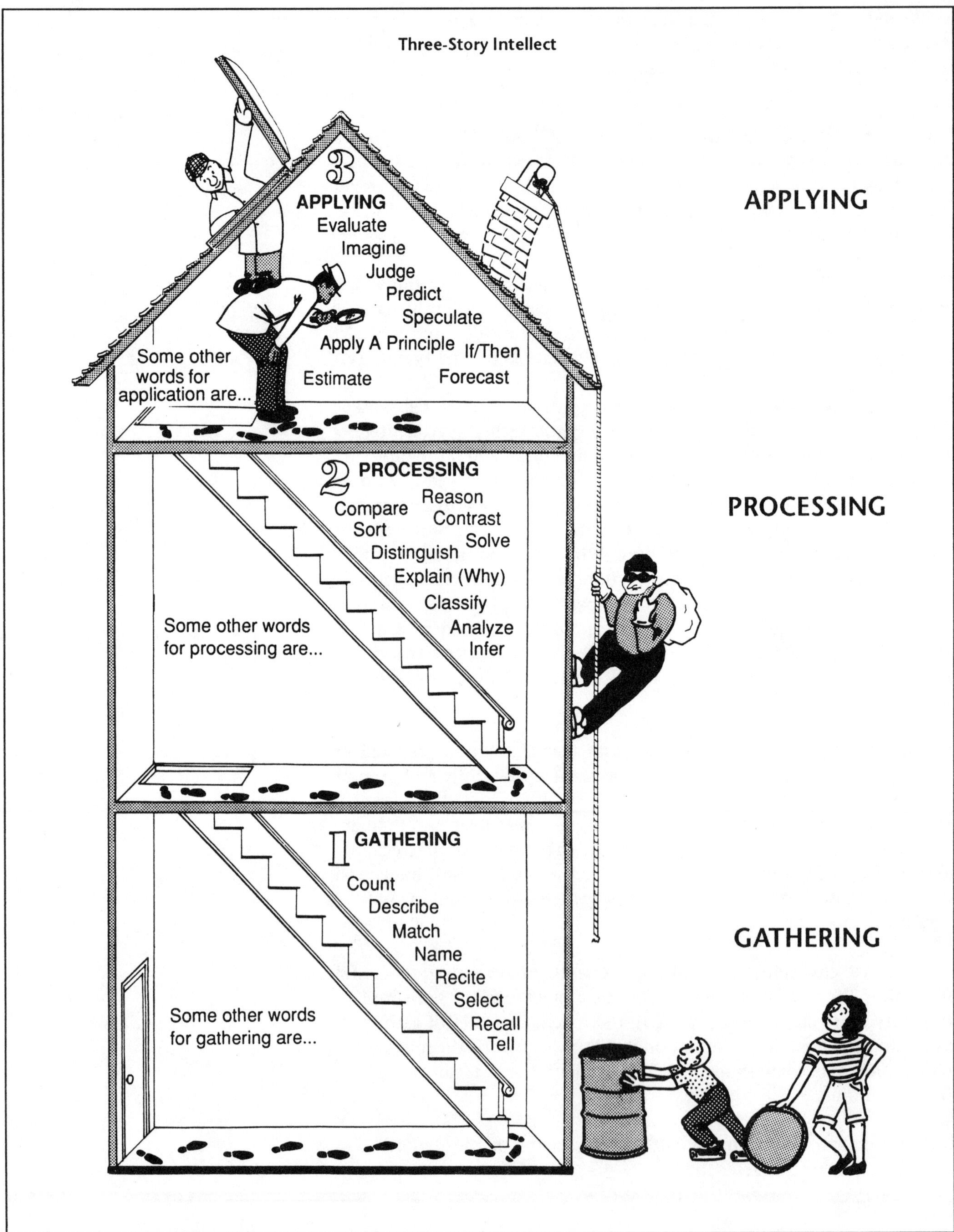
Three-Story Intellect
3
APPLYING
Evaluate
Imagine
Judge
Predict
Speculate
Apply A Principle
If/Then
Estimate
Forecast
Some other words for application are...
2
PROCESSING
Compare
Reason
Contrast
Sort
Solve
Distinguish
Explain (Why)
Classify
Analyze
Infer
Some other words for processing are...
1
GATHERING
Count
Describe
Match
Name
Recite
Select
Recall
Tell
Some other words for gathering are...
APPLYING
PROCESSING
GATHERING

- ✔ Perseverance
- ✔ Reflectiveness
- ✔ Metacognition
- ✔ Problem posing
- ✔ Carefulness
- ✔ Use of prior knowledge
- ✔ Precise language
- ✔ Enjoyment of thinking
- ✔ Transference

Given the identification of the curriculum goals, the renewal committee has two major tasks. First, it must identify the concept of teaching transfer, which will anchor each course of study. This means it has to remove such activities as long division to the ninth place, the memorization of the top 200 vocabulary words in sophomore biology and the identification of 320 basic reading skills as items for testing.

In place of these lowest-level tasks, each committee of second-wave or experienced teachers who are trained in a specific skill, course or content (third-grade reading, middle-grade geography, etc.), frames thinking and transferring objectives for its curriculum. For instance, a third-grade math team would have the authority to throw out a minimal list and time-wasting objective such as, "Each student will calculate three-digit problems to the ninth place." In its place they would prepare a problem-solving objective such as, "Students will demonstrate the long division skill to solve a variety of two-step word problems taken from real-world situations."

In biology, the committee of trained biology teachers would abandon objectives that stress recall of key vocabulary words. The replacement objectives would require students to do such thinking tasks as, "*Explain* why a concept is important," "*Hypothesize* about the problem-solving methods for conducting experiments," and "*Predict* outcomes of procedures in a given task."

The key concept to transfer is having the committee understand the essential transfer principles of hugging and bridging.

The immediate cry of woe that springs up when thinking and transferring objectives are created is that "lower-ability" students won't have the ability. "They can't do the low-level work; how can you expect them to think?" is one classic complaint. "You'll damage their self-concepts," is another. At the level of both complaints is the essence of low expectations. Low expectations not only dissenfranchise the youngsters who have a more difficult time playing the memory game, but they also haul every student down to the lowest level of thinking.

The contrast is clear. Set expectations high with a transfer curriculum. These expectations challenge the most able students to stretch well beyond anything they are being asked to do now. Equally as important, the thinking and transferring objectives present new opportunities for every child. Thus, in this context, never set low expectations. Even if a student does not reach the high expectations set by the teacher, most likely he/she will go far beyond the lower expectations imposed by the recall curricula.

Implicit in framing a curriculum that highlights concept transfer is sufficient instructional time for explicit instruction of thinking skills. Thinking skill lessons not only require 50 to 70 minutes for explanation and demonstration, but also daily interactive and guided practice sessions that allow for teacher feedback and student metacognition. (This time allotment varies—according to student age, ability and motivation—from one week of explicit follow-up lessons focused only on one thinking skill, to four or five weeks of such lessons.) When students demonstrate satisfactory mastery of a thinking skill, the curriculum encourages interactive application lessons that enable students to practice the thinking skill across the curriculum.

Advanced training for thinking in the cooperative class prepares the curricular team to plan those components of the transfer curriculum which highlight the cooperative-cognitive skills. The advanced training program, *Patterns for Thinking— Patterns for Transfer,* focuses on the explicit thinking skills of brainstorming, predicting, visualizing, analyzing, attributing, classifying and prioritizing. Cognitive organizers (such as decision trees and sequence blocks), and metacognitive strategies (such as PMI) are used within a structured framework to focus lessons on the development of thinking and transferring patterns that are applicable across the curricula. On the following pages one patterned lesson is modeled; it is designed for the important cognitive skill of determining cause and effect.

DETERMINING CAUSE AND EFFECT

C HOOSE A SITUATION

H AVE POSSIBLE OUTCOMES IN MIND

A DVANCE ONE IDEA

I NDICATE THE 'CHAIN OF EVENTS'

N OTE THE CAUSE/EFFECT RELATIONSHIP OR

S TART AT OUTCOME AND WORK BACKWARD

Cause-Effect lesson excerpted from *Teach Them Thinking*

DETERMINING CAUSE AND EFFECT

☐ Creative Thinking  ☒ Critical Thinking

PROGRAM : Skill: Cause and Effect Relationship

PASSWORD : Acronym: **CHAINS**

DATA BASE : Definition: To determine cause and effect relationships.

LIST : Synonyms: action — consequence; catalyst — outcome; chain — reaction concept; cause — result.

SCAN : Examples: drop match in woods; ignites leaves; spreads to trees → forest fire [loss of natural resource results in wood and by-products price increase.]

ie. match causes effect of forest fire → which causes prices to rise on wood products.

ENTER : When to use:
- — planning a course of action; options.
- — analyzing the cause of a particular consequence, result or effect.

MENU : How to use:

Choose a situation
Have possible outcomes in mind
Advance one idea
Indicate the 'chain of events'
Note the cause/effect relationship or
Start at outcome and work backward

DEBUGGING : What to do if:
- — cannot decide on outcome; work through several probable outcomes; prepare for both.
- — tracing backward and have several possible causes; check each one further to clarify or narrow to most probable cause.

Cause-Effect lesson excerpted from *Teach Them Thinking*

VISUAL LAYOUT : Patterns: Cause-Effect Chain
Flow Chart

FILE : Sample Lesson:

Earth Science: Effects of Weather

Record March snowfalls have left heavy coverage on the ground. What effects can be anticipated in the spring? Why? What can farmers do to prepare? Explain.

Choose situation: Heavy snows

Have outcomes in mind: quick thaw, slow thaw

Advance one idea: quick thaw

Indicate chain of events: quick thaw → floods → wet ground → late planting → late crops → farmers have financial problems

Note cause/effect relationship: heavy March snow → thaw → flood → or

Start at end: financial problems → late crop → flood → snow

INDEX : Suggested Applications:

MATH:
- Statistics
- Probabilities
- Stock Market
- Logic — If . . . then

LANGUAGE ARTS:
- Analyzing Events In A Story
- Constructing Alternate Plots & Outcomes

SCIENCE:
- Chemical Reactions
- Environmental Issues
- Physics — Action/Reaction

SOCIAL STUDIES
- Economics
- Current Events (political)
- History — "What if . . ."
- Government — Law

Cause-Effect lesson excerpted from *Teach Them Thinking*

A MENTOR PROGRAM With a core of teachers who have completed the basic (*Thinking in the Cooperative Classroom: Basic*) and advanced (*Patterns for Thinking—Patterns for Transfer*) applications, and who have worked on the restructuring of the curriculum to focus on transfer, a school is ready to initiate its mentor program.

In the mentor program, those teachers who have led the way in initiating the transfer curriculum become the turnkey mentor-trainers. With additional training of trainers preparation, each adopts three to five volunteers to initiate the next round of training in the school. Rather than use a six-hour-a-day workshop approach, the input, demonstration and guided coaching practice sessions of basic training span a period of 12 to 24 weeks. In a second sequence, the mentors work equal amounts of time to train teams on advanced application. This allows each small team to make immediate and intense use of model lessons, develop classroom tools and build a small, but intense support group.

In larger schools, the trained team may repeat the process, having mentors perform small-team trainings over the course of several years until all volunteers are trained at both levels. School leaders find that as the critical mass of teachers prepares to use the transfer curriculum, assistance diminishes until less than 5 percent hold out. At this point, it becomes an administrative perogative to address the issue of those who say, "No way."

Throughout this three- to five-year change/process, the principal's role is critical, especially if the last, crucial step is to become a reality.

Let's examine the principal's role in the full development of the transfer curriculum.

a. The principal identifies a core of leader-teachers for the first basic training program. These teachers, well-experienced in the classroom and familiar with the student population, are the front-runners. They initiate the first applications of thinking in the cooperative classroom, the first peer-assistance teams, the first curriculum renewal and the first mentor work.

b. The principal structures the application phase by identifying substitute teachers, scheduling peer observations and team meetings, and by keeping the pressure off the core team. As the program moves ahead, the principal ensures that the budget supports all phases of the professional development. In return for the teachers' professional commitment to carry out this difficult process of change, the principal sees that the teachers receive professional treatment. This includes evaluating programs and providing adequate time in the workday for teachers to attend all training programs and special meetings, and plan lessons.

c. The principal encourages and supports the team members as they "try out" new patterns of instruction. Giving daily support, encouraging discussions, solving application problems and reinforcing successes are a must.

d. The principal leads the team in planning the curriculum renewal process. This planning may entail negotiating with the district or state education officials for variances from mandates. It may also require negotiations with union leaders for variances from the contract.

e. The principal monitors the application process and provides progress reports to the district, union and/or state officials.

f. The principal leads the team in its planning for the training of trainers and the subsequent mentor coaching program.

g. The principal communicates with the parents and community about the restructuring process, its benefits and its results.

h. The principal ensures that the assessment process provides quality information on the effects of the transfer curriculum in student learning, thinking, and transferring and other areas determined by the school's leadership team.

i. The principal leads the team of teachers in forming a vision as they continue to restructure the school for the 21st century and develop a strategic plan.

j. The principal communicates to the entire staff the high expectations for collaborative development and application of the transfer curriculum. By word, action and active participation in the learning program, the curriculum renewal process and the development of the strategic plan, the principal leads every step of the process.

A STRATEGIC PLAN FROM THE INSIDE OUT The beginning of the change process can start if staff members have restructured curriculum and instruction in the classroom. Once the classroom is restructured, teachers' readiness to restructure other aspects of the school to meet the learner's needs follows almost automatically. The goal of this fifth phase is to restructure the school from the inside out.

Restructuring from the inside out is an honor that comes through professional staff development, teacher-centered curriculum renewal and site-based strategic planning that asks which administrative structures will best support and extend cooperative classrooms and which thinking skills are the paramount goals. When focus is on the learner and the professionals who school the learner, there is, in fact, a redefinition of the restructuring process—change in schooling is not from the top down, not from the outside in, but from the inside out.

☐ ☐ ☐

Update your task sequence on page 348.

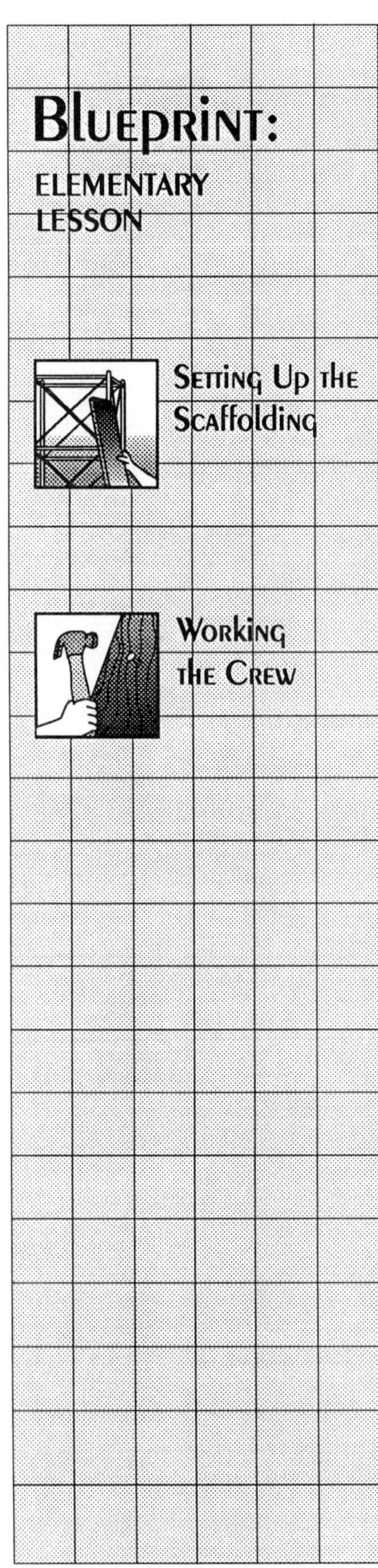

IN THE EARLY YEARS: MY FUTURE SCHOOL

Lead a discussion about the future. Get students thinking about the year 2000. Use the video "Future World, Future School" or other media that present a future vision. Have students scout for pictures and information about the future. Develop a mind-set for looking ahead and envisioning what schools might be like in the year 2000.

Arrange the class into partners. Have students face their partners. In turn (rotating speaker/listener roles), they are to talk about and explore ideas for shaping the school of the future. Suggest that their conversation might begin with the idea . . .

> "If I ran the school, I'd change things from the inside out. I'd look into tomorrow with tomorrow's eyes and this is what I'd see . . . ."

Ideas should include:

- WHO: Adults and kids
- WHERE: The school and classroom
- WHAT: Content of what they're learning
- WHEN: When they go to school
- WHY: Why they would involve these
- HOW: How this school is restructured from the inside out

After sufficient warm-up and pre-writing dialogue, instruct students to write a first draft of their future visions.

If I ran the school, I'd change things from the inside out. I'd look into tomorrow with tomorrow's eyes and this is what I'd see . . . My future school . . . .

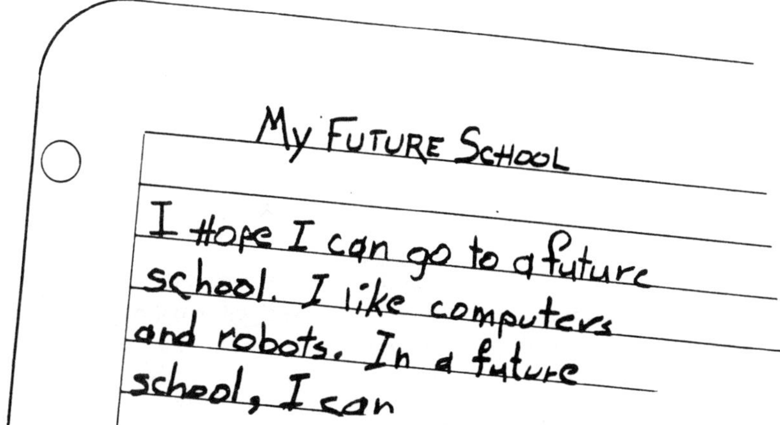

My Future School
I Hope I can go to a future school. I like computers and robots. In a future school, I can

To process affectively, do a wraparound with this lead-in:

The hardest thing about visualizing the future school is . . . .

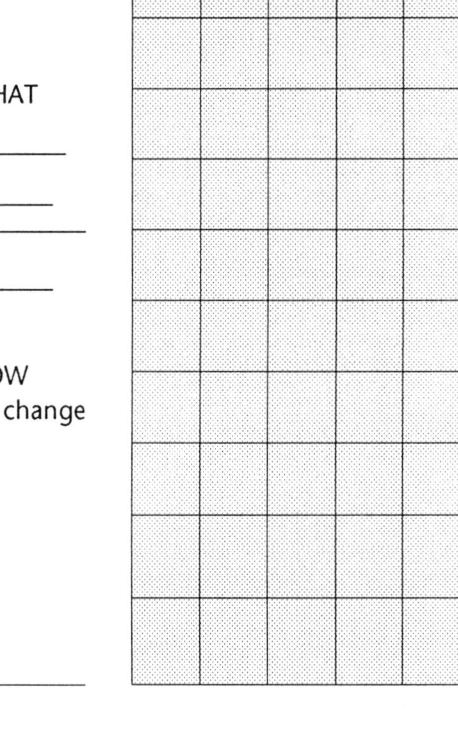

To process the social skill of encouraging others in their visions, have each student describe "a dream come true" experience.

To process cognitively, ask students to complete the following fish bone by adding the critical attributes of the school of the future. Students are to list their ideas on the "bones" with the appropriate headings— i.e., who, what, where, when, why and how.

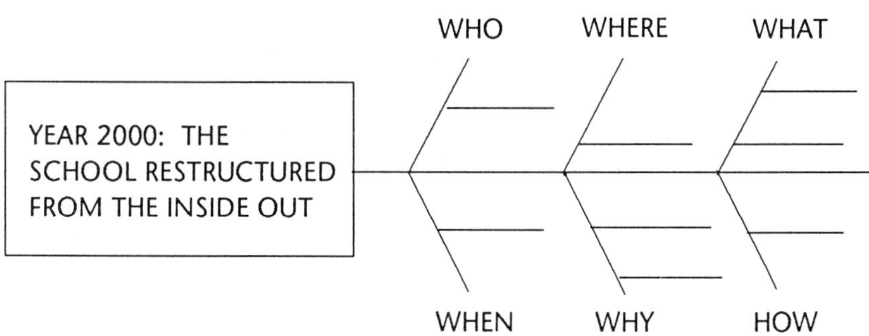

To process metacognitively, have students talk about what it means to change from the inside out.

□ □ □

IN THE MIDDLE YEARS: IF I RAN THE SCHOOL . . .

Use the video "Future World, Future School" or other media that present a future vision. Have students scout for pictures and information about the future. Develop a mind-set for looking ahead and envisioning what schools might be like in the year 2000.

Arrange the class into partners. Have students face their partners. In turn (rotating speaker/listener roles), they are to talk about and explore ideas for shaping the school of the future. Suggest that their conversation might begin with the idea . . .

> "If I ran the school, I'd change things from the inside out. I'd look into tomorrow with tomorrow's eyes and this is what I'd see . . . ."

Ideas should include:

- WHO: Adults and kids
- WHERE: The school and classroom
- WHAT: Content of what they're learning
- WHEN: When they go to school
- WHY: Why they would involve these
- HOW: How this school is restructured from the inside out

After sufficient warm-up and pre-writing dialogue, instruct students to write a first draft of their future visions.

IF I RAN THE SCHOOL . . .

If I Ran the School...

If I ran the school, I'd change things from the inside out. I'd look into tomorrow with tomorrow's eyes and this is what I'd see...

To process affectively, do a wraparound with this lead-in:

The hardest thing about visualizing the future school is . . . .

To process the social skill of praising another's idea, have students describe situations in which their good ideas "saved the day."

To process cognitively, ask students to complete the following fish bone by adding the critical attributes of the school of the future. Students are to list their ideas on the "bones" with the appropriate headings— i.e., who, what, where, when, why and how.

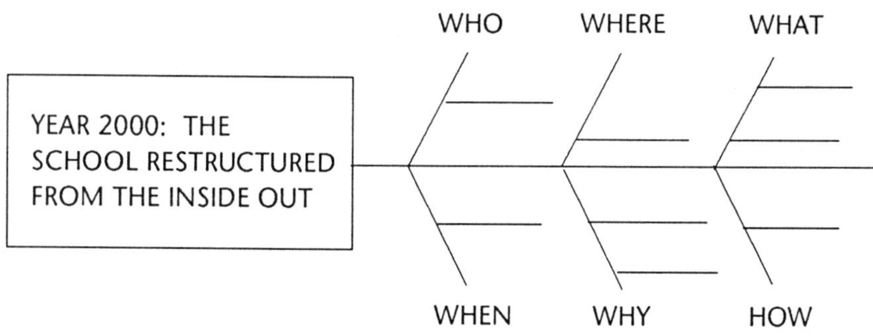

To process metacognitively, have students talk about what it means to change from the inside out.

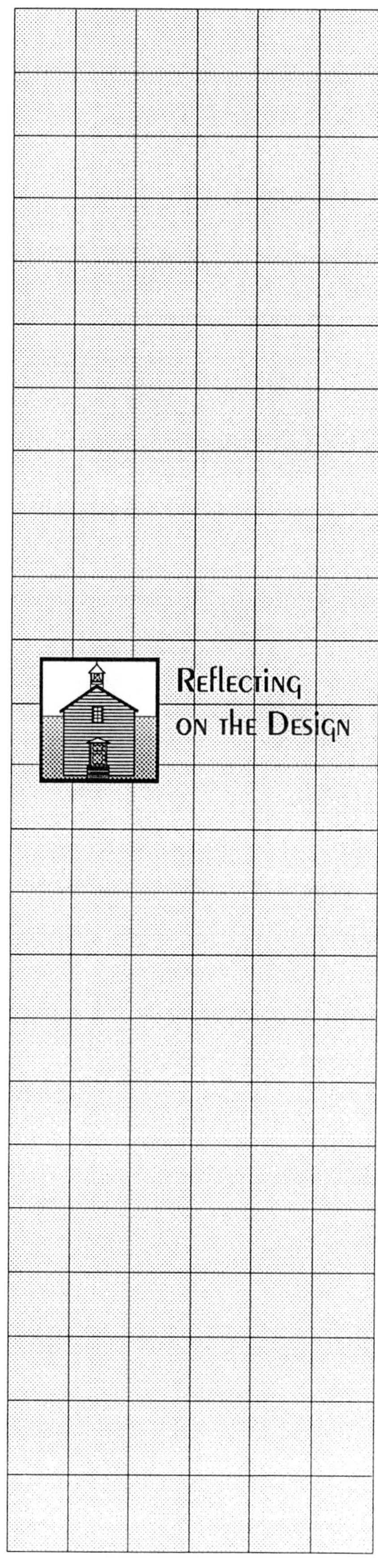

IN THE SECONDARY YEARS: BENEFITS OF THE FUTURE SCHOOL

Use the video "Future World, Future School" or other media that present a future vision. Have students scout for pictures and information about the future. Develop a mind-set for looking ahead and envisioning what schools might be like in the year 2000.

Arrange the class into partners. Have students face their partners. In turn (rotating speaker/listener roles), they are to talk about and explore ideas for shaping the school of the future. Suggest that their conversation might begin with the idea . . .

> "If I ran the school, I'd change things from the inside out. I'd look into tomorrow with tomorrow's eyes and this is what I'd see . . . ."

Ideas should include:

- WHO: Adults and kids
- WHERE: The school and classroom
- WHAT: Content of what they're learning
- WHEN: When they go to school
- WHY: Why they would involve these
- HOW: How this school is restructured from the inside out

After sufficient warm-up and pre-writing dialogue, instruct students to write a first draft of their future visions.

IF I RAN THE SCHOOL . . .

If I ran the school, I'd change things from the inside out. I'd look into tomorrow with tomorrow's eyes and this is what I'd see . . . Benefits of the future school . . . .

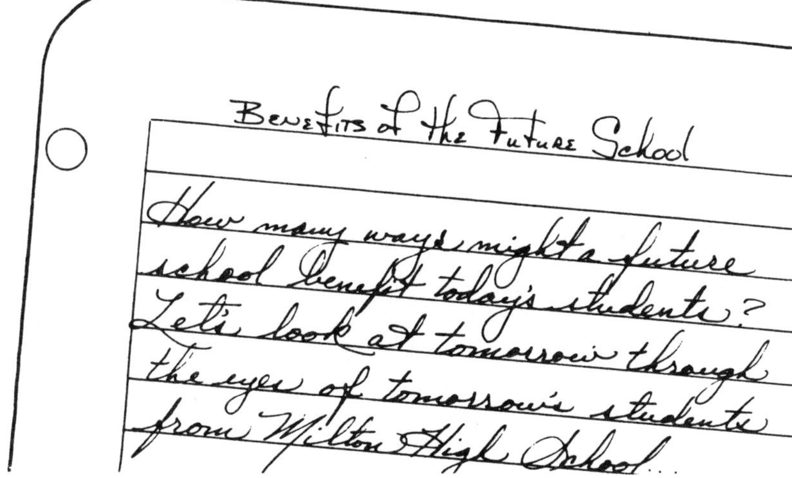

Benefits of the Future School
How many ways might a future
school benefit today's students?
Let's look at tomorrow through
the eyes of tomorrow's students
from Milton High School...

To process affectively, do a wraparound with this lead-in:

The hardest thing about visualizing the future school is . . . .

To process the social skill of adding your own ideas to the group, have students relate experiences in which their good ideas were preempted by someone else.

To process cognitively, ask students to complete the following fish bone by adding the critical attributes of the school of the future. Students are to list their ideas on the "bones" that have the appropriate headings; i.e., who, what, where, when, why and how.

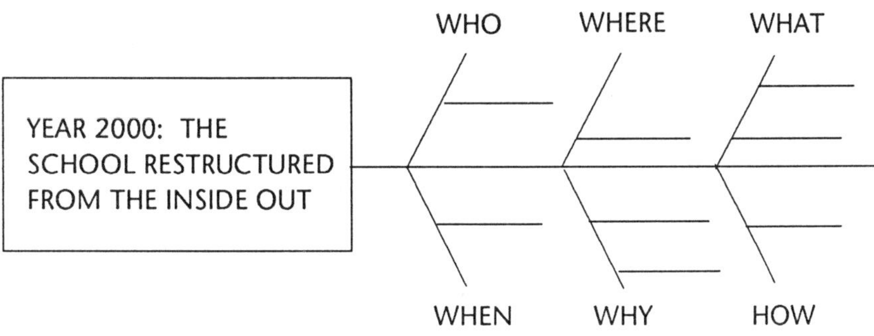

To process metacognitively, have students talk about what it means to change from the inside out.

□ □ □

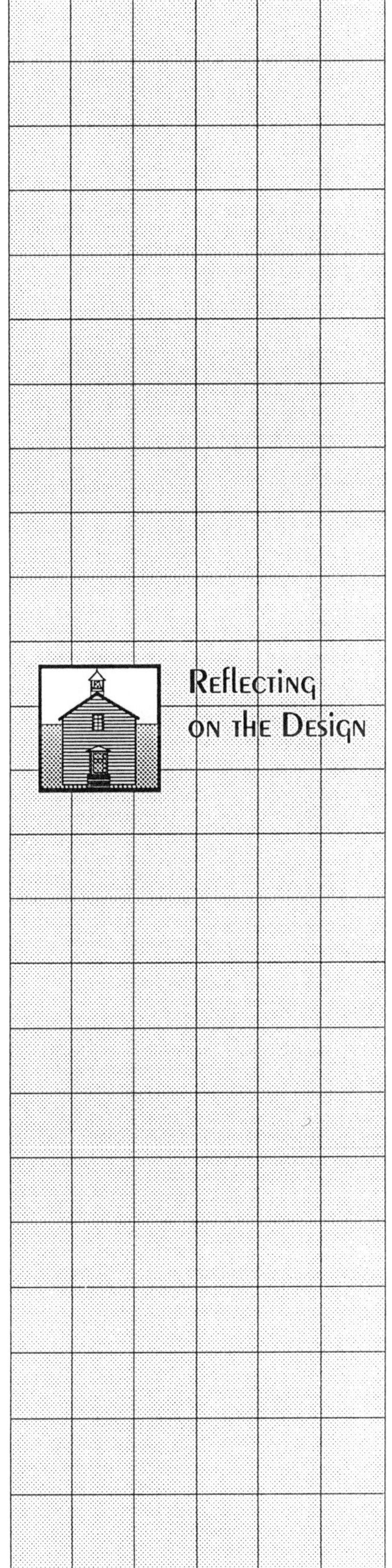

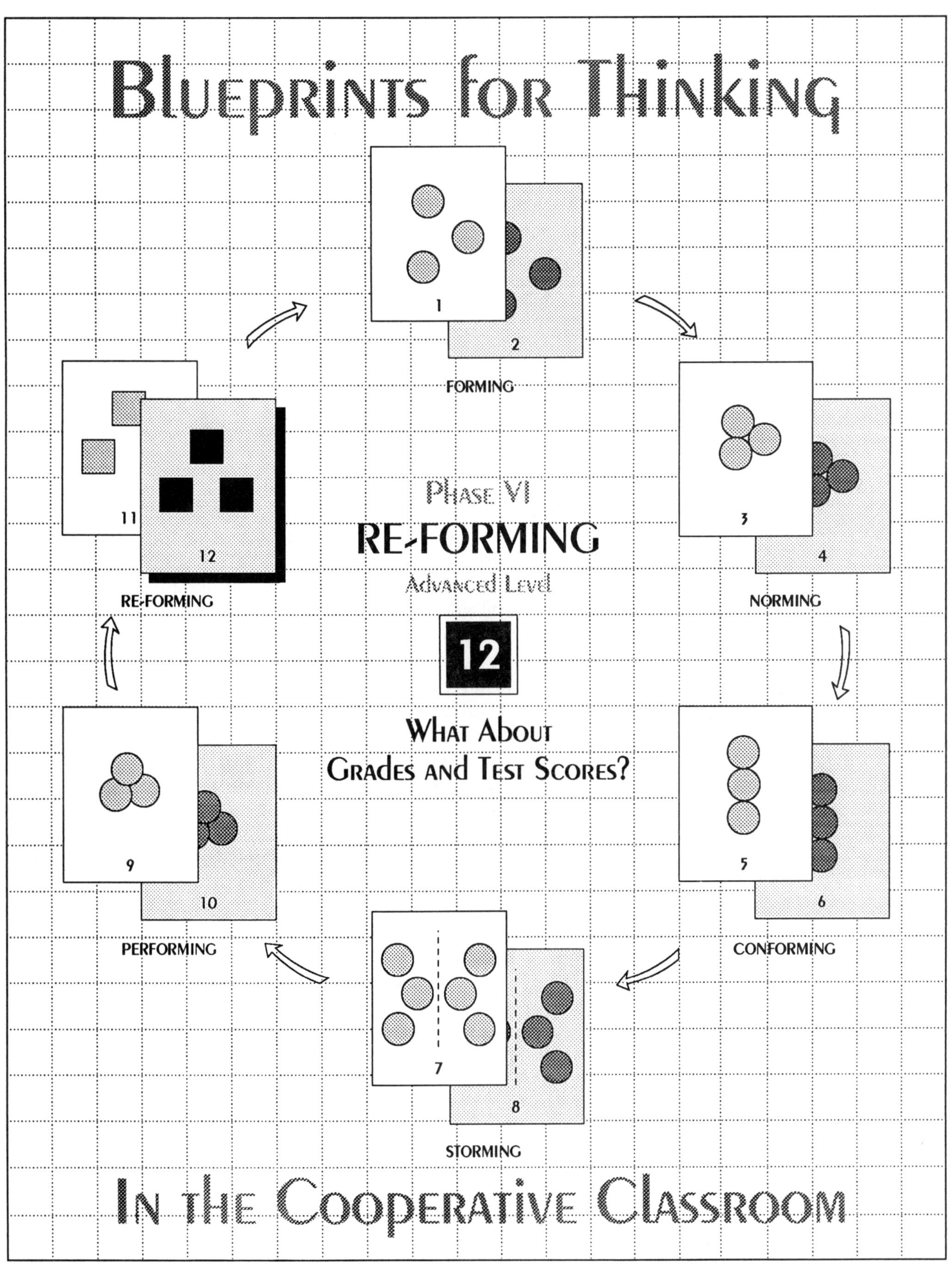
Blueprints for Thinking
1
2
FORMING
3
4
NORMING
5
6
CONFORMING
7
8
STORMING
9
10
PERFORMING
11
12
RE-FORMING
Phase VI
RE-FORMING
Advanced Level
12
What About
Grades and Test Scores?
In the Cooperative Classroom

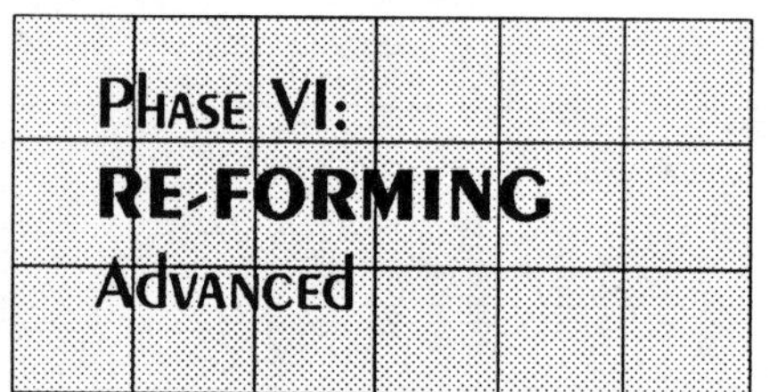

What About Grades and Test Scores?

There are days when spelling tuesday simply doesn't count.
—Rabbit in *Winnie the Pooh,* A.A. Milne

Draft

In this age of accountability, classroom teachers feel an inordinate amount of pressure to test and measure. With the current mania for standardized test results, that pressure is most often translated into confusion about instructional priorities. The confusion surfaces in the question, "But what do I do about tests and grades for cooperative learning and critical thinking?" Behind this question is the teacher concern: "I am expected to make sure all my students do well on the standardized tests for basic skills. The tests don't measure cooperative learning or thinking. If I spend time on thinking and cooperating, I will have to take instructional time from the basic skills. If I take time from the basic skills, my students may not do as well on the standardized tests. If they do poorly on tests, I will be blamed. . . ." Such concern is both earnest and legitimate. On the one hand, the teacher sees the opportunities for learning inherent in the thinking and cooperative classroom. On the other hand, the standardized tests may not relieve the pressure for accountability. Even more, the teacher wants to be accountable. The teacher wants the tests to match what the students are learning *and* he/she wants to do the best teaching possible.

There are legitimate answers to this problem. A teacher who sees the value of learning from a cognitive and cooperative perspective *can* measure student performance in effective ways. While not yet readily acceptable as valid measuring devices by those who understand little about the science of educational measurement, the methods are described by many researchers as more "authentic" and certainly more supportive of the total learning process.

What does *authentic assessment* mean? According to the dictionary, authentic means reliable, trustworthy, supported by unquestioned evidence. Assessment means appraisal, evaluation, estimation of value. In a broader sense, authentic assessment means the evaluation of a student's learning through a *broad array* of unquestionable evidence. This evidence may include portfolios of student work, logs, student artifacts and yes, test scores. It means weighing not only what students do, but also how they plan a task, how they make decisions during a task and how they themselves evaluate a task. It uses evidence gathered from a variety of sources to paint a portrait of a student's growth as a thoughtful learner. The assessment is not limited to standardized tests. It looks to see the whole performance and not reduce the student to a single number, test score or grade.

Authentic assessment forgoes reducing a student to a single grade or test score.

How does a teacher evaluate what a scantron won't? It is easy to advocate the use of logs, student artifacts and thoughtful discussions. It is more difficult, however, to actually use them. There are several steps, all time-worn and mostly predating the accountability mania, that provide solid assessments of student performance, even of such esoteric processes as thinking and cooperating.

☐ SET THE CRITERIA FOR EACH EVALUATION

SPECS

Knowing what the teacher is going to evaluate is helpful to students as well as the teacher. For instance, when it comes to the measurement of thinking, there are two essential approaches.

DISPOSITIONS FOR THINKING

One approach follows the lead of Costa. He recommends that the teacher identify the dispositions of thinking. Following are *characteristics* of intelligent behaviors that Costa believes teachers and parents can teach, observe and assess:

✓ Persistence
✓ Decreasing impulsivity
✓ Empathic listening
✓ Flexibility in thinking
✓ Metacognitive awareness
✓ Checking for accuracy
✓ Questioning
✓ Problem posing
✓ Drawing on past knowledge
✓ Application to new situations
✓ Precision of language and thought
✓ Using all the senses
✓ Ingenuity, originality, insightfulness and creativity
✓ Inquisitiveness, curiosity
✓ Enjoyment of problem solving

SPECIFIC THINKING PROCESSES

The second approach to measuring student thinking concerns identifying *specific thinking processes* that the teacher wants the students to use with the subject matter. The Three-Story Intellect model provides a framework for those skills.

GATHERING	PROCESSING	APPLYING
Count	Compare	Evaluate
Describe	Sort	Imagine
Match	Distinguish	Judge
Name	Explain (why)	Predict
Recite	Classify	Speculate
Select	Analyze	Apply a principle
Recall	Infer	If/then
Tell	Reason	Forecast
	Contrast	Estimate

☐ QUANTITY AND QUALITY

Once the teacher has selected the criteria, the next task in planning for assessment is to pinpoint the quantity and quality of evidence that is desired. Consider these examples:

FLUENCY

Fluent thinkers are able to come up with a greater number of ideas. When the teacher asks the students to gather information (name the characters, list the cities, describe the attributes, etc.), he/she need only count the number of responses. For instance, a simple gathering task may ask the students to list the colors seen in a picture; a more complex gathering task would ask students to identify the positive characteristics of a literary character such as Ebenezer Scrooge. The grade for the individual or the group depends on the number of items listed.

FLEXIBILITY

Flexible thinkers can identify a wide range of divergent responses to a question. Not only does the teacher look for fluency (quantity), but also for how different the responses may be. For instance, if students are asked to gather information about botanical diseases found on pine trees that grow in a certain climate, the teacher would look for samples of common trees and rare trees. If students are assigned a more complex task such as providing reasons for the disease, the teacher would look for a variety of arguments and viewpoints.

PRECISION AND PERSEVERANCE

In mathematics and other convergent subjects, precision and perseverance are important traits. When assessing precision, the teacher looks for the exact and detailed application of a standard. For example, in science, did the students weigh each chemical to the exact decimal given? In math, did students use each of the steps as given? When assessing perseverance, the teacher sees how long students stay with a difficult task and how many different tries they make in order to solve the given problem. For instance, when students are working on a three-step word problem, how many tries do they take before giving up or asking for help?

THOROUGHNESS AND LOGIC

When looking for application of thoroughness, the teacher first counts the number of appropriate examples students provide in making an argument or in defending a point. For instance, if students are assigned an expository essay to describe a historic event, the teacher looks for completeness and full coverage of the event. If students are assigned an argumentative essay about a critical social issue, the teacher counts how many pros and cons are given. Going beyond the numbers of examples given, the teacher evaluates the appropriateness of the examples by applying the rules of logic to each example. For instance, if the students are arguing against increased local taxes to fund schools, the teacher would reject a biased argument that attacked the governor for his beliefs about abortion.

TRANSFERENCE

The teacher *can* assess the students' ability to transfer ideas. Narrow transfers, which simply duplicate ideas, receive lower grades than "fat" transfers, which show more creativity and individuality. For instance, if the class is studying appropriate uses of a word processing program that demonstrates a cut-and-paste procedure and the teacher asks the students to provide examples of times they could use this procedure, one student might repeat an example already given in the text; another might describe the use of the procedure in preparing research documents in another class. The latter's idea shows a greater breadth and depth of transfer.

☐ SELECT THE MEDIA

The third step in planning for assessment is to select the media through which students will provide the evidence. When the teacher attempts to apply criteria to students' thoughtful work, it is helpful for him/her to work from models which provide concrete examples of the *degrees* of quality expected. Not only do models help the teacher measure the quality of each student's work, but also they provide a concrete way to give students accurate feedback. Following are some examples for gathering evidences:

QUIZZES AND TESTS

Quizzes and tests ask students to define the thinking skill, to identify strong uses of the skill, to give a demonstration of the skill in a concrete problem or to write instructions for another use of the skill.

LOGS AND JOURNALS

Logs and journals ask students to discuss what they have learned about a topic, questions they have on a burning issue, feelings about tasks they are doing, ways to plan how to think through a problem, thoughts monitored while developing a concept, how they used a specific thinking skill, evaluations of their thinking dispositions and sketches of the ways they might think about a project (see example on opposite page).

AD CAMPAIGNS

Ad campaigns ask students to use two or three different media (e.g., posters, magazines, video) to sell a concept that they have learned (e.g., photosynthesis, whole numbers, tragedy).

PRODUCT PORTFOLIOS

Product portfolios encourage each student to keep a representative collection of completed assignments and products (e.g., a series of writing assignments) and to prepare an explanation of the changes noted over the year—including a semester review of the changes that have occurred over the four months and an evaluation of the changes with a PMI chart.

EXTENDED PROJECTS

Extended projects have students pull together a key concept for the year—for example, in science, a project on nuclear energy and its community effects can demonstrate students' problem-solving ability and how it has changed through the project.

Thinking Log Task: In your log, write about how you thought through the lab experiment today.	
Student: ***Limited Response*** *I had to figure out the different ways the frogs ate bugs.*	Teacher Comment You have identified the first step in the problem-solving model. I would like you to tell me more by using the chart for problem solving on page 9. How would you use the other steps?
Student: ***Incomplete Response*** *I followed the seven steps and checked off each one. After I checked it off, I made sure that I had an example for each one.*	Teacher Comment I am pleased that you followed the seven-step model. That is a great start. I would like to have you give some of the examples here and tell how you decided on which example each time.
Student: ***Adequate Response*** *The first thing I did was figure out the different kinds of food the frog ate. I brainstormed some other ideas. Then the facts told me that the real problem was to know the ways the frog ate insects. Once I had this idea, I began to look in two articles for the best reasons. I used the quote from the scientist to make my choice. He is the expert. After that, it was easy to pick out the others.*	Teacher Comment I like the several different types of thinking you identified: problem identification, brainstorming, judging expert opinion. You have a start in explaining in more detail what you thought about. I would like you to say more about some of the ways you used the quote to help you choose.
Student: ***Complete Response*** *When I read the first paragraph about the frog's eating habits, I thought of the ways my little brother eats in the highchair. He has all sorts of ways to attack food. So does the frog. The question is, which way is best? Obviously, the frog and my brother will have different best ways. To figure out the best way for the frog, I thought about Dr. Pink's argument. Since he has studied the frog for 24 years, I accept him as reliable. I thought about questioning his theory, but I didn't have time to research the answers. I do still have the question in my head.*	Teacher Comment I liked the personal touch in the comparison to your brother. It brings your thinking to life. I also like how you keep asking questions and looking for several answers to each question. Another plus is how you thought about the expert. I am interested and would like to hear the questions.

LOG/JOURNAL EXAMPLE

Adapted from *Reading & Responding: Evaluation Strategies for Teachers by* Jeroski, Brownlie & Kaser

Note that the media described look like student projects. That is accurate. The key is to use the projects as a means or medium to help students think about how they approach learning tasks and expend a conscious effort to communicate how they plan, monitor and evaluate their thinking. With the criteria in hand, measurement of students' thinking within the media becomes an easier task.

DRAFT

☐ GRADING COOPERATION IN THE CLASSROOM

In any situation, grading is a two-edged sword. On the one hand, good grades can motivate students who care about grades. On the other hand, grades can have little or no effect on students, usually the ones who have a record of *C's, D's* or *F's*. If a teacher elects to use grades for cooperation, here are some suggestions and guidelines:

- ✓ Grade demonstrated behavior. After teaching a social skill, use checksheets to observe students' use of the T-chart behaviors.
- ✓ Grade individuals for observed contributions to the group. What behavior helped? did not help?
- ✓ Grade groups very carefully. Group grades for cooperation need to reflect how all members contributed and supported each other in a task. It is best to use group social skills as a *bonus* above task scores.
- ✓ Never use group grades to punish the group. Punishment would include lowering academic grades for poor use of social skills.
- ✓ When group members demonstrate a commitment to work together, consider how group grades for the task may help.

SPECS

New users of cooperative learning often ask about grading and testing. In the age of "hard" measurement—with standardized tests and scantrons—there is little leeway for "soft" (i.e., hard-to-measure) evaluations on topics such as cooperation, thinking and transference. If one respects teachers' judgments about student performance, there are many valued answers to the questions about assessing student performance. If one is searching for teacher-proof evaluation methods, the field of opportunities is very small.

The assessment of cooperation, thinking and transfer *is* possible. Moreover, well-done assessment can end in solid grades of student performance. The catch is in the teacher's willingness to go beyond standardized tests and to use a variety of tools *with* the scantrons.

The most important reason for assessing student thinking and learning is almost always the most forgotten: constructive feedback enables students to refine and develop their thinking patterns. More likely, assessment results get jumbled in state mandates, real estate appraisal competition, school report cards and other less important factors. When the teacher has assessed the students' thinking, immediate written feedback, as quickly as possible, is a major motivator. Delayed and general feedback has little effect on students' desire to improve. One task returned with extensive and thought-producing comments is far more effective than five returned with little more than *A+* or "good job" or *C*.

INDIVIDUAL GRADES

When it comes to thinking and cooperating in the classroom, there is little to justify the use of grades other than to summarize or to report to parents how a student is doing in the class or to motivate those students for whom grades are important. If the teacher must provide grades, it is possible to do so for both individual work and for group work in the classroom. The teacher can assess *any* classroom task. If clear criteria for performance have been established, it is simple to attach a letter grade to each criterion. For instance, in the previous log sample, the limited response might receive a *D* while the complete response would merit an *A*. For a thinking task in which fluency is the criterion, students with five responses might receive a *C*, seven responses a *B* and ten responses an *A*.

GROUP GRADES

Some teachers elect to enhance and reward cooperative work by using group grades. This practice is full of danger. It can just as easily backfire as not. When using group grades, consider these procedures:

Raise the Group Average First, assign student groups to work together for several grading rounds. In the beginning rounds, determine the average grade of each group for each task. Add bonus points for improvement of a group's average in subsequent rounds. For instance, in a series of weekly spelling quizzes, each student can have one point added to his/her individual score for each point the group average is raised. A variation of this method has the teacher identify individuals' base scores in each quiz area (e.g., vocabulary, spelling, grammar, math, science, reading).

Raise Individual Scores Based on Improvement In this variation, each individual receives as many bonus points as other members of the group have earned. For instance, in a math exam, the teacher sets the criteria for a *B* grade at 85 percent. For every student in the group who scores higher than 85, each student earns two bonus points. A variation on this method has each member earn the bonus points only for the students who typically score below 85 but who scored higher on this test.

Increase Individual Mastery with Team Assistance In *Teams, Games, Tournaments* Slavin has extended the group grade concept. Team members correct each other's practice work. Once a student has scored more than 80 percent, he/she takes a final test which is scored by a student monitor. Test scores and the number of tests completed each week contribute to the team score. Students receive the grade earned on the final tests and may receive bonus rewards for being part of the highest-scoring team.

Give a Bonus for Cooperative Skills Some teachers base bonus points only on the observed use of cooperative skills. The teacher or a student observer uses an observation checklist during class work to tabulate observed social skills. A preset number of observed cooperative behaviors merits bonus points (e.g., five behaviors = one point). Other teachers provide bonus points based on the quality of group processing. This bonus approach requires that a preset criterion be announced to the class.

The Pitfalls of Group grades Before teachers use group grades, it is important that they review the pitfalls of group evaluation. For example, when the teacher uses a group grade for a heterogeneous group of high and low achievers, the high achievers must have the social skills to resolve conflict and encourage equal participation. By asking a very able student to work with a resistant or less able student, a teacher is risking not only the success of the less able student, but frustration by the more able. Save group grades until all students demonstrate they are able to work together using cooperative skills.

Check the water temperature with parents, especially the parents of the class' high achievers. If the more able students' parents perceive that their children's grades are dependent only on how well the students work together or how their children succeed with less able children, the principal will be the first to face the storm. The wise teacher makes sure that the parents know what this thing called cooperative learning is and how it benefits their children.

Keeping students in the dark about the grading criterion causes difficulties. If group grades are used, then it's important to announce the success criteria at the start of the task.

Rather than fool with the many pitfalls of group grades, it is often more appropriate to grade the low-level products of cooperative work on an individual basis. Students first work in the cooperative groups to learn vocabulary, practice computation or answer recall questions. The common work they do is checked in the group and reviewed by the teacher. After the students study the teacher feedback and correct the work, each takes an individual test or quiz and receives an individual grade in the grade book. As students move to more complex, higher-level thinking in the cooperative groups, it is easier to give a group grade. This happens because, as was shown in the earlier chapters on thinking, the higher-level tasks encourage greater united teams and individual learning as part of the lesson. When the teacher uses the broad array of procedures to structure the higher-level lessons, grades become a secondary concern to the students.

NO GRADES

If a teacher should elect not to use grades as a motivator for cooperative learning, a variety of other tools can ensure a high degree of individual learning in the cooperative classroom.

Include a Tight Checker By structuring the tight checker to check short lists of basic information (vocabulary words, steps in a task, etc.) in small parts and again before students take the test, then the short, guided reviews (massed practice) enhance short-term recall, lead to increased mastery and model a way to memorize.

Assign a Traveler When a group gets stuck with a concept, send one student to another group to find out other options. This person could be the low achiever who is given special recognition in this role.

Perform Trust Activities When the cooperative skills lag, return to the trust activities or the team identity tasks (reviewing group goals, creating team flags, making a team ad, etc.).

Review the Social Skills or Introduce New Ones By introducing a high-energy, high-involvement activity as the hook for a review of needed social skills, the teacher can review the skills without a heavy hand.

Work Directly on the Students' Self-Concept By structuring activities for goal setting (individual and group), building encouragement, strengthening team identity and discovering personal likes, cooperative learning helps students experience classroom success, which is of paramount importance to building high self-esteem.

Tighten Other Aspects of Group Structure Be specific about what is expected from each person in the jigsaw or the group wraparound. Each of these can tighten group work without making a big noise. As Pat Taylor, a geometry teacher in Richmond, Virginia, tells her students, "You are each accountable for every concept you learn in your cooperative groups." To back this up, she uses a variety of techniques to ensure that their focus is not on "What grade did you get?" but on "What did you learn about this math topic?"

Practices in individual learning communicate to each student his/her personal responsibility for learning the concepts and skills taught. In addition to the ideas described, here are samples of other usable transfer for increasing individual learning:

1. *Answer a random oral quiz.* Pick one person from the group to answer the question.
2. *Take a post-activity quiz.* Have all students take a quiz at the end of the lecture or activity. Instead of grading the quizzes, have students compare and discuss their work.
3. *Write a paper.* Have all students write an essay, letter or memo to summarize the lesson.
4. *Sign on the line.* Have each student sign the idea he/she contributed or the problem he/she solved.
5. *Explain to a neighbor.* Select one half of the class to explain why an answer was correct or wrong to the other half of the class or orchestrate a human graph (see blackline on page 335).
6. *Get signatures from all.* Have everyone in the group sign the statement: "I made my best contribution." ______________________________
7. *Hold a tournament.* Teams that raise the quiz scores of all its members earn points.
8. *Use a group evaluator.* Give one student in the group a checklist with which to observe and give feedback on participating, idea sharing and other social skills.
9. *Complete homework practice.* After successful group practice, assign and collect individual "homework" practice.

10. *Make a test.* Have each group make a test on a topic. Rotate group tests.
11. *Evaluate a neighbor.* Use a PMI chart or Mrs. Potter's questions for groups to evaluate individual performances in the group.
12. *Give round-robin answers.* Use a round robin (also called forced response and wraparound) with different lead-ins to check skills.
13. *Share group products.* Have each group present its product to the class. All members have a role in their presentation.
14. *Explain the answers.* After one student gives an answer, select another to explain why it is or is not correct.
15. *Coach a partner.* Instruct groups that finish a task first to coach groups still working.
16. *Do a jigsaw or expert jigsaw.* After instructing student groups to jigsaw material (see blackline master on page 336), have them do an expert jigsaw in which students form expert groups to research the same material. They review and confirm their information before returning to their base groups to teach group members the material.

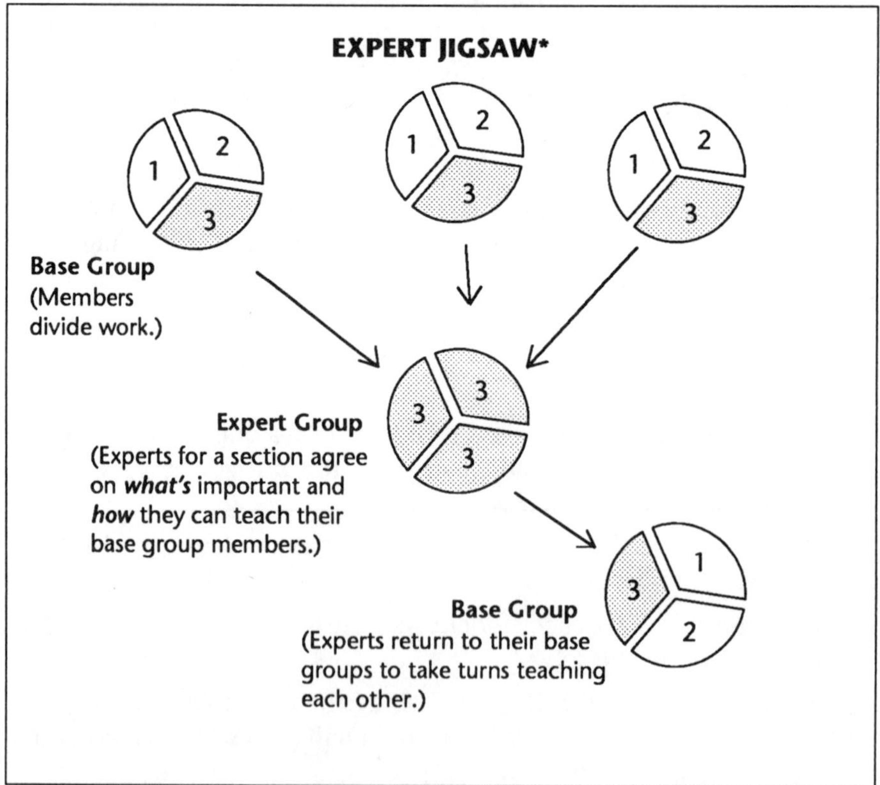
EXPERT JIGSAW*
1
2
3
Base Group
(Members
divide work.)
Expert Group
(Experts for a section agree
on ***what's*** important and
how they can teach their
base group members.)
Base Group
(Experts return to their base
groups to take turns teaching
each other.)

17. *Create Individual Applications.* Have each student brainstorm a way to apply or transfer a concept.
18. *Make Log Entries.* At the end of each lesson, have students complete the stem, "I learned...," in their logs. Randomly check their entries.
19. *Use a Teacher-Observer.* Tell the class which participation skills will be observed. Wander through the class, make notes and give feedback.
20. *Make a Team Ad.* Have students list the positive contributions of each team member on a team ad.

*page 337

IN CONCLUSION

When all else is said and done about tests and grades, there is a growing amount of evidence that *thinking in the cooperative classroom* shows the most powerful effects on learning even with the most traditional measuring tools. When studying the research on cooperative learning and the research on thinking, it is hard to ignore that many of the studies use only standardized test measures to assess performance. As Joyce points out in his meta-study:

> *So further, with the gains in achievement, school liking, retention, self-esteem and problem solving measured by Johnson and Johnson, Slavin and others, the sum total tells us that the question to ask about grades, checks and tests is, 'Which ways can we measure?' If we accept that there are multiple ways, not just the standardized test, then we are on the right track.*

However, it is also clear that the cooperative model provides a wonderful window of opportunity, especially when teachers BUILD individual learning into every lesson for evaluating student performance in many new dimensions.

□ □ □

Update your task sequence on page 348.

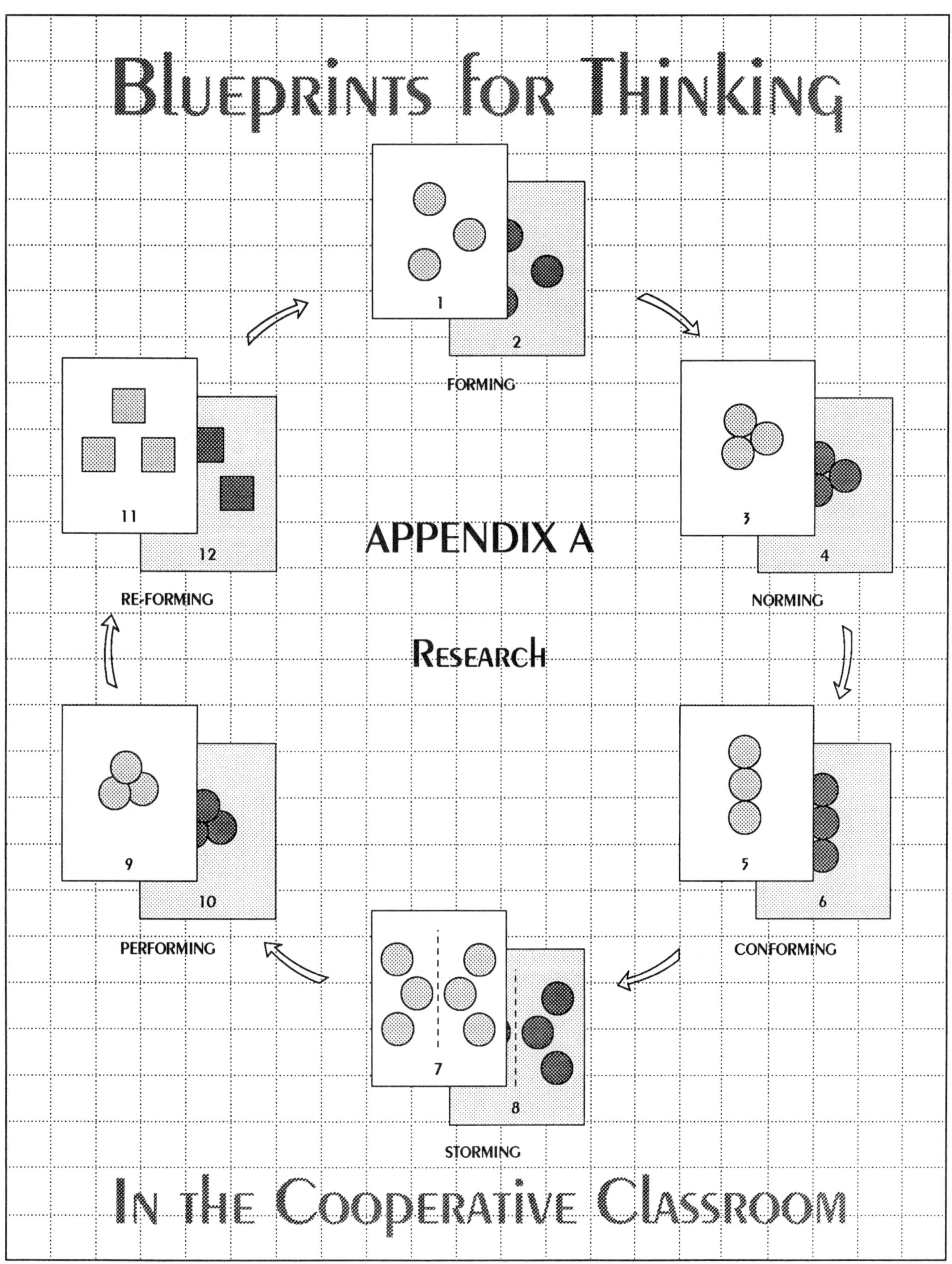
Blueprints for Thinking
1
2
FORMING
3
4
NORMING
5
6
CONFORMING
7
8
STORMING
9
10
PERFORMING
11
12
RE-FORMING
APPENDIX A
Research
In the Cooperative Classroom

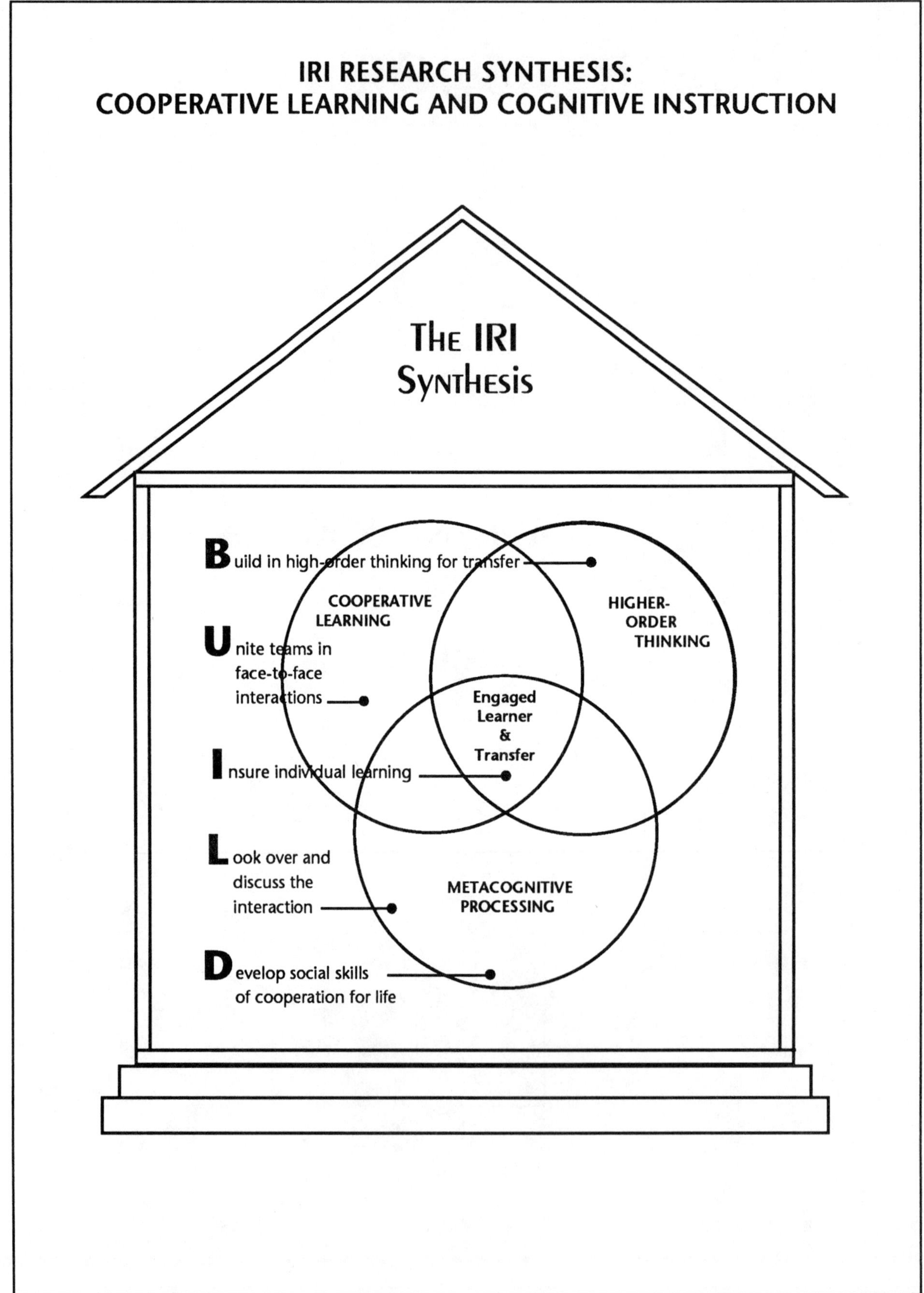
IRI RESEARCH SYNTHESIS:
COOPERATIVE LEARNING AND COGNITIVE INSTRUCTION
The IRI
Synthesis
Build in high-order thinking for transfer
COOPERATIVE
LEARNING
HIGHER-
ORDER
THINKING
Unite teams in
face-to-face
interactions
Engaged
Learner
&
Transfer
Insure individual learning
Look over and
discuss the
interaction
METACOGNITIVE
PROCESSING
Develop social skills
of cooperation for life

APPENDIX A: RESEARCH

THE BIG PICTURE: THE RESEARCH AND THE RATIONALE

A brief look at the research provides the rationale and theoretical foundations for cooperative learning and cognitive instruction as the undergirding themes in *Blueprints*. These theoretical girders that support the ideas presented in *Blueprints* are categorized into two major sections: Cooperative Learning Research and Cognitive Instruction Research. Within section I, four schools of cooperative learning are presented along with a fifth and final model, the IRI model, which synthesizes the critical elements of the other four and addresses the additional element of higher-order thinking in cooperative tasks. In section II, cognitive instruction is separated into four distinct areas: explicit thinking skills, cognitive organizers, metacognition and transfer.

Section I: Cooperative Learning
- Four models
- IRI synthesis

Section II: Cognitive Instruction
- Explicit thinking skills
- Cognitive organizers
- Metacognition
- Transfer

Each of these broad areas of research is presented in a separate section for teachers to use as a quick reference to the findings. In conclusion, the theoretical bases are synthesized briefly into a final piece that weaves the separate strands together in the fabric called *Blueprints*. Please refer to the following sections for an in-depth look at the theory and research that support this effort.

What It's All About

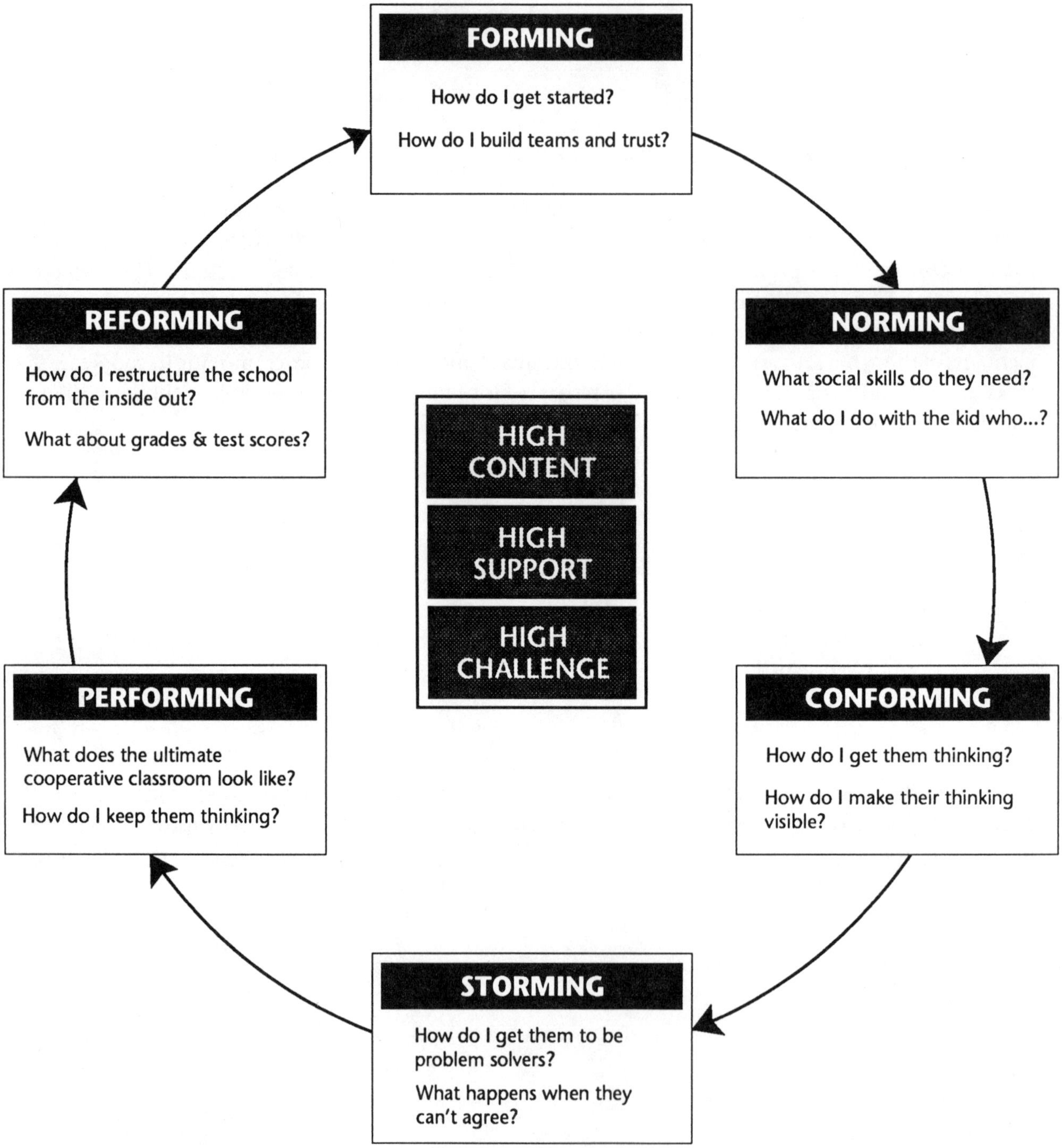

FORMING

How do I get started?

How do I build teams and trust?

NORMING

What social skills do they need?

What do I do with the kid who...?

CONFORMING

How do I get them thinking?

How do I make their thinking visible?

STORMING

How do I get them to be problem solvers?

What happens when they can't agree?

PERFORMING

What does the ultimate cooperative classroom look like?

How do I keep them thinking?

REFORMING

How do I restructure the school from the inside out?

What about grades & test scores?

HIGH CONTENT

HIGH SUPPORT

HIGH CHALLENGE

Beginning with the nitty-gritties of *forming* cooperative learning groups, developing trust during the *norming* phase, building self-concept and self-esteem through the *conforming* phase, and learning strategies for coping with the conflicts of the *storming* phase, higher-order thinking functions smoothly in the *performing* stage and the cycle is reignited each time new groups are formed.

Section I

COOPERATIVE LEARNING RESEARCH

A LOOK BACK

Any naysayer who says that cooperative learning is just a fad or another new wrinkle, may find the following bit of history interesting. In the earliest settlements, the pioneer families knew the benefits of tutoring their children in groups. Very often, older students paired with the younger "to cipher the slates," read stories and review their bible lessons. In the pioneer schools, several families bunched their children into one room. The young teacher, very often one of the oldest students, relied heavily on the children to help each other with lessons. Well into the 20th century in rural America, the one-room schoolhouse with cross-age tutors, cooperative learning groups and group investigations were the norm. Not until the urban school emerged and the modern factory arrived did schools adopt the assembly line model of teaching and learning. Even at that time, educational leaders such as Francis Parker, superintendent of Quincy Public School (1875-80), John Dewey, Carlton Washborne and Martin Deutch were strong advocates of the cooperative learning model. As early as 1889, Pepitone, Twiner and Triplett were conducting the first formal studies. Today, thanks to the work of Johnson and Johnson, Slavin and others, numerous studies document the powerful effects of cooperative learning as well as the specific elements needed to make cooperation work in the classroom. No other instructional method used today can claim the quantity or quality of research highlighting its success.

In the 1970s, two major school issues gave birth to a concentrated focus on cooperative learning. The first was the mainstreaming issue; the second was the integration challenge.

When Public Law 94-142 was passed by Congress in the 1970s, schools had to restructure classrooms to include the handicapped. Many students previously separated from regular classroom life were mainstreamed. Regular teachers, not knowing how to "handle" students who had physical disabilities, learning and behavioral problems were concerned. The first concern focused on how the "regular" and the "special" students would get along. Many of the mainstreamed students lacked "social skills" and could easily antagonize their peers; many regular students who were equally lacking in these social skills, estranged their new classmates.

Following the integration directions established by the Supreme Court in Brown vs. Board of Education, 1954, schools across the nation were challenged to restructure student assignment patterns. "Separate but equal" schools were out. As students from different racial groups were mixed into unsegregated schools and classrooms, the concerns focused on how these young people would "get along."

Roger and David Johnson, two brothers at the University of Minnesota, proposed a solution that applied to both challenges—direct instruction of social skills with guided classroom practice. They theorized that students taught to work cooperatively in small groups would develop positive social skills. This in turn, they speculated, would speed the integration of students who saw each other as different.

To everyone's pleasant surprise, the data gathered in these early programs not only showed that their methods worked as planned for improving student-to-student interaction, but also had two unpredicted side effects—dramatic increases in the academic achievement of students and positive effects in students' self-esteem.

From these early studies sprang more than 500 studies by Johnson and Johnson and others. Over and over, with a consistency and reliability remarkable for a school methodology, the studies have demonstrated how and why cooperative learning is one of the most powerful teaching and learning tools available. In his meta-study of research on the various models of teaching, Bruce Joyce wrote: "Research on cooperative learning is overwhelmingly positive, and the cooperative approaches are appropriate for all curriculum areas. The more complex the outcomes (higher-order processing of information, problem solving, social skills, and attitudes), the greater are the effects."

No instructional tool has held the researchers' attention more than the cooperative model. Johnson and Johnson, perhaps the most prolific researchers of cooperative learning, claim we know more about cooperative learning than any other instructional methodology. They further point out that the results hold true across age, subject matter, race, nationality, sex and every other discriminator.

THE MAJOR FINDINGS

- Students who learn in the cooperative model perform better academically than students who learn in the individualistic or competitive models. The Johnsons' 1981 meta-analysis of 122 studies shows that cooperative learning tended to give higher achievement results than the other two methods, especially with such higher-level tasks as problem solving, concept attainment and predicting. Further studies indicate why this superior success occurs.

- Because of the quantity of "cognitive rehearsal," all students of all ability levels in cooperative learning groups enhance their short- and long-term memory as well as their critical thinking skills. (Johnson, 1983)

- Because cooperative experiences promote positive self-acceptance, students improve their learning, self-esteem, school liking and motivation to participate. (Johnson, 1983)

- Because cooperative learning leads to positive interaction among students, intrinsic learning motivation and emotional involvement in learning are developed to a high degree. (Johnson, 1989)

- Because cooperative learning nurtures positive peer relationships and structures positive interactions, students in cooperative learning classrooms develop stronger scholastic aspirations, more pro-social behavior and more positive peer relationships. (Johnson, 1979; Johnson and Matross, 1977)

There are a variety of successful approaches to cooperative learning. Although it is clear to the researchers that classrooms organized for cooperative learning produce superior academic, social and personal results, they do debate on which is the "best" approach—at least as measured by research standards. Because few practitioners have the luxury to isolate classroom practice to the "purity" desired by the researchers, most classroom teachers adopt a single approach or a combination of approaches that works best with their own teaching style and their students. Ironically, the research on staff development tells us that the most effective practitioners are more likely to pull the best from each approach and create their own approaches.

THE FIVE APPROACHES

A brief look at the major approaches will help teachers clarify the pluses and minuses of each and understand the tremendous wealth of successful cooperative tools that have been developed.

Cooperative Learning: Five Models

MODEL	CREATOR	DESCRIPTION	PLUSES	MINUSES
The Conceptual Approach	Johnsons Cohen	Theories of cooperation, competition and expectation-state theory	+ creative teachers create + can easily enhance what experienced teacher already does	- time away from content - no recipes - extra planning time - not step-by-step - unskilled teachers - full commitment
Curriculum Packages Approach	Slavin	Curriculum packages that have cooperative learning structured into the materials	+ easy to train + daily + pretested strategies + instructional variety (HOT/Dir. instruction)	- no direct teaching of social skill - discourages transfer - not a lot of curriculum packages available
A Structures Approach	Kagan	A repertoire of interactive strategies	+ simplicity in structures + easy to use + builds repertoire of strategies	- cutesy - assumes transfer - if restricted to low level tasks
The Group Investigation Model	Sharan & Sharan	The ultimate classroom jigsaw	+ inquiry + social skills + creative problem solving + facilitates skills + gives depth to content	- not good for curriculum coverage - if students have poor social skills - if parents want same assignment for all
The IRI Synthesis with HOT	Bellanca Fogarty	A synthesis of the four cooperative learning approaches with higher order thinking focus	+ synthesis + creative application + transfer	- needs training - needs commitment from school & district

MODEL 1: THE CONCEPTUAL APPROACH

Roger Johnson, a science educator, and his brother, David Johnson, a social psychology researcher, use their early studies of cooperative learning to frame the conceptual approach. They argue that all effective cooperative learning is marked by five critical characteristics. If all five are present, there is cooperative learning; if any one attribute is missing, there may be group work, but not cooperative learning.

Johnsons' Five Elements of Cooperative Groups

1. **Face-to-Face Interaction.** The physical arrangement of students in small, heterogeneous groups encourages students to help, share and support each other's learning.
2. **Individual Accountability.** Each student is responsible for the success and collaboration of the group and for mastering the assigned task.
3. **Cooperative Social Skills.** Students are taught, coached and monitored in the use of cooperative social skills, which enhance the group work.
4. **Positive Interdependence.** Students are structured by a common goal, group rewards, role assignments and other means to assist each other in completing the learning task.
5. **Group Processing.** Students reflect on how well they work as a group to complete the task and how they can improve their teamwork.

In any cooperative lesson, these characteristics overlap. They are identified to reinforce the notion that all groups are not cooperative groups. As mental "coat hooks," the characteristics provide a framework for designing strong and effective cooperative learning tasks. They also provide an umbrella under which a large variety of cooperative strategies, structures and activities may be gathered. As the teacher designs a cooperative lesson, these characteristics are the checklist to ensure the greatest success.

Pluses and Minuses

For teachers who dislike recipe and workbook teaching, the conceptual model is a delight. In effect, the Johnsons' research acts as a touchstone against which the experienced teacher can measure what he/she already does with groups and make quick, positive adjustments that result in greater student-to-student teamwork. For the teacher who has never used groups, the approach provides definite standards that point out some sure ways to start. The Johnsons recognize—as do adult learning researchers such as Fullan, Knowles and Krupp—that a teacher is most likely to add to his/her repertoire of skills and strategies when there are street lights to guide the progress.

There are several definite minuses to the conceptual model. First, it requires extra time for planning lessons. Even when used only as guided lesson practice, this approach requires time to restructure lesson plans. When the teacher is taking a bolder step to prepare an inquiry or group investigation, even more time is needed "up front."

Second, the conceptual approach doesn't work well for teachers who want a workbook, ditto masters for step-by-step procedure manuals, absolute quiet or straight rows of desks. This approach requires a teacher who is most comfortable creating lessons in and around required concepts and skills. The teacher who cannot tolerate ambiguity and chance that a lesson might go flat without a step-by-step procedure manual, workbooks or blackline masters, shouldn't start here.

Third, the conceptual model may end up as poison for the bright child. When a teacher restricts most of the cooperative learning to low-level recall tasks (vocabulary review, computational practice, etc.), the gifted child never gets the chance to soar. Instead, he/she ends up as a substitute teacher doing work for the other children, never reaping any of the social or intellectual benefits.

Fourth, the conceptual model requires a full commitment to learning and transfer. The teacher needs time to learn the model, to develop the skills, strategies, and structures and to redesign the classroom. As Bruce Joyce has pointed out, this instructional change process requires not only well-taught demonstrations, but also a solid peer coaching program and administrative support for implementing the changes.

Fifth, because there is no prepared day-to-day cooperative learning curriculum, the conceptual model sometimes is used only as filler for "What do we do on Friday afternoons?" and "Let's play a cooperative game."

Finally, the conceptual approach does bump against the "coverage" curriculum. It does take more time in the crowded day to teach lessons in the conceptual model of cooperative learning. Where does the social skill instruction fit in? Where is the time for group processing? The conceptual approach demands time away from content coverage to ensure successful learning by all students.

MODEL 2: THE CURRICULUM APPROACH

Slavin's research, conducted with colleagues at the Johns Hopkins University Center for Research on Elementary and Middle Schools, focuses on cooperative learning and basic skill instruction. Slavin and his colleagues have developed a series of cooperative curriculum programs in math and language arts. They have prescribed specific cooperative strategies that teachers can easily learn as they promote heterogeneous cooperation. Because they desire to find workable alternatives to tracking and ability grouping practices, especially where those practices are detrimental to poor and minority children, they stress packages that all teachers can easily use.

Slavin's Curriculum Packages

1. Team Accelerated Instruction (TAI)
2. Cooperative Integrated Reading and Composition (CIRC)
3. Teams, Games, Tournaments (TGT)
4. Student Teams, Achievement Division (STAD)

1. **Team Accelerated Instruction (TAI)** is a mathematics program that combines cooperative learning with individualized instruction in a heterogeneous classroom. Designed for grades three to six, TAI utilizes the students to tutor each other, to encourage accurate work, to produce positive social effects and to handle the record-keeping logistics of individualized instruction or programmed learning. Each eight weeks, teams of high, middle and low achievers take achievement tests for placement in the individualized program. In the teams, students help each other through the material. Each day, the teacher pulls students from the

heterogeneous groups for focused instruction. Students work in teams and across teams to progress through the material. Each week, progress scores are established for each team. Pre-criteria are established for the degrees of recognition each team receives.

TAI is most notable for dispelling the myth that math instruction *must* be done by track or ability group. One look at the results clearly shows how TAI students of all abilities do better at computation in concepts and at applications with supportive effects in math self-concept, math liking, behavior, relations and acceptance of differences. (Slavin, 1985)

2. **Cooperative Integrated Reading and Composition (CIRC).** In preparing a cooperative curriculum for language arts, grades three and four, Slavin's group used cooperative methods for reading groups (eight to fifteen students) and reading teams (two or three students). As students work in their teams, they earn points for their groups. Points based on scores from quizzes, essays and book reports allow students to earn certificates. As some teams use a variety of strategies, the teacher monitors progress or instructs other teams in comprehension strategies (e.g., predicting, comparing, drawing conclusions). Included in the strategies are partner reading, story prediction, words aloud practice, spelling review, partner checking and team comprehension games. At times, students work individually doing independent reading, basal work or book reports.

   CIRC research results are most notable for showing the benefits of cooperative learning with mainstreamed handicapped students, without detriment to the highest-performing students. In the studies, high, medium and low performers showed equal gains, although the mainstreamed handicapped gains were most impressive. (Slavin et al., 1988)

3. **Teams, Games, Tournaments,** maybe the most widely known of the Slavin/Hopkins curricular approaches, is adaptable to any curricular area, K–12. In this format, students work in groups to master content provided by the teacher. After practicing on worksheets, students demonstrate mastery of the content in weekly tournaments. Students compete in teams against other teams of equal ability (e.g., top achievers vs. top achievers).

4. **STAD (Student Teams, Achievement Division).** STAD was designed by Slavin and the Hopkins Group in 1982. In these heterogeneous groups, four or five students who are mixed by ability, ethnic and gender differences work on worksheets that already have the answers provided. The common goal is to understand the answers, not fill in the blanks. The teams quiz each other until all members understand the answers. The task is completed when the teacher gives an individual quiz to each member. The team score is the sum of the improvement points earned by each individual. Special recognition is given to the teams with the greatest improvement.

Pluses and Minuses

There are seven pluses for the curriculum approach to cooperative learning: (1) It is easy to train teachers. The lessons and strategies are preset for a beginning level training program and show how to use the set curriculum. (2) The approach builds in daily cooperative learning that needs little pre-planning on the teacher's part. By setting out daily lessons, there is higher probability that they will be used. (3) The strategies are pretested as appropriate to each content. The teacher can worry less about "doing the right thing." (4) The curriculum has built-in instructional variety. Small-group, large-group and individual activities are balanced with direct instruction by the teacher. (5) The programs take a "higher-order" thinking approach to direct instruction and guided practice of content. (6) Most of the critical attributes of cooperative learning outlined by the Johnsons are inherent within each curriculum. And, (7) it gets results in self-esteem as well as academic achievement.

The minuses most frequently discussed regarding the curriculum approach center on social skill instruction. In the model, social skills are developed indirectly. There is no room *given* for direct instruction to students on how to work cooperatively. While the approach works very well with skilled classroom managers and with students who are well-behaved, many teachers report that it breaks down when competition (as in TGT or CIRC) between groups becomes too intense, the teacher lacks strong management skills, or the students have little experience or valuing of cooperative learning.

The second minus derives from the first curriculum thrust. The detailed, step-by-step procedure for implementing cooperative learning within a set curriculum discourages transfer of the approach to other curricular areas. For instance, if the teacher is using CIRC for math, he/she may not see any way to use cooperative elements in reading or social studies.

The third minus is the very small number of developed cooperative curricula available for the classroom. Although some major educational publishers are suggesting some cooperative activities within science and language arts texts, the scope of well-developed cooperative curricula is limited.

MODEL 3: THE STRUCTURAL APPROACH

Since 1967, Spencer Kagan has focused his research on the structural approach to cooperative learning. This approach is based on the creation, analysis and application of *content-free* structures that cause students to interact in positive ways in the classroom. Content-free structures, usable with any content, enable the teacher to make multiple applications of a single structure in a variety of subjects. (The debate about content-free structures and content-specific structures is heard, it seems, whenever skill-theorists get together. Their debates on study skills, thinking skills, social skills and reading skills have very similar dialogues. While there is clear evidence that both content-free and content-specific structures produce positive effects, there is little proof one method is superior to the other.)

Kagan's structures fall into three groups:

Kagan's Structures

A. **In Turn.** The teacher structures a task in which individuals take a turn in a prescribed order. Included among these are "round robin" or "response in turn," "round table," "four corners" and "three-step interview."

B. **Jigsaw.** The teacher structures the task so that each student in the group has part of the information to study. When all members teach each other their material, the whole is greater than the parts. "Level I jigsaw," "level II jigsaw," "co-op–co-op," and "think-pair-share" all follow this format.

C. **Match-Ups.** The teacher structures student-to-student tasks, which formally and informally create cooperative situations. Included here are "match mine," "numbered heads together," "co-op cards" and "partners."

Pluses and Minuses

The pluses and minuses of the structural approach begin with its simplicity. Each structure is easy to use. This means it takes less than a staff-development hour to master a single structure and to develop a variety of appropriate activities. The new structures blend quickly with lecture format and provide practical ways to develop "quick," informal student interactions and well-structured discussions.

Just as teachers easily switch to cooperative structures from more traditional classroom methods, students also easily adapt to the new methods. Because of the number of structure options, a teacher can introduce more variety into the daily regimen and thus boost motivation.

As the teacher builds a more extensive repertoire of cooperative structures, he/she can find a number of ways to create multi-dimensional lessons. For example:

ANTICIPATORY SET: The teacher calls a student to the front of class and interviews the student. "Who are you? What is your age? Where were you born? When did you start school here? Why do you think I am asking you these questions?" Answer to the why question: to model an interview that uses the basic five questions of who, what, when, where and why.

OBJECTIVE: The teacher shows the lesson objective on the overhead: "To develop interview questions in preparation for a news article."

INPUT: The teacher shows the newspaper model on the overhead, explains the key questions and demonstrates how the parts of the graphic are used. She uses the questions asked in the anticipatory set to demonstrate.

CHECKING FOR UNDERSTANDING: The teacher tells the students to **turn to a neighbor**. Next, he/she has one student in each pair explain to the partner how to use the newspaper model to generate the questions. After three minutes, the groups stop. Several different listeners from the pairs describe what they heard. Other students give corrective feedback as needed.

GUIDED PRACTICE: The teacher distributes one copy of the model to each pair. A **recorder and a worrier-checker** are assigned. The **pairs review** roles and **cooperative guidelines** as the teacher monitors and assists the pairs as needed. After this round, several pairs describe the questions they asked and explain why they made each selection. Again, corrective feedback is encouraged. A second round of models is given out for additional practice.

UNGUIDED PRACTICE: For homework, all students are given a blank sheet of instructions for interviewing a household member of their choice.

CLOSURE: On the next day, **each pair joins a second pair** and they review and critique each other's interview questions. This is followed by an all-class discussion about interview questions. Which questions are most important? Why? What benefits the writer?

The third plus is that the structures readily lend themselves to problem solving and the application of thinking tasks. For example, partner structures can work at any level of thinking.

Thinking Level I: Gathering Information

1. Assign each pair in a team a list of vocabulary words. Have the pairs coach and quiz each other on the meanings of assigned words. If any pair is unsure of a definition, have it "travel" to another pair for advice.
2. When all pairs are ready, have a final check for mastery in each team. Follow this with a quiz in which teams compete against each other.

Thinking Level II: Processing Information

1. Have each pair use the vocabulary words to create a story about the current season of the year. If any pair gets stuck, let it "travel" for help to another pair.
2. Have each pair share its story with the team. Encourage the team to *explain why* each story was done well.

Thinking Level III: Applying Information

1. Have each pair hypothesize changes that might occur to this season of the year if global warming increases in the next decade.
2. Have pairs share their hypotheses in a team. Assign one person in a team to list the hypotheses on a sheet of newsprint. Encourage the teams to discuss and rank their hypotheses based on which effect would be most disastrous.

The simplicity of the structural approach is a double-edged sword. Because the structures look "fun and cute," a teacher may save the structures for Friday afternoon fillers. Consequently, the students get the message that these are play activities, and they reap little value from the potential richness of the cooperative structure.

The second minus is that the structural approach assumes a great deal about student transfer of the cooperative ethic, cooperative skills and cooperative behaviors. Much is left to the teacher's enthusiasm, assertiveness and ability to design a variety of lessons with each content area—that is, if the teacher's classroom management skills and enthusiasm are to "hook" students into cooperative tasks. However, because the structural approach works best as a "hook," the cooperative skills are transferred more by osmosis than by formal instruction. As with the curriculum approach, the lack of formal group-processing and formal social-skill instruction limits the transfer of the cooperative skills beyond the specific task to the super learners.

The third minus of the structural approach occurs when the teacher restricts the use of cooperative structures to low-level and routine classroom tasks (spelling words, worksheets, computation drill and practice, etc.). Students quickly perceive such limited use as a gambit to manipulate quick interest.

MODEL 4: THE GROUP INVESTIGATION APPROACH

A classroom teacher who used both the conceptual approach and the structural approach called group investigation the "ultimate jigsaw." "For my classes," she wrote, "group investigation is the most powerful and empowering of the cooperative methods." In group investigation, students work together to plan how they will find answers to key questions about a topic of mutual interest. The group breaks down the work into individual or pair investigation tasks. Each person gathers the assigned information and brings it to the group for discussion, synthesis and reporting to the class. The teacher plays the major facilitating role through each stage of this inquiry process.

Sharan & Sharan's Group Investigation Model

Stage 1: Posing the Big Question and Forming Groups by Interest. The teacher frames the broad topic, which the students investigate as a "big" question.

- What do you think will happen if the U.S. produces twice as much nuclear waste per year each year for the next decade?
- How would our American society be different today if we had lost World War II?
- What can we learn from a study of plant life?

After the big question, students are encouraged to brainstorm *what they want to know* about the topic. If they need stimulation, the teacher provides a potpourri of print or video materials, a guest lecturer or a field trip. Generated questions are reviewed in teams, and then classified and synthesized into subtopics for small-group investigation.

Stage 2: Identifying the Inquiry Problem and Planning How to Research. Each student selects a subtopic to investigate. The subtopic teams formulate the problem statement and help each other discuss and plan the search process.

Stage 3: Dividing Up the Work and Gathering Information. The groups divide up the research. Members research their information, analyze it and draw tentative conclusions.

Stage 4: Preparing the Report. The groups translate their results into a class report. The teacher schedules the reports.

Stage 5: Presenting and Evaluating the Report. As the groups make formal presentations, the teacher guides discussions on their results. Finally, students evaluate their work.

Pluses and Minuses

If the teacher wants the optimum structure for encouraging inquiry, student-to-student interaction, cooperative social-skill development, creative problem-solving and communication skills, this approach provides it. If the teacher wants the maximum opportunity to use his/her facilitation skills with students, group investigation provides it. If the teacher wants students to delve deeply into a concept in the curriculum, then he/she will find no better motivator.

On the other hand, if the teacher is concerned about curriculum coverage, a supervisor who expects quiet students in seat rows or to know what each student is doing every moment, then group investigation will not work. If students are not well prepared for positive interaction, question asking, problem solving and consensus seeking, or if they cannot handle the open-ended tasks, the group investigation will fall flat. And if parents expect uniform assignments, daily quizzes and grades, grades, grades, don't even think about group investigation. In short, the minuses of this approach focus on lack of order and recall; its pluses focus on abundant cognitive rehearsal.

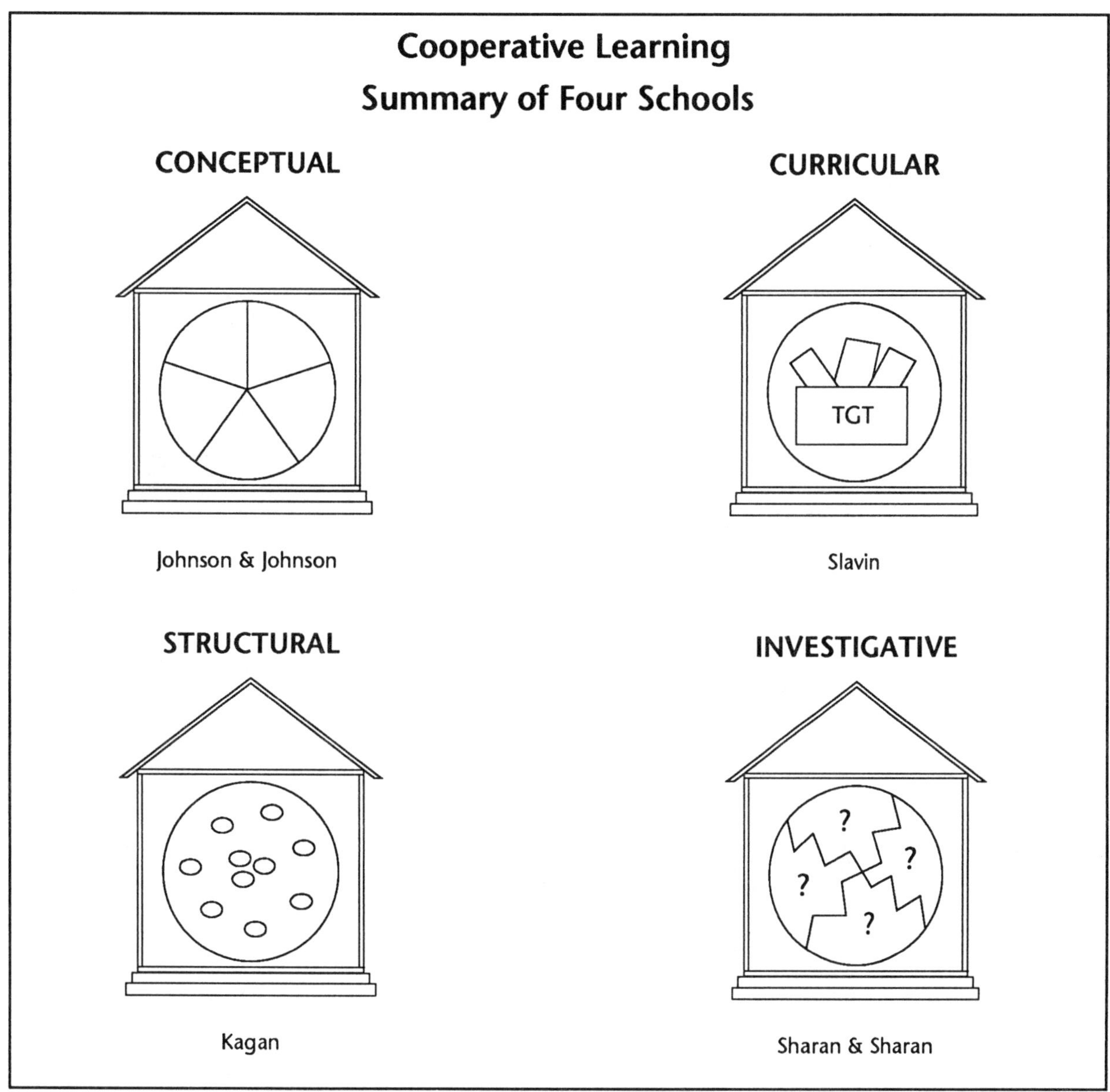

MODEL 5: IRI SYNTHESIS APPROACH

A study of these various approaches shows that no *one* approach is sufficient or superior. Obviously, cooperative learning in some form is a necessary tool for use in every effective classroom. In this context, it serves the practical teacher to live with a design that borrows the best from each approach.

As we have listened and worked with teachers in their classrooms, it has become more and more clear that a synthesized model that ties cooperative learning with a critical and creative thinking context of learning for transfer is needed. We look at cooperative learning as an essential ingredient for developing students who are more able to think critically and creatively. We sometimes sketch the picture of cooperative learning as a jet engine: critical and creative thinking skills are the fuel. When put together, they produce a powerful thrust for soaring to new frontiers of discovery and adventure.

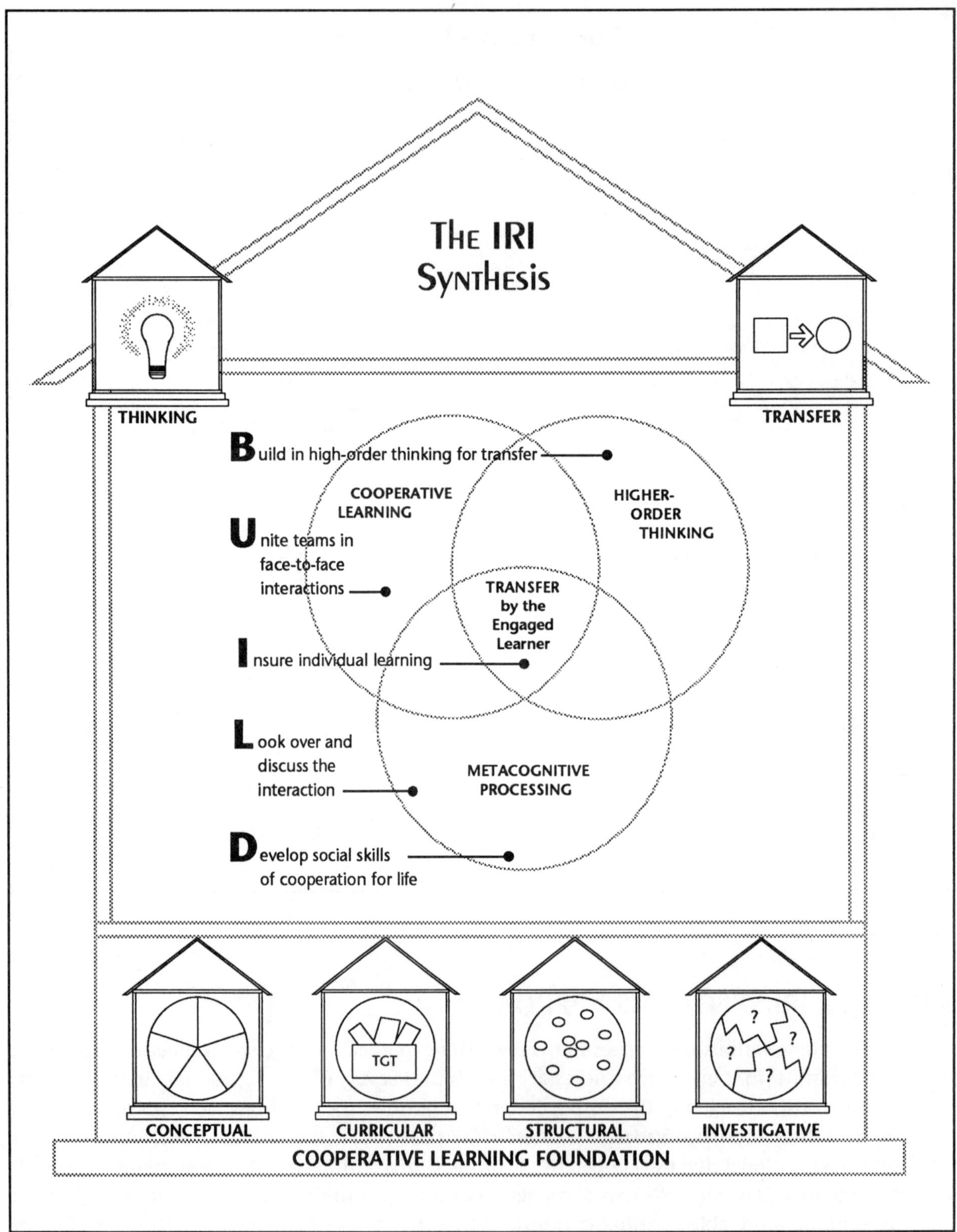

The IRI transfer model of cooperative learning synthesizes the most effective elements of the earlier models with the more recent research on explicit thinking skills, metacognition, cognitive organizers and learning for transfer for staff as well as for students. Using the acronym BUILD, the IRI Synthesis is summarized in the diagram above.

The Essential Concepts Plus One

The Johnson and Johnson model outlines the five essential ingredients that distinguish cooperative learning from other forms of group work and which are necessary for making cooperative learning succeed in the classroom. When combined with cognitive processing (so lessons focus on higher-order thinking tasks) the additional element of thinking for transfer is also added. And when each and every lesson is structured from this transfer perspective, even more dynamic changes occur in the classroom.

What the Kagan model calls cooperative structures, trainers in other fields such as Kenneth Blanchard, Thomas Peters and University Associates (business training and development), Jack Canfield (self-esteem), Louis Raths (values clarification) and Joel Goodman (creative problem-solving) have called "strategies." Whichever name is used, the common element is that the "strategies" approach to staff development encourages the quickest transfer and use without falling into the workbook mentality. In the IRI synthesis model, an inductive approach is used. First, teacher trainees begin with basic strategies that are easy to apply and use. This is the practical element. The integrated staff development program begins with participants working together to plan how to weave these basic strategies into the classroom. After the trainees have experienced strategies, both as students and as teachers, they explore the conceptual framework; the concepts prevent the strategies from being isolated games. Later, in an advanced program, after intensive classroom application, the trainees focus on the more sophisticated strategies. These require students with higher-level social skills and concentration on inert cognition, problem solving and reasoning in a variety of contents (e.g., math reasoning, language arts, science). In the final stage, trainees concentrate on two leaders for mentor coaching and curriculum renewal. Both extend the use of cooperative learning and cognitive instruction to teamwork and problem solving as key components for effective transfer.

Pluses and Minuses

The IRI transfer model asks for a long-term and intense commitment to staff development. Moreover, it expects that what happens in the training program, as well as what happens in the classroom, will be used. With this synthesis, teachers can begin switching from a focus on recall and quick-answer tests to a focus on transferring knowledge and skills across the curriculum and into life outside the school walls.

This model takes time. In an already crowded curriculum, with more and more coverage being required, where is the time for group processing, metacognition or social skills? To do these functions well, content coverage must give way.

The teacher who uses this model needs a high tolerance for ambiguity. If the classroom is a world of one right answer, the first precondition for developing the intelligent behaviors and social skills is lacking. In this model, greater emphasis is placed on helping youngsters process and apply information than on having students memorize great quantities of detailed information. The teacher most often is asked to challenge and extend thinking and less often to inoculate students with information.

The teacher using the IRI model also needs strong planning skills and a creative beat. He/she will not have a page-by-page recipe or a lock-step teacher's guide. The teacher must feel comfortable with his/her own ability to design lessons that incorporate not only cooperative learning, but also intelligent behavior and reasoning skills.

The IRI model requires intense and supportive staff development for most implementors. This means the district will need to spend money not only for intensive training days, but also for coaching teams, administrative inservice and opportunities to restructure curriculum.

The IRI model is difficult to test with standardized instruments. This is especially true when trying to measure students' transfer of concepts, their ability to reason *and* their acquisition of knowledge. To succeed, assessments other than scantron tests are needed. The IRI transfer model advantageously asks students to strive for intelligent behavior, not test results. This is well outside the norms imposed by the current and fanatical interest in quick tests of isolated facts and skills.

The IRI model will push a school on essential curricular change. Thinking and cooperating require more time for in-depth exploration of concepts, in-depth practice of skills and an emphasis on inquiry rather than answers. When the coverage curriculum is the norm and isolated facts the king, there is not time for quality thinking or intense cooperation. Unless the school district is ready to challenge the restrictive time limits and coverage of materials, and unless it is ready to redesign curricula with transfer in mind, teachers can expect students to have a more difficult time with transfer.

The IRI model does not, however, necessitate the total curricula changeover. But it does facilitate change by encouraging teachers to set new priorities in their curricula—i.e., "What are the most important concepts to establish firmly vs. what are the facts to cover more quickly?"

It also encourages teachers to think about thinking skills as tools for unifying and integrating their curriculum. For instance, they can teach prediction in depth with language arts lessons and use science, math and social studies materials for students to practice thinking skills in cooperative groups.

In effect, the combination of cooperative learning and cognitive development is not just equal to a math computation in addition (cooperation plus thinking is not the same as 3+3=6), but rather a multiplication of components (3x3=9) in the classroom. Add still another factor, a transfer-based staff-development program with structured coaching and support, and a powerful, exponential change process that produces effective, multi-dimensional results (3x3x3=27) is engaged.

Now, to look at the cognitive research . . . What is the research? What does it tell us? . . . The research that springs from cognitive development actually comes from four distinct bodies of literature:

- Explicit Thinking Skills
- Cognitive Organizers
- Metacognition
- Transfer

The explicit instruction of a thinking skill is the initial body of research that served as a catalyst to the thinking skills movement in the early 1980s. Coupled with the emerging information on left/right brain hemispheres and the notion of cognitive maps and visual representations to aid memory and learning, cognitive strategies began finding their place in the classroom. At the same time, the research on reading focused on the concept of thinking strategically about how one thinks. This theory, called "metacognition," emerged not only as a driving force in approaching the task of reading, but also as a mirroring technique to help learners reflect on all aspects of their own thinking and behavior.

Subsequently, the metacognitive strand sparked additional theory and research on transfer. By stepping outside a situation and "looking in" one extracts the pieces that can be generalized for transfer within the content, across disciplines and into life situations. To understand the impact of these four distinct areas of cognitive research, following are elaborations upon each theory.

Section II

COGNITIVE INSTRUCTION RESEARCH

EXPLICIT THINKING SKILLS

A steady current of experts favor explicit skill instruction for the thinking curriculum. In thinking about a thinking skill program there is strong agreement. In some areas, consensus among the many thinking skills advocates and references in *Developing Minds* (ASCD) embody these beliefs:

Explicit Thinking Skills

1. Thinking most often is taught indirectly, but a direct approach is needed.
2. Learning how to think is not an automatic by-product of studying certain subjects.
3. Students will not learn to think better simply by being asked to think about a subject or topic.
4. Youngsters do not learn how to engage in critical thinking by themselves.
5. There is little reason to believe that competency in critical thinking can be an incidental outcome of instruction directed, or that appears to be directed, at other ends.
6. Instructions for the skills must be direct and systematic prior to, during and following students' introduction to and use of them in our classrooms.

However, there seem to be two obstacles impeding the momentum of a stronger flow toward consensus on how to teach thinking explicitly. The first obstacle is a philosophical issue that must be addressed before the second obstacle can even be approached. This primary issue is the debate over *whether or not explicit thinking skills should be taught separate from or infused into the existing subject area curriculum*. There are, of course, pros and cons for each instance.

	PROS	CONS
Thinking Infused Into Content	• Easy transfer • Carries content	• Teachers may be unskilled in the teaching of thinking skills
Thinking Taught Separately	• Spot and slot for thinking • Targeted to test and grade therefore will teach	• No time • No transfer

Although both approaches—thinking as a separate program and thinking infused into the content—are successfully implemented in various settings, we favor the infused model. Our focus is always and foremost on the *transfer of learning* for all children, and the infused model eases the way for fruitful transfer, creative application and relevant student use throughout the curriculum. The separate model seems to reinforce for students the "little boxes" theory of curriculum: in little boxes, math is not art, art is not science and thinking is not any of these—the curricula are fragmented.

However, once the decision has been made in terms of how to deliberately include thinking in the curricula, the next obstacle stubbornly emerges: how does one know which program is best? An overview of the spectrum of thinking models provides some food for thought. Just as in cooperative learning, the various programs tend to cluster into four distinctive categories: the conceptual models, the strategic approaches, the curriculum packages and the model-building designs. The following presents the thinking skill programs as they appear to cluster in patterns.

CLUSTERS OF THINKING SKILLS PROGRAMS

Conceptual, Strategic, Curricula, Models

CONCEPTUAL MODELS

- Patterns for Thinking—Patterns for Transfer - Fogarty and Bellanca
- Tactics in Thinking - Marzano and Arredondo
- Dimensions in Thinking - Marzano
- Thoughtful Education Training Series - Hansen, Silver and Strong
- Models of Teaching - Joyce and Weil
- Teaching for Intelligent Behaviors - Costa

STRATEGIC/SKILLS APPROACH

- CoRT - de Bono
- Catch Them Thinking - Bellanca and Fogarty
- Start Them Thinking - Fogarty and Opeka
- Teach Them Thinking - Fogarty and Bellanca
- Synectics - Gordon
- Strategic Reasoning - Upton
- Practical Strategies for the Teaching of Thinking - Beyer
- Project Impact - Winocour

CURRICULUM PACKAGES

- Philosophy for Children - Lipman
- Instrumental Enrichment - Feuerstein
- HOTS - Pogrow
- SOI - Meeker
- Great Books - Will (Adler)
- Future Problem Solving - Torrence
- Odyssey - Project Zero (Harvard)
- Midwest: Critical Thinking - Black and Black

MODEL BUILDING WITH PROTOTYPES

- Knowledge as Design - Perkins
- Keep Them Thinking I, II, II - Opeka, Fogarty, Bellanca
- Breakthroughs - Jones
- Guided Design - Nardi, Wales
- Connections - Perkins
- Creative Problem Solving - Parnes

The major categories that delineate the four types of thinking skill programs have definite characteristics which distinguish one from the other. Each program has a flavor of its own, yet each category is also easily recognized by its distinguishing critical attributes.

Conceptual Models

In the conceptual models, broad guidelines set the framework within which more specific ideas are set forth. For example, in *Patterns for Thinking—Patterns for Transfer*, the four broad guidelines framing the program are teaching *for, of, with* and *about* thinking: setting the climate *for* thinking, teaching the explicit skills *of* thinking, structuring interactions to teach *with* thinking and teaching metacognitively *about* thinking. Within that framework, specific thinking skills and strategies are used to demonstrate the conceptual model.

Likewise, in *Models of Teaching*, Joyce and Weil conceptualize instructional models into families: information processing, personal, social and behavioral. Within that framework, specific models are explored. For example, within the personal family the synectics approach is elaborated. It begins with a scenario that presents the model, followed by an introduction to the basic structure, theory, demonstration, practice and feedback. It ends with coaching and extended application that help teachers learn the instructional techniques.

While conceptual models allow great freedom on the part of the teacher for innovative and highly relevant content-specific use, less skilled or less confident staff may find the freedom within the conceptual structure *too* vague.

Strategic/Skills Approach

The strategic/skills approach, on the other hand, provides tried and true, teacher-tested techniques that are ready for immediate back-home use. In the strategic/skills approach, a menu of specific and fully delineated methods are presented to the teacher for explicit instructional use.

Usually, these strategies/skills are introduced in what is often called a "content-free" lesson. In reality, this content-free lesson does indeed have a content focus. However, the content is usually familiar, almost generic in nature. It is used merely as a vehicle to carry the strategy or skill under study. For example, in teaching the explicit thinking skill of classification, the familiar content focus might be on solids, liquids and gases. Using these generic categories, the classification skill, not the science, becomes the focus of the lesson.

Similarly, in teaching the strategy PMI (plus, minus, interesting), de Bono uses the generic or familiar content of buses. The initial lesson requires students to generate pluses, minuses and interesting aspects of buses that have *no* seats. Again, by using content that is simple and well-known, the emphasis can be placed on the PMI strategy itself.

While the strategic/skills approach usually has immediate appeal to practitioners because it easily applies directly to the classroom, caution must be taken that the strategies/skills lessons are not merely taken per se into the classroom as a cutesy Friday afternoon activity. If the strategy or skill is used only once as modeled in the teacher training, it is an *activity*. If, however, teachers introduce the strategy or skill as modeled, practice it in another situation and transfer it into still another situation, then and only then can we call it a *strategy*. An activity is a one-time shot. A strategy is used over again; it is placed in our repertoire of instructional techniques, our bag of teaching tricks to be used over and over, whenever appropriate.

Curriculum Packages

As indicated by the cluster title, curriculum packages provide a ready-made set of materials for classroom use. These materials are, more often than not, specifically designed for explicit instruction as separate and disparate pieces in the classroom. While the curriculum package provides a neat and tidy unit for deliberate placement in the instructional day, "a spot and a slot" for explicitly addressing thinking skills and strategies, often the subsequent transfer needed for continued and relevant use does not occur.

Examples of fine curriculum packages might include Feuerstein's *Instrumental Enrichment* in which specific and strategic thinking techniques are taught through pencil-and-paper tasks. By metacognitively processing and talking about how students approached a particular task, future application and transfer are mediated for the students.

Another curriculum package is Lipman's *Philosophy for Children* program in which skillfully written, highly motivating and extremely relevant scenarios are used to engage students in Socratic dialogue. Using the fictional situations as springboards, further discussion is encouraged as students attempt to draw philosophical principles into other academic situations or into life's circumstances.

While curriculum packages have strong appeal because of their completeness as a package, their use can be limiting if transfer is not addressed with vigor.

Model Building with Prototypes

The final cluster of thinking skill programs, model building with prototypes, provides a generic piece or model as a prototype. That is, the generalizable model is presented through a content-specific lesson, with the implicit understanding that it is a *model* and should be used as such. Transfer to other content is built in explicitly. Examples of model building with prototypes are the *Breakthrough* program by Zaner-Bloser and *Knowledge as Design* by Perkins.

In the *Breakthrough* program, for example, a lesson on garbage is presented in a fully designed, ready-to-use lesson format. However, in model building a specific prototype is set up. The lesson features specific strategies for modeling collaborative learning, reciprocal teaching and cognitive mapping. The expectation is that although garbage is the lesson's content focus, the *real* lesson extends beyond that with definite attention to instructional methodology.

Perkins' *Knowledge as Design* uses the same model-building approach. Perkins poses four questions that can be applied across content, subject matter and life situations:

1. What is its purpose (or purposes)?
2. What is its structure?
3. What are model cases of it?
4. What are arguments that explain and evaluate it?

In applying the four questions, a model for thinking emerges. Perkins claims these questions can be applied to ecology, Boyle's law, the Bill of Rights and to understanding a common screwdriver.

This last cluster, model building with prototypes, may have the most transfer power of all the clusters.

THINKING SKILL PROGRAMS		
TYPE	**PROS**	**CONS**
Conceptual Models	• Deep understanding results in creative application • Can easily adapt, mix and match the best from many models	• Full commitment to long-term change from building or district • Needs explicit attention to transfer
Strategic/Skills Approach	• Easy for teachers to learn • Immediate application • Transfer power inherent (if noted explicitly)	• Can appear as "cutesy" • Superficial activities rather than generic, transferrable strategies for the instructional repertoire
Curriculum Packages	• Stand alone • Spot and slot in curriculum • Teacher preparation minimal	• Narrow in focus • Needs (and often overlooks) attention to transfer • Separated from content; more to teach
Model Building with Prototypes	• Procedural learning or heuristics taught and modeled for easy application and transfer • Straightforward approach with transfer built in	• Can be narrow in focus • Transfer embedded but can be slighted

Briefly, without belaboring the decision-making processes that must be employed to reach consensus, there are some major considerations to weigh in the selection process.

CONSIDERATIONS FOR SELECTING A PROGRAM

1. What is the purpose of the program?
2. Should an explicit thinking skill program be introduced separate from or infused into the subject matter content?
3. What are the experiences and competencies of the teachers?
4. What are the available resources in terms of time and funds for training and materials?
5. What is the commitment level for long-term change toward cognitive instruction?
6. What kinds of results are expected?

How to Teach the Skills

After consideration of these key issues, program selection becomes easier. By targeting the needs and expectations, several programs will seem more appropriate than others. Once the final choice is made, the subsequent decisions on how to teach the skills seem to fall into place.

To that end, to teach explicit thinking skills, according to Beyer (1989), we must provide the following:

HOW TO TEACH EXPLICIT SKILLS

1. Examples (or products).
2. Introduction of components of the thinking skill in a systematic manner.
3. Demonstration of the basic attributes of the skill.
4. Discussion of the operation and how to do the operation.
5. Opportunity for related practice and feedback.
6. A broadening of the skill beyond the original components.
7. Generalization and transfer of the skill with application in a variety of situations.

EXPLICIT SKILL INFORMATION

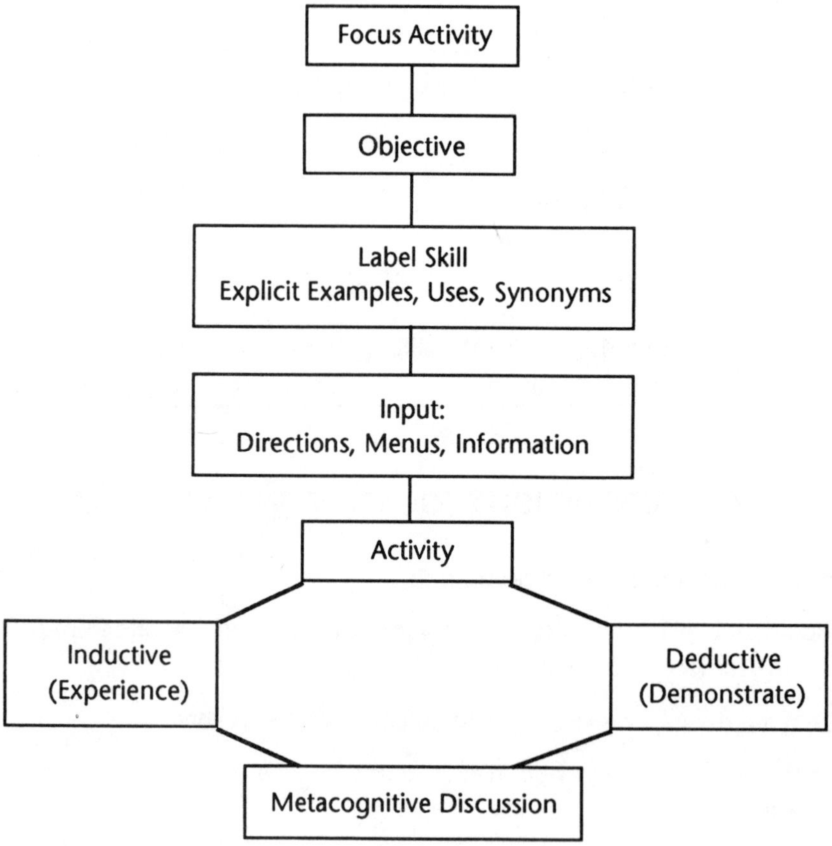

Focus Activity

Objective

Label Skill
Explicit Examples, Uses, Synonyms

Input:
Directions, Menus, Information

Activity

Inductive
(Experience)

Deductive
(Demonstrate)

Metacognitive Discussion

(Based on Beyer's model)

The research on the need for explicit attention to thinking in the curriculum is clear:

Knowing that . . .

...Schools do make a difference (Edmonds)

...Intelligence is modifiable (Feuerstein)

...Learners can monitor and control their own performance (Brown)

...Learners are active, strategic, planful and constructive (Anderson, Hiebert, Scott, Wilkinson, Schoenfield, Silver, Bransford, Sherwood and Vye)

... then cognitive instruction must include explicitness in both the thinking skill and the transfer of the thinking skill.

COGNITIVE ORGANIZERS

The concept of cognitive organizers is rooted in Ausubel's (1978) theory of "meaningful reception learning." Simply put, Ausubel believes that information is stored by nature, hierarchically in the brain. For instance, highly generalized concepts seem to cluster together, followed by less inclusive concepts and finally specific facts and details.

Ausubel advocates the idea of the advance organizer in which information is graphically displayed prior to the reading of the text. In Ausubel's terms, this advance visual depicts information in hierarchical order and is called a *structured overview.*

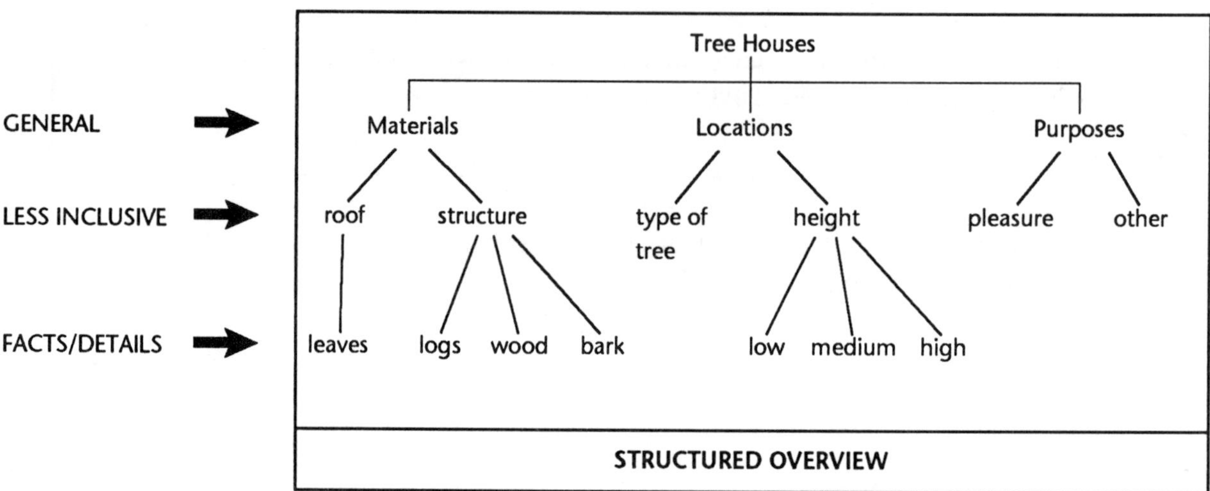

STRUCTURED OVERVIEW

The structured overview always shows vocabulary in relation to more inclusive vocabulary. However, don't think of the cognitive structure as passive. It is really quite dynamic. As new information and experiences are assimilated by the learner, it is reorganized cognitively and the graphic display reflects the shifts.

Mapping

Cognitive maps or organizers, as studied by Ambruster and Anderson (1980), Dansereau (1979), Davidson (1982) and Vaughn (1982), demonstrate success in improving the retention of information. Lyman and McTighe (1988) demonstrate the use of cognitive maps in a discussion of "theory-imbedded tools" for cognitive instruction. They suggest that the ability to organize information and ideas is fundamental to thinking. Graphic displays or cognitive maps aid in the development of organizational skills for students of all ages and abilities and across all content.

Cognitive organizers provide a holistic picture of the concept, complete with relationships and interrelationships. Lyman and McTighe suggest that cognitive maps help students:

- represent abstract or implicit information in more concrete forms,
- depict the relationships among facts and concepts,
- generate elaborate ideas, and
- relate new information to prior knowledge.

Maps and Minds-Together

From kindergarten to college, cognitive organizers are employed to help students organize, retain and assimilate concepts and ideas. Perhaps the most widely used cognitive organizer is the web.

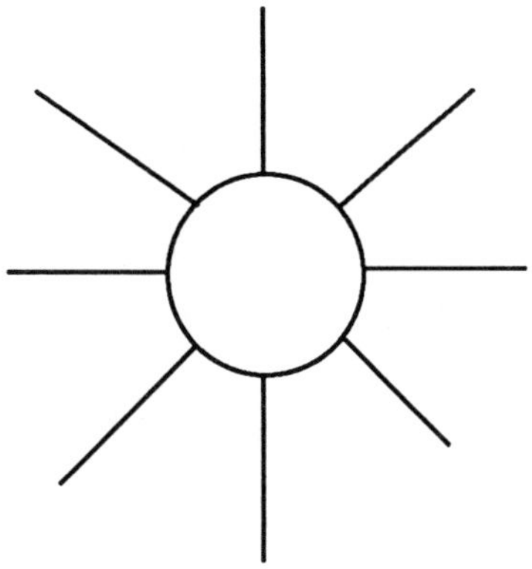

The web targets a concept and provides structures for analyzing attributes. Other types of maps include sequence chains, vector charts, story maps, analogy links, flow charts, matrices, Venn diagrams and ranking ladders. These cognitive organizers provide frameworks for class or small-group discussions and written work. According to Lyman (1986), when used in conjunction with think-pair-share cooperative strategies and metacognitive cues, these cognitive maps are even more powerful in helping students learn.

Perhaps most importantly, the use of cognitive organizers provides a deliberate technique for allowing students to interact personally with the information. These theory-embedded tools, called maps, make the thinking visible for both the students and the teacher. Ausubel suggests that learning is easier for a person whose knowledge is clear, stable and organized. Cognitive organizers facilitate just that sort of thinking—clear, stable and organized.

METACOGNITION—A SUPERORDINATE KIND OF THINKING

According to Swartz and Perkins (1989), metacognition refers to knowledge about, awareness of and control over one's own mind and thinking. Costa (1985) calls this "thinking about thinking." Marzano and Arredondo (1986) also speak of awareness and control over one's own thinking, while Brown and Palincsar (1978) describe the metacognitive process in relationship to the reading process.

They allude to the good reader who reads and reads and reads and suddenly hears a little voice inside his head saying, "I don't know what I just read." The words on the page had been read, they had been spoken in the mind, but in a "word-calling" sense, no meaning had been conveyed. Suddenly, the reader becomes aware of this deficit. He realizes he has lost contact with the context of the text and his mind signals him to adapt a recovery strategy: reread the beginning of the paragraph, recall a thought, scan the text for key words . . . .

On the other hand, the poor reader reads and reads and reads and never knows he doesn't know. He has not noticed that he is getting no meaning from the text because he has never gotten meaning from text. He word calls in his mind, but he is a nonreader in the real sense of reading.

Learning to understand and articulate our own mental processes is a necessary link to fruitful transfer—or as Costa suggests about metacognition, having the ability to know what we know and what we don't know, and wondering why we are doing what we are doing. That's the metacognition we want to promote for all learners.

More specifically, planning, monitoring and evaluating the learning activity are the components of metacognitive processing. Students become aware of their own thinking and what goes on inside their heads when they are thinking prior to, during and after a learning activity.

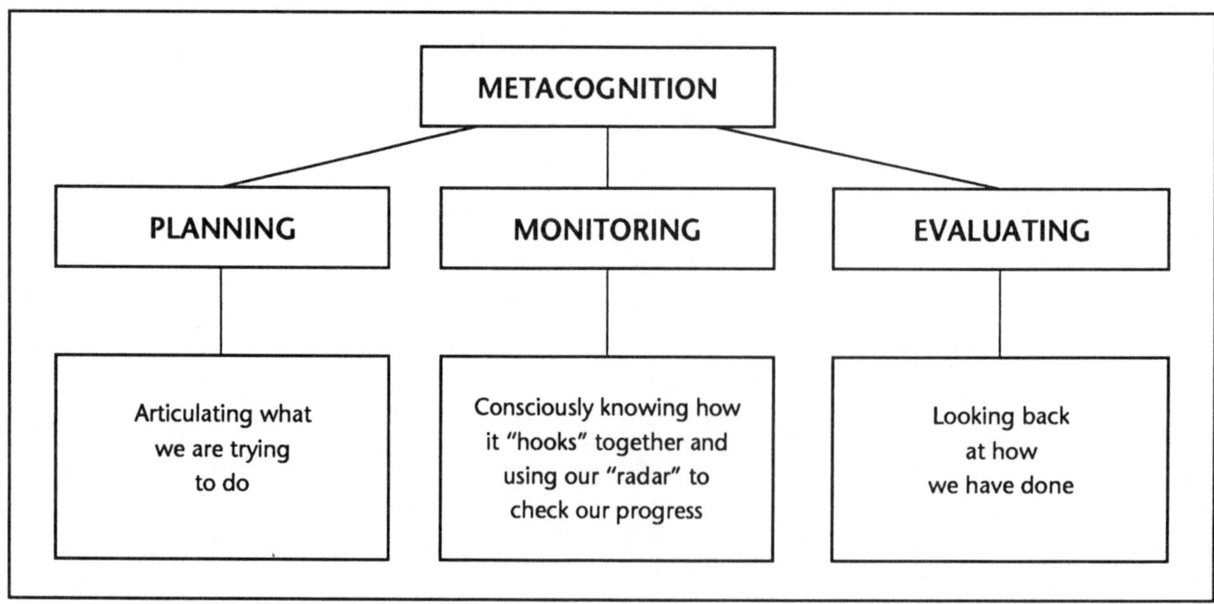

In the most current writings about metacognition, Swartz and Perkins (1989) gauge the sophistication of thinking by four distinctive levels that are increasingly metacognitive in nature:

Tacit Use: doing a kind of thinking without thinking about it
Aware Use: conscious that/when one is doing a certain kind of thinking
Strategic Use: organizing thinking by conscious strategy
Reflective Use: reflecting upon thinking before, during and after the process; pondering how to proceed and how to improve

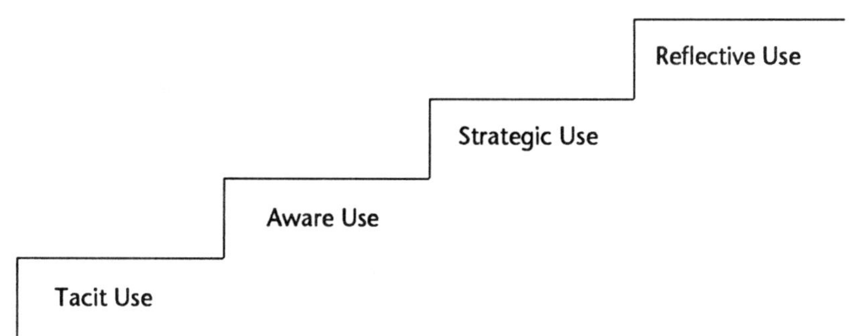

A sophisticated example of paying explicit attention to metacognition is seen in Whimbey's model of paired partner think-alouds. In this strategy, a problem solver thinks aloud as he/she works through a situation. The monitor cues the "thinking aloud" with specific questions or prompts. Thus, instead of *tacitly* solving the problem, unaware of the strategies used, *awareness* is brought to a conscious level. In addition, over time, *strategic* use is mapped out by both the problem solver and the monitor as problem-solving patterns emerge. Reflective use is inherent in the think-aloud technique. In fact, all four metacognitive levels are clearly evidenced in the strategy.

By using metacognitive *prompts* we can help students monitor and direct their own thinking as they move toward reflective thinking. Beyond teaching about thinking, metacognitive questions also promote the kind of metaphorical thoughts, generalizations and mindful abstractions that Perkins and Salomon (1988) suggest are powerful bridges for complex transfer.

In addition, Beyer elaborates on a cueing technique to prompt metacognition. Questions Beyer (1987) suggests to foster metacognitive behavior are:

- What am I doing?
- Why am I doing it?
- What other way can I do it?
- How does it work? Can I do it again or another way?
- How would I help someone else do it?

These questions and similar questions lead students to examine their own thinking and behavior in ways that press the generalization process. Additional lead-ins that may be discussed within the group or reflected upon individually in a log entry are:

- How is ______________ like ____________________?
- I wish I'd known this when ______________________.
- Next time, I am gonna . . . .

Mrs. Potter's Questions (Bellanca and Fogarty, 1989) are the standard metacognitive questions that promote reflective thinking and foster future applications. The IRI version of the metacognitive questions, called Mrs. Potter's Questions, are suggested for repeated use to process student thinking during cooperative learning tasks in the classroom.

As the story goes, Mrs. Mimi Potter was Jim Bellanca's "critic" teacher when Jim was completing his student teaching in Champaign-Urbana, Illinois. In this high school English class, regardless of what lesson Jim taught or how successful the lesson seemed, Mrs. Potter would always sit Jim down and ask him to reflect on these questions:

"Now, Jim:

"What were you trying to do?

"What do you think went well?

"What would you do differently, next time?

"Do you need any help?"

Mrs. Potter's Questions

1. What were you expected to do?
2. In this assignment, what did you do well?
3. If you had to do this task over, what would you do differently?
4. What help do you need from me?

In the self-analysis and in answering these four questions, Jim was asked to reflect on his own teaching behavior for future transfer and successful use. Inadvertently, in Jim's own teaching situations, he discovered that he began asking the very same questions of his students. In turn, they became reflective about their own thinking and behavior in his classes. Mrs. Potter's Questions can be posted and used repeatedly as reminders of the metacognitive nature needed for the transfer process. They can easily become part of the processing that follows a cooperative task.

In addition, Beyer (1989) suggests modeling direct instruction of a thinking skill and thinking guides to promote planning, monitoring and evaluating. A viable tool that students can readily use to assess their own behavior is a strategy based on de Bono's PMI (1978). In this procedure, students look at the affective, cognitive and metacognitive levels for processing their thinking. This evaluation is tied directly to the learning situation.

Affective: How did it feel?

P (+)	
M (-)	
I (?)	

Cognitive: Assessing answers and/or strategies.

What answer did you get?
What else?
Tell me more.
Give an example.
Please illustrate.

Metacognitive: Why bother? How can I use this?

Can I:
- **Duplicate?**
- **Replicate?**
- **Integrate?**
- **Map?**
- **Innovate?**

Regardless of the means or measures used for the metacognitive process, the evidence is clear that explicit attention to the metacognitive—the stuff beyond the cognitive answers—promotes transfer and application of knowledge, skills, concepts and attitudes in novel situations.

BO PEEP, BLACK SHEEP AND THE GOOD SHEPHERD—THE TALES OF TRANSFER

Isn't all learning for transfer? The question is so generic to the teaching/learning process, one wonders why talk of transfer has become this seemingly unending tale of controversy and confusion. To transfer learning means to use what is learned in one situation in another situation that is either quite like the initial learning situation or even perhaps quite different from the situation in which the learning originally took place.

That seems quite straightforward. In learning to drive a car, we, in essence, transfer that learning to driving all cars. In learning to survey a book, we, in essence, learn the art of survey as an overview methodology. Of course, we learn things so we can use that learning in other places. Learning has relevance and usefulness.

However, as the tale of transfer unfolds, the complexity of the issue becomes more evident and the concern for transfer takes on added dimensions. On the one hand, experts throughout the past 25 years seem to agree that there is a natural dichotomy to this concept called transfer. There appears to be transfer that is simple and another type of transfer that is more complex. The research suggests many terms to describe this dichotomy. For the simple transfer there is: simple (Fogarty, 1989), near (Wittrock, 1987), horizontal (Joyce and Showers, 1983), automatic (Perkins, 1986), lowroad (Salomon and Perkins, 1988), similar (Hunter, 1973; Beyer, 1989), spontaneous (Sternberg, 1984), and practiced (Feuerstein). For the complex transfer there is: complex (Fogarty, 1989), far (Wittrock, 1987), vertical (Joyce & Showers, 1983), mindful (Perkins, 1986), highroad (Salomon and Perkins, 1988), cued (Beyer, 1987) guided and scaffolded (Sternberg, 1984), and mediated (Feuerstein, 1980).

DICHOTOMY IN TRANSFER

LOW LEVEL	HIGH LEVEL
simple	complex
near	far
horizontal	vertical
automatic	mindful
lowroad	highroad
similar	cued
spontaneous	guided and scaffolded
practiced	mediated

This seems to be fairly easy to sense and deal with. Yet, there is another dichotomy in thinking about transfer that seems to take precedence over all else. In fact, to explore the division in thinking, the controversy over whether or not transfer is best served with *generic generalizable teaching* rather than with teaching that has a *content-specific focus*, we must look historically into the issue.

Bo Peep Theory

"Leave them alone and they'll come home wagging their tails behind them." According to Perkins (1988), this represents the standard instructional practice today. This is the basic position that holds the educational community in its grip at the present time—i.e., teach the content, give students practice that is both immediate and spaced over time, and the transfer of learning is sure to follow.

For example, by teaching students the Periodic Table of Elements and giving them practice in recognizing and analyzing the atomic structure of the elements, it is presumed that this factual information somehow transfers into relevant application. With sufficient and varied practice, this may actually occur. And, then again, it may not. It may also be presumed that students who learn the Periodic Table of Elements also somehow transfer concepts about patterns, symbolic notation and about charting information by simply working with the actual table in fact-oriented tasks. While there is some possibility of the first presumption occurring as a result of varied practice, there is slim possibility of the second type of transfer occurring. *Bo Peep* has lost her sheep here.

Black Sheep Theory

In fact, again according to Perkins (1990), over time, transfer has become not only the lost sheep, but the *black sheep* of the educational community. Let's unravel the tale from the beginning to see how this black sheep theory has evolved to the point that it somehow overrides all other evidence.

Historically, the educational dogma dictating curricula adhered to the adage: Latin, geometry (and the like) train the mind. However, in the early 1900s Thorndike and others presented convincing evidence that suggested that "training the faculties" indeed did not transfer in generalized ways. These researchers favored schooling in which the initial learning situation simulated as closely as possible the anticipated transfer situation. In fact, they advocated learning that encompassed identical elements for the two situations. Training would be specific and transfer would occur.

Diametrically opposed to that view, in the early 1900s Polya advocated the position that a general, generic, heuristic approach to problem solving in math was the key to the transfer of learning in diverse settings. And so that tale begins, the arguments for transfer from specific, similar contexts versus transfer from generalizable heuristics are cast and the curricular war is waged. Unfortunately, buried within the embers of the fading controversy is one illuminating fact. Neither side—context-bound, specific training nor generalizable principles and rules—shows overwhelming and convincing evidence of transfer.

Perkins' summation: "Transfer ain't that great, right now. We're not getting the transfer we want." In fact, the transfer is so lacking, so rare, that transfer has become what Perkins now calls the "black sheep" of education. If it doesn't work, if we can't seem to get the transfer we want, then let's just do better in highly focused subject-oriented lessons. Thus, transfer has been ignored. If transfer can't be there, it's not a big issue. Let's just teach well, what we can teach.

Good Shepherd Theory

Fortunately, the transfer embers, close to becoming forgotten ashes, have recently been stirred by the winds of curricular change. A number of voices from the thinking-skills movement are focusing on the transfer issue again, igniting sparks of urgent concern and emerging agreements.While the controversy surrounding "transfer-as-context-bound" or "transfer-as-generalizable" remains a somewhat unresolved issue, agreements about transfer of learning do show evidence of promise for the educational community.

Teaching Latin does not seem to transfer in terms of a more disciplined mind, yet it is now agreed that Latin may not have transferred because Latin had not been taught to cultivate transfer. And while teaching general heuristics such as steps to math problem-solving do not seem to transfer into problem-solving steps in the writing process even though transfer had been expected, intricate and powerful implications have emerged from work in both areas.

In essence, what current transfer research suggests is that when teachers pay attention to transfer in contextual learning situations, transfer does occur. And when general, bare strategies are accompanied with self-monitoring techniques, transfer does in fact occur. In both context-bound teaching and a general heuristics approach, transfer must be shepherded.

Thus, there is Perkins' *good shepherd theory*: when transfer is provoked, practiced, and reflected on, transfer is fairly easy to get. Transfer *can* be mediated. With the good shepherd theory, comes a new hope for transfer. And with that new hope, of course, comes the new responsibility of teaching for transfer—for after all, isn't all learning for transfer?

Hugging and Bridging for Transfer

To get the desired transfer, to change Perkins' adage "transfer ain't that great, right now," to "transfer is greater than ever, right now," a microscopic look at transfer reveals two critical elements that seem to foster the transfer phenomenon. Salomon and Perkins (1988) refer to lowroad, automatic transfer and highroad, abstracted transfer. They further describe two mediation strategies for lowroad/highroad transfer which they label "hugging and bridging."

Hugging means teaching so as to better meet the resemblance conditions for lowroad or "automatic" transfer. *Bridging* means teaching to better meet the conditions for highroad transfer by mediating the needed processes of abstraction and making connections (Perkins and Salomon, 1988).

While Beyer refers to mediation as cueing what to do, when to do it and how to do it, his cues take the content lesson's thinking skill into new contexts. Perkins (1989) further suggests that anticipatory tactics and retrieval tactics promote transfer. Using these categories—anticipatory tactics and retrieval tactics—the following are suggested:

TRANSFER TACTICS		
	ANTICIPATORY	RETRIEVAL
Highroad	• abstracting rules • anticipating applications	• reflect by generalizing the problem • focus retrieval in one particular context • make metaphors
Lowroad	• immediate practice • varied practice • matching lesson to target outcome	• spaced, varied practice over time

(Adapted from Perkins' *Knowledge As Design*, 1986)

The Transfer Curriculum

In looking at the transfer of learning by adult learners in staff development programs, Joyce and Showers suggest that while horizontal transfer shifts directly into the classroom teaching situation, vertical transfer requires adaptation to fit the conditions. High transfer requires understanding of the purpose and rationale of the skill and know-how to adapt it with executive control. Still, looking at adult learners, Fogarty (1989) suggests a continuum of transfer behavior within the dichotomy of simple and complex transfer. The learner levels, originally indicative of adult creative transfer are also similarly applied to student transfer as depicted in the charts on the following pages.

A Continuum

FROM TRAINING TO TRANSFER: LEARNER SITUATIONAL DISPOSITIONS

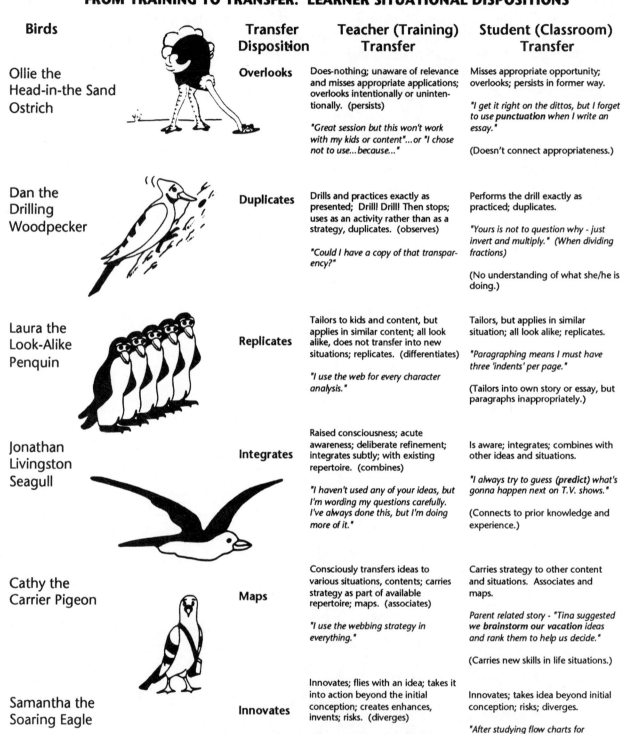

Birds	Transfer Disposition	Teacher (Training) Transfer	Student (Classroom) Transfer
Ollie the Head-in-the Sand Ostrich	Overlooks	Does-nothing; unaware of relevance and misses appropriate applications; overlooks intentionally or unintentionally. (persists) *"Great session but this won't work with my kids or content"...or "I chose not to use...because..."*	Misses appropriate opportunity; overlooks; persists in former way. *"I get it right on the dittos, but I forget to use* ***punctuation*** *when I write an essay."* (Doesn't connect appropriateness.)
Dan the Drilling Woodpecker	Duplicates	Drills and practices exactly as presented; Drill! Drill! Then stops; uses as an activity rather than as a strategy, duplicates. (observes) *"Could I have a copy of that transparency?"*	Performs the drill exactly as practiced; duplicates. *"Yours is not to question why - just invert and multiply." (When dividing fractions)* (No understanding of what she/he is doing.)
Laura the Look-Alike Penquin	Replicates	Tailors to kids and content, but applies in similar content; all look alike, does not transfer into new situations; replicates. (differentiates) *"I use the web for every character analysis."*	Tailors, but applies in similar situation; all look alike; replicates. *"Paragraphing means I must have three 'indents' per page."* (Tailors into own story or essay, but paragraphs inappropriately.)
Jonathan Livingston Seagull	Integrates	Raised consciousness; acute awareness; deliberate refinement; integrates subtly; with existing repertoire. (combines) *"I haven't used any of your ideas, but I'm wording my questions carefully. I've always done this, but I'm doing more of it."*	Is aware; integrates; combines with other ideas and situations. *"I always try to guess* ***(predict)*** *what's gonna happen next on T.V. shows."* (Connects to prior knowledge and experience.)
Cathy the Carrier Pigeon	Maps	Consciously transfers ideas to various situations, contents; carries strategy as part of available repertoire; maps. (associates) *"I use the webbing strategy in everything."*	Carries strategy to other content and situations. Associates and maps. *Parent related story - "Tina suggested we* ***brainstorm our vacation*** *ideas and rank them to help us decide."* (Carries new skills in life situations.)
Samantha the Soaring Eagle 	Innovates	Innovates; flies with an idea; takes it into action beyond the initial conception; creates enhances, invents; risks. (diverges) *"You have changed my teaching forever. I can never go back to what I used to do. I know too much. I'm too excited."*	Innovates; takes idea beyond initial conception; risks; diverges. *"After studying flow charts for computer class student constructs a Rube Goldberg type invention."* (Innovates; invents; diverges; goes beyond and creates novel.)

Teacher Levels of Transfer

Ollie the Head-in-the-sand Ostrich **OVERLOOKS**  Does nothing; unaware of relevance and misses appropriate applications; overlooks intentionally or unintentionally. (persists) *"Great session but this won't work with my kids or content"...or "I chose not to use...because..."*	**Dan** the Drilling Woodpecker **DUPLICATES**  Drills and practices exactly as presented; Drill! Drill! Then stops; uses as an activity rather than as a strategy; duplicates. (observes) *"Could I have a copy of that transparency?"*
Laura the Look-alike Penguin **REPLICATES**  Tailors to kids and content, but applies in similar content; all look alike, does not transfer into new situations; replicates. (differentiates) *"I use the web for every character analysis."*	**Jonathan** Livingston Seagull **INTEGRATES**  Raised consciousness; acute awareness; deliberate refinement; integrates subtly; with existing repertoire. (combines) *"I haven't used any of your ideas, but I'm wording my questions carefully. I've always done this, but I'm doing more of it."*
Cathy the Carrier Pigeon **MAPS**  Consciously transfers ideas to various situations, contents; carries strategy as part of available repertoire; maps. (associates) *"I use the webbing strategy in everything."*	**Samantha** the Soaring Eagle **INNOVATES**  Innovates; flies with an idea; takes it into action beyond the initial conception; creates enhances, invents; risks. (diverges) *"You have changed my teaching forever. I can never go back to what I used to do. I know too much. I'm too excited."*

Student Levels of Transfer

Ollie **the Head-in-the-sand Ostrich** **OVERLOOKS**	**Dan** **the DrillingWoodpecker** **DUPLICATES**
 Misses appropriate opportunity; overlooks; persists in former way. *"I get it right on the dittos, but I forget to use punctuation when I write an essay."* (Doesn't connect appropriateness.)	 Performs the drill exactly as practiced; duplicates. *"Yours is not to question why—just invert and multiply."* (When dividing fractions, has no understanding of what she/he is doing.)
Laura **the Look-alike Penquin** **REPLICATES**  Tailors but applies in similar situation; all look alike; replicates. *"Paragraphing means I must have three 'indents' per page."* (Tailors into own story or essay, but paragraphs inapproriately.)	**Jonathan** **Livingston Seagull** **INTEGRATES**  Is aware; integrates; combines with other ideas and situations. *"I always try to guess (predict) what's gonna happen next on T.V. shows."* (Connects to prior knowledge and experience.)
Cathy **the Carrier Pigeon** **MAPS**  Carries strategy to other content and situations. Associates and maps. *Parent-related story—"Tina suggested we brainstorm our vacation ideas and rank them to help us decide."* (Carries new skills into life situations.)	**Samantha** **the Soaring Eagle** **INNOVATES**  Innovates; takes ideas beyond initial conception; risks; diverges. *"After studying flow charts for computer class student constructs a Rube Goldberg type invention."* (Innovates; invents; diverges; goes beyond and creates novel.)

Awareness of the learner's transfer level and monitoring of that transfer through appropriate cueing questions seem to promote creative transfer, which is increasingly complex. For example, for the learner who is simply "duplicating" the learned skill or strategy, which is a somewhat low level of transfer, the teacher might cue with a question such as, "Can you think of an adjustment you can make so that this idea is useful in another context?" This cue may be enough to spark movement toward "replicated" transfer in which the learner personally tailors the idea to suit his/her needs.

This reflective questioning based on transfer levels is analogous to a student who always draws figures in an identical way, almost as if they were produced in a cookie-cutter fashion. Simply by suggesting that the learner might change the eyes or hair on the figure, or even the size of it, the teacher propels the student toward creative divergence and more complex transfer. The metacognitive reflection questions can be self-monitored or peer-monitored with both adult and student learners. Note the shifts that are required as one wrestles with the following transfer cueing questions.

TRANSFER CUEING QUESTIONS

OVERLOOKING

Think of an instance when the skill or strategy would be inappropriate.
"I would not use _________ when _________."

DUPLICATING

Think of an "opportunity passed" when you could have used the skill or strategy.
"I wish I'd known about _________ when _________."

REPLICATING

Think of an adjustment that will make your application of _________ more relevant.
"Next time I'm gonna _________."

INTEGRATING

Think of an analogy for the skill or strategy.
"_________ is like _________ because both _________."

MAPPING

Think of an opportunity to use the new idea.
"Next _________, I could use _________ when _________."

INNOVATING

Think of an application for a "real-life" setting.
"I could use _________ when _________."

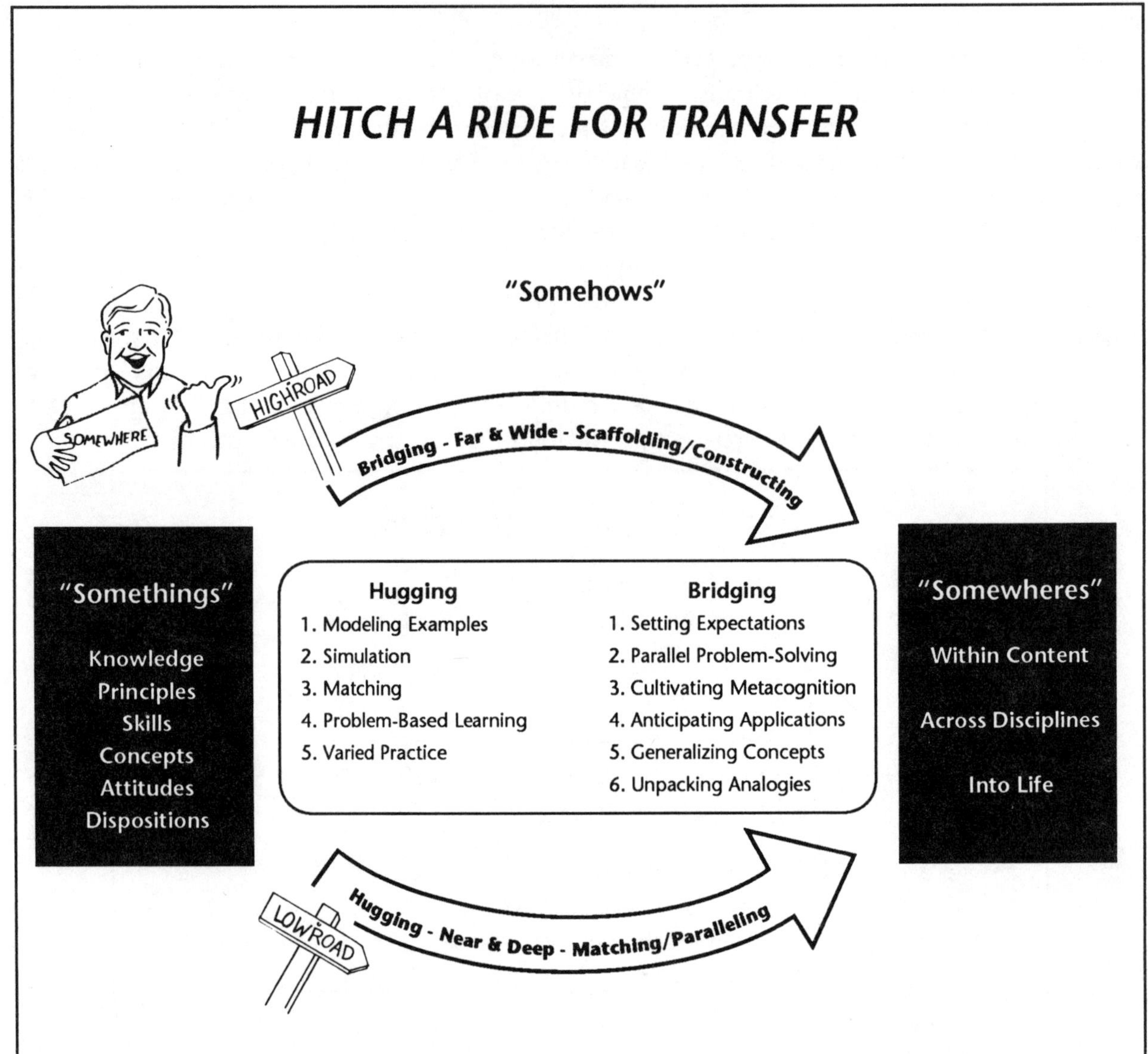

Shepherding Transfer

Some of the most current thinking on transfer is addressed by Perkins, Fogarty and Barell (1989)—they look at the topic of teaching for transfer as the key to more thoughtful instruction. By focusing curricula on the "somethings" to be transferred (the knowledge, skills, concepts, principles, attitudes, dispositions) and the "somewheres" that teachers want them transferred to (within content, across disciplines and into life), instruction is expertly tailored by mediating the "somehows" of the hugging and bridging strategies.

By working with the model of "somethings" to transfer "somewhere," the instructional strategies of the "somehows" take on greater emphasis in the teaching/learning situation. In essence, the curricula is reshaped with the pieces, which have what Fogarty calls *transfer power*, and teaching for transfer becomes an explicit part of the lesson.

THE MODEL		
Something	**Somehow**	**Somewhere**
CONCEPTS **SKILLS** **ATTITUDES** **KNOWLEDGE** **DISPOSITIONS** **CRITERIA:** ☐ ____________ ☐ ____________ ☐ ____________	**HUGGING:** bring instructional experience closer to target you want Modeling Simulating Matching Problem-based Learning Practicing **BRIDGING:** use mindful abstractions Expectations Problem Solving Metacognition Applications Generalizations Analogies	**WITHIN LESSON CONTENT:** Subtraction Addition Multiplication Fractions **ACROSS DISCIPLINE:** Math Science Social Studies Language Arts **INTEREST LIFE:** Personal School Work Family

Knowing that (1) the *Bo Peep theory* leads only to the loss of one of the key aspects of the learning situation, the transfer of learning; (2) by ignoring transfer as the *black sheep* of the instructional cycle we again miss the essence of learning, (which of course is the transfer, use and application of learning in new settings); and (3) if we pay attention to transfer and guide it like a *good shepherd* herds his sheep, then we will take learning to new heights for learners of all ages and in all situations—knowing *all* this, we can pay attention to transfer. Isn't all learning for transfer?

CONCLUSION

One final look is needed in bringing the research together as we consider cooperative learning models and the cognitive instruction pieces of cognition, metacognition and transfer. Bruce Joyce sums it up best with this statement:

Research on cooperative learning is overwhelmingly positive and the cooperative approaches are appropriate for all curriculum areas. The more complex the outcomes (higher-order processing of information, problem solving, social skills and attitudes), the greater are the effects.

The marriage between cooperative learning and cognitive instruction provides the master blueprint for instructional excellence. To illustrate the various components and how they fit together in an instructional design for the classroom, note the following diagram:

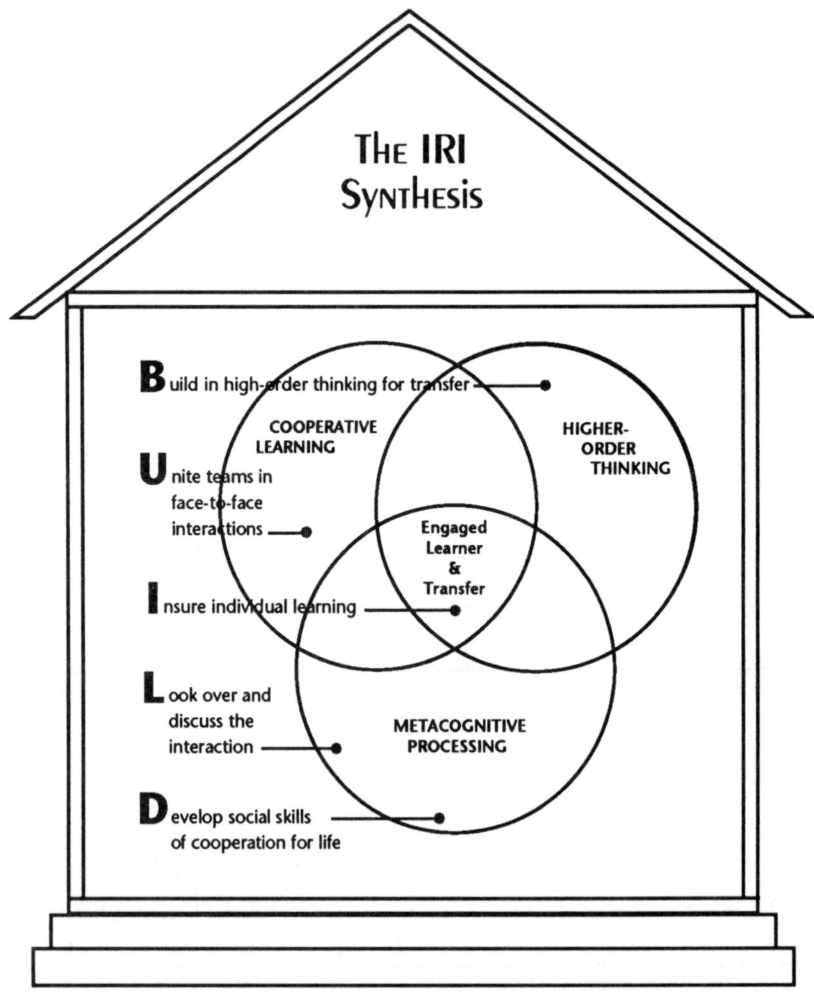
The IRI Synthesis
Build in high-order thinking for transfer
Unite teams in face-to-face interactions
Insure individual learning
Look over and discuss the interaction
Develop social skills of cooperation for life
COOPERATIVE LEARNING
HIGHER-ORDER THINKING
Engaged Learner & Transfer
METACOGNITIVE PROCESSING

The collaborative skills of the cooperative learning model are linked with the thinking skills and cognitive organizers. These major instructional concepts are further intertwined with the metacognitive strategies of reflective use. Together, the three—cooperative learning, higher-order thinking skills and metacognitive processing—provide the blueprint for the transfer of learning. By blending these key elements together in varying and unique instructional designs, teachers have blueprints for thinking in the cooperative classroom.

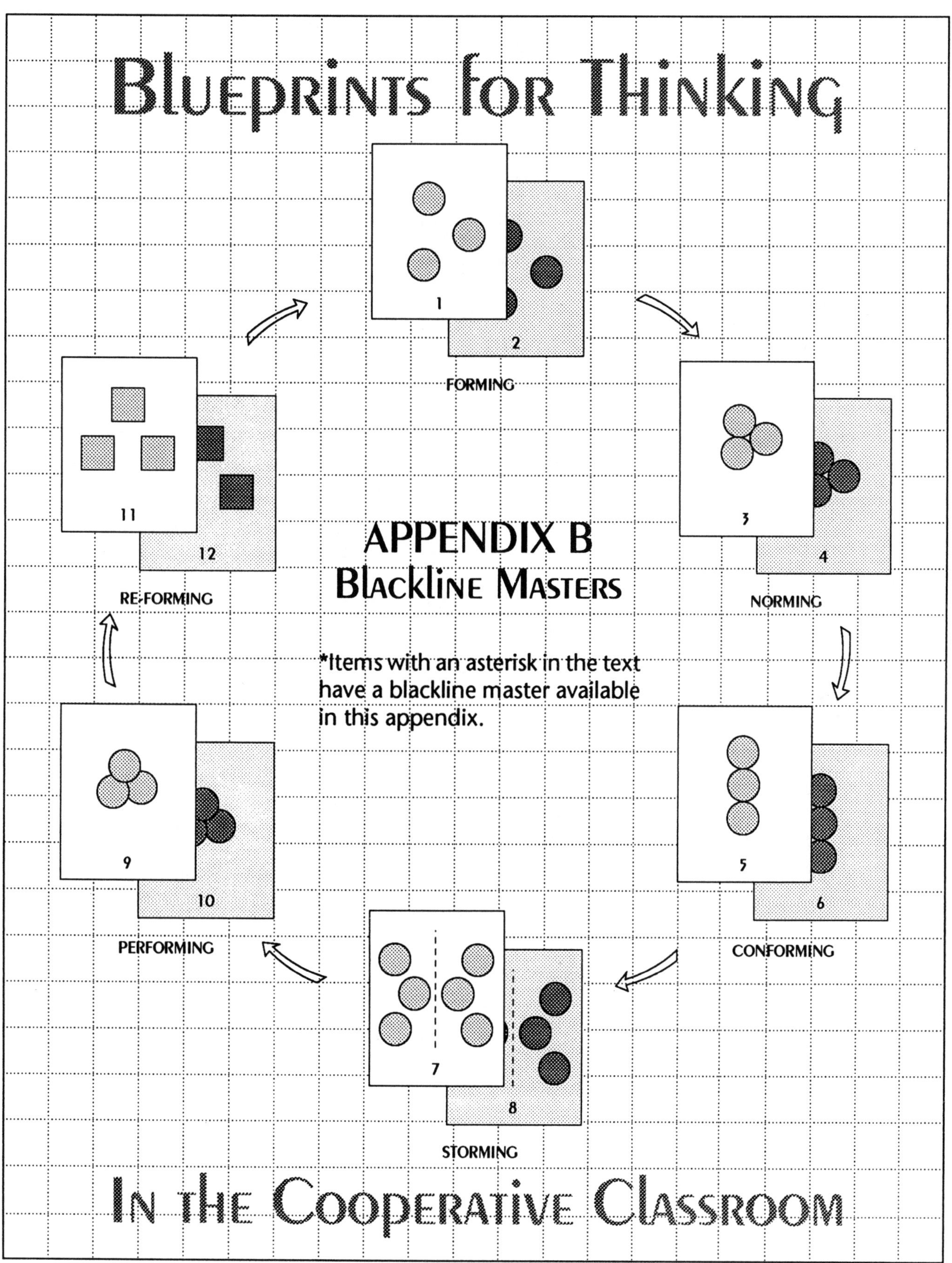
Blueprints for Thinking
1
2
FORMING
3
4
NORMING
5
6
CONFORMING
7
8
STORMING
9
10
PERFORMING
11
12
RE-FORMING
APPENDIX B
Blackline Masters
*Items with an asterisk in the text have a blackline master available in this appendix.
In the Cooperative Classroom

Role Cards

WORRIER

"Let's review our task."

ENCOURAGER

"What do you think?"
"Tell me more."
"What's your idea?"
"Would you help, please?"

CHECKER

"Explain..."
"Summarize..."
"What are our agreements?"
"Give an example of..."
"How did you get that answer?"
"Let's review..."

EXAMPLES OF FORMING SOCIAL SKILLS

Elementary Example

- Use 6" voices
- Listen to your neighbor
- Stay with the group
- Look at the speaker
- Don't hurt feelings

SKYLIGHT PUBLISHING

EXAMPLES OF FORMING SOCIAL SKILLS

Middle School Example

- Use 6" voices
- It's OK to think
- Don't interrupt others
- Help your neighbor
- Know and do your job
- Listen to all ideas
- Use encouraging words

EXAMPLES OF FORMING SOCIAL SKILLS

Secondary School Example

- Control your voice
- Think for yourself
- Respect others' opinions
- Carry your weight
- Help each other stay on task
- Explore different points of view
- Include all members

SUMMARY OF COOPERATIVE GROUPS

	Primary Use	Make-Up	Selection	Duration
Informal Task Groups	Content-Review Activities & Processing Academic Content	Quick, Random Groupings	Turn to Your Neighbor	Until End of Academic Review/ Processing Activity
Formal Task Groups	Daily Classroom Work & Special Research Projects	Heterogeneous Ability Groups & Homogeneous Interest Groups	Teacher Makes Groups Based on Student Interest & Ability	Until end of lesson, unit or project
Base Groups	Support/ Bonding Activities & Social Skill Practice	Homogeneous Peer Relationships & Heterogeneous Personality Characteristics	Based on Student-Peer Relations *(with teacher monitoring)*	Whole Quarter/ Semester/ Year *(as long as groups are working well)*

WHAT WE KNOW-KWL

What we **know**	What we **want** to know	What we **learned**

WHAT WE KNOW-KWL

What we **know**	What we **want** to know	What we **learned**

WHAT WE KNOW-KWL

What we **know**	What we **want** to know	What we **learned**

Chapter 2, page 32

PREDICTION PAIRS

What will happen next	Reasons from reading

PREDICTION PAIRS

What will happen next	Reasons from reading

PREDICTION PAIRS

What will happen next	Reasons from reading

SKYLIGHT PUBLISHING

MAIL-GRAM

To: ________________________

From: ________________________

Message: **I learned...** ________________________

____

____

____

Signed________________________

MAIL-GRAM

To: ________________________

From: ________________________

Message: **I learned...** ________________________

____

____

____

Signed________________________

MAIL-GRAM

To: ________________________

From: ________________________

Message: **I learned...** ________________________

____

____

____

Signed________________________

Chapter 2, page 33

FAT AND SKINNY QUESTIONS

FAT QUESTIONS	*SKINNY QUESTIONS*
Before 1.__________ __________ 2.__________ __________	Before 1.__________ __________ 2.__________ __________
During 3.__________ __________ 4.__________ __________	During 3.__________ __________ 4.__________ __________
After 5.__________ __________ 6.__________ __________	After 5.__________ __________ 6.__________ __________

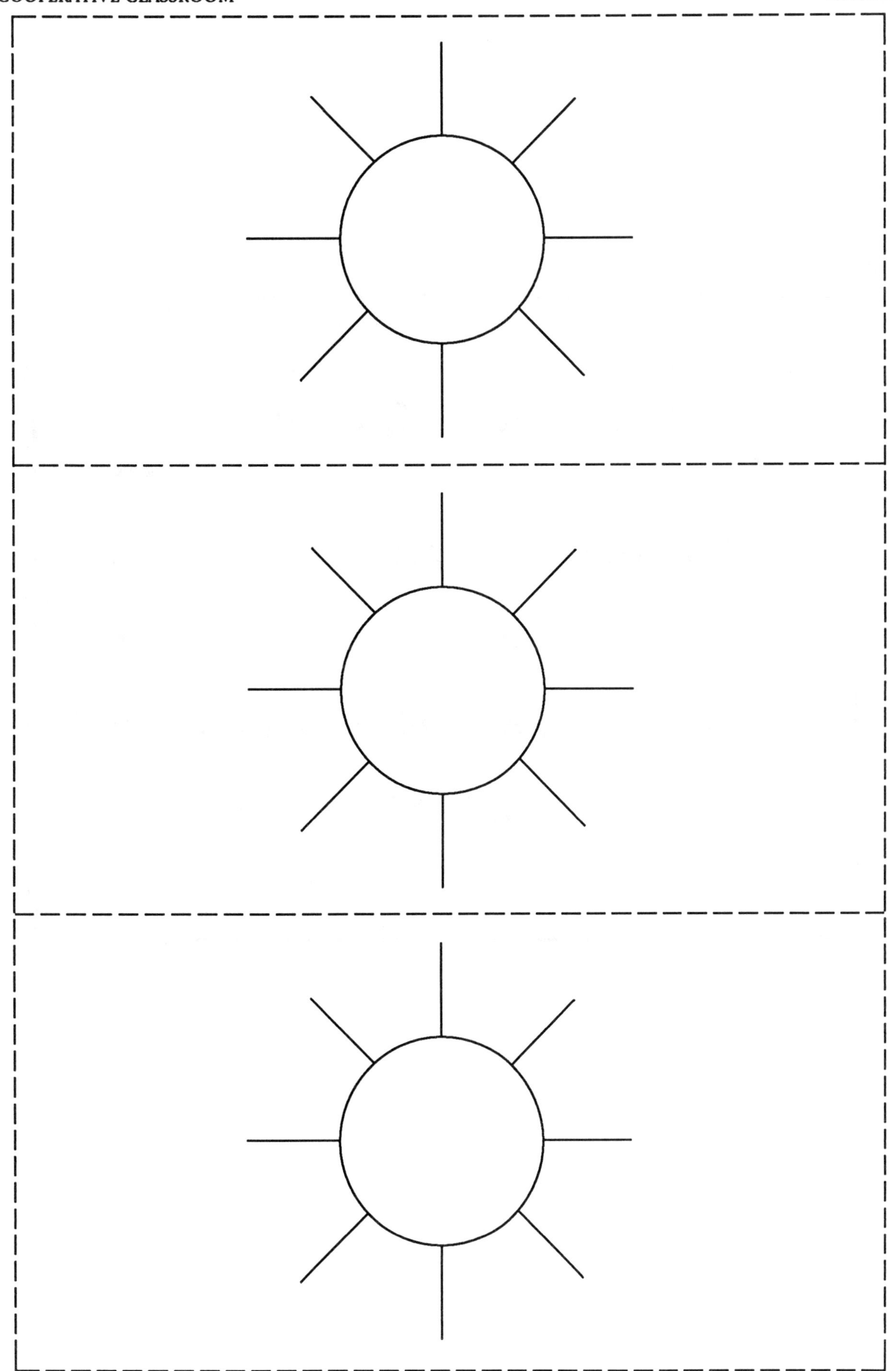

Mrs. Potter's Questions

1. What were you supposed to do?
2. What did you do well?
3. What would you do differently next time?
4. Do you need any help?

SKYLIGHT PUBLISHING

PEOPLE SEARCH

Find Someone Who . . .

Can distinguish between base groups and task groups (both formal & informal) ________________	Has a favorite way of encouraging all students ________________
Has a great success story about student thinking in the classroom ________________	Can name 3 social skills his/her students lack ________________
Can explain why trust building is important in cooperative learning ________________	Can describe a special "group" experience outside of the classroom ________________

IALAC

IALAC

IALAC

STORY ONE

The large plane carried a crew of seven people—pilot, co-pilot, navigator, head cabin manager, and three assistant cabin managers. One-half the way from New York to Chicago they ran into a heavy thunder storm. Lightning struck the plane and damaged the tail gears.

STORY TWO

The football team was playing for the league championship. At half time, seven members of the offense and both coaches became very ill. The team doctor said they could not return to the field.

STORY THREE

On the way to a very important tennis match, the van with the girls' team was struck by a bus. No one was injured. However, all the racquets, except two were destroyed.

STORY FOUR

The students in Professor Swartz's law class had formed their own study groups. It was now time for the final exam. The last assignment was to review the second half of the textbook, including five chapters not covered in class. There were two days for the review.

STORY FIVE

The firefighters in station 25 had worked together for 12 years. They were organized in five teams of seven. Due to retirements and reorganization of the department, there were five vacancies in the station. Two workers were assigned to the station.

STORY SIX

The first pair of paramedics arrived at the accident at 6:10 p.m. It was already dark. Three adults were standing at the edge of the pond. Twenty-five feet out there was a hole in the ice. A young boy was in the water and holding onto a fallen tree. When the medics called for assistance, they were told everyone was at a fire across town. They could expect no backup for at least 15 minutes.

STORY SEVEN

The construction crew had two days to finish rebuilding the road before a "late fine" was imposed by the state highway department. The crew estimated that the job would take at least 20 hours with the equipment they had.

SKYLIGHT PUBLISHING

THAT'S A GOOD IDEA

1. Use DOVE guidelines:
   Defer judgment
   Opt for original
   Vast number of ideas are best
   Expand by piggybacking

2. Respond in turn with:
   a) "That's a good idea because..."
   b) Your idea

3. Allow students to say, "I pass."

4. Keep going around the circle until everyone has had a chance to respond.

5. Record all ideas and reasons on a chart.

TOPIC	
Idea	**Reason**
1.	1.
2.	2.
3.	3.

SKYLIGHT PUBLISHING

OBSERVER'S CHECKLIST

Desired Social Skill	Group A	Group B	Group C	Group D
1				
2				
3				
4				

Date:________________ Observer: ____________________________

Chapter 4, page 66

PARTNER A-1

Your task is to describe the following figure to a partner. Your partner must sit back-to-back with you and may not (a) see your sketch, or (b) talk with you. Your partner must reproduce your sketch using your instructions. You will have five minutes.

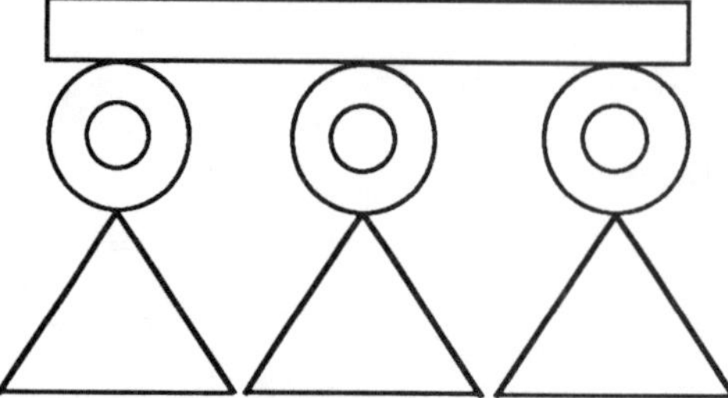

PARTNER A-1

Your task is to describe the following figure to a partner. Your partner must sit back-to-back with you and may not (a) see your sketch, or (b) talk with you. Your partner must reproduce your sketch using your instructions. You will have five minutes.

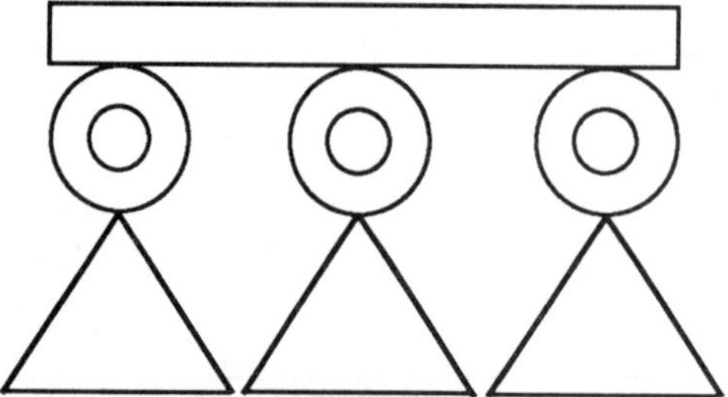

PARTNER A-1

Your task is to describe the following figure to a partner. Your partner must sit back-to-back with you and may not (a) see your sketch, or (b) talk with you. Your partner must reproduce your sketch using your instructions. You will have five minutes.

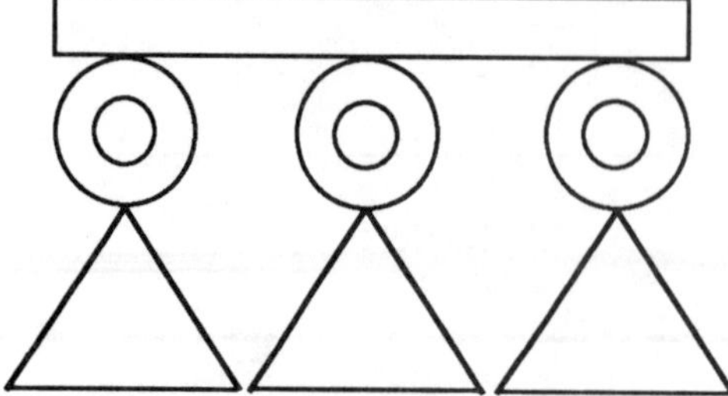

PARTNER B-1

Your task is to sketch the figure as instructed by your partner. You may not talk with your partner or see the original. You will have five minutes.

PARTNER B-1

Your task is to sketch the figure as instructed by your partner. You may not talk with your partner or see the original. You will have five minutes.

PARTNER B-1

Your task is to sketch the figure as instructed by your partner. You may not talk with your partner or see the original. You will have five minutes.

PARTNER A-2

You may not see the sketch. You may ask clarifying questions about the instructions and discuss how you are sketching.

PARTNER A-2

You may not see the sketch. You may ask clarifying questions about the instructions and discuss how you are sketching.

PARTNER A-2

You may not see the sketch. You may ask clarifying questions about the instructions and discuss how you are sketching.

PARTNER B-2

You may not show this sketch to your partner. You may answer your partner's questions about your instructions. You have five minutes.

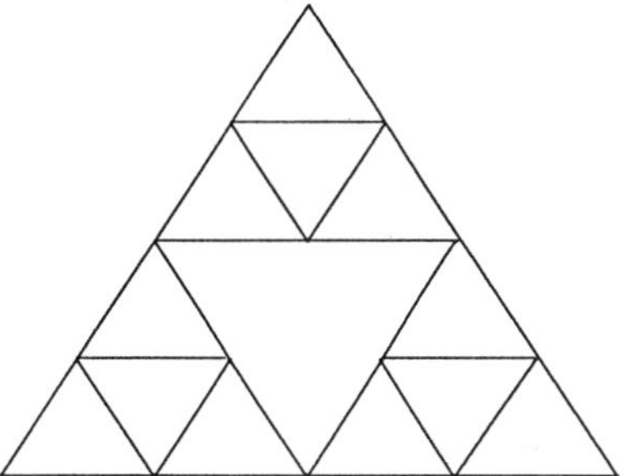

PARTNER B-2

You may not show this sketch to your partner. You may answer your partner's questions about your instructions. You have five minutes.

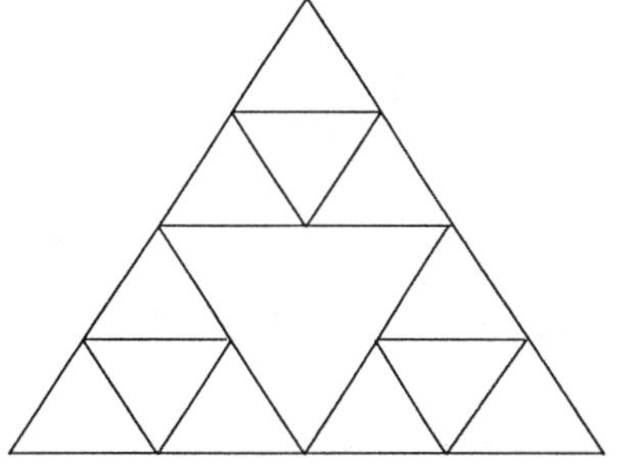

PARTNER B-2

You may not show this sketch to your partner. You may answer your partner's questions about your instructions. You have five minutes.

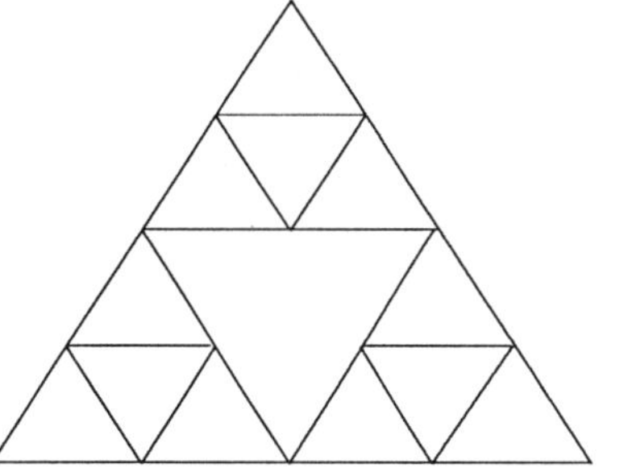

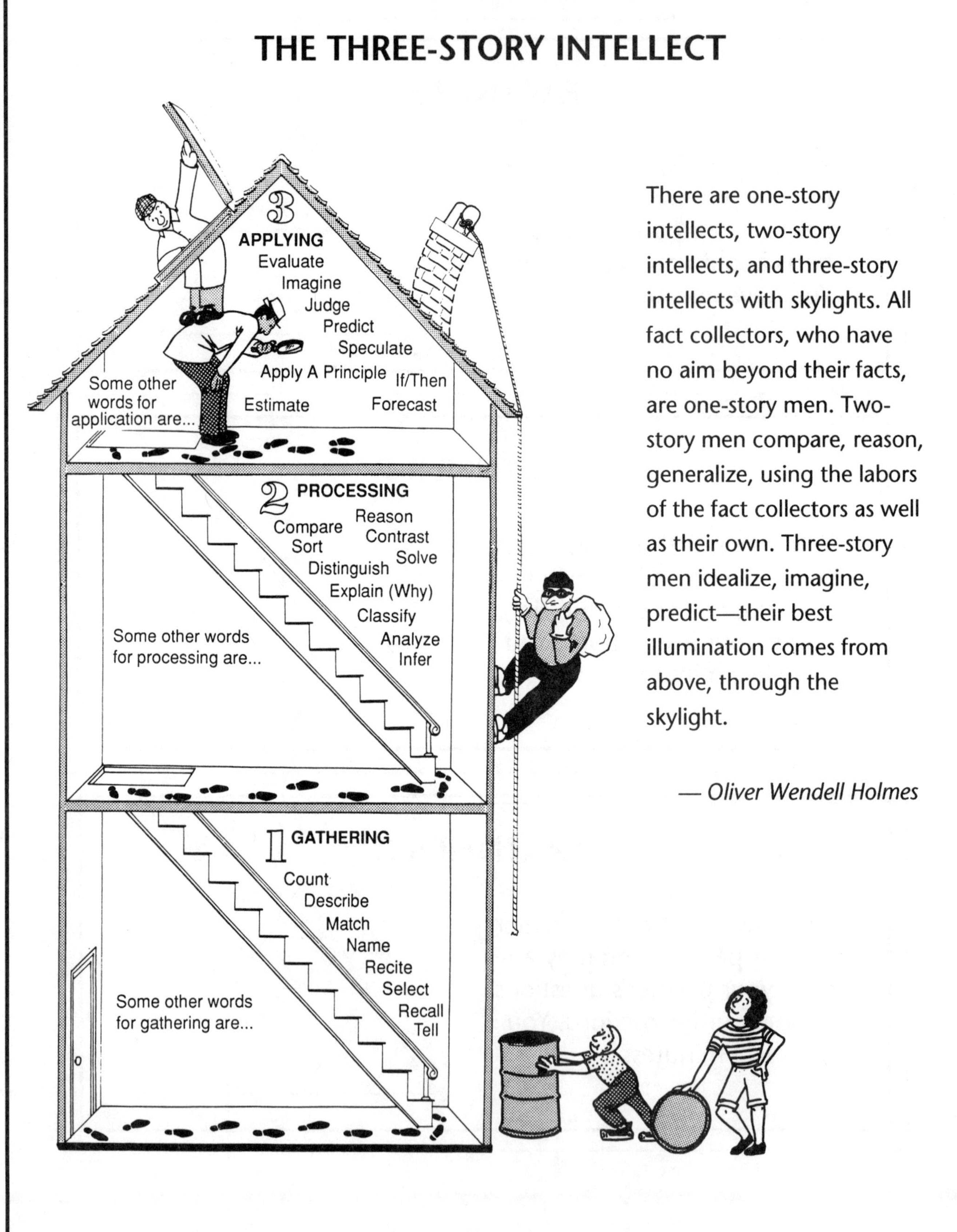
THE THREE-STORY INTELLECT
3
APPLYING
Evaluate
Imagine
Judge
Predict
Speculate
Apply A Principle
If/Then
Estimate
Forecast
Some other words for application are...
2
PROCESSING
Compare
Reason
Contrast
Sort
Solve
Distinguish
Explain (Why)
Classify
Analyze
Infer
Some other words for processing are...
1
GATHERING
Count
Describe
Match
Name
Recite
Select
Recall
Tell
Some other words for gathering are...
There are one-story intellects, two-story intellects, and three-story intellects with skylights. All fact collectors, who have no aim beyond their facts, are one-story men. Two-story men compare, reason, generalize, using the labors of the fact collectors as well as their own. Three-story men idealize, imagine, predict—their best illumination comes from above, through the skylight.
— Oliver Wendell Holmes

SKYLIGHT PUBLISHING

FILL IN THE BUTTONS

FILL IN THE BUTTONS

FILL IN THE BUTTONS

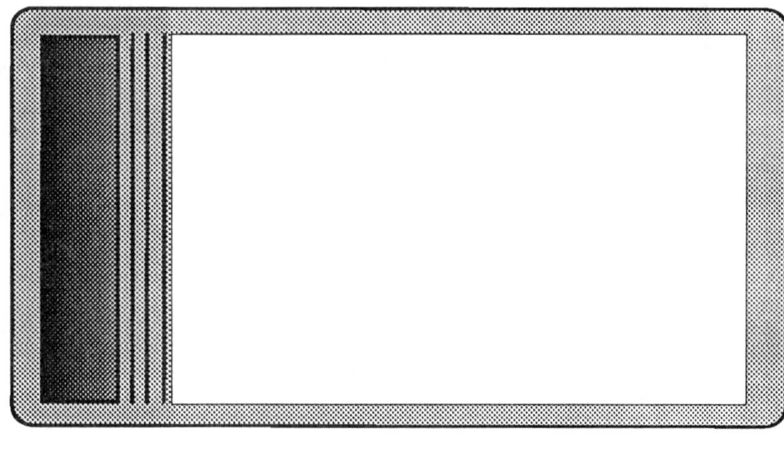

CREATE A CREATURE CLASSIFICATION LAB

	A	B	C	D	E	F
	BODY SYMMETRY	SEGMENTATION	FORM OF LOCOMOTION	SENSORY ORGANS	SUPPORT STRUCTURES	BODY COVERING
1						
2						
3						
4						
5						
6						

SKYLIGHT PUBLISHING

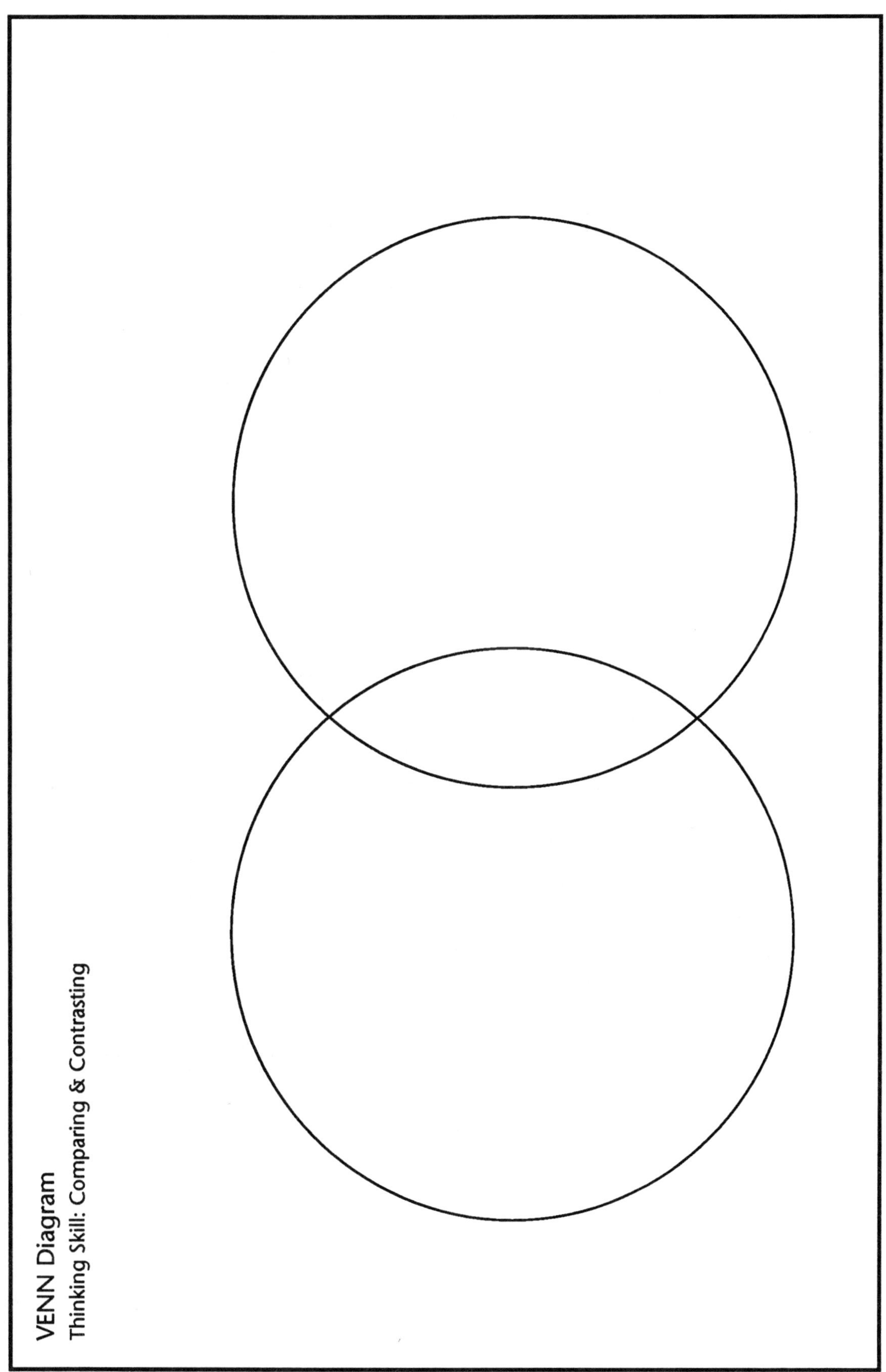
VENN Diagram
Thinking Skill: Comparing & Contrasting

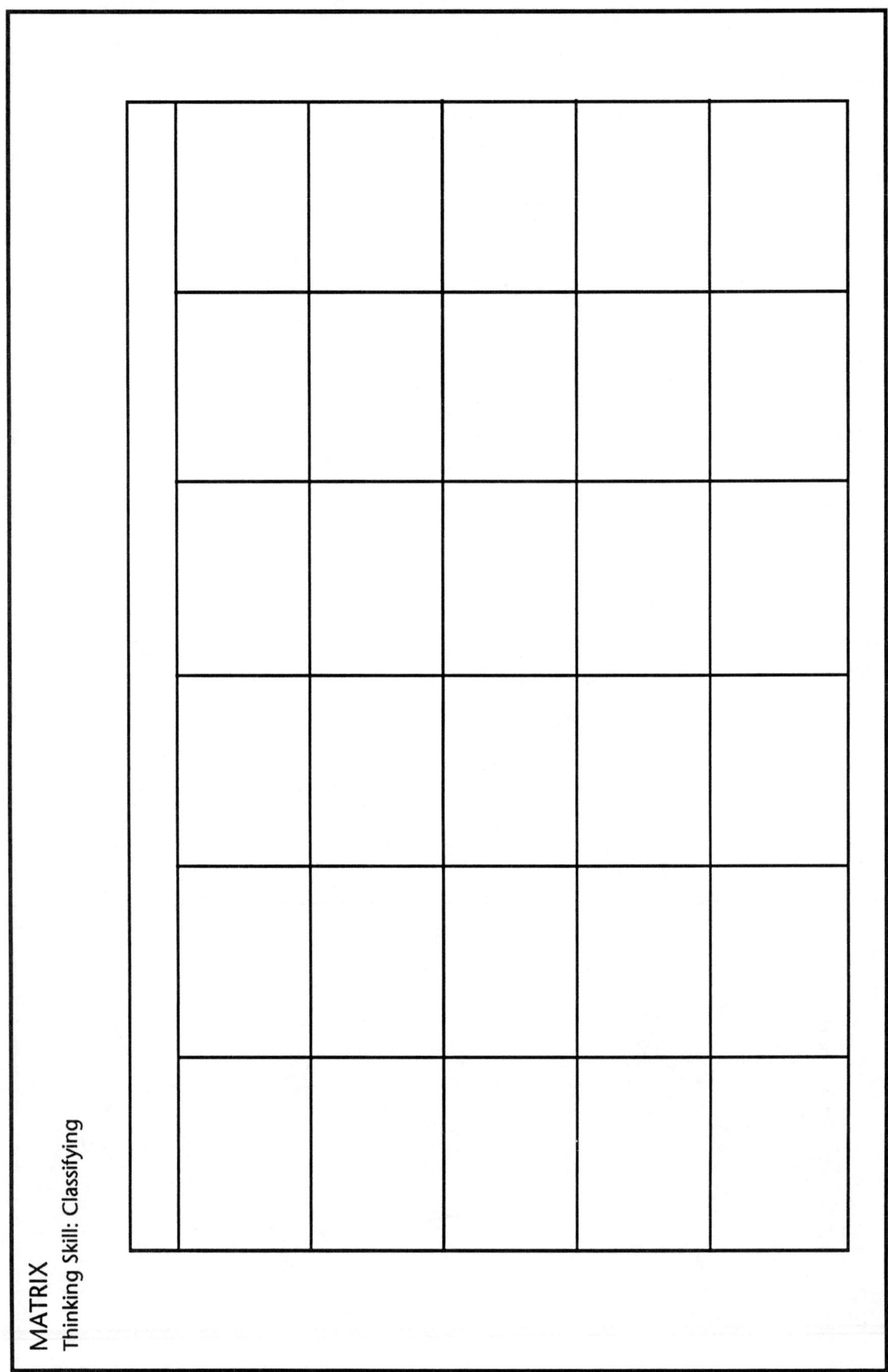
MATRIX
Thinking Skill: Classifying

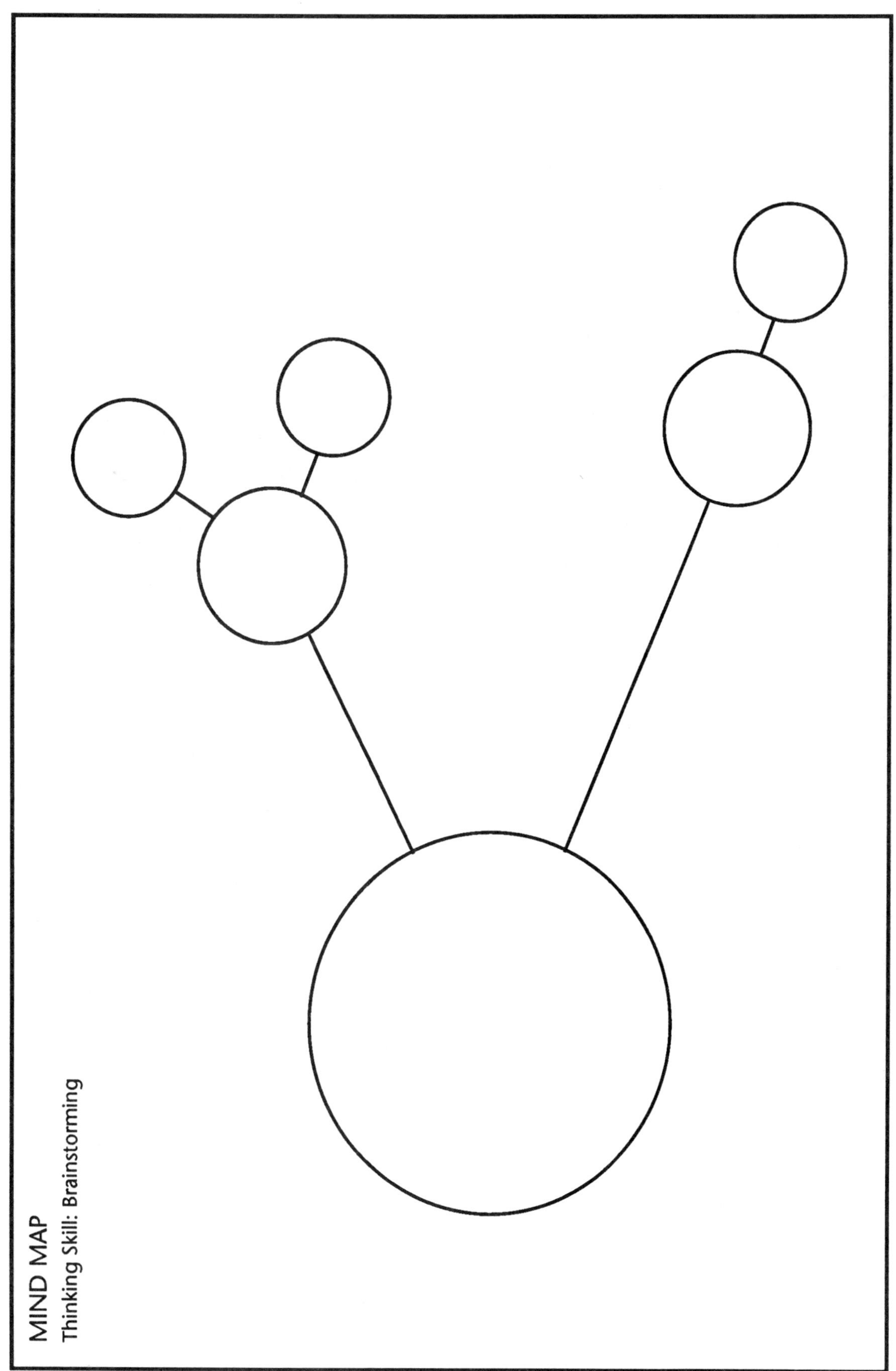

Chapter 6, page 107

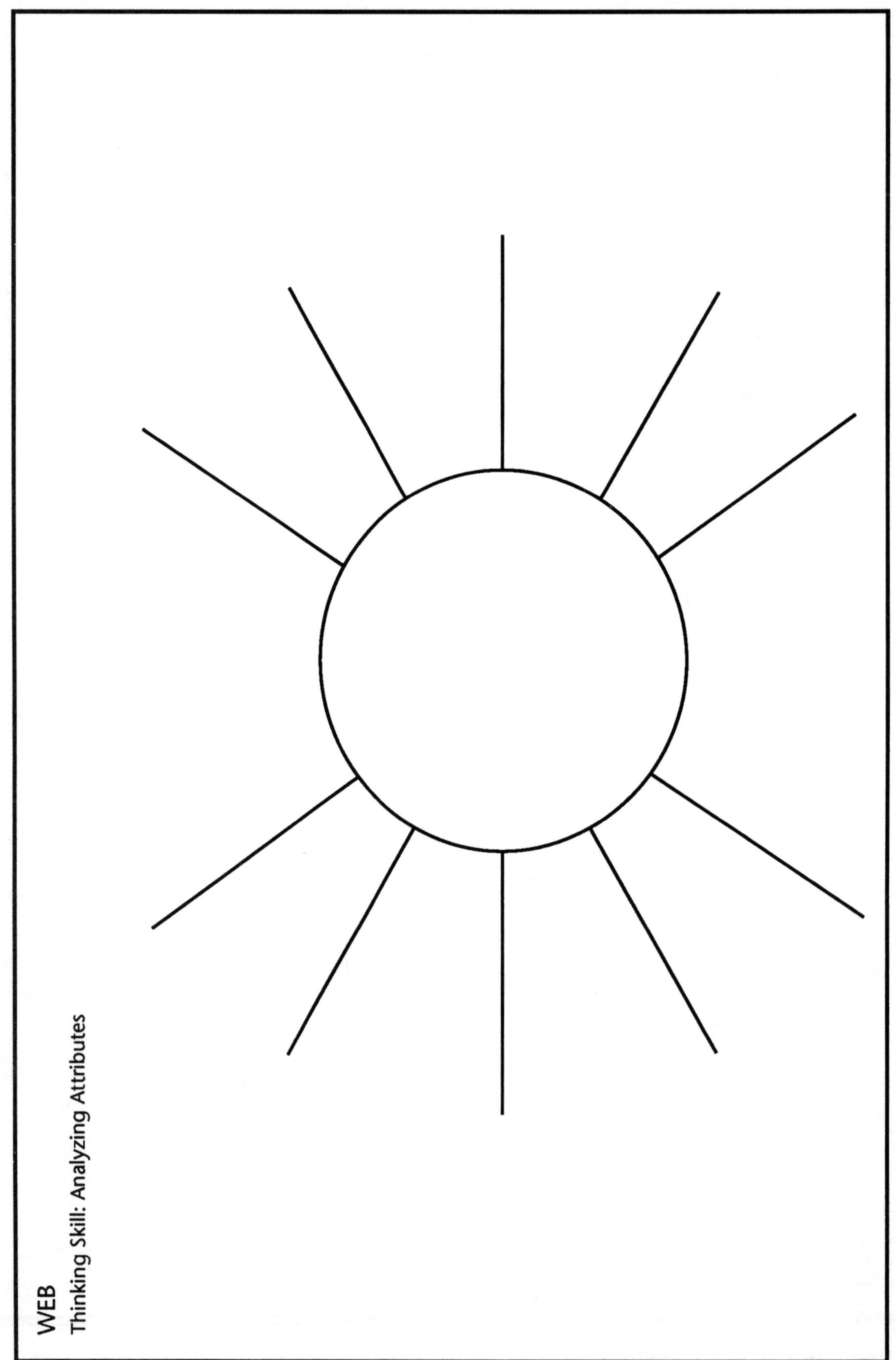
WEB
Thinking Skill: Analyzing Attributes

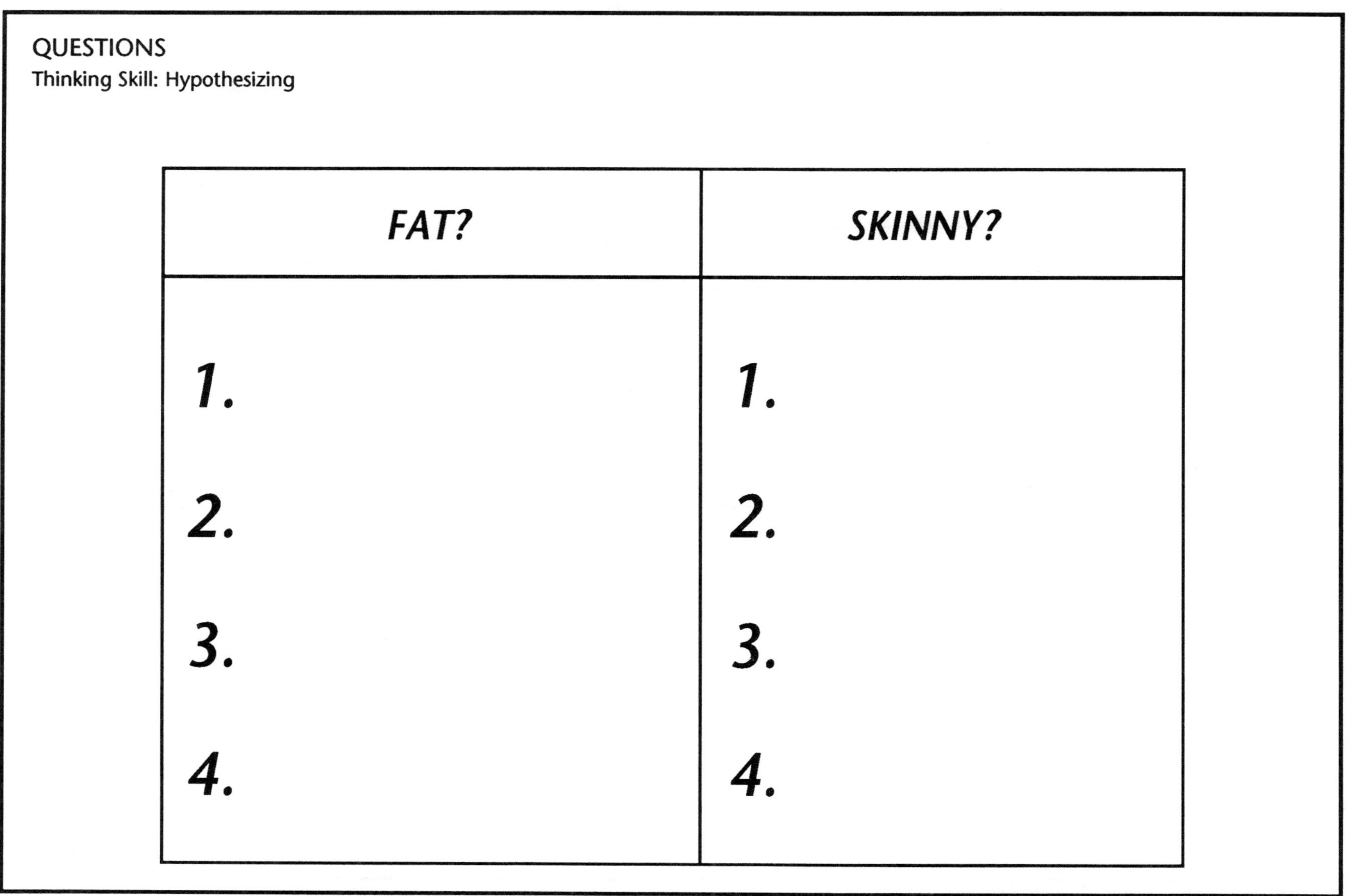
QUESTIONS
Thinking Skill: Hypothesizing
FAT?
SKINNY?
1.
1.
2.
2.
3.
3.
4.
4.

RANKING

Thinking Skill: Prioritizing

1.

2.

3.

4.

SKYLIGHT PUBLISHING

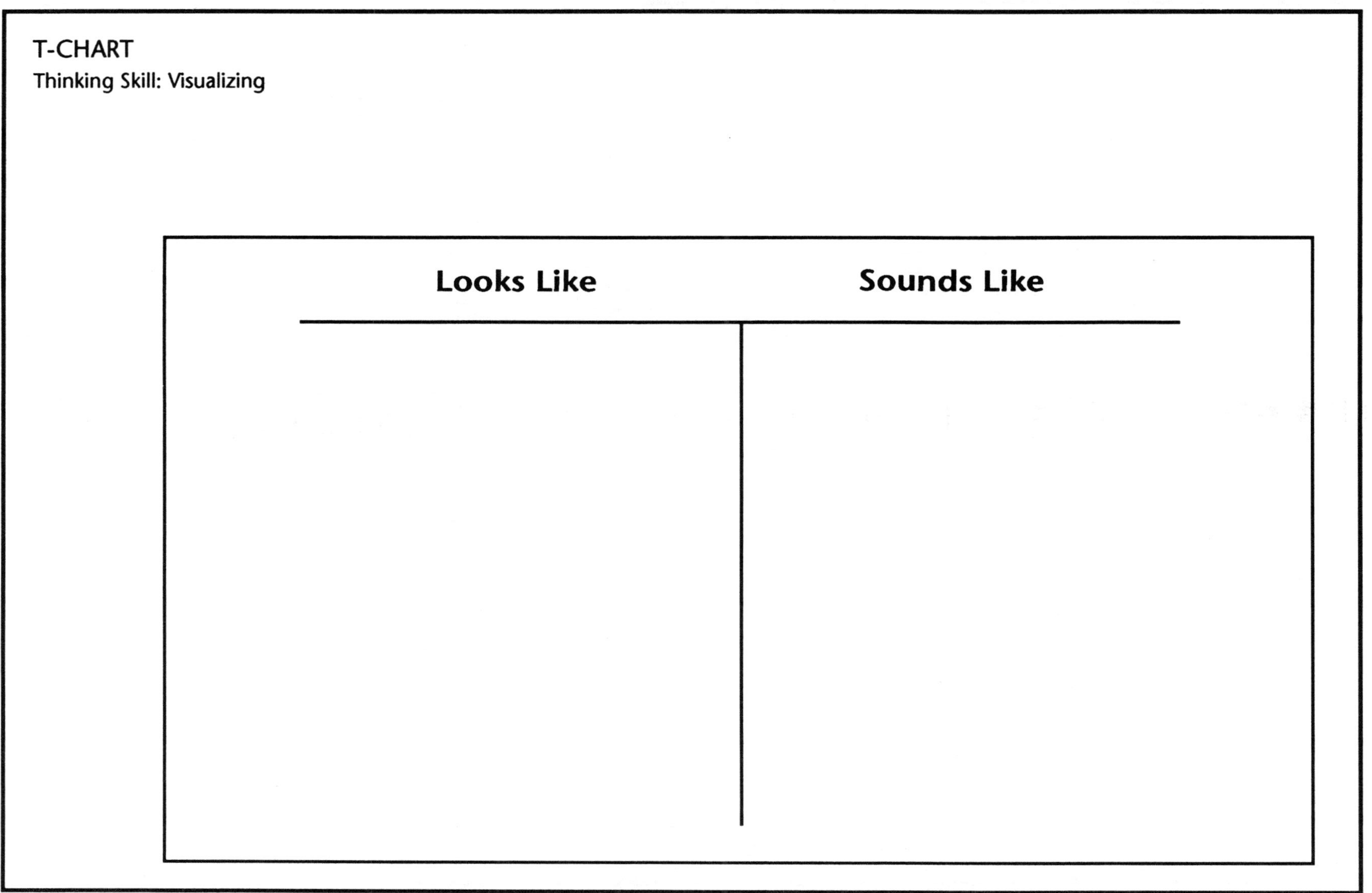

Chapter 6, page 107

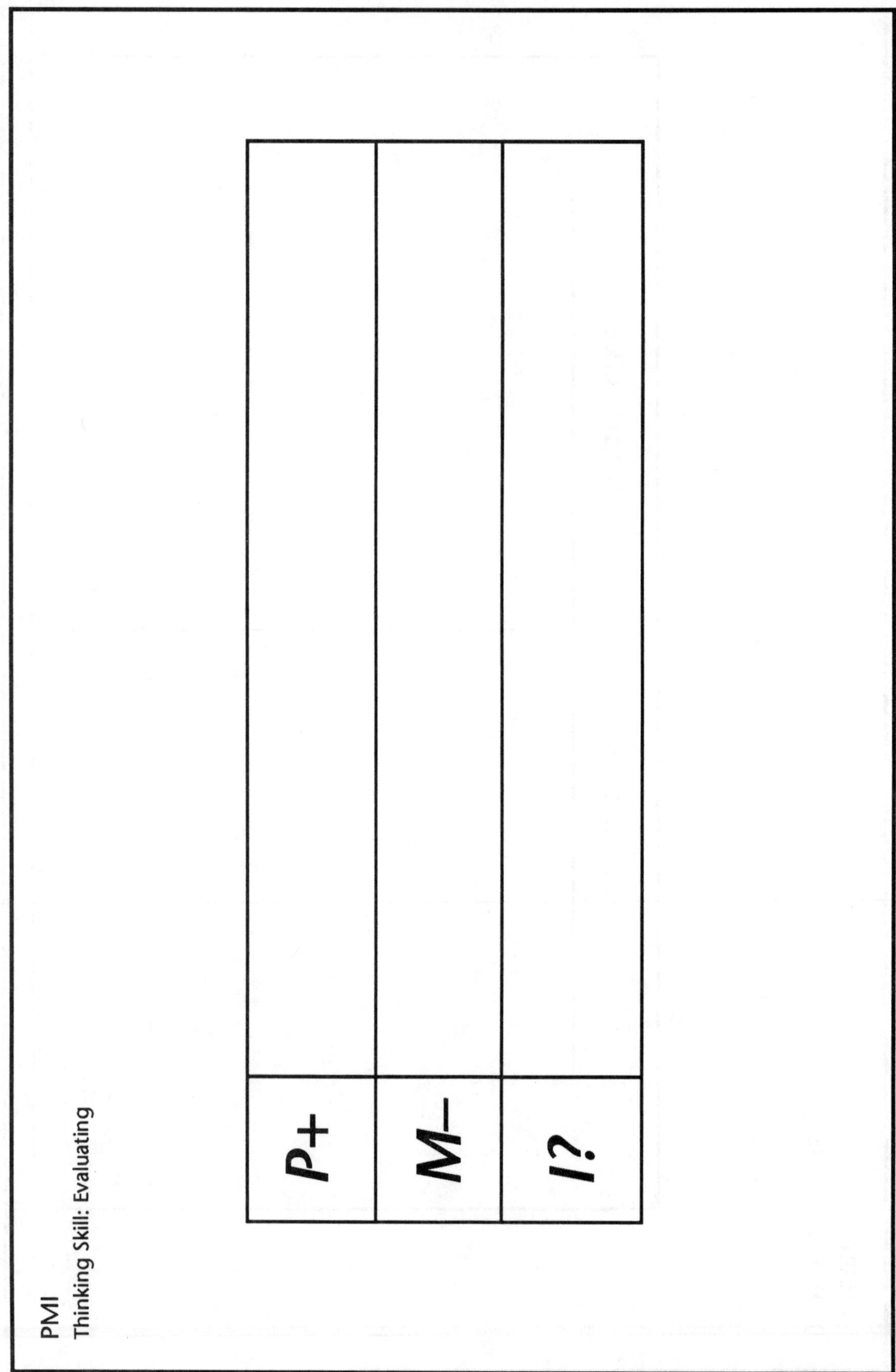

SKYLIGHT PUBLISHING

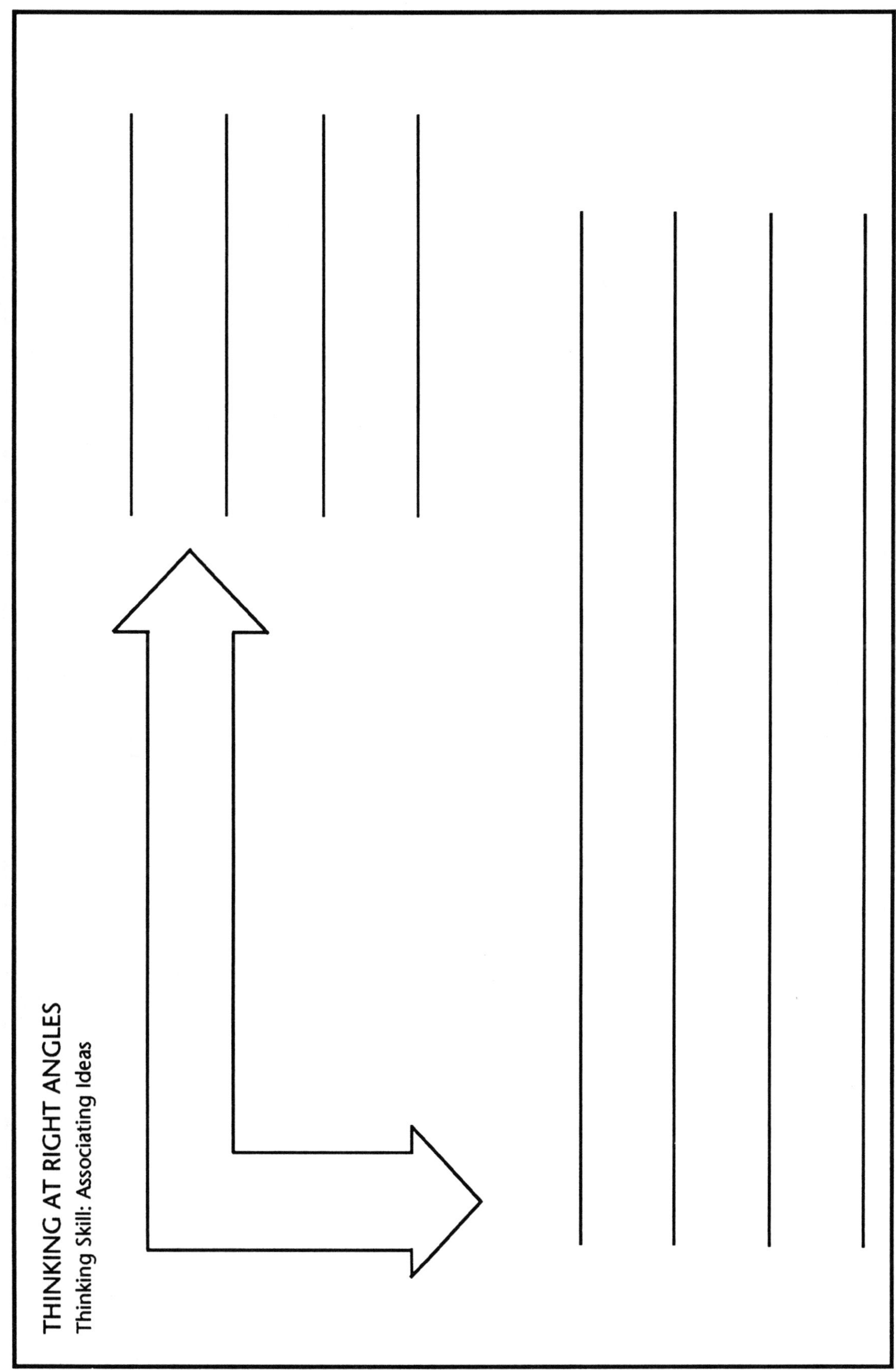

Chapter 6, page 107

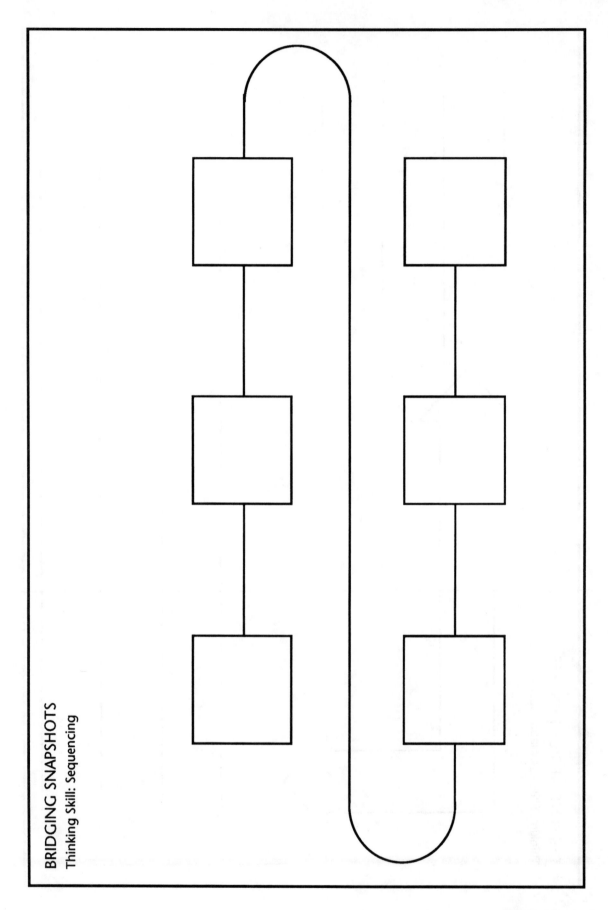

BRIDGING SNAPSHOTS

Thinking Skill: Sequencing

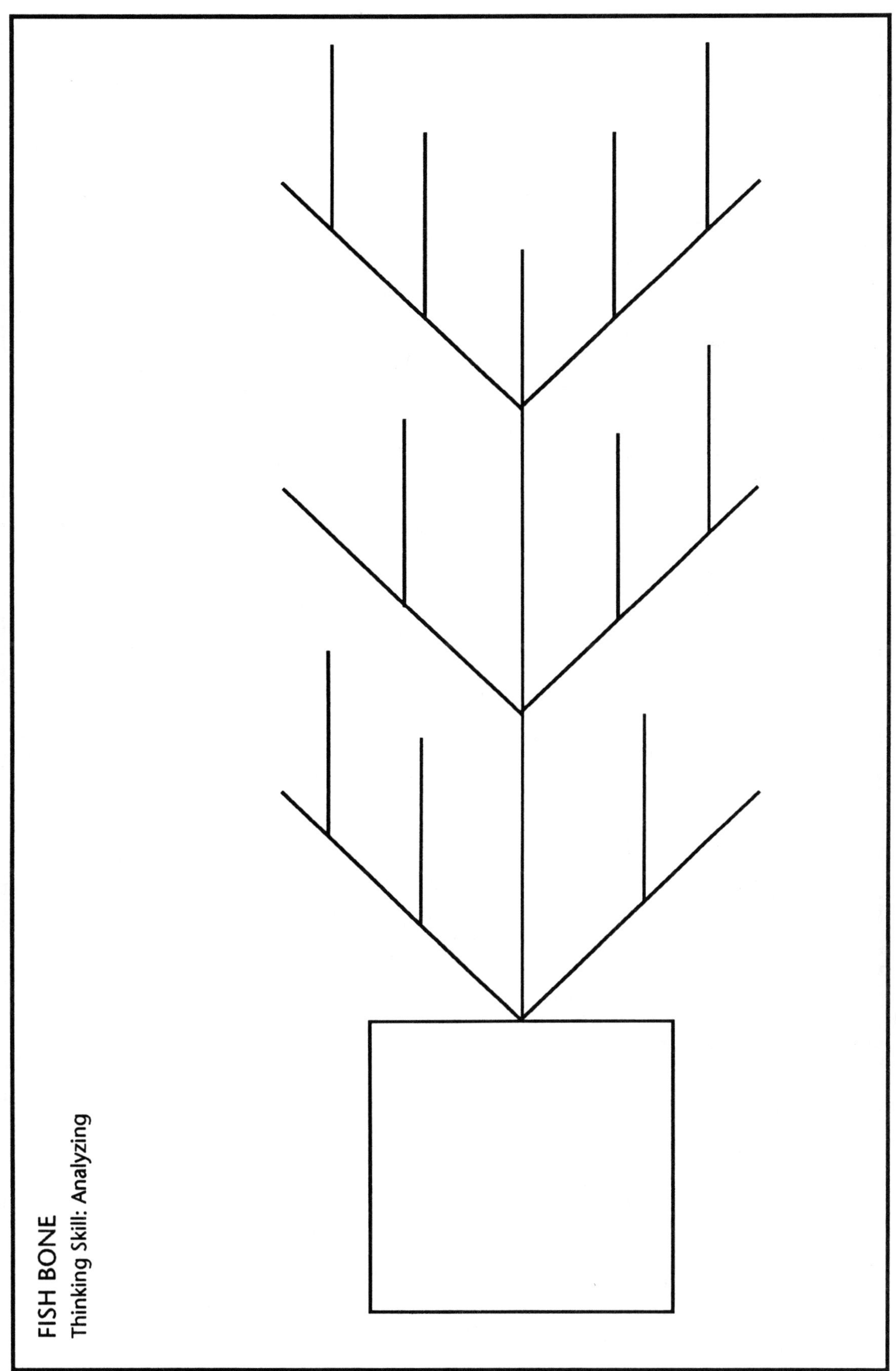
FISH BONE
Thinking Skill: Analyzing

KWL
Thinking Skill: Predicting/Evaluating

What We **Know**	What We **Want** to Find Out	What We **Learned**

AFRICAN & ASIAN ELEPHANTS

Elephants are the largest of all land animals, and they are among the strangest-looking animals in the world, with their long trunks, big ears and pointed tusks. There are two basic kinds of elephants—African elephants and Asian (or Indian) elephants. It is rather easy to tell one kind from another.

Asian elephants have smaller ears than African elephants. They have a high forehead with two rather large "bumps" on it. The back of the Asian elephant bends up in the middle, and usually only the males have tusks.

African elephants have very large ears. Their foreheads don't have big bumps on them. The back of an African elephant bends down in the middle, and both the males and females have tusks.

African elephants are larger than Asian elephants, and the males of both kinds are larger than the females. The average Asian male is about 9 feet (2.74 meters) tall at the shoulder and weighs about 10,000 (4,535 kilograms). African males average about 10 feet tall (3 meters) and weigh about 12,000 pounds (5,443 kilograms).

However, some elephants grow much larger than this. The largest African male on record was more than 12 1/2 feet tall (3.66 meters) and weighed about 22,000 (9,979 kilograms). The single elephant weighed as much as 150 average-sized people.

Male elephants are called bulls, and females are called cows. Young elephants are called calves. When an elephant calf is born, it is already a big animal. It is about three feet tall (1 meter) and weighs about 200 pounds (90 kilograms). Baby elephants are covered with hair, but as they grow they lose most of it.

Elephants can live a very long time. Asian elephants may live as along as 80 years, and African elephants may live for 60 years.

Chapter 6, page 113

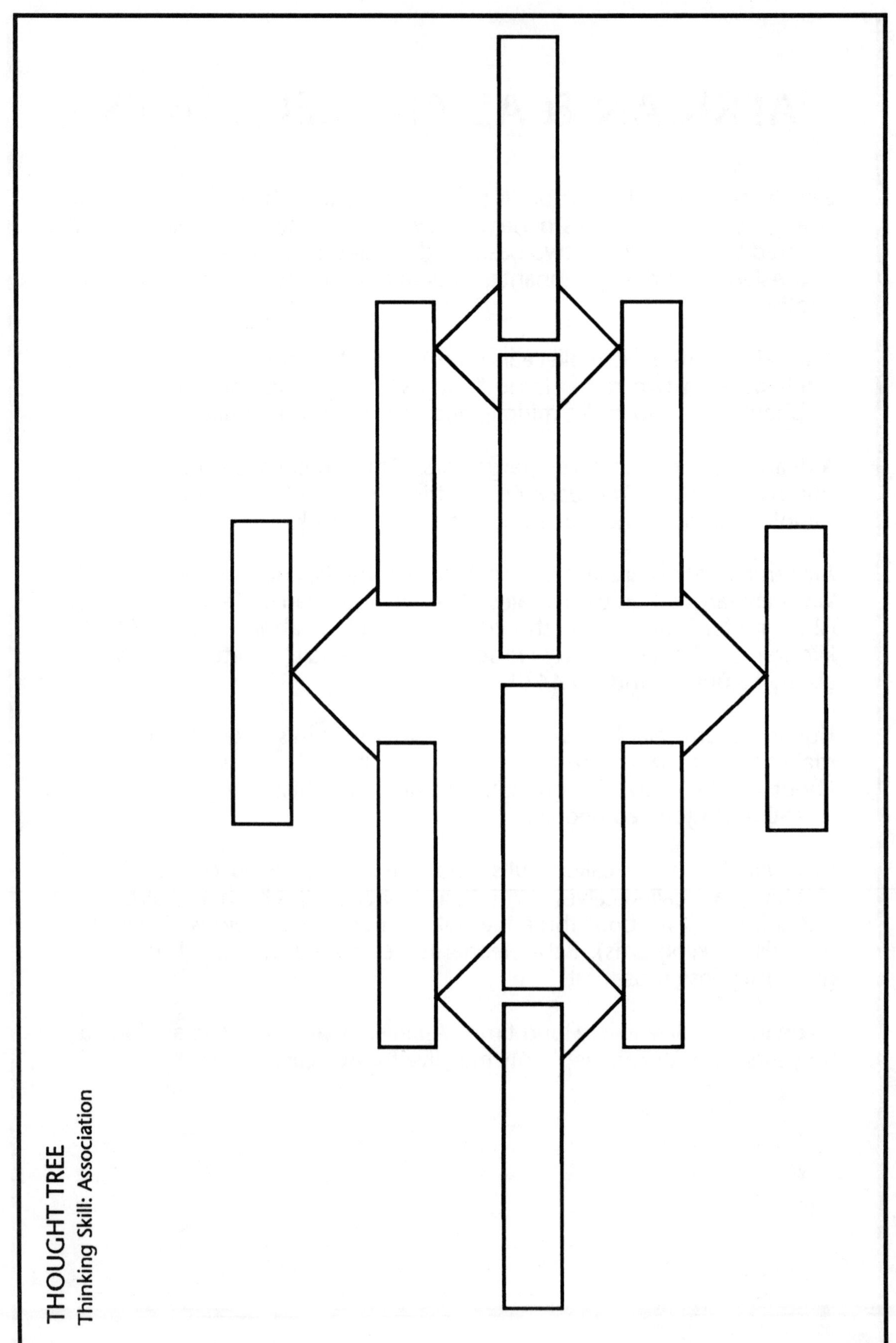
THOUGHT TREE
Thinking Skill: Association

Chart A Challenge

Choose one problem area and create a problem scenario

1	2	3	4	5	6	7
SENSE THE PROBLEM	FIND THE PROBLEM	BRAINSTORM IDEAS	PRIORITIZE SOLUTIONS	SELL TO OTHERS	PLAN THE ACTION	FACE NEW CHALLENGE
Family						
Siblings						
Parents						
Car						
Appearance						
Grades						
Future						
Teachers						
Peers						
Self-Image						
	"Could it be...?"	"Ways out"	"Best one"	"Convincing others"	"First steps"	"Now what?" "What next?"

SKYLIGHT PUBLISHING

PROBLEM-SOLVING MODEL

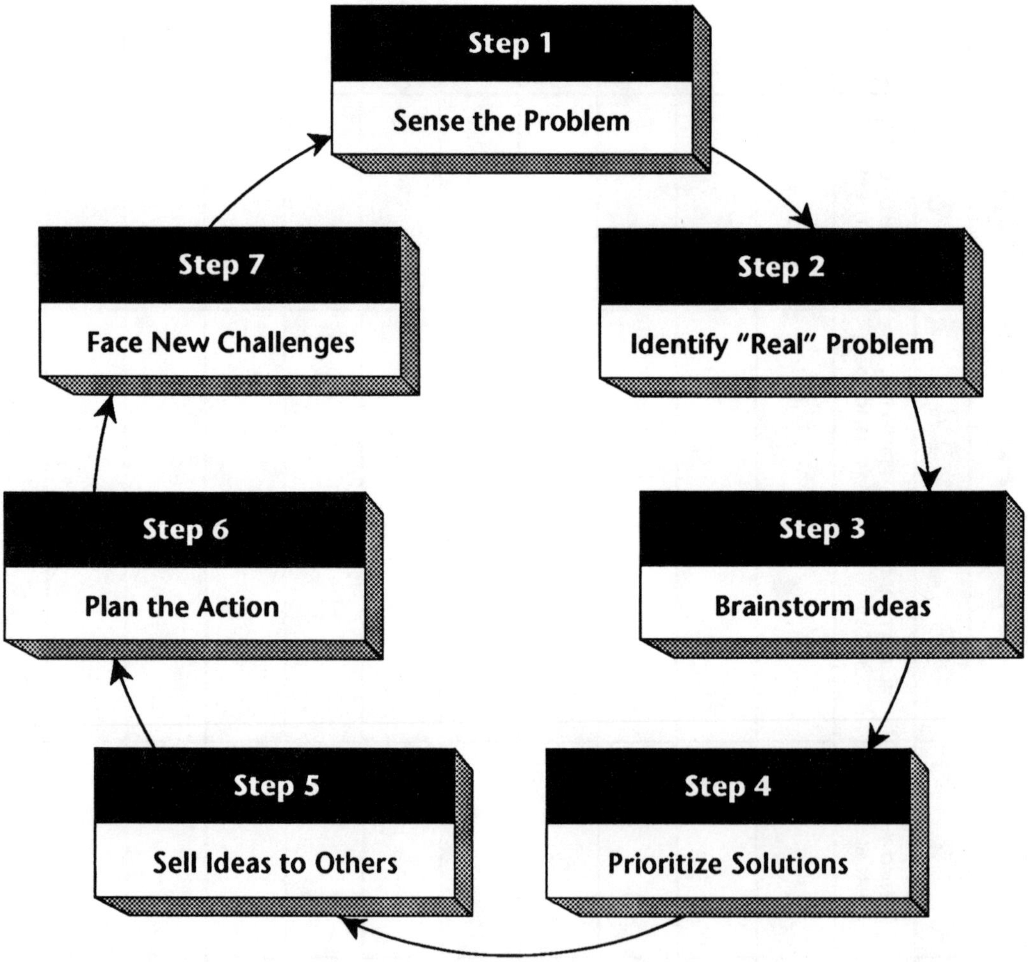

Step 1
Sense the Problem

Step 2
Identify "Real" Problem

Step 3
Brainstorm Ideas

Step 4
Prioritize Solutions

Step 5
Sell Ideas to Others

Step 6
Plan the Action

Step 7
Face New Challenges

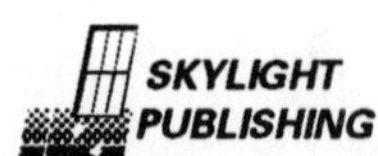

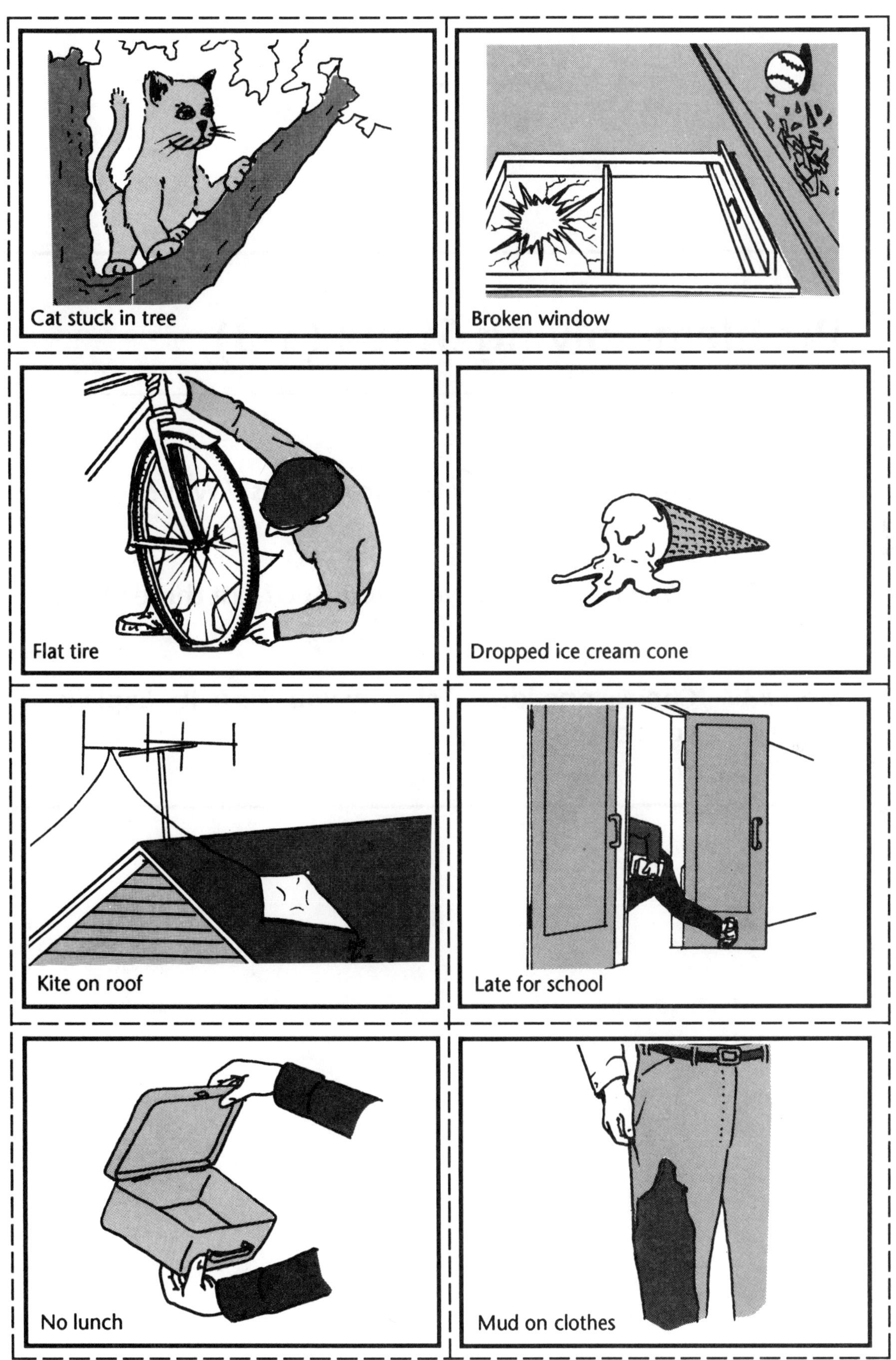
Cat stuck in tree
Broken window
Flat tire
Dropped ice cream cone
Kite on roof
Late for school
No lunch
Mud on clothes

Problem-solving Steps (1-3)

Step #1	What do you think the problem is? Why?
Step #2	What do you think you should do? List three ideas.
Step #3	Choose one idea. Tell why you chose it; Explain your criteria.

"What If Quote"

"Trust is the result of a risk successfully survived!"

-Jack R. Gibb

Chapter 7, page 128

PROBLEM-SOLVING STRATEGIES

Strategy Used ______________________

☐ Will never use

☐ Would like to try

☐ See definite possibilities

☐ Frequent use anticipated

☐ An all-time favorite

I marked ______________________

____

because ______________________

____

What do you do when you disagree?

Check the strategies you used.

- ❑ Argue - stand firm
- ❑ Persuade - justify, reason, appeal to
- ❑ Vote - majority rules
- ❑ Compromise - combine, modify
- ❑ Mediate - neutral party facilitator
- ❑ Arbitrate - agree to abide by decision of arbitrator
- ❑ Delay - table it, sleep on it, wait
- ❑ Reconceptualize - rethink, find new angles
- ❑ Negotiate - give and take
- ❑ Give In - give up, cave in, play martyr
- ❑ Seek Consensus - talk, cajole, juggle, adjust, modify
- ❑ Humor - veer away from confrontation
- ❑ Avoid - ignore or postpone indefinitely

What do you do when you disagree?

Check the strategies you used.

- ❑ Argue - stand firm
- ❑ Persuade - justify, reason, appeal to
- ❑ Vote - majority rules
- ❑ Compromise - combine, modify
- ❑ Mediate - neutral party facilitator
- ❑ Arbitrate - agree to abide by decision of arbitrator
- ❑ Delay - table it, sleep on it, wait
- ❑ Reconceptualize - rethink, find new angles
- ❑ Negotiate - give and take
- ❑ Give In - give up, cave in, play martyr
- ❑ Seek Consensus - talk, cajole, juggle, adjust, modify
- ❑ Humor - veer away from confrontation
- ❑ Avoid - ignore or postpone indefinitely

What do you do when you disagree?

Check the strategies you used.

- ❑ Argue - stand firm
- ❑ Persuade - justify, reason, appeal to
- ❑ Vote - majority rules
- ❑ Compromise - combine, modify
- ❑ Mediate - neutral party facilitator
- ❑ Arbitrate - agree to abide by decision of arbitrator
- ❑ Delay - table it, sleep on it, wait
- ❑ Reconceptualize - rethink, find new angles
- ❑ Negotiate - give and take
- ❑ Give In - give up, cave in, play martyr
- ❑ Seek Consensus - talk, cajole, juggle, adjust, modify
- ❑ Humor - veer away from confrontation
- ❑ Avoid - ignore or postpone indefinitely

TUG O'WAR THINKING CREED

We pledge to...

Tug at ideas, not people.

Examine all sides of the issue.

Actively listen and clarify.

Modify our position when appropriate.

Seek the best decision,
not the winning position.

Conflict Resolution Puzzle - All Levels

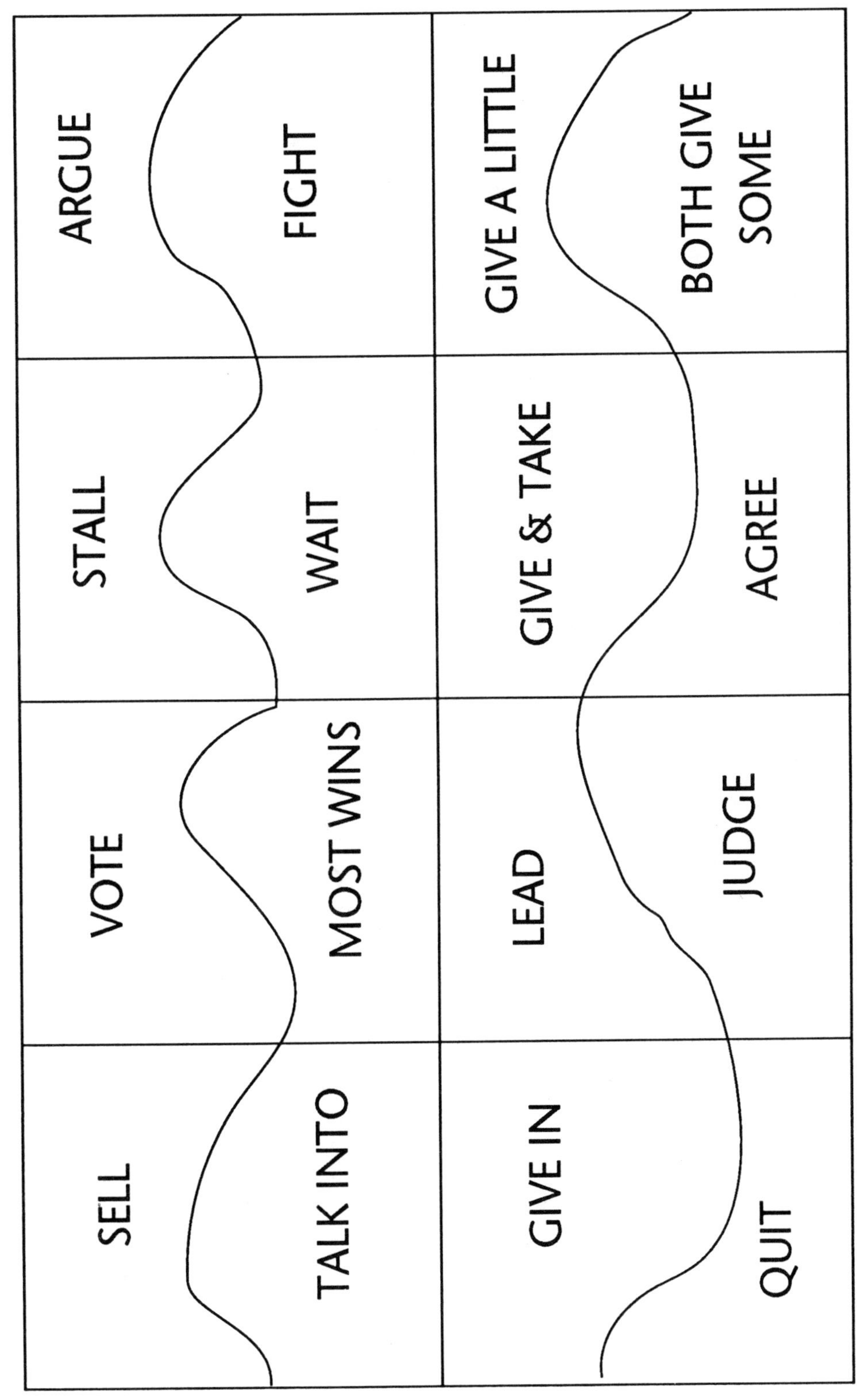

DOVE

Defer judgment; anything goes

Opt for original; different ideas

Vast number is needed

Expand by piggybacking on other's ideas

Conflict Resolution Puzzles - All Levels

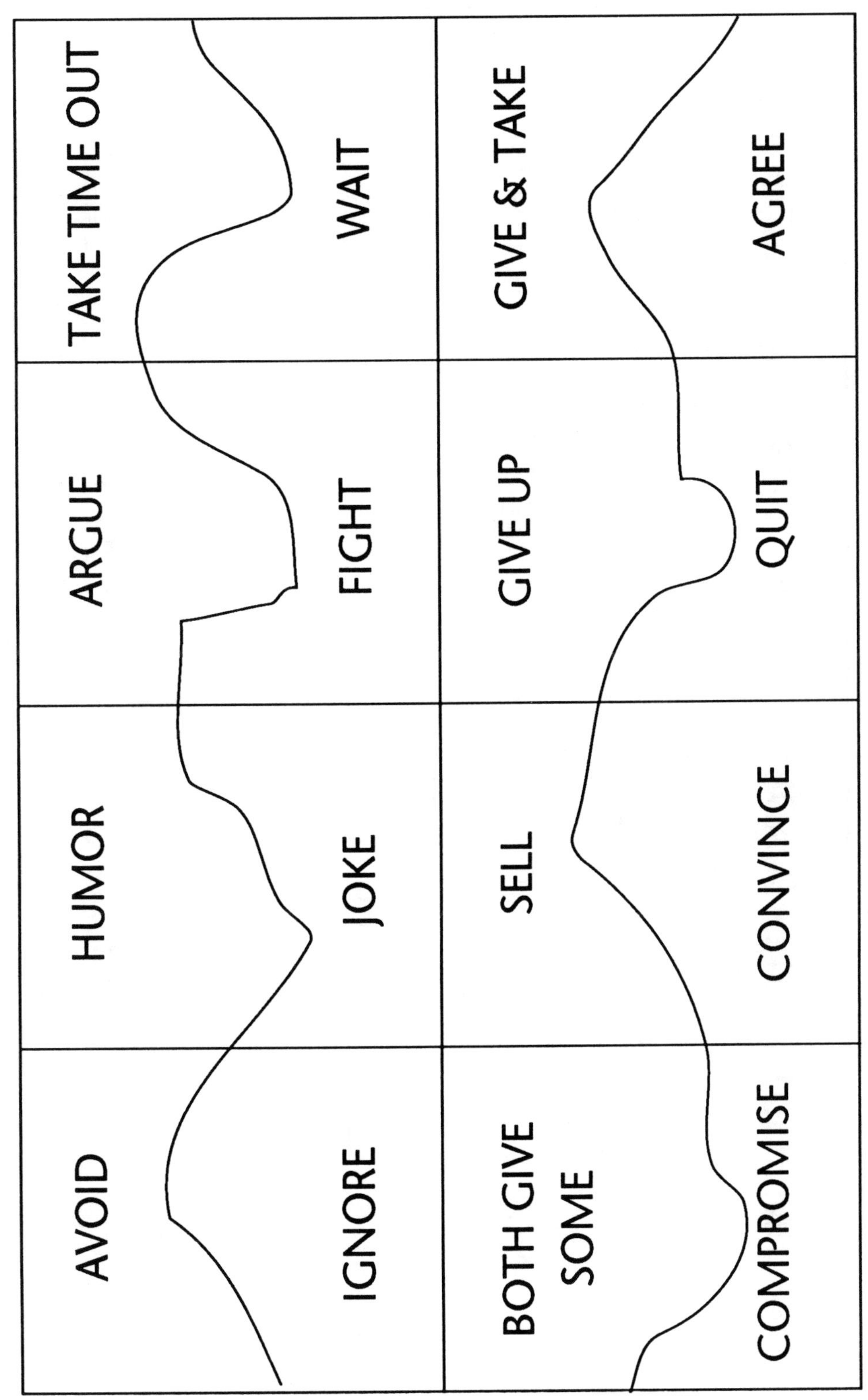

Chapter 8, page 148

Conflict Resolution Puzzles - Middle and Secondary Levels

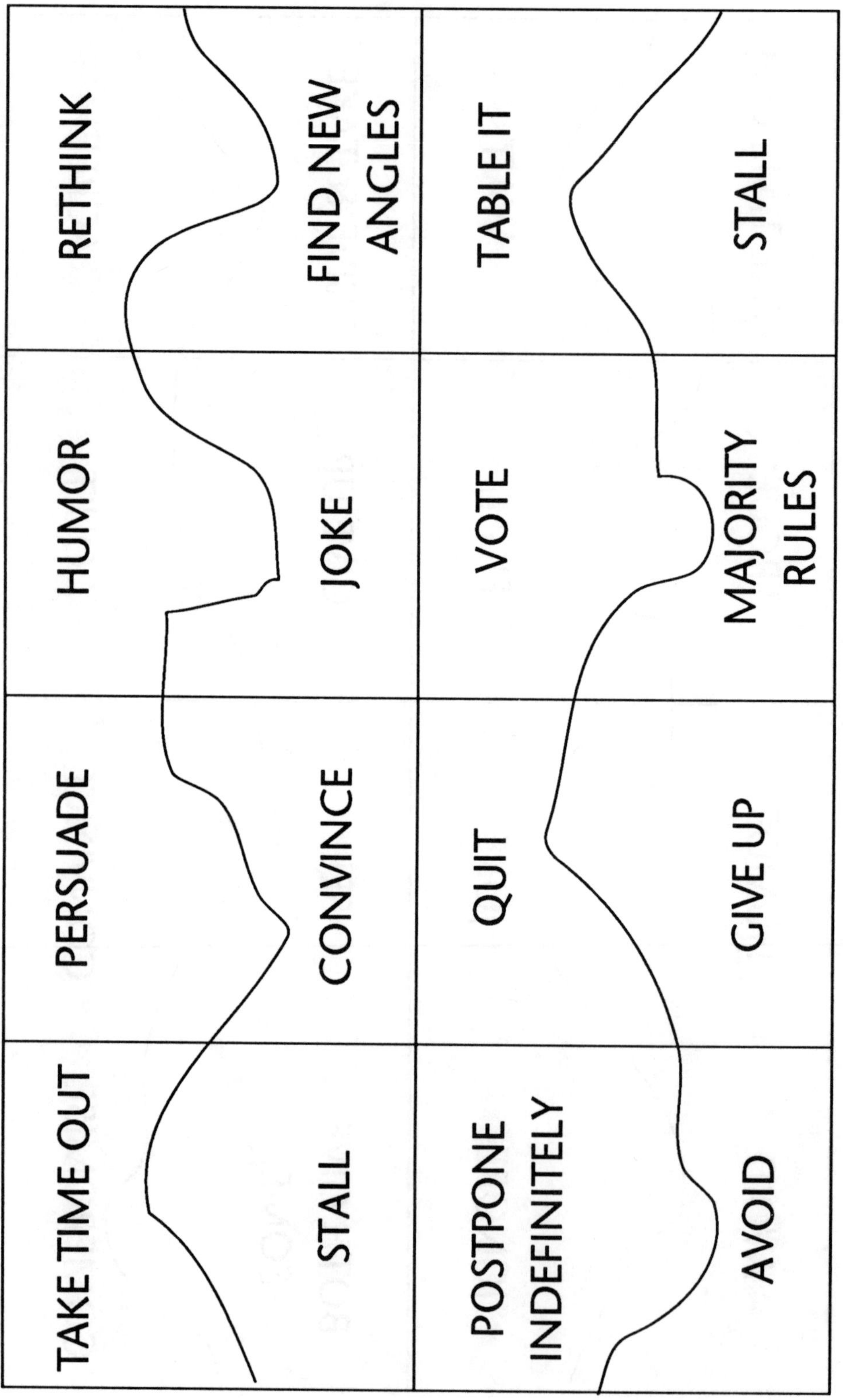

RETHINK / FIND NEW ANGLES	TABLE IT / STALL
HUMOR / JOKE	VOTE / MAJORITY RULES
PERSUADE / CONVINCE	QUIT / GIVE UP
TAKE TIME OUT / STALL	POSTPONE INDEFINITELY / AVOID

Conflict Resolution Puzzles - Secondary School Level

PERSUADE APPEAL TO	MEDIATE USE NEUTRAL FACILITATOR	VOTE MAJORITY RULES	RECONCEP-TUALIZE RETHINK
HUMOR VEER FROM CONFRONTATION	ARGUE STAND FIRM	NEGOTIATE GIVE & TAKE	COMBINE COMPROMISE

Create your own conflict resolution puzzles

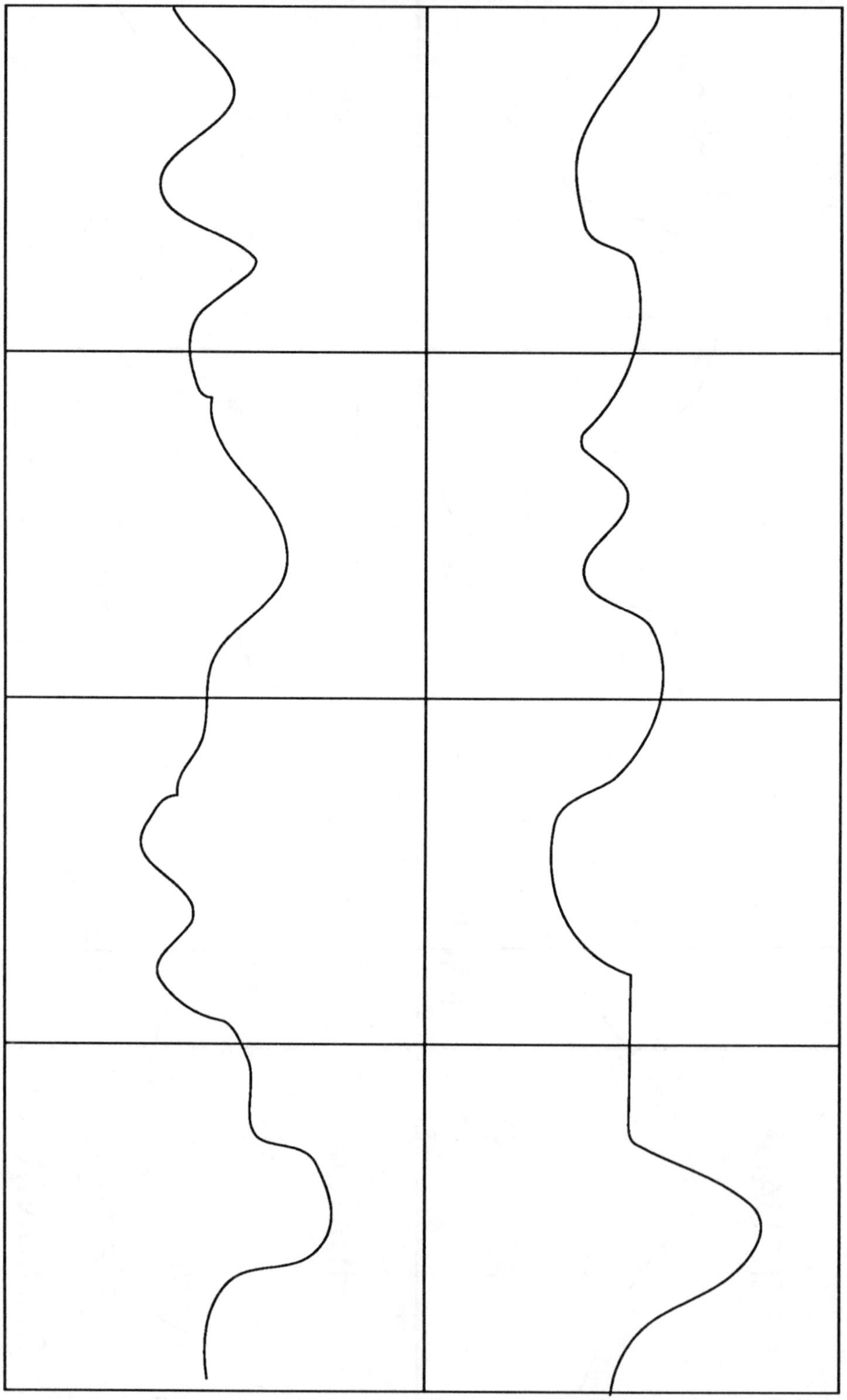

QUICK REFERENCE: COOPERATIVE LESSON PLANNING

	B	U	I	L	D
	Build in High-Order Thinking	**Unite Teams**	**Insure Individual Learning**	**Look Over & Discuss**	**Develop Social Skills**
	Problem Solving Decision Making Creative Ideation	*Build Trust & Teamwork*	*Insure Individual Learning & Responsibility*	*Plan, Monitor & Evaluate*	*Communication Leadership Conflict Resolution*
1					
2					
3					
4					
5					
6					
7					
8					
9					
10					

WAYS TO TEACH ANOTHER

- Tell
- Model
- Demonstrate
- Draw
- Give Examples
- Use Visuals
- Make Analogies
- Quiz

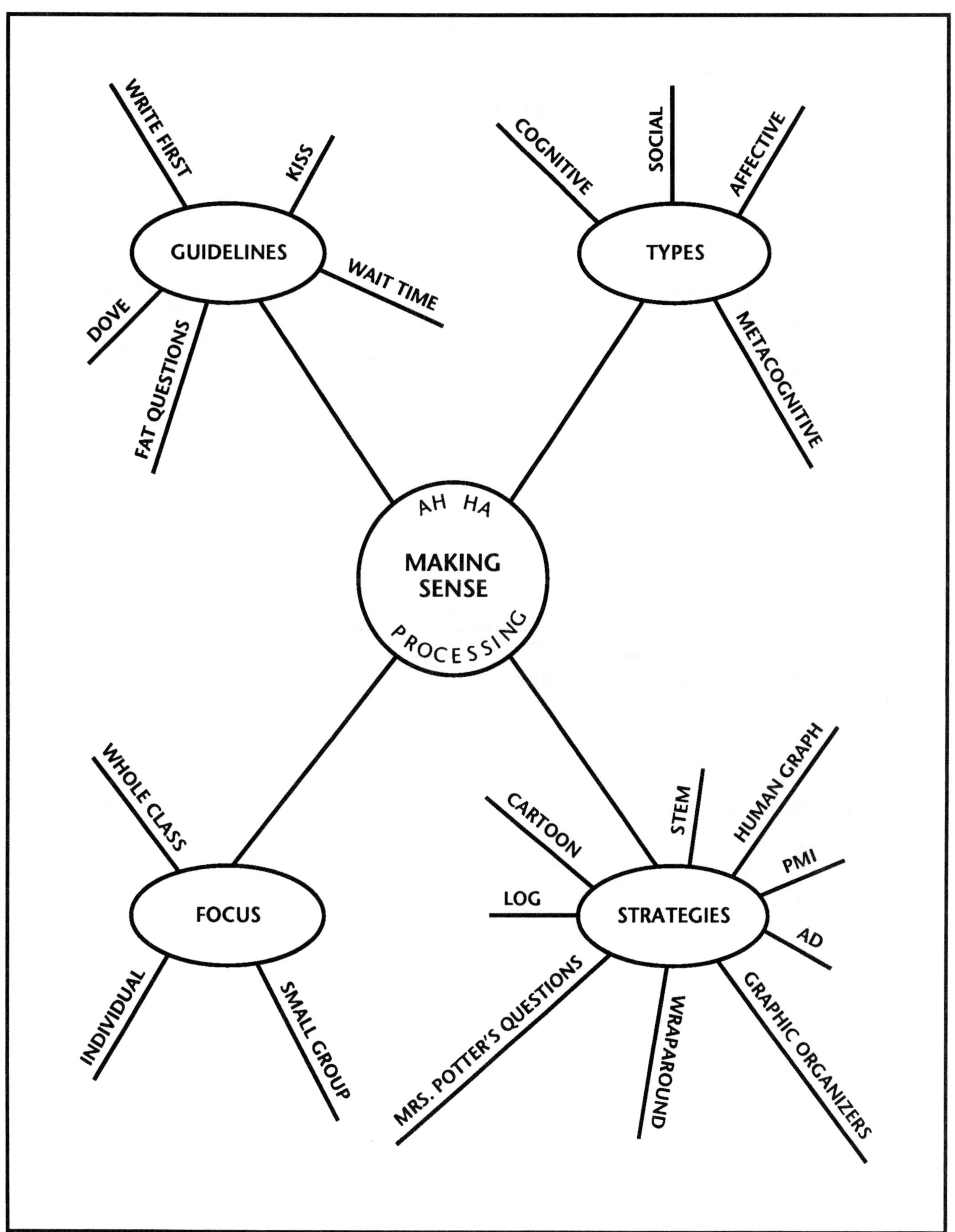
MAKING SENSE
AH HA
PROCESSING
GUIDELINES
WRITE FIRST
KISS
WAIT TIME
FAT QUESTIONS
DOVE
TYPES
COGNITIVE
SOCIAL
AFFECTIVE
METACOGNITIVE
FOCUS
WHOLE CLASS
INDIVIDUAL
SMALL GROUP
STRATEGIES
CARTOON
STEM
HUMAN GRAPH
PMI
LOG
AD
MRS. POTTER'S QUESTIONS
WRAPAROUND
GRAPHIC ORGANIZERS

Design A Decade - Secondary School

List three words for each decade.				Rank
1900-09	______,	______,	______	______
1910s	______,	______,	______	______
1920s	______,	______,	______	______
1930s	______,	______,	______	______
1940s	______,	______,	______	______
1950s	______,	______,	______	______
1960s	______,	______,	______	______
1970s	______,	______,	______	______
1980s	______,	______,	______	______
1990s	______,	______,	______	______
2000-09	______,	______,	______	______

List three words for each decade.				Rank
1900-09	______,	______,	______	______
1910s	______,	______,	______	______
1920s	______,	______,	______	______
1930s	______,	______,	______	______
1940s	______,	______,	______	______
1950s	______,	______,	______	______
1960s	______,	______,	______	______
1970s	______,	______,	______	______
1980s	______,	______,	______	______
1990s	______,	______,	______	______
2000-09	______,	______,	______	______

SKYLIGHT PUBLISHING

HUMAN GRAPH

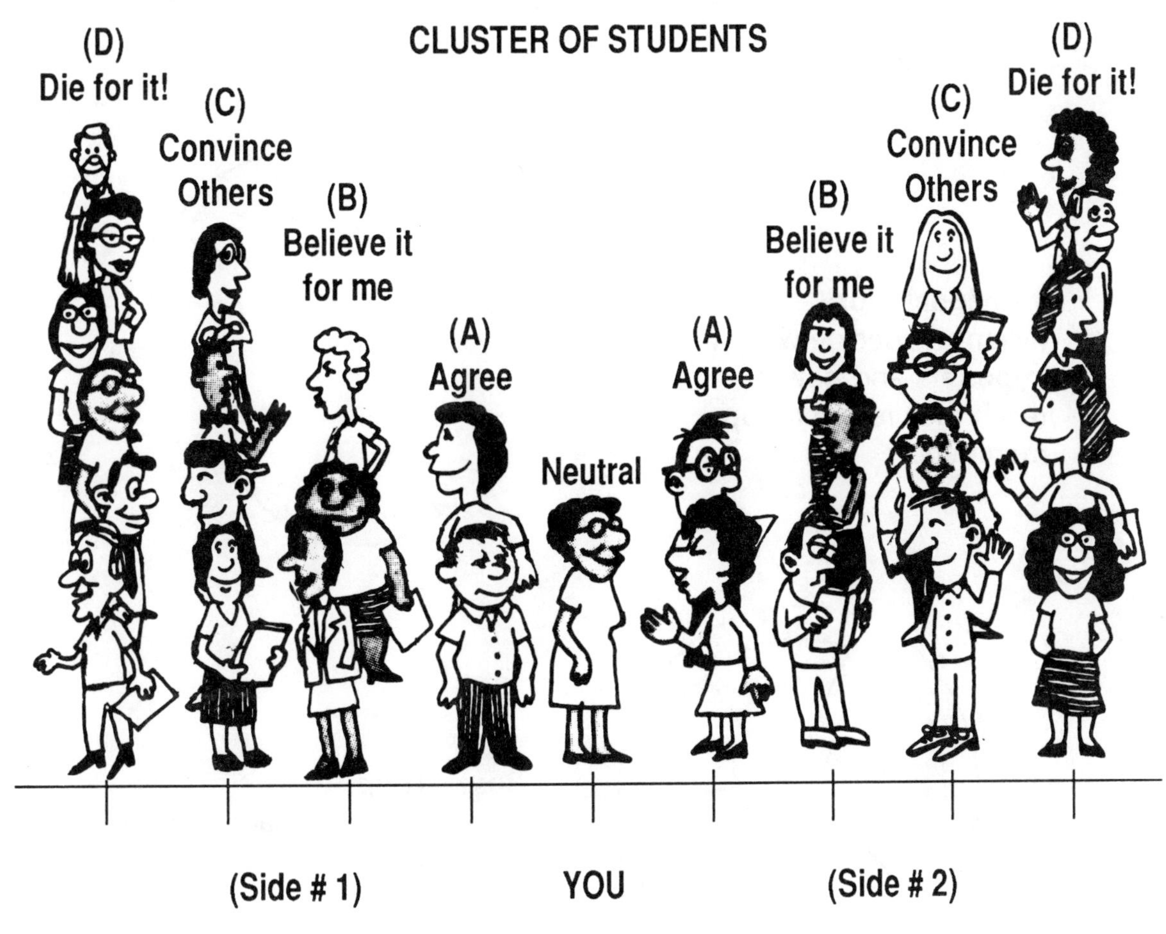
CLUSTER OF STUDENTS
(D)
Die for it!
(C)
Convince
Others
(B)
Believe it
for me
(A)
Agree
Neutral
(A)
Agree
(B)
Believe it
for me
(C)
Convince
Others
(D)
Die for it!
(Side # 1)
YOU
(Side # 2)

JIGSAW

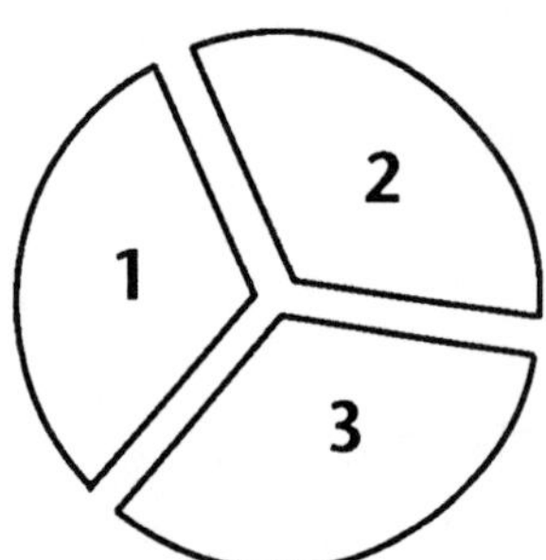

Base Group
(Members divide work.)

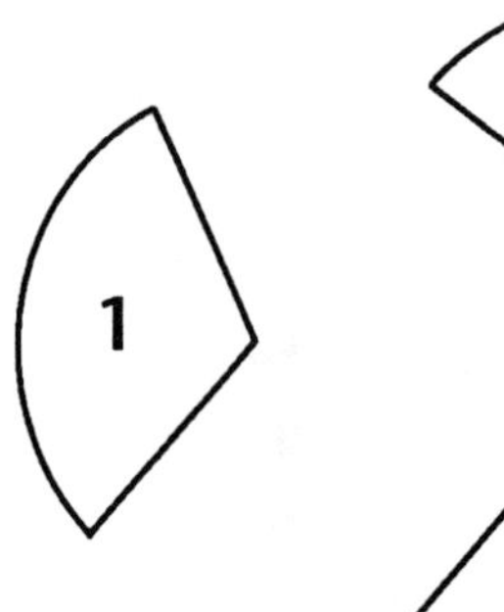

Individual Work
(Members decide *what's* important and *how* to teach their fellow group members.)

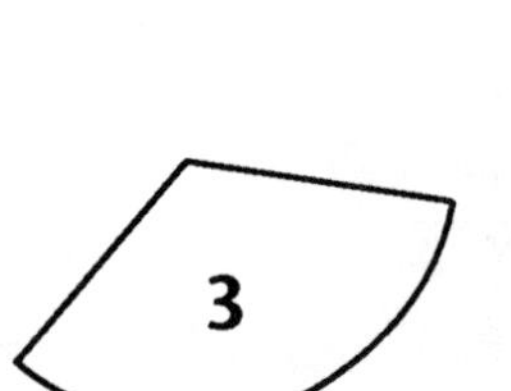

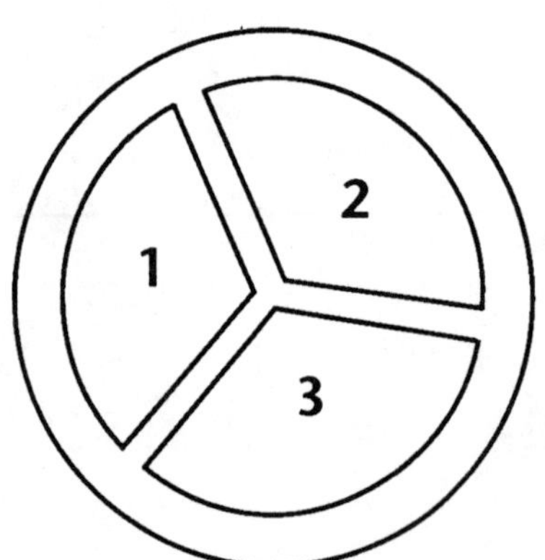

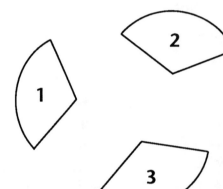

Base Group
(Members teach each other.)

TWO DECISIONS

#1 What to teach . . .

#2 How to teach it . . .

EXPERT JIGSAW

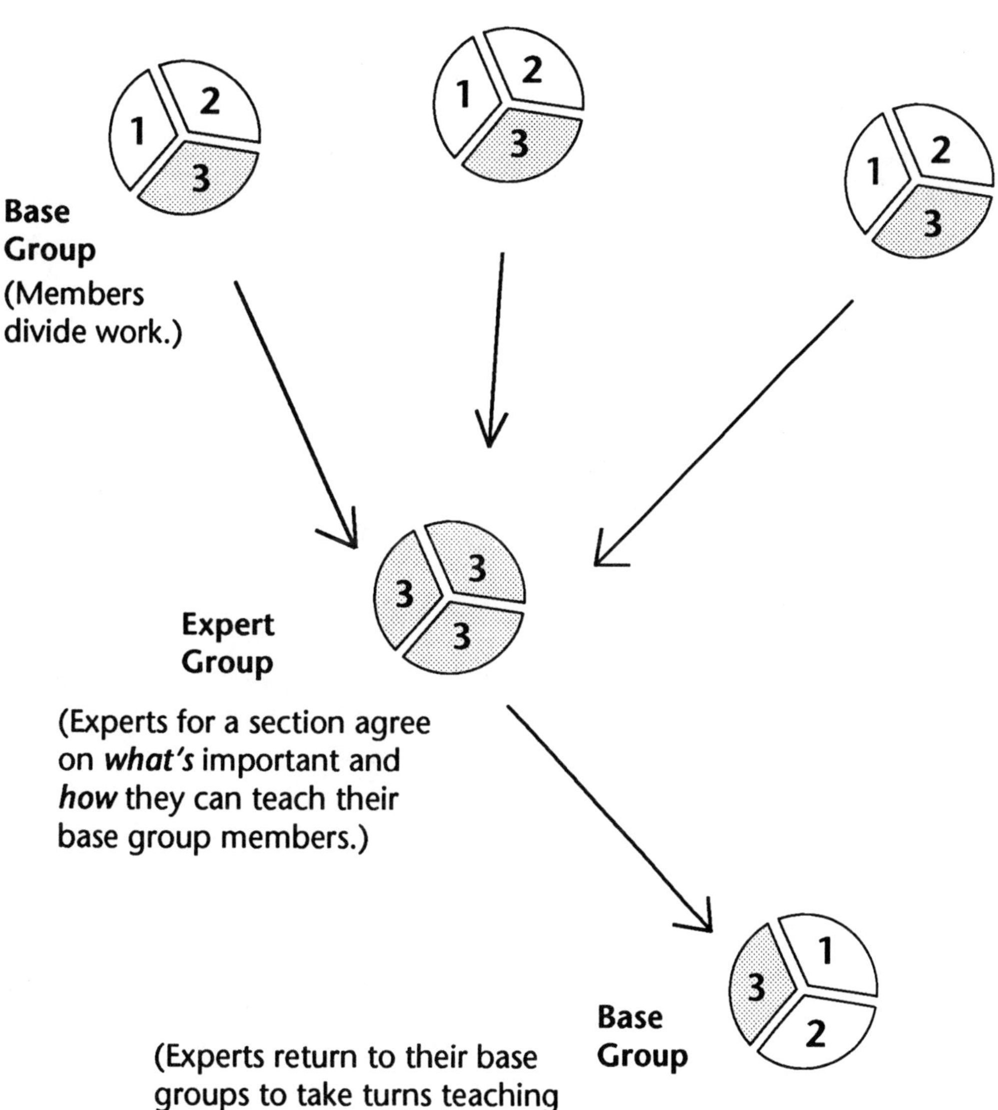
1
2
3
Base
Group
(Members
divide work.)
1
2
3
1
2
3
3
3
3
Expert
Group
(Experts for a section agree
on *what's* important and
how they can teach their
base group members.)
3
1
2
Base
Group
(Experts return to their base
groups to take turns teaching
each other.)

TWO DECISIONS

#1 What to teach . . .

#2 How to teach it . . .

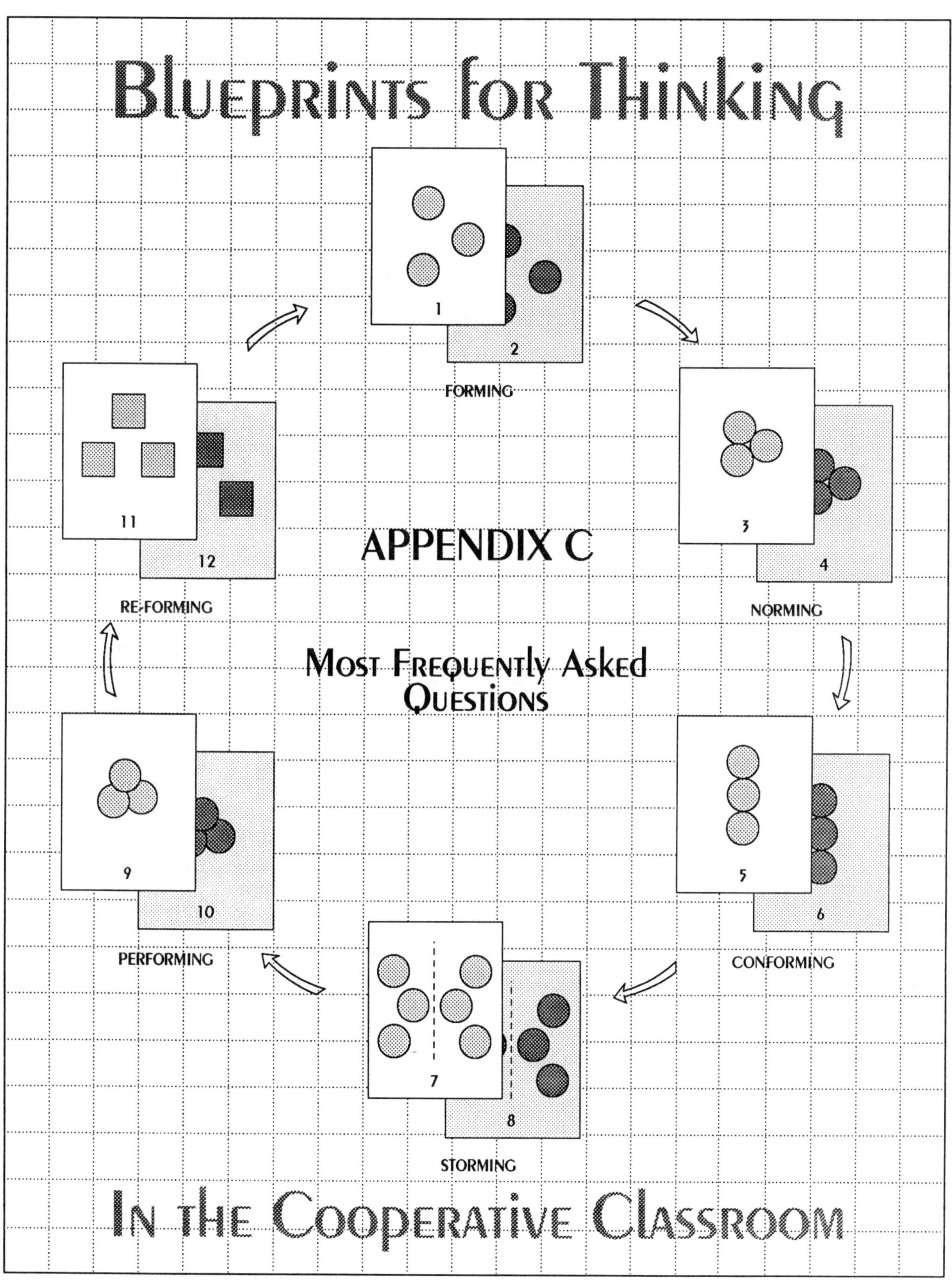
Blueprints for Thinking
1
2
FORMING
3
4
NORMING
5
6
CONFORMING
7
8
STORMING
9
10
PERFORMING
11
12
RE-FORMING
APPENDIX C
Most Frequently Asked Questions
In the Cooperative Classroom

WHEN DO I START USING COOPERATIVE GROUPS?

Chapter 1, page 2

RIGHT AWAY

It takes time to develop cooperative groups. The sooner you start them the better off you will be:

1) Prepare your classroom to *signal* a cooperative atmosphere through its bulletin boards, role cards, signals, room arrangement and visible guidelines.

2) Take 30 to 40 minutes to introduce the concept and teach the basic procedures. See pages 22-25 for lessons you can adapt to your students.

3) Expand the use each day (see chapter 2) until 50 to 60 percent of students' time is spent in cooperative groups.

WILL YOU MODEL A LESSON THAT ILLUSTRATES B-U-I-L-D?

Chapter 1, page 3

PORTMANTEAU

Literal: A large leather suitcase with two hinged compartments; coatcarrier.
Literary: Words from different concepts put together to form another word with a separate meaning.

"A number of words originally coined or used as nonsense words have taken on specific meanings in subsequent use. Renowned among such words is *jabberwocky*, used by Lewis Carroll in *Through the Looking Glass* as the title of a nonsense poem about a fantastic monster called a *jabberwock*. A meaningless nonsense word itself, *jabberwocky* appropriately enough became a generic term for meaningless speech or writing.

"Carroll was very fond of coining blends or, to use his term, 'portmanteau' words, so called because blending words is like packing them into the same traveling bag. Thus Carroll not only added to the English language a number of blend words, he also gave us a new sense for *portmanteau*, and we can now use it as an adjective to mean 'combining more than one use or quality.' Among the portmanteau words coined by Carroll which have become useful members of the language are *chortle* and *galumph*. *Chortle*, a blend of *chuckle* and *snort*, means 'to sing, chant, laugh, or chuckle exultantly.'" (Excerpted from *Webster's Word Histories*. 1989. Springfield, MA: Merrian-Webster, p. 246.)

Analysis of BUILD strategies used in the Portmanteau lesson	
B	1) drawing a definition (a creative thinking skill) 2) having to teach others what you have learned 3) making connections to prior knowledge and experience
U	1) jigsaw (dividing the material among team members) 2) assigned role for each team member 3) limited time (more to learn as a team in short time than could be learned alone)
I	1) individual learning/teaching time 2) random oral quiz 3) checking in the teams
L	1) processing questions on how the team worked well together 2) teacher feedback/observations 3) discussing ways to improve team's effectiveness
D	1) keeping on task 2) encouraging team members during the task 3) checking the team for understanding

LESSON INSTRUCTIONS:

1. Divide the class into groups of three. Assign the roles of worrier, encourager and checker.

2. Distribute three different portmanteau words to each member in a group (see sample words on next page). Allow time for group members to study the definitions of their words and to draw a picture of each definition to serve as a memory and teaching aid.

3. When all students are ready, have each encourager teach the group the three words on his/her card using visual aids. Remind students that they will have a final quiz which will focus on *definitions*, not spellings. For the quiz, all members of the group are accountable to know the definitions of all nine words in the group!

4. After this first round of teaching, have the checkers check to see if their group members all understand.

5. Have the worriers begin the second round of teaching. And again, have the checkers check for understanding.

6. Then allow the third and final member, the checker, to finish the round-robin teaching with his/her three words.

7. After all rounds are done, have checkers check for understanding of *all* the words.

8. Pull the whole class back together. Instruct the teams to put away their definitions and pictures. Conduct a brief, random oral quiz with the groups choosing one member of each team to define one of the nine portmanteau words. Ask the rest of the class if the answer is correct.

9. After testing each team, have the teams discuss their experience of working together:
   - What did we do to help each other in this lesson?
   - What can we do next time to help each other even more?

10. Give the class your feedback and observations about how they worked together. Have team members shake hands and offer thanks for help with this lesson.

Portmanteau Student Cards

(These lists were created by students after learning about portmanteaux.)

CHATEAUINCINERADE
The very, very well done steak that was accidently left in the microwave for three hours

LINEBIND
When you go to the bank and are delighted that the line is short only to discover the person in front of you is depositing $500 in pennies

CUSTOMERANIA (or CUSTOMEPHRENIA)
The tendency of every salesperson in a store to ask "May I help you?" when you are "just looking"

MCLAG
Being at a fast-food hamburger joint and having to wait longer for your order than at a restaurant

AUSSIFICATION
What happens to most Americans who spend a long time in Australia

ACCELERYELLER
The person who thinks that when the stoplight changes to yellow it means to step on the gas

LEAFTOVER
The tiny piece of greenery stuck between someone's front teeth after eating spinach salad or soufflé

DEFIZZICATION
What happens to any opened carbonated drink after sitting around for three days

SOCDROOP
The tendency of socks which have lost their elastic to work their way down below the ankle

HOW DO I SELECT THE GROUPS?

Chapter 1, page 7

RANDOMLY, THEN BY MIXING ABILITY LEVELS

In the first few lessons, do random mixes that signal "this is a cooperative classroom, no cliques." Mark role cards for group membership and make a different mix for each cooperative task. In later lessons, you can divide the class into thirds by ability or motivation and assign one student from each third to a group (three to a group is preferred).

HOW DO I EVALUATE LEARNING IN COOPERATIVE GROUPS?

Chapter 1, page 15

THE SAME AS YOU DO INDIVIDUAL AND COMPETITIVE LEARNING

For the first year, use the same methods you now use to measure academic performance. If you grade *individual* quizes, tests, projects or essays, do that. If you check mastery of each student's learning, do that. Use *cooperative groups* for learning the material and for developing social skills (see chapters 3 and 4), but assess each individual. At least for the first year, *avoid group grades*. As you and the students become more comfortable and skilled with cooperative learning, you may consider when group grades are OK to use (see chapter 12).

WHAT DO I DO WITH STUDENTS WHO WON'T COOPERATE?

Chapter 1, page 15

HONOR THEIR RIGHT TO WORK ALONE

Start with the understanding that every child has a right to learn alone. It is a *privilege* to work together. If you honor the right, you will avoid needless power conflicts with the rare student who really doesn't want to work with peers (see chapter 4).

HOW DOES COOPERATIVE LEARNING FIT WITH THE HUNTER (ITIP) LESSON DESIGN?

Chapter 2, page 34

COOPERATIVE LEARNING CAN BE TAUGHT WITH A DIRECT INSTRUCTION MODEL (Thinking Skill Focus)

LESSON OBJECTIVE: To apply the thinking skill of *prioritizing.*

ANTICIPATORY SET: Tell students, "Turn to your neighbor and rank order your three favorite subjects in school. Explain to your neighbor your priority."

INPUT/DEMO: Display and explain to students the menu of operations for prioritizing, definition and synonyms for prioritizing, and appropriate times to use. (Lecture with notes)

CHECK: Now, tell students, "Turn to your neighbor and explain (a) the steps in prioritizing and (b) why ranking is an important thinking skill." Sample students' responses.

GUIDED PRACTICE: Use task grids with a worksheet of sample items to rank. Have students prepare explanations for each ranking once they have agreed upon the final rank.

DISCUSSION AND CHECK: Assign and discuss group reports.

CLOSURE: Allow time for students to make journal entries.

HOW DOES COOPERATIVE LEARNING FIT WITH THE INQUIRY MODEL?

Chapter 2, page 34

COOPERATIVE LEARNING CAN BE TAUGHT WITH THE INQUIRY MODEL (Content Focus)

LESSON OBJECTIVE: To elicit attributes of magnets.

ANTICIPATORY SET: Have students collect objects from home or the garage in baggies.

GATHERING INFORMATION: With the assortment of objects, student pairs test the items with a magnet. They sort items that are attracted to the magnet and items that are not.

PROCESSING INFORMATION: Using a Venn diagram as a graphic organizer, students list attributes of items that are and are not attracted to a magnet.

APPLYING INFORMATION: Students make generalizations and predict which new objects will or will not be attracted to the magnet.

CLOSURE: Complete the stem, "Magnets are like _____ because both _______________."

WHEN ARE THE BEST TIMES FOR BASE GROUPS TO MEET?

Chapter 2, page 35

SELF-CONTAINED CLASSROOMS

- Daily as start-up "sponge" activity
- Daily at the end of the day to share journals, do social skill processing for the day or to summarize the day's learning
- Three times a week to practice social skills (see chapter 3)
- As a daily mid-day sharing session or self-concept activity

MIDDLE SCHOOL

- At least twice a week in adviser/advisee periods for social skill work
- In each class before a unit (goal setting) and after a unit (review for the test)
- Fifteen minutes each Monday and Friday for social skill review, learning to learn, practice or topical interest discussion

HIGH SCHOOL

- Once a week in homeroom for social skill lessons, study skill practice, self-esteem activities or problem-solving sessions
- In each class before a unit (goal setting) and after a unit (review for the test)
- In each class for projects, lab experiments or practice in thinking skills applied to course content

HOW OFTEN SHOULD I USE COOPERATIVE GROUPS?

Chapter 2, page 37

FOR AT LEAST 60 PERCENT OF STUDENTS' LEARNING TIME (Devoutly to be wished)

As you begin cooperative learning, you may wonder "How often should I use groups?" or "Will students tire with too much cooperation?"

To get the best achievement and social skill results that the research (see Appendix A) shows can occur, it is best to get to the 60 percent mark. This means 60 percent of the students' time will be spent in learning together, not alone.

When you start, you will want at least forty minutes in the first week to set up basic procedures, guidelines and expectations for cooperative learning. In the second week, use *at least* two informal tasks each day (elementary) or once a day in the upper grades (middle, high school). By the third week, add your formal task groups at least for guided practice (three cooperative practices, ten minutes each, in the week), unit review, vocabulary (see page 34, jigsaw) mastery. By the fourth week, you will be ready to start base groups with a social skill's hook lesson (see chapter 3) and daily social skill practices. As appropriate, in the elementary classroom, increase to three or five formal cooperative tasks blended with a variety of informal groups, base groups, discussions and formal presentations. In the upper grades, plan to use task groups for more complex tasks throughout the week.

A 60% ELEMENTARY MODEL
(1 Morning)

8:30 Sponge: Math homework, pair review
8:40 Base groups: "Me Bag" activity
9:00 Math
a. All-class homework review
b. New lesson lecture and board demo
c. Guided practice: math trios with observer
d. Check and assign homework
9:15 Reading
a. Individual silent reading
b. Reading trios: read story and make a play
c. Trios practice for play
9:30 Nutrition break
9:40 Reading
a. Trios give play presentations
b. Class feedback "What I liked about their play"
10:15 Recess
10:40 Reading
a. Continue plays and feedback
b. Small-group processing
11:15 Writing
a. Individual journal entries
b. Journal sharing in trios
11:45 Social skill practice
a. All-class discussion "Ways I encouraged"
12:00 Lunch

A 60% UPPER-GRADE MODEL
(1 Week: Freshman English Novel Unit)

Monday
- Introduce unit goals and agenda
- Base groups: goal setting
- All-class demonstration "Selecting character traits" with web organizer
- Check for understanding
- Homework reading assignment: chapter jigsaw

Tuesday
- Jigsaw task groups: prepare character web

Wednesday
- Character webs presented to class and "I learned" wraparound

Thursday
- Continue presentations and wrap around class for reactions
- Trios review with jigsaw

Friday
- Individual quiz on characters
- All-class summary discussion
- Base groups: assess members' performance in group

WHAT SOCIAL SKILL AREAS NEED TO BE ADDRESSED?

Chapter 3, page 50

COMMUNICATION, TRUST, LEADERSHIP AND CONFLICT RESOLUTION

Communication: Skills in articulation and listening; expressive language and receptive language; both verbal and non-verbal communication strategies.

Trust building: Skills needed to enhance teamwork and maintain effective working relationships; fostering comaraderie.

Leadership: Skills for accepting responsibility, accepting and encouraging others; problem solving and decision making.

Conflict resolution: Skills needed to challenge each other's ideas; skills of reasoning, justifying, seeking consensus, constructing controversies, and seeking solutions and alternatives.

WHAT DO I DO IF THERE ARE MANY STUDENTS NOT BEHAVING AFTER I HAVE TAUGHT THE SOCIAL SKILLS?

Chapter 4, page 66

WORK SOME MORE WITH THE WHOLE CLASS

If there are many students not behaving after you have moved through the social skills and used the quick stop and timeout strategies, first spend more time working with the *whole* class on the cooperative social skills. Refocus and reteach the social skills to all the students. The goal redirection strategies work best when the classroom *norm* is cooperation and you only have one or two students who need the more complex help in cooperating. Second, see if the missing social skills need a simpler model. Go back to using *pairs* and make think-pair-share the core. Throughout a lesson (approximately every ten minutes), instruct students to "turn to your partner and agree upon an answer to this question . . . ." Then process the pairs. Seek several responses each time. Pair review, prediction pairs and explain why exercises (see chapter 2, pages 31-33) help students get used to working together.

Start Here ➡

1. Get up my nerve
2. Believe in the cooperative way
3. Understand why cooperative learning works so well
4. See it in practice
5. Design a bulletin board
6. Make role cards
7. Teach roles
8. Post social skill guidelines
9. Rearrange room
10. Teach signals
11. Select incentives
12. Teach value lesson
13. Send a parent letter explaining cooperative learning
14. Use think/pair/share (<u>when</u>)
15. Do partner pair intros (business cards, KWL, etc.)

Keep it up

16. Do other informal groups
17. Do starter jigsaw
18. Practice vocabulary jigsaw
19. Have jigsaw groups chart progress
20. Start short formal groups
    - •reading
    - •science
    - •math
    - •writing
    - •social studies
    - •other
21. Start base groups and use
    - •bonding
    - •group goals
    - •lesson reviews
    - •social skill practice
    - •other
22. Teach and model fat and skinny questions; use in content areas
23. Select first social skill
24. Teach movement into groups
25. Post T-chart
26. Do hook lesson
27. Do guided practice
28. Use student observer
29. Observe student skill use

⬅ **Don't stop now**

30. Blend skill into lessons
31. Select rewards for use of social skill
32. Set up timeout procedures
33. Post "rights" sign
34. Confer with time-out student
35. Contract time-in with student
36. Diagnose student misbehavior
37. Test reactions to misbehavior
38. Select strategies
39. Work on class misbehavior with problem-solving model
40. Increase social skill lessons and practice
41. Practice wait time and equal response
42. Practice fat and skinny questions

Way to go!

43. Select organizers (repeat as needed)
    - •Venn Diagram
    - •Matrix
    - •Mind Map
    - •Web
    - •Questions
    - •Ranking
    - •T-Chart
    - •P.M.I.
    - •Right Angles
    - •Bridging Snapshots
    - •Fish Bone
    - •KWL
44. Plan lesson with organizer
    - •explain organizer without content
    - •model for use
    - •check for understanding
    - •guide practice
    - •aid independent practice
45. Select grading procedure
    - •communicate criteria
    - •show media models
46. Design content lesson with BUILD
47. Select responsibility methods
48. Share lesson w/peer
49. Review lessons and results with peer
50. Concentrate on transfer, etc.
51. Etc.

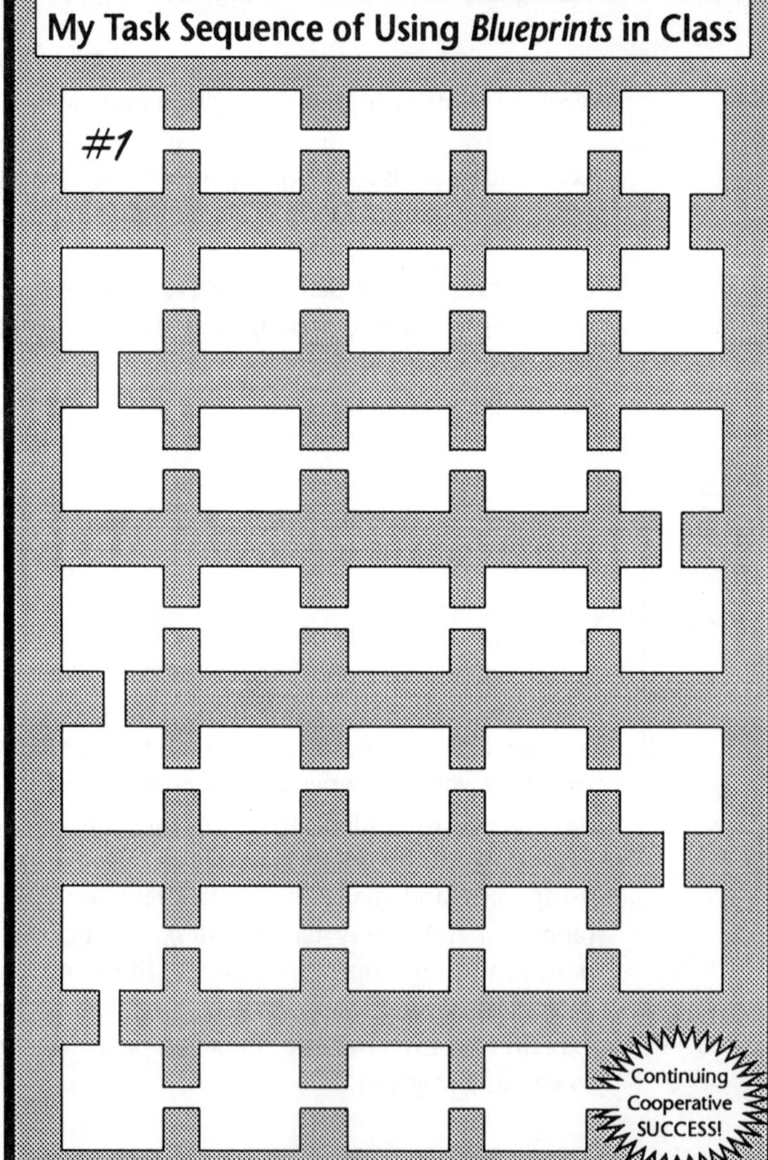

Bibliography

† Denotes that the resource is available from Skylight Publishing.

Adler, M. J., & Van Doren, C. (1972). *How to read a book.* Simon & Schuster.

† Archibald, S., & Bellanca, J. (1988). *Early stars: Skills for saying "yes" to health.* Palatine, IL: Skylight.

Aronson, E. (1978). *The jigsaw classroom.* Beverly Hills, CA: Sage Publications.

Baron, F., Joan, B., & Robert J. Sternberg, eds. (1987). *Teaching thinking skills: Theory and practice.* New York: W.H. Freeman.

Barron, F. (1969). *Creative person and creative process.* New York: Holt, Rinehart and Winston.

Becoming a nation of readers. (1984). *The report of the commission on reading:* NIE.

† Bellanca, J. (1989). *Team stars.* Palatine, IL: Skylight.

† Bellanca, J. (1990). *The cooperative think tank.* Palatine, IL: Skylight.

† Bellanca, J. (1990). *Keep them thinking: Level III.* Palatine, IL: Skylight.

† Bellanca, J., & Fogarty, R. (1986). *Catch them thinking: A handbook of classroom strategies.* Palatine, IL: Skylight.

Belonging (16 mm film) (1980). Edina, MN: Interaction Book Company.

Berman, P., & McLaughlin, M. (1978). *Federal programs supporting educational change, Vol. VIII: Implementing and sustaining innovations.* Santa Monica, CA: Rand Corporation.

Beyer, B.K. (1983, November). Common sense about teaching thinking skills. *Educational Leadership, 41:3,* 44-49.

Beyer, B.K. (1984, March). Improving thinking skills—defining the problem. *Phi Delta Kappan,* 65:7, 486-490.

Beyer, B.K. (1984, April). Improving thinking skills—a practical approach. *Phi Delta Kappan,* 65:8, 556-560.

Beyer, B.K. (1985). Critical thinking: What is it? *Social Education,* 4, 270-276.

Beyer, B.K. (1985, January). Teaching thinking skills: How the principal can know they are being taught. *NASSP Bulletin.*

Beyer, B.K. (1985, April). Teaching critical thinking: A direct approach. *Social Education,* 49:4, 297-303.

† Beyer, B.K. (1987). *Practical strategies for the teaching of thinking.* Boston, MA: Allyn & Bacon.

† Beyer, B.K. (1988). *Developing a thinking skills program.* Boston: Allyn & Bacon

Beyer, B.K., & Charlton, R.E. (1986, April). Teaching thinking skills in biology. *The American Biology Teacher,* 48:4, 207-212.

Black, H., & Black, S. (1987). *Building thinking skills: Books 1-3.* Pacific Grove, CA: Midwest Publications.

Blake, R., & Mouton, J. (1961). Comprehension of own and outgroup positions under intergroup competition. *Journal of Conflict Resolution,* 5, 304-310.

Bloom, B. (1981). *All our children learning.* New York: McGraw-Hill.

Brandt, R. (1988, April). On teaching thinking: A conversation with Arthur Costa. *Educational Leadership,* 45:7, 11.

Brown, A.L. (1978). Knowing when, where, and how to remember: A problem of metacognition. In R. Glaser (ed.), *Advances in instruction psychology (1).* Hillsdale, NJ: Erlbaum.

Brown, A.L. (1982). Learning how to learn from reading. In J.A. Langer and M.T. Smith-Burke (eds.), *Reader meets author/bridging the gap: A psycholinguistic and sociolinguistic perspective.* Newark, DE: International Reading Association.

Brown, A.L., Campione, J.C., & Day, J.D. (1981, February). Learning to learn: On training students to learn from texts. *Educational Researcher,* 10:2, 14-21.

Bruner, J. (1960). *The process of education.* New York: Vintage Books.

† Burns, M. (1976). *The book of think or how to solve a problem twice your size.* Boston: Little, Brown and Co.

Campbell, J. (1965). *The children's crusader: Colonel Francis W. Parker.* Doctoral dissertation, Teachers College, Columbia University.

Chase, L. (1975). *The other side of the report card.* Glenview, IL: Scott Foresman.

† *Circles of Learning* (16 mm film) (1983). Edina, MN: Interaction Book Company.

Costa, A.L. (1981, October). Teaching for intelligent behavior. *Educational Leadership*, pp. 29-32.

Costa, A.L. (1984, November). Mediating the metacognitive. *Educational Leadership*, pp. 57-62.

† Costa, A.L. (Ed.) (1985). *Developing minds.* Alexandria, VA: Association for Supervision and Curriculum Development.

Costa, A. (1985). *Teaching for intelligent behavior: A course syllabus.* Orangevale, CA: Search Models Unlimited.

Costa, A.L. (1988, Winter). What human beings do when they behave intelligently and how they can become more so. *California ASCD Journal* 1:1 (original title: *Search for Intelligent Life*).

Costa, A.L., & Garmston, R. (1985, March). *The art of cognitive coaching: Supervision for intelligent teaching.* Paper presented at the Annual Conference of the Association for Supervision and Curriculum Development, Chicago.

† Costa, A., & Lowery, L. (1989). *Techniques for teaching thinking.* Pacific Grove, CA: Midwest Publications.

de Bono, E. (1967). *New think.* New York: Basic Books.

de Bono, E. (1973). *Lateral thinking: Creativity step by step.* New York: Harper and Row.

de Bono, E. (1976). *Teaching thinking.* New York: Penguin Books.

Deutsch, M. (1949). An experimental study of the effects of cooperation and competition upon group processes. *Human Relations*, 2, 199-232.

Deutsch, M. (1973). *The resolution of conflict.* New Haven, CT: Yale University Press.

DeVries, D., & Edwards, K. (1973). Learning games and student teams: Their effects on classroom process. *American Journal of Educational Research,* 10, 307-318.

DeVries, D., Slavin, R., Fennessey, G., Edwards, K., & Lombardo, M. (1980). *Teams-games-tournament.* Englewood Cliffs, NJ: Educational Technology.

Dewey, J. (1933). *How we think.* Boston: D.C. Heath & Co.

† Dishon, D., & O'Leary, P. (1984). *A guidebook for cooperative learning.* Holmes Beach, FL: Learning Publications.

Durkin, D. (1978-79). What classroom observations reveal about reading comprehension instruction. *Reading Research Quarterly,* 12, 481-533.

Eisner, E.W. (1983, October). The kind of schools we need. *Educational Leadership,* pp. 48-55.

Elbow, P. (1981). *Writing with power.* New York: Oxford University Press.

Elbow, P. (1973). *Writing without teachers.* New York: Oxford University Press.

Ferguson, M. (1980). *The aquarian conspiracy.* Los Angeles: J.P. Tarcher.

Feuerstein, F. (1979). *The dynamic assessment of retarded performance: The learning potential assessment device, theory, instruments, and technique.* Baltimore: University Park Press.

Feuerstein, R. (1980). *Instrumental enrichment.* Baltimore, MD: University Park Press.

Flavell, J. (1976). Metacognitive aspects of problem solving. In Resnick (Ed.), *The nature of intelligence.* Hillsdale, NJ: Lawrence Erlbaum Associates.

Flavell, J. (1977). *Cognitive Development.* Englewood Cliffs, NJ: Prentice-Hall.

Fogarty, R. (1989). *From training to transfer: The role of creativity in the adult learner.* Doctoral dissertation, Loyola University of Chicago.

† Fogarty, R. (1990). *Keep them thinking: Level II.* Palatine, IL: Skylight.

† Fogarty, R., & Bellanca, J. (1986). *Planning for thinking: A guidebook for instructional leaders.* Palatine, IL: IRI Group.

† Fogarty, R., & Bellanca, J. (1986). *Teach them thinking.* Palatine, IL: Skylight.

† Fogarty, R., & Bellanca, J. (1989). *Patterns for thinking—Patterns for transfer.* Palatine, IL: Skylight.

† Fogarty, R., & Haack, J. (1986). *The thinking log.* Palatine, IL: Skylight.

† Fogarty, R., & Haack, J. (1986). *The thinking/writing connection.* Palatine, IL: Skylight.

† Fogarty, R., & Opeka, K. (1988). *Start them thinking.* Palatine, IL: Skylight.

Frankenstein, C. (1979). *They think again.* New York: Van Nostrand Rheinhold.

Fullan, M. (1982). *The meaning of educational change.* New York: Teachers College Press, Columbia University.

Gardner, H. (1983). *Frames of mind: The theory of multiple intelligences.* New York: Basic Books.

Gibbs, J. (1987). *Tribes.* Santa Rosa, CA: Center Source Publications.

Glaser, R. (Ed.) (1978). *Advanced instructional psychology.* 2 vols. Hillsdale, NJ: Lawrence Erlbaum Associates.

† Glasser, W. (1986). *Control theory in the classroom.* New York: Harper & Row.

Goodlad, J. I. (1984). *A place called school, prospects for the future.* New York: McGraw-Hill.

Gordon, W.J. (1961). *Synectics: The development of creative capacity.* New York: Harper & Row.

Graves, D.H. (1983). *Writing: Teachers and children at work.* Portsmouth, NH: Heinemann Educational Books.

Guilford, J.P. (1977). *Way Beyond IQ.* Buffalo, NY: Creative Education Foundation.

Hart, L. (1983). *Human brain and human learning.* White Plains, NY: Longman Publishing.

Hart, L. (1975). *How the brain works.* New York: Basic Books.

Hord, S., & Loucks, S. *A concerns-based model for delivery of inservice.* CBFM Project - Research and Development Center for Teacher Education, the University of Texas at Austin.

Hunter, M. (1971). *Transfer.* El Segundo, CA: Tip Publications.

Hunter, M. (1982). *Teaching for transfer.* El Segundo, CA: Tip Publications.

Jeroski, S., Brownlie, F., & Kaser, L. (At press). *Reading & Responding: Evaluation Strategies for Teachers.* Scarborough, Ontario: Nelson Canada.

Johnson, D.W. (1971). Role reversal: A summary and review of the research. *International Journal of Group Tensions,* 1, 318-334.

Johnson, D.W. (1975). Affective perspective-taking and cooperative predisposition. *Developmental Psychology,* 11, 869-870.

Johnson, D.W. (1980). Constructive peer relationships, social development, and cooperative learning experiences: Implications for the prevention of drug abuse. *Journal of Drug Education,* 10, 7-24.

Johnson, D.W. (1980). Group processes: Influences of student-student interactions on school outcomes. In J. McMillan (Ed.), *Social psychology of school learning.* New York: Academic Press.

Johnson, D.W. (1981). Student-student interaction: The neglected variable in education. *Educational Researcher,* 10, 5-10.

Johnson, D.W. (1986). *Reaching out: Interpersonal effectiveness and self-actualization.* Englewood Cliffs, NJ: Prentice-Hall.

Johnson, D.W. (1987). *Human relations and your career: A guide to interpersonal skills* (second edition). Englewood Cliffs, NJ: Prentice-Hall.

Johnson, D. W., & Johnson, R. (1974). Instructional goal structure: Cooperative, competitive, or individualistic. *Review of Educational Research,* 44, 213-240.

† Johnson, D. W., & Johnson, R. (1978). Cooperative, competitive, and individualistic learning. *Journal of Research and Development in Education,* 12, 3-15.

Johnson, D. W., & Johnson, R. (Eds.) (1978). Social interdependence within instruction. *Journal of Research and Development in Education,* 12:1.

Johnson, D. W., & Johnson, R. (1979). Conflict in the classroom: Controversy and learning. *Review of Educational Research,* 49, 51-70.

Johnson, D. W., & Johnson, R. (1982, October). Cooperation in learning: Ignored but powerful. *Lyceum.*

Johnson, D. W., & Johnson, R. (Eds.) (1984). *Structuring cooperative learning: The 1984 handbook of lesson plans for teachers.* Edina, MN: Interaction Book Company.

† Johnson, D. W., & Johnson, R. (1986). *Circles of learning: Cooperation in the classroom.* Alexandria, VA: Association for Supervision and Curriculum Development.

Johnson, D. W., & Johnson, R. (1987). *Joining together: Group theory and group skills* (third edition). Englewood Cliffs, NJ: Prentice-Hall.

Johnson, D.W., & Johnson, R. (1987). *Learning together & alone: Cooperative, competitive & individualistic learning.* Englewood Cliffs, NJ: Prentice-Hall.

Joyce, B.R. (1986). *Improving America's schools.* White Plains, NY: Longman Publishing.

Joyce, B.R., & Showers, B. (1980, February). Improving inservice training: The message of research. *Educational Leadership,* p. 380.

Joyce, B.R., & Showers, B. (1983). *Power in staff development through research and training.* Alexandria, VA: Association for Supervision and Curriculum Development.

Joyce, B.R., & Weil, M. (1985). *Models of learning.* Englewood Cliffs, NJ: Prentice-Hall.

Kagan, S. (1977). Social motives and behaviors of Mexican American and Anglo American children. In J. L. Martinez (Ed.), *Chicano psychology.* New York: Academic Press.

Kagan, S., Knight, G. P., Martinez, S., & Espinoza Santana, P. (1981). Conflict resolution style among Mexican children: Examining urbanization and ecology effects. *Journal of Cross-Cultural Psychology,* 12:2.

Kagan, S., & Madsen, M. C. (1972). Rivalry in Anglo American and Mexican children. *Journal of Personality and Social Psychology,* 24, 214-220.

Kohlberg, L. (1981). *The meaning and measurement of moral development.* Worcester, MA: Clark University Press.

Krupp, J.A. (1981). The adult learner. *Adult learning and development.* Connecticut.

Krupp, J.A. (1982). Adult development. *Adult learning and development.* Connecticut.

Lipman, M., Sharp, A., & Oscanyan, F. (1980). *Philosophy in the classroom* (second edition). Philadelphia: Temple University Press.

Lochhead, J., & Clement, J. (Eds.) (1979). *Cognitive process instruction.* Philadelphia: The Franklin Institute Press.

Luria, A.R. (1976). *Cognitive development: Its cultural and social foundations.* Cambridge, MA: Harvard University Press.

Machado, L.A. (1980). *The right to be intelligent.* New York: Pergamon Press.

MacKinnon, D.W. (1978). *In search of human effectivenss: Identifying and developing creativity.* Buffalo, NY: The Creative Educational Foundation, Inc., in association with Creative Synergetic Associates, Ltd.

† Marcus, S.A., & McDonald, P. (1990). *Tools for the Cooperative Classroom.* Palatine, IL: Skylight.

Marzano, R. (1988). *Tactics for teaching thinking.* Alexandria, VA: Association for Supervision and Curriculum Development.

Marzano, R., & Arredondo, D.E. (1986, May). Restructuring schools through the teaching of thinking skills. *Educational Leadership,* 43:8, 23.

Marzano, R., et al. (1988). *Dimensions of thinking: A framework for curriculum and instruction.* Alexandria, VA: Association for Supervision and Curriculum Development.

McTighe, J. (1987). Teaching for thinking, of thinking, and about thinking. In Heiman and Slomianko (Eds.),*Thinking skills instruction: Concepts and techniques.* Washington, D.C.: National Education Association.

Meeker, M.N. (1969). *The structure of intellect: Its interpretation and uses.* Columbus, OH: Charles E. Merrill.

Nickerson, R.S. (1982). *Understanding understanding* (BBN Report No. 5087).

Nickerson, R.S. (1983). Computer programming as a vehicle for teaching thinking skills. *Journal of Philosophy for Children,* 4:3 & 4.

Nickerson, R.S., Perkins, D.N., & Smith, E.E. (1984). *Teaching thinking,* (BBN Report No. 5575).

Nickerson, R.S., Perkins, D.N., and Smith, E.E. (1985). *The teaching of thinking.* Hillsdale, NJ: Lawrence Erlbaum Associates.

Nickerson, R.S., Salter, W., Shepard & Herrnstein, J. (1984). *The teaching of learning strategies,* (BBN Report No. 5578).

Noller, R. (1977). *Scratching the surface of creative problem solving: A bird's eye view of CPS.* Buffalo, NY: D.O.K.

Noller, R., Parnes, S., & Biondi, A. (1976). *Creative action book.* New York: Charles Scribner & Sons.

Noller, R., Treffinger, D., & Houseman, E. (1979). *It's a gas to be gifted or CPS for the gifted and talented.* Buffalo, NY: D.O.K.

† Norris, S.P. & Ennis, R.H. *Evaluating critical thinking.* Pacific Grove, CA: Midwest Publications.

Ogle, D. (1986). K-W-L: A teaching model that develops active reading of expository text. *The Reading Teacher,* 6, 564-570.

† Opeka, K. (1990). *Keep them thinking: Level I.* Palatine, IL: Skylight.

Osborn, A.F. (1963). *Applied imagination.* New York: Charles Scribner & Sons.

Palincsar, A. (1984). The quest for meaning from expository text: A teacher guided journey. In G. Duffy L., Roehler, and J. Mason (Eds.), *Comprehension instruction: Perspectives and suggestions.* White Plains, NY: Longman Publishing.

Parnes, S. (1972). *Creativity: Unlocking human potential.* Buffalo, NY: D.O.K.

Parnes, S. (1975). *Aha! Insights into creative behavior.* Buffalo, NY: D.O.K.

Pearson, C. (1980, February). Can you keep quiet for three minutes? *Learning.*

Perkins, D.N. (1983). *The mind's best work.* Cambridge, MA: Harvard University Press.

Perkins, D.N. (1986). *Knowledge as design.* Hillsdale, NJ: Lawrence Erlbaum Associates.

Perkins, D.N. (1988, August 6) *Thinking frames.* Alexandria, VA: Paper delivered at ASCD conference on approaches to thinking, pp. 14-15.

Perkins, D.N. & Leondar, B., (Eds.) (1977). *The arts and cognition.* Baltimore, MD: Johns Hopkins University Press.

Perkins, D.N. & Salomon, G. (1987). Transfer and teaching thinking. In D.N. Perkins, J.C. Lochhead, and J.C. Bishop (Eds.), *Thinking: The second international conference.* Hillsdale, NJ: Lawrence Erlbaum Associates.

Perkins, D.N. & Salomon, G. (1988, September). Teaching for transfer. *Educational Leadership,* pp. 22-32.

Perkins, D.N. & Salomon, G. (1989, January-February). Are cognitive skills context bound? *Educational Researcher,* pp. 16-25.

Peters, T. & Austin, N. (1985). *Passion for excellence.* New York: Random House.

Peters, T. & Waterman, R., Jr. (1982). *In search of excellence.* New York: Warner Communications.

Piaget, J. (1972). *The psychology of intelligence.* Totowa, NJ: Littlefield Adams.

Polette, N. (1981). *Exploring books for gifted programs.* Metuchen, NJ: Scarecrow Press.

Posner, G.J., Strike, K.A., Hewson, P.W., & Gertzog, W.A. (1982). Accommodation of a scientific conception: Toward a thoery of conceptual change. *Science Education 66,* pp. 211-227.

Posner, M.I. & Keele, S.W. (1973). Skill learning. In Robert M. W. Travers, (Ed.) *Second handbook of research on teaching.* Chicago: Rand McNally College Publishing Company, pp. 805-831.

Raths, Louis, et al. (1986). *Teaching for thinking: Theories, strategies and activities* (second edition). New York: Teachers College Press, Columbia University.

†Rico, G.L. (1983). *Writing the natural way.* Los Angeles: J.P. Tarcher.

Rosenshine, B.V. (1986, April). Synthesis of research on explicit teaching. *Educational Leadership,* 43:7, 60-69.

Rumelhart, D.E. (1981). Schemata: The building blocks of cognition. In J.T. Guthrie (Ed.), *Comprehension and teaching: Research reviews.* Newark, DE: International Reading Association.

Salomon, G. (1981). *Communication and education: Social and psychological interactions.* Beverly Hills, CA: Sage Publications.

Schmuck, R., Chesler, M., & Lippit, R. (1966). *Problem solving to improve classroom learning.* Chicago: SRA.

† Schmuck, R., & Schmuck, P. (1983). *Group processes in the classroom.* Dubuque, Iowa: Wm. C. Brown.

Schoenfeld, A.H. (1980). *Teaching problem-solving skills.* American Mathematical Monthly, 87: 10, 794-805.

Schoenfeld, A.H. (1983). Metacognitive and epistemological issues in mathematical understanding. In E.A. Silver (Ed.),*Teaching and learning mathematical problem solving.* Hillsdale, NJ: Lawrence Erlbaum Associates.

Segal, J.W., Chipman, S.E., & Glaser, R., (Eds.) (1985). *Thinking and learning skills.* 2 vols. Hillsdale, NJ: Lawrence Erlbaum Associates.

Sergiovanni, T. (1987, May). Will we ever have a true profession? *Educational Leadership,* 42:1, 44-49.

Sharan, S. (1980). Cooperative learning in small groups: Recent methods and effects on achievement, attitudes, and ethnic relations. *Review of Educational Research,* 50, 241-271.

Sharan, S., Hertz-Lazarowitz, R., & Ackerman, Z. (1980). Academic achievement of elementary school children in small-group versus whole class instruction. *Journal of Experimental Education,* 48, 125-129.

Sharan, S., & Sharan, Y. (1976). *Small-group teaching.* Englewood Cliffs, NJ: Educational Technology Publications.

Sigel, I.E. (1984, November). A constructivist perspective for teaching thinking. *Educational Leadership,* 42:3, 18-22.

Slavin, R. E. (1977). Classroom reward structure: An analytic and practical review. *Review of Educational Research,* 47:4.

Slavin, R. E. (1977). Student team approach to teaching adolescents with special emotional and behavioral needs. *Psychology in the Schools,* 14:1.

Slavin, R. E. (1979). Effects of biracial learning teams on cross-racial friendships. *Journal of Educational Psychology,* 71, 381-387.

† Slavin, R. E. (1980). *Using student team learning (rev. ed.).* Baltimore, MD: Center for Social Organization of Schools, Johns Hopkins University.

Slavin, R. E. (1983). *Cooperative learning.* New York: Longman.

Slavin, R. E. (1983). When does cooperative learning increase student achievement? *Psychology Bulletin,* 94, 429-445.

Slavin, R. E., & Hansell, S. (1983). Cooperative learning and intergroup relations: Contact theory in the classroom. In J. Epstein & N. Karweit (Eds.), *Friends in school.* New York: Academic Press.

Slavin, R. E., & Oickle, E. (1981). Effects of cooperative learning teams on student achievement and race relations: Treatment by race interactions. *Sociology of Education,* 54, 174-180.

Smith, F. (1986). *Insult to intelligence: The bureaucratic invasion of our classrooms.* New York: Arbor House.

Stauffer, R. (1969). *Reading as a thinking process.* New York: Harper & Row.

Sternberg, R.J. (1981, October). Intelligence as thinking and learning skills. *Educational Leadership.* pp. 18-21.

Sternberg, R.J. (1984, September). How can we teach intelligence? *Educational Leadership,* 42:1, 38-48.

Sternberg, R.J. (1985). Critical thinking: Its nature, measurement and improvement. In Frances R. Link, (Ed.), *Essays on the intellect.* Alexandria, VA: Association for Supervision and Curriculum Development, pp. 45-65.

Sternberg, R.J. (1985, November). Teaching critical thinking, part I: Are we making critical mistakes? *Phi Delta Kappan,* pp. 194-198.

Sternberg, R.J. (1986). *Intelligence applied: Understanding and increasing your intellectual skills.* New York: Harcourt Brace Javanovich.

Sternberg, R.J., & Detterman, D.K. (Eds.) (1986). *What is intelligence?* Norwood, NJ: Ablex.

Swartz, R.J. (1986). Restructuring curriculum for critical thinking. *Educational Leadership,* 43, 43-44.

Swartz, R.J. (1987). Critical thinking attitudes and the transfer question. In Heiman and Slomianko (Eds.), *Thinking skills instruction: Concepts and techniques*. Washington, DC: National Education Association.

Swartz, R.J., & Perkins, D.N. (1987). Teaching for thinking: A developmental model for the infusion of thinking skills into mainstream instruction. In Baron and Sternberg (Eds.), *Teaching thinking skills: Theory and practice*. New York: W.H. Freeman and Co.

Swartz, R.J., & Perkins, D.N. (1989). Structured teaching for critical thinking and reasoning in standard subject area instruction. Forthcoming in Perkins, Segal, and Voss (Eds.), *Informal Reasoning and Education*. Hillsdale, NJ: Lawrence Erlbaum Associates.

† Swartz, R.J., & Perkins, D.N. (1989). *Teaching thinking: Issues and approaches*. Pacific Grove, CA: Midwest Publications.

Taba, H. (1942). The evaluation of critical thinking. In Howard Anderson, (Ed.), *Teaching critical thinking in the social studies*. Washington, D.C.: National Council for the Social Studies.

Taba, H. (1965, May). The teaching of thinking. *Elementary English,* 42, 534-542.

Torrance, E.P. (1979). *The search for satori and creativity*. Buffalo, NY: Creative Education Foundation, and Great Neck, NY: Creative Synergetics Associates.

Tyler, R.W. (1986, December-1987, January). The five most significant curriculum events in the twentieth century. *Educational Leadership*, 44:4 36-37.

Upton, R. (1985). *Strategic reasoning*. Bloomington, IN: Innovative Sciences, Inc.

U.S. Department of Education (1986). *What works: Research about teaching and learning.* Washington, D.C.: Author.

† von Oech, R. (1983). *A whack on the side of the head.* New York: Warner Books.

† von Oech, R. (1986). *A kick in the seat of the pants.* New York: Harper & Row.

Vygotsky, L.S. (1962). *Thought and language.* Cambridge, MA: Institute of Technology Press.

Walberg, Franette. (1980). *Puzzle thinking*. Philadelphia: Franklin Institute Press.

Warner, Sylvia Ashton. (1972). *Teacher.* New York: Vintage Books.

Whimbey, A. (1975). *Intelligence can be taught.* New York: Innovative Science.

Whimbey, A. (1977, December). Teaching sequential thought: The cognitive skils approach. *Phi Delta Kappan,* 59:4, 255-259.

Whimbey, A., & Lochhead, J. (1982). *Problem solving and comprehension* (third edition). Philadelphia: The Franklin Institute Press.

Whimbey, A., & Lochhead, J. (1984). *Beyond problem solving and comprehension.* Philadelphia: Franklin Institute Press.

Winocur, S. (1983). *Project impact.* Costa Mesa, CA: Orange County School District.

Wittrock, M.C. (1967). Replacement and nonreplacement strategies in children's problem solving. *Journal of Educational Psychology*, pp. 69-74.

Index

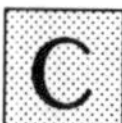

There are
one-story intellects,
two-story intellects, and three-story
intellects with skylights. All fact collectors, who have
no aim beyond their facts, are one-story men. Two-story men compare,
reason, generalize, using the labors of the fact collectors as well as
their own. Three-story men idealize, imagine, predict—
their best illumination comes from above,
through the skylight.

—Oliver Wendell
Holmes

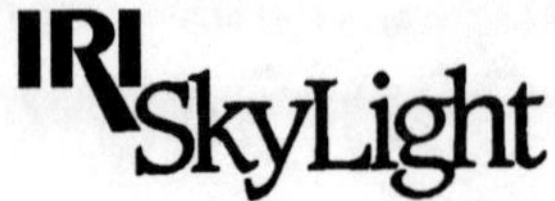